What Causes War?

An Introduction to Theories of International Conflict

Greg Cashman

Lexington Books
An Imprint of Macmillan, Inc.
New York

Maxwell Macmillan Canada
Toronto

Maxwell Macmillan International
New York   Oxford   Singapore   Sydney

Library of Congress Cataloging-in-Publication Data

Cashman, Greg.
    What causes war? : an introduction to theories of international
conflict / Greg Cashman.
        p.   cm.
    ISBN 0-669-21215-6
    1. War.   I. Title.
    U21.2.C37   1993
    327.1'6—dc20   92-40643
                                                                CIP

Lexington Books
An Imprint of Macmillan, Inc.
866 Third Avenue, New York, N. Y. 10022

Maxwell Macmillan Canada, Inc.
1200 Eglinton Avenue East
Suite 200
Don Mills, Ontario M3C 3N1

Macmillan, Inc. is part of the Maxwell Communication Group of Companies.

Printed in the United States of America

printing number
1   2   3   4   5   6   7   8   9   10

For Linda

Contents

Preface and Acknowledgements

Academic textbooks can frequently trace their parentage to necessity and frustration. So it is with this project. When I began teaching a course on the causes of war in the late 1970s, I was frustrated by my inability to gather for my students in a single volume a truly representative selection of writings from the various theories and approaches to war. One might find a serviceable text on international relations theory, but the relevant portions dealing directly with theories of war might account for only a third of the book. Edited readers concerning war excluded whole areas of investigation, addressing only certain levels of analysis and omitting analyses from certain academic disciplines. Thus I began this project by writing short summarizations for my students to fill the various gaps in their reading assignments. The students seemed receptive, and I kept on expanding the summaries.

I had several goals in mind as this project developed. First, I wanted the book to be as comprehensive as possible, providing students of international conflict with the broadest survey possible of theories that attempt to explain the causes of war. Second, almost by definition the work would have to be cross-disciplinary. Insights and theories from political science would be combined with those from biology, ethology, psychology, sociology, anthropology, economics, geography, and history. Third, I hoped to be able to give some guidance to students in sorting out the relative merits of these competing theories. I wanted to offer empirical evidence side by side with theoretical arguments. Fourth, I have attempted to present these theories as simply and concisely as possible, avoiding the more odious usages of social science jargon (I will apologize in advance for my occasional lapses in this area). Writing this book has proved to be a tremendously useful (though inordinately prolonged) experience; I hope it proves as valuable to the reader as it has been to me.

This book would not be possible without the efforts of a large community of international scholars who have pushed back the frontiers of our knowledge on issues of war and peace. This book really belongs to them. I owe significant intellectual debts to my own teachers, both at Ohio University and the University of Denver, especially Karen Feste, Arthur Gilbert, Harold Molineu, and the late Fred Sondermann. I also owe a debt of gratitude to several scholars who read drafts of several chapters. Karen Feste read my earliest efforts and was kind enough to offer cogent criticism and good-hearted encouragement. Several colleagues at Salisbury State University read chapters and offered generous assistance and advice. I thank especially Michael O'Loughlin, Harry Basehart, Cyril Daddieh, Barry Shreeves, and Lynne Carroll. I have benefitted over the years as well from the wisdom of Phil Bosserman, both on issues of international violence and on uncooperative word-processing software. I also thank my students who have responded so favorably to my writings and who have continued to initiate provocative discussions about the causes of war—usually just at that point when I had thought I had everything figured out. Salisbury State University provided a fall semester sabbatical that enabled me to start this project in earnest. Paul O'Connell, Peter Doherty, Bruce Nichols, Charles Hanson, and Carol Mayhew of Lexington Books have been generous with their help. My most profound thanks goes to James Rosenau for his timely, insightful, and penetrating comments as he trudged through my drafts. His graceful combination of firmness and tact persuaded me to reconsider and rewrite significant portions of this work. This is surely a better book than it might have been because of him. Finally, I owe an enormous debt of gratitude to my wife, Linda, who has contributed mightily to the maintenance of my mental balance during the long process of writing and rewriting. It is to her that this book is dedicated.

1
Empirical Theory and the Causes of War

What is called wisdom is concerned with primary causes.
—Aristotle

This is a book about the causes of war. More specifically, it is a book about the causes of *interstate war*—large-scale organized violence between the armed forces of states. It should be understood that organized violence can take many forms, for instance: gang wars, intercommunal wars, civil wars, wars of secession, and wars of national liberation, as well as interstate wars. To attempt to analyze the causes of all these forms of organized violence would be to force on them more uniformities and commonalties than they possess. These various forms of conflict are significantly different and their causes are also analytically distinct. We will focus therefore only on interstate wars to the exclusion of other forms of warfare.

Most of what follows is based on the assumption that, all things being equal (which, of course, almost never is the case), wars should be tenaciously avoided. Although wars have been with us for many centuries, the increasing ability of governments to mobilize their peoples for war coupled with greatly enhanced technology of mass violence have substantially increased the destructiveness of twentieth-century wars. The central imperative of our times is therefore to avoid wars of mass destruction; all other goals suffer in comparison. As Jacques Cousteau has mused, "Why protect fish if the planet is going to be destroyed?"[1] If the central imperative of our times is the avoidance of war, the primary dilemma of our times is how to achieve this. One theme of this book is that if we can understand the causes of war, we should be better able to prevent their occurrence.

Empirical Theory

Since this is a book about theories of war, one good place to start is to figure out just what is meant by the term "theory."[2] We quite often hear our friends

1

say, "I have a theory about why we lost the basketball game," or "I have a theory about why George Bush was elected president." In most cases, what they mean by theory is what we would call a hunch, an educated guess. In this book the term "theory" will refer to something more than a hunch. Social scientists who analyze war are concerned with two kinds of theory: normative theory and empirical theory.

Normative theory deals with how things *ought* to be. They deal with ethics and morals and value judgments. They are concerned with questions about what is right and wrong, what behaviors are morally acceptable or unacceptable. Normative theories of war would deal with questions such as: Can wars be just (morally acceptable), and if so, under what conditions? What kinds of practices and techniques of fighting are acceptable in war and which are unethical or immoral? Such questions are within the realm of political philosophers. Although such questions will inevitably arise in the course of this book, we will be addressing primarily the second kind of theory, empirical theory.

Empirical theories—also known as causal theories—deal not with how things *ought* to be but why things *are* the way they are. They are concerned with what causes certain behaviors and outcomes. The goal of empirical theory is the explanation of behavior—in this case, war. Although there are numerous methods of explanation, empirical theory—at least in political science—has implied the use of the "scientific method" of inquiry. Discovering and verifying the cause (or causes) of political phenomena cannot be based on sheer hunch or intuition; it must be based instead on rigorous tests of proof. Social sciences such as political science have adapted the scientific method used in the "hard sciences" like physics, chemistry, and biology for purposes of research in political behavior. This methodology involves a step-by-step process, which is applied in an effort to discover the cause(s) of any particular phenomenon. Since many of the theories of war examined in this book have been developed and tested through the application of the scientific method—especially those in Chapters 5–9—it might be useful to provide a brief introduction to social science research.

The Scientific Method

Theories in the social sciences are essentially explanations concerning the causes of human behavior. Theories of war consist of explanations about what causes war and why this cause-and-effect relationship exists. Logically, theories may be constructed in three different ways: through induction, deduction, or a combination of the two. In *induction* the analyst constructs the theory on the basis of observation of the facts (or data), working from the specific to the general. As the investigator learns more about specific wars, and as hypotheses are tested, theories are constructed and refined. In *deduc-*

tion the theory is constructed on the basis of logical reasoning, usually prior to the investigation of the relevant facts. This probably involves deducing the theory of war from a more comprehensive, general theory about international relations or politics. In reality, theories are probably constructed by scholars working in both directions, from the bottom up through induction from the facts about specific wars and from the top down from more general theories and principles.

How are theories tested? In the social sciences it is likely that no theory can ever be conclusively proven true. But theories can be proven false. Essentially, theories are tested by testing hypotheses that are derived deductively from them. If the hypotheses are proven to be incorrect, then either the deduction is wrong or the theory is flawed. If the hypotheses cannot be disconfirmed, then the theory is tentatively confirmed. It continues to be accepted until disproved at a later time. Theories therefore tend to "expire" for two reasons: (a) they lack confirmation, or (b) they are replaced by better theories.

A quick guide to the use of the scientific method follows.

Step One: The Formulation of Empirical Definitions for Concepts

Each theory of war identifies concepts or factors that are deemed important to the understanding of the cause of war. Certain lines of inquiry are specified as being more fruitful than others. The determination of which questions to ask and which factors are important or unimportant can be achieved inductively from studying the data or deductively from general principles, but each theory identifies certain concepts as more relevant to the causes of war than others.

Concepts are terms or words that identify general classes of things or ideas. War itself is a concept; so are tanks, decision-makers, diplomats, perceptions, arms races, mobilizations, and alliances. Specific persons or things are not concepts: though presidents and wars are concepts, President Bush and World War II are not. These terms refer to particular and specific persons and things rather than to a general class of phenomena.

For purposes of research, concepts must be given *operational definitions*; they must be defined in terms of something that is directly observable and measurable. For concepts that are directly observable, such as tanks, diplomats, mobilizations, and wars, this poses few problems. Other concepts, however, are more abstract and are not directly observable. For instance, the concepts of power, status, deterrence, hegemony, democracy, and liberalism are not directly visible and observable. The construction of operational definitions for these concepts is a little trickier.

Concerning the concept of interstate war, it is usually desirable to make some kind of operational definition in order to be able to determine what is a war and what military actions belong to categories of military action short of war—like border skirmishes, for instance. In collecting data on international wars between 1816 and 1980 for the Correlates of War (COW) project, J. David Singer and Melvin Small operationally define interstate war as a conflict involving at least one member of the interstate system on each side and in which the battle-connected deaths of all combatants together surpass 1,000. This has become the standard operational definition of interstate war. Some theories may require that we know more than just whether a war was present at a particular time or not. It may be necessary to define the concept of war more specifically in terms of the war's severity, its magnitude, or its intensity. Singer and Small devise simple indicators for each: *severity* is measured by the total number of battle-connected deaths suffered by all participants in the war combined; *magnitude* is measured by the combined number of months each nation spent at war; and *intensity* is indicated by the number of battle deaths per nation-month.[3]

Some concepts are best defined through the use of more than one indicator. National capabilities (referred to crudely as "power") is a good example. Conceptually, power is based on much more than just military strength. So when we devise an operational definition of national strength we will want to include indicators of several different properties of national power. We might construct an index of national strength that takes into account:

1. Geographic size—as measured in square miles
2. Population size—as measured by numbers of citizens
3. Technological development—as measured by yearly iron and steel production and/or energy consumption.
4. Military strength—as measured by number of men in armed forces and/or annual defense spending
5. Political stability—as measured by the number of months since the last unconstitutional change of regime

Likewise, the concept of democracy might be operationalized by constructing a scale of the degree of democracy present in a country based on such indicators as:

1. The degree of press freedom—as measured by the number of "independent" newspapers per capita
2. The degree of freedom of opposition—as indicated by the number of political parties or the number of political prisoners in jail per capita
3. The degree of electoral freedom—as measured by the presence or absence of direct popular elections for the chief executive and the national legislature, the degree of regularity in national elections, the average

number of candidates running per office, and the presence or absence of referenda, secret ballot procedures, and universal suffrage

4. The degree of individual freedom—as indicated by the presence of constitutional guarantees of individual civil and political rights such as freedom of speech, assembly, and suffrage, and freedom from unlawful search and seizure

5. The absence of a role for the military in the political process—as indicated by presence or absence of military candidates for public office, and the presence or absence of military action to negate election results

It should be obvious that the scores for different nations will differ considerably on these indicators. Nations vary on the amount of power they have, the degree of democracy they have, and the amount of war they have experienced. These concepts can therefore be called *variables*. Variables are things that vary—concepts that can take different values. The major goal of theory is to explain variation. For instance, why do some states experience more wars (or wars of greater severity) than other states? Without variation there is nothing to explain. If, for instance, all states were equally warlike and if the incidence of war was constant over time, there would be little need for scientific inquiry.

Step Two: Construction of Hypotheses

Hypotheses are unproved propositions; they are essentially guesses about the casual relationship of certain variables. In other words they are guesses that a particular outcome or behavior (a *dependent variable*) is determined or caused by a certain factor or set of factors (*independent variables*). Hypotheses may be arrived at inductively through the observation of events, facts, and data. Or they may be arrived at deductively, working backward from a general causal theory. Usually, hypotheses are constructed through a combination of deductive and inductive reasoning.

Hypotheses may take several forms. They may, for instance, be *universal* (absolute) or they may be *probabilistic*. Let's look at some examples. Drawing either inductively from our knowledge of the past or deductively from our understanding of democratic theory (or both), we may wish to hypothesize that there is a causal link between democratic states and peace— and conversely between nondemocratic states and war. Let us use this as an example to illustrate the construction of hypotheses. H_1 places the hypothesis in universal form:

$$H_1 = \text{All democracies are peaceful.}$$

We may readily admit, however, that this is not likely to be the case in reality, that there are exceptions to this "rule," and we should therefore loosen the form of the hypothesis to admit these exceptions. In the social sciences in general we find very few universal truths, and we therefore tend to use probabilistic hypotheses to reflect this reality. A better hypothesis might therefore be:

$$H_2 = \text{Democracies tend to be peaceful.}$$

This hypothesis introduces the notion of probability into the relationship. Rather than stating that democracies are always peaceful, it suggests that democratic states are probably peaceful most of the time. H_3 states the hypothesis in slightly different form.

$$H_3 = \text{If a state is democratic, then there is a high}$$
$$\text{probability that it will be peaceful.}$$

This reformulates the hypothesis in the classic "if . . . then" statement of the relationship between independent and dependent variables. H_4 states a slightly different variation of the same proposition.

$$H_4 = \text{The more democratic the state, the less war it should experience.}$$

This formulation incorporates the idea that neither democracy nor war are absolutes; both may be placed along a continuum in which some cases contain more or less of the particular quality. In other words, it includes the idea of variation. States may vary in the amount of democracy they experience; they may also vary in the amount of war they experience over time. The hypothesis suggests that variation in one variable (the independent variable, democracy) explains, accounts for, or causes the variation in the second variable (the dependent variable, war).

Step Three: Gathering Data

Step Four: Testing Hypotheses

Once hypotheses have been formulated, they must be tested against the evidence of the real world. This is the essence of the scientific method. We need to know whether our hypotheses are in fact correct or incorrect. Does the relationship between the two variables we have proposed exist in reality? Is there in fact an association between the two variables? All of this presumes that one has evidence from the real world against which one may test the hypothesis. Sometimes this requires an extensive effort to develop "data sets" concerning things like when wars have occurred, which nations fought in them, how many casualties were suffered, the degree of democracy that existed in particular countries at particular times, the power capabilities of each state, and so one. If one is lucky, other researchers will already have done this kind of legwork.

Testing of hypotheses must be rigorous. That is, you must try through a variety of methods to prove that the relationship *does not* exist! It is incumbent on the researcher to try to prove that his own hypothesis is false. Hypotheses are not proved by scavenging through the historical record to find examples of supporting evidence.[4] You can't validate hypotheses by simply citing facts to support them; this is too easy. You must actively search for examples which would *disprove* the hypothesis. Only if your search for this contrary evidence is futile may you claim success.

How might we go about testing our hypotheses concerning the postulated relationship between democracy and peace? If we start with the universal hypothesis that all democracies are peaceful, our immediate tasks are to determine which states are democracies and to determine what constitutes peace. These are matters of operational definition. Let us resolve them quickly, for argument's sake, in a relatively simplistic way. Democracies are those states which have in the last twenty years an uninterrupted record of regular election of a national legislature in which candidates from two or more political parties have participated. Peace will be defined as the absence of war participation in the last twenty years, with war defined as the presence of military combat with another state which involves more than 1,000 combat-related deaths for the states involved.

If the universal hypothesis is true we should find, on inspection of the data, that no democracy was involved in war and that all states which were involved in war were nondemocratic. Table 1.1 is a simple two-by-two table which depicts how we would expect the data to be dispersed if the universal hypothesis was correct.

We have already conceded that this outcome is quite unlikely in the real world and that some type of probablistic hypothesis would be more desirable. Let us look, therefore, at H_4—the more democratic a state is, the less war it should experience. Once again our immediate task (in addition to the accumulation of the relevant data) is to determine operational definitions of democracy and war. Democracy and war are no longer dichotomous variables. That is, they are no longer two-dimensional variables whose values are either O (absent) or X (present). Now the two variables must be put in a form in which they can be given values along a numerical scale—either on an *ordinal* (rank order) scale or an *interval* scale in which the numbers represent

Table 1–1
Hypothesized Universal Relationship between Democracy and War

	Democratic states	Nondemocratic states
Peace	X	O
War	O	X

real values. Let's assume that through diligent spade work and good "horse sense" we can create a rough 1–9 ordinal scale for such indicators of democracy as freedom of the press, freedom of opposition, electoral freedom, and individual rights. And let's assume that a good indicator of overall democracy would be to average a country's score on these four separate indicators. Let us select as our measure of war the number of wars a country has been involved in during the past twenty years. We have then an ordinal level measure of democracy and an interval level measure of war. We can now conduct several tests of varying sophistication to determine the validity of our hypothesis.

We might start by simply arranging the data in a way which helps us to analyze it visually. A three-by-three table suffices for this task, but it does not require some arbitrary judgements. So let's arbitrarily decide that countries that score from 0 to 3.0 on our scale of democracy are nondemocratic states; those that score from 3.1 to 6.0 can be classified as mildly democratic; and those that score from 6.1 to 9.0 can be described as democratic. Let's proceed similarly with our other variable, war. If the average number of wars that nations engaged in over the twenty-year period was one, let's define peace as zero wars; one war as mildly warlike; and two wars and above as warlike. In order for our hypothesized relationship to not be proven wrong, the three-by-three table ought to look something like Table 1.2.

Simply arraying the data in two-by-two or three-by-three tables as we have done is good for a start, but tests of greater sophistication will also be required. Researchers will want to use a variety of statistical tests to asses the degree of association between the independent and dependent variable and to determine whether this association might exist on the basis of pure, random chance. Perhaps it is better to stop at this point, however, before we get into hotter water than we presently find ourselves with regard to methodological problems.

We have said that a variety of tests should be performed. There are certainly many ways of testing the same basic hypothesis. For instance, a logical assumption based on our theorized relationship between democracy

Table 1–2

Hypothesized Relationship between Degrees of Democracy and Degrees of War

	Democratic states	Mildly democratic states	Nondemocratic states
No wars	Many cases	Some cases	No cases
One war	Some cases	Some cases	Some cases
Two or more wars	No cases	Some cases	Many cases

and war is that any specific country's war involvement will vary along with its change in the level of democracy. This suggests that for any given country, wars should be more prevalent during periods of time in which the government was nondemocratic than during periods in which it was democratic. Nations ought to become more peaceful once they become (more) democratic. And democratic nations that revert back to authoritarianism should then become more highly involved in war. Furthermore, since democratic states are presumed to be relatively peaceful, war between two democratic states should be extremely rare or nonexistent. Examination of these related hypotheses ought to strengthen (or weaken) our confidence in the correctness of the original tests.

Two warnings need to be issued at this point. First, while we have been using a single variable explanation of war merely for the sake of simplicity, *multivariate* explanations of war are likely to be much more powerful. Since social and political behaviors are extremely complex, they are almost never explainable through a single factor. Decades of research have led most analysts of international relations to reject *monocausal* explanations of war. For instance, international relations theorist J. David Singer suggests that we ought to move away from the concept of "causality" since it has become associated with the search for a single cause of war; we should instead redirect our activities toward discovering "explanations"—a term that implies not only multiple causes of war, but also a certain element of randomness or chance in their occurrence.[5]

The second warning is that statistical correlations between independent and dependent variables do not automatically mean a causal relationship has been established. For instance, one may find an inverse statistical relationship between the quantity of cranial hair in Soviet leaders and propensity toward "liberal" reforms. (Lenin, Khrushchev, and Gorbachev were bald reformers; Stalin, Brezhnev, and Chernenko were hairy conservatives.) Or one might find a positive statistical relationship between the number of garment workers in New York City and the severity of wars in the international system. This doesn't mean that baldness causes the political reform or that a booming miniskirt industry causes wars of great severity. Causal inferences may be drawn only if (1) there is a time lag between the independent and dependent variable—logically, the potential causal factor must precede the thing being caused; (2) other variables can be proven *not* to be related to the variation in the dependent variable; and (3) a theory can logically and plausibly explain the relationship that is found to exist.

Theory Revisited

If the hypothesis is confirmed repeatedly by different observers using different tests, then it achieves the status of a *law* or *generalization*. Laws are confirmed hypotheses that state a relationship between two variables. Laws may be universal or probabilistic, like the hypotheses on which they are based. However, laws only state that there is an association between two (or more) variables. They do not explain *why* that association exists. *Theories* are needed to provide this explanation. As political scientists are fond of saying, "The data never speak for themselves." Without a theory there is no real explanation. Suppose we find a strong relationship between wars and the prior existence of arms race. What then? How are we to interpret this? What is it about arms races that may make war more likely? Likewise, suppose it turns out that there is indeed a relationship between democratic states and peace—how is this condition to be explained? This is the realm of theory.

We have stated previously that theories often fall by the wayside only when they are replaced by better theories. The reader needs to be aware that more than one theory can appear to explain a set of facts and relationships. We may find that several theories simultaneously contend with each other to explain the same set of facts. If we discover, for instance, a relationship between arms races and war, several theories might purport to explain how arms races "cause" war. Probably the reigning theory is that arms races induce war because they heighten the tension, suspicion, and mutual fear between the countries involved. This initiates or exacerbates a spiral of hostility between the arms racers. The hostility spiral escalates until greater and greater levels of conflict and violence are achieved—leading to an all-out war. Arms races are therefore associated with wars, but they don't directly cause them. They only compound and intensify other conditions that are more directly related to the cause of war. Alternatively, however, the relationship between arms races and war might be more direct. It is possible to argue that a tremendous buildup in arms leads to bureaucratic pressures to use those arms that have been accumulating. Military institutions and their political and industrial supporters may feel the need to justify the expensive purchases of weapons by regularly demonstrating that massive arms supplies are actually needed. The only real way to demonstrate this need is to engage in large-scale fighting. Military, political, and industrial elites initiate arms races in order to reap economic benefits and to increase their power and status within their respective institutions. They then use their influence to push the nation into the actual use of military force in order to preserve their power and increase their economic gains.

These two explanatory theories proceed along very different lines of reasoning and in fact operate at quite different levels of analysis. They also lead to quite different hypotheses and tests so that it is logically possible to determine which of these theories—if either—is correct. Eventually, these conflicts between contending theoretical explanations get sorted out.

We have said that theories tend to be replaced over time by better theories; let us return to the question of what makes one theory better than others.

Evaluation and Comparison of Theories

Not all theories are equally good. Since the reader will be faced in the balance of this work with a series of contending theories that purport to explain the occurrence of war, it is essential to have in mind some criteria for judging the relative worth of these theories. Some characteristics of a good theory are listed below. While these criteria are in no particular order, those which the author sees as the most important appear at the end of the list.

1. Good theories are well-defined concepts that can be operationalized.
2. Good theories are clear and precise.
3. Good theories are simple, or parsimonious; they explain the phenomena with as few variables and as little complexity as possible. (One should probably not be excessively picky about this particular criteria; the world itself is not particularly simple and parsimonious. Oversimplification in a theory may result in a loss of explanatory power.)
4. Good theories should be plausible. They should make intuitive sense and not challenge too vigorously our sense of the possible and probable.
5. Good theories must be logically consistent.
6. Good theories must be testable and verifiable (and therefore falsifiable.)
7. The best theories are usually those which have the greatest empirical evidence to support them. As we shall soon discover, the evidence concerning the validity of most theories of war is rather mixed and sometimes contradictory. The quality and quantity of confirming evidence constitutes a major tool in evaluating and comparing theories of war.
8. Good theories are usually able to explain "anomolies" in other theories—gaps, or things that are unexplainable or are poorly explained in other theories.
9. The more general the theory, the better. Good theories explain more than previous theories; they have greater range and wider applicability. The goal of theory construction is to create a general theory of war that would be applicable to interstate conflicts in all geographic regions of the world across the historical lifespan of states. Such a theory would have as few cultural, geographic, or temporal boundaries as possible.
10. Good theories frequently build bridges to other theories. They provide a way of linking several theories across different levels of analysis. As the reader approaches the final chapters in this book, it will become evident that actors and phenomena at many levels will play important roles in war causation. Single-factor theories of war and single-level theories of war have all proven inadequate to the task. Therefore, a truly comprehensive theory of war must take into consideration factors at multiple levels of analysis.

"Islands of Theory"

International relations theories have been for the most part *"middle range" theories* rather than *"grand theories"* of a more comprehensive nature that attempt to explain a wide range of phenomena. Most theories of war address a limited range of behaviors at a single level of analysis with as few variables as possible. For instance, middle-range theories might attempt to explain the relationships between alliances and war, deterrence and war, the perceptions of decision-makes and war, economic modernization and war, and so on. Though the connections between these middle-range theories are at present only faintly sketched in, the assumption made by most theorists is that eventually the accumulation of midrange theories at different levels of analysis will lead to the construction of theories of greater and greater sophistication and complexity. Nevertheless, Snyder and Diesing's famous analogy remains apt:

> In our teaching and research, we are like travelers in a houseboat, shuttling back and forth between separate "islands" of theory, whose relatedness consists only in their being commonly in the great "ocean" of "international behavior." Some theorists take up permanent residence on one island or other, others continue to shuttle, but few attempt to build bridges, perhaps because the islands seem too far apart.[6]

Prediction

Finally, a word about prediction is necessary. One of the goals of theorizing about war is the ability to be able to predict with some degree of certainty when and where wars will occur. The development of theories about the causes of war may be helpful in this regard, but theory is not always necessary for prediction. We do not have to know *why* the sun has risen every morning in the east for the past several millennia to predict that it will also rise in the east tomorrow morning at pretty much the same time that it did today. Nor do we need to know what causes the ebb and flow of tides to be able to predict their occurrences with any accuracy. It is enough to have identified the relationships and patterns without being able to explain why the relationship exists.

On the other hand, unique events cannot be predicted—only regular, patterned events. In fact, if all events are unique, they have unique causes and there is little use trying to explain and predict classes of events like wars in a general way. One of the chief assumptions made by political scientists is that events are not unique and political phenomena do not occur randomly; instead, recurring patterns and trends can be identified. Definite similarities can be discovered in the behavior of nations. If these assumptions are false, it would be possible only to explain the causes of each individual war, and the cause of each war would be essentially different.

Levels of Analysis

Clues to the cause of war may be found in a variety of different locations. The causes of war may be said to exist at several levels of analysis. While there are different views of the number and identity of levels of analysis, we will examine theories of war at five levels: the individual, the small group, the state, the interaction between two states, and the international system. These levels of analysis can be viewed as essentially levels of aggregation. Each level is made up of larger and larger units than the preceding level. Small groups are aggregations of individuals, states are aggregations of many groups, dyads are made of two states, international systems are made up of the combined interactions of many states.

At each level different types of theories purport to explain the causes of war. At the *individual level,* the basic contention is that wars are due to the nature of mankind or to the specific nature of certain individual leaders who take their states into war. At the *small-group level,* the argument is that individuals are rarely responsible for decisions to go to war, and that these decisions are instead made by relatively small groups of officials within national governments. If one wishes to understand the cause of war, one needs to understand the processes by which these small groups come to their decisions. At the level of the *nation-state,* the basic premise is that there is something about the nature of particular states that causes them to be more warlike or aggressive than those that lack these attributes. At the *dyadic interaction level,* it is not the nature of particular states or individuals that are responsible for war; it is how two states interact with each other which determines whether war will occur or not. The focus is primarily on patterns of interaction that escalate in intensity and hostility and lead to war. Finally, at the level of the *international system,* war is deemed to be a product of some aspect of the structure of the international system itself—the balance of power within the system, the hierarchical structure of status and prestige in the system, or cycles of economic growth and decline imbedded in the structure of the international system.

We will proceed in this book from the individual level on through the international system level in search of the causes of war. Chapters 2 and 3 deal with the individual level of analysis, Chapter 4 with government decision-making by small groups, Chapter 5 with national attributes, Chapters 6 and 7 with dyadic interaction between pairs of states, and Chapters 8 and 9 focus on the international system. Chapter 10 will bring together some of the insights from each of these levels of analysis.

2

The Individual Level of Analysis: Human Aggression

> We used to wonder where war lived, what it was that made it so vile. And now we realize that we know where it lives, that it is inside ourselves.
>
> —Albert Camus

We frequently hear comments such as: "There will always be wars because men are just aggressive animals; as long as there are men there will be wars." Or, "As long as there are lunatics like Hitler or Saddam Hussein running governments, there is going to be aggression." These views reduce the cause of war to either the nature of man in general or the nature of particular men. While these statements discern the causes of war within individual humans, they illustrate two very different types of theories. In fact, they point to a level of analysis distinction *within* the individual level of analysis.[1]

Those who believe that the fundamental cause of war is that humans are naturally aggressive take the position that all men (and women) are the same. National leaders who make the decisions to go to war are no different from the masses: they share with *all* mankind the same aggressive traits that characterize humans as a species. This collective characteristic of human aggression affects the process of war at the *macro level* of collective action.

On the other hand, those who believe that the root cause of war must be found in the personal, psychological characteristics of particular national leaders argue that men are *not* all alike. The individual makes a difference. It matters whether Adolf Hitler or Helmut Kohl leads Germany, just as it matters whether the (former) Soviet Union is ruled by Mikhail Gorbachev or Josef Stalin. Aggression is seen as an individual characteristic rather than a collective characteristic, and its effect on war is felt at the *micro level* of decision-makers who hold in their hands the ability to choose war or peace.

Let us develop the two ideas separately. Aggression as a common characteristic of the human race is the subject of Chapter 2. Individual and psychological sources of war will be explored in Chapter 3.

14

Are Human Beings by Nature Aggressive?

Philosophers and theologians through the ages have sought to explain the aggressiveness of man by explaining the nature of mankind.[2] In his classic of political philosophy *Leviathan*, the seventeenth-century English philosopher Thomas Hobbes described living conditions in the "state of nature" (that is, in primitive societies before the creation of government) as "a war of everyman against everyman." This constant conflict stemmed, according to Hobbes, from the nature of mankind. Men were self-seeking, selfish, and greedy; they were only concerned with satisfying their own desires. Personal gain and glory were man's basic motivations. St. Augustine also noticed man's great capacity for mayhem and slaughter. This propensity for evil seemed to Augustine to require a theological explanation: original sin. Man's aggressive nature was related directly to the fall from grace in the Garden of Eden. Alternatively, Spinoza, the seventeenth-century Dutch philosopher, perceived a great struggle going on within man between the forces of passion and rationality. Unfortunately, passion frequently won out over reason.

Early psychologists like William James noticed that combat and war seemed to satisfy deep-rooted needs of individuals and societies, needs that were presumed to be inherent in all humans. This aggressive drive could not be suppressed, but it might be redirected and diverted toward more peaceful activities that involved similar challenges and exertions. Thus, James suggested the need to create a "moral equivalent of war."[3] Youths might be conscripted to plant trees and build roads or dams rather than to kill the young men of other societies. Such programs would inoculate them with the same "social vitamins" as war without causing the same destruction to life and property.

Sigmund Freud also believed the aggressive behavior of mankind stemmed from deep-seated unconscious drives. Indeed, aggression seemed to be a behavioral trait of all humans. Freud suggested that an explanation for such aggressiveness might be related to the existence in man of the *life instinct* (Eros), which seeks to preserve and unite, and the *death instinct* (Thanatos).[4] The death instinct presumably has as its goal the removal of all tension, stimulation, and excitement in the individual. This death instinct is centered inward, and the logical outcome of its hold is suicide—aggression directed toward the self. But these drives do not exist in isolation; they interact with each other and modify each other. Man lives because the life instinct counters the death instinct and channels the drive away from the self and toward others. Overt aggression is thus the result of internal aggressive drives being redirected at others. Freud argued that aggression must not only be released in some way or another but that man gains a certain amount of satisfaction from the release. In other words, man *needs* to satisfy these aggressive drives, though not necessarily by means of overt aggression.

In more recent times a major debate has been fought in academic circles and in the popular literature about the source of human aggressiveness at the macro level. The debate centers on the issue of whether mankind's propensity for intramural mayhem can be attributed primarily to some universally inherent (and probably genetic) trait or to the specific culture and environment in which some groups of humans are raised. Those who take the former position are primarily ethologists; those who take the latter are usually anthropologists. The debate is usually characterized as the nature-nurture debate.

The Nature–Nurture Debate

Nature: Ethology

Ethology, the study of animal behavior, is a relatively new field. The publication of Konrad Lorenz's *On Aggression* in 1966 brought its theories widespread attention.[5] And writer Robert Ardrey's popular summarizations (*African Genesis, The Territorial Imperative, The Social Contract*) of the work of Lorenz and other ethologists added to the awareness of these new ideas.[6] The major thesis of the ethologists is that man is a product of two million years of biological evolution. Lionel Tiger, an anthropologist, argues that men remain "fine-honed machines for the efficient pursuit of game." We are "biologically or genetically wired for hunting—for the emotions, excitements, curiosities, the fears and the social relations that were needed in the hunting way of life."[7] The most extreme formulation of this position has been by Raymond Dart (and by Ardrey, who has popularized much of Dart's work). Dart, an anatomist, has argued that man is a direct descendant of a killer ape, *Australopithecus africanus*. On the basis of Dart's investigation of the fossil remains of africanus, he concludes that this particular ape was not only carnivorous, but cannibalistic as well—an instinctual killer who may have killed for the enjoyment of it.[8] (It appears now that Dart may have been mistaken. The existence of a large number of hominid remains that had incurred significant fracturing and puncturing was taken by Dart to be evidence of widespread interpersonal violence among africanus. The fossil evidence has now been reexamined by others who believe the damage is more likely due simply to the compression of bones and other debris over a lengthy period of time.)[9]

For Lorenz the concept of aggression refers only to *intraspecific aggression*—fighting between members of the same species. When two species fight (as when one species kills another for food), aggression is not involved. Perhaps the best example of aggression is seen when animals defend their territory against another of the same species.

Ethologists see aggression as an *instinct* (an innate drive) that once helped to ensure the survival of the individual and the species. As such, it was passed down from generation to generation as part of our hereditary makeup. The problem is, of course, that the presence of such a drive in the modern age—with its weapons of mass destruction—may be extremely counterproductive.

Aggression is believed to have several species-preserving functions:

1. It keeps a balance in the territory between the needed resources on the one hand and the number of individuals to be supported on the other.
2. It aids in defense of the young.
3. It contributes to the survival of the fittest through the process of sexual selection.
4. It contributes to the establishment of stable social relations through the creation of dominant-subordinant systems such as the well-known "pecking system."

An interesting feature of this intraspecific aggression, however, is that it is generally not aimed at killing or extermination. Ethologists point out that intraspecific aggression among animals usually does not result in death for the loser. On the other hand, the behavior of man is quite different. Apart from rats, which also engage in "clan" wars and murder members of their own species, Lorenz identifies man as the only species that routinely slaughters its own kind. In reality, Lorenz was probably wrong about this. We now know that several species also occasionally kill their own kind. For instance, Edward Wilson discusses the notoriously aggressive behavior of ant colonies toward one another and of "colony warfare" both within and between species. Colonies of the common pavement ant defend their territories with pitched battles conducted by masses of workers. Murder and cannibalism among the vertebrates also seem to be more prevalent than previously believed. Lions sometimes kill other lions, and there are reports of the killing and cannibalism of cubs after one of their protector males had died and the territory was invaded by other prides. Indeed, man may not even be the most aggressive species—the hyena is often granted this distinction now.[10]

At any rate, what could account for this seeming difference between man and most other animals? The answer is that intraspecific aggression among most animals is highly ritualized. The combatants do battle within the strictures of routine and symbolic patterns. As the course of the battle demonstrates the relative prowess of the contestants, the inferior competitor will engage in *appeasement gestures* or *releasing signals*, which will signal deference and submission, thus inhibiting further violence and preventing the combat from continuing to the death. The most frequently cited example of such inhibiting mechanisms is that of the wolf's baring his neck during combat, an act that would presumably leave him vulnerable to be killed, but instead acts as a kind of surrender signal to the opponent, who then ends the contest.

Man apparently lacks such inhibiting mechanisms. Why? The answer given by ethologists is that in the early stages of his evolution he had no need for them. Unlike the saber-toothed tiger and other predators, man was unable to kill his fellow-men quickly; without claws and fangs he simply did not have the tools for it. The sheer difficulty of hand-to-hand killing meant that most men would give up the effort long before death resulted. If the physical difficulty was surmountable, presumably the aggressor would also be dissuaded by the anguished pleading of his opponent. However, assisted by the development of a greatly enlarged brain, humans later devised tools and weapons that could be used to slay their enemies—even at great distances—thereby reducing both the physical and emotional constraints on killing. By this time, however, it was too late for man to develop those inhibiting gestures that lower relations had possessed for millenia.

Instead of these "instinctual" mechanisms passed down through genetic imprinting, mankind has been forced to rely on other measures to inhibit killing: morality, religion, ethics, and cultural prohibitions. It would be an understatement to say that these have proven to be ineffective. The result is that while aggressive instincts were once species preserving, they no longer serve the function—just the opposite. Man's aggressive instincts, combined with the lack of instinctual inhibitory mechanisms and the ability to develop weapons of long-range destruction, mean constant conflict and death.

Lorenz summarizes how aggression influenced human development:

> . . . it is more than probable that the destructive intensity of the aggression drive . . . is the consequence of a process of intra-specific selection which worked on our forefathers for roughly forty thousand years, that is, throughout the Early Stone Age. When man had reached the stage of having weapons, clothing, and social organization, so overcoming the dangers of starving, freezing and being eaten by wild animals, and these dangers ceased to be the essential factors influencing selection, an evil intra-specific selection must have set in. The factor influencing selection was now the wars waged between hostile neighboring tribes.[11]

Thus, from the perspective of the ethologist, wars provide an outlet for the aggressive tendencies that are inherent in human beings. Indeed, Lorenz sees aggression as a drive that must seek release; in other words, man has an innate "need" for aggression. Some have referred to this conception of aggression as the *drive-discharge model*—aggression is seen as a drive that seeks release or discharge, thus impelling man toward aggressive activities. Others call it the *hydraulic model* analogous to the pressure created by water that is held in check by a dam.[12] In other words, a kind of energy accumulates in the instinct center of the animal, generating pressure for its discharge. Aggression is in this sense spontaneous. Its source is internal to the organism, not external.

There is some dispute among ethologists (and others) about how these aggressive actions are set off. The question centers around the stimuli needed to elicit such a response. Lorenz and psychiatrist Anthony Storr suggest that although the physical mechanism of aggression is inborn, it is still usually triggered from the external environment. But they also argue that the fact that aggression needs an outside stimulus to set it off does not imply that man can escape the need to behave aggressively. Lorenz maintains that the longer the aggressive energy is dammed up, the lower the threshold value of the stimulus needed to elicit the aggressive response. Indeed, he speculates that following an extensive period of damming, aggression can be performed *without* the presence of an external stimulus.[13] Storr agrees, suggesting that when no external stimulus exists that is capable of stimulating aggression, man will actually seek out such a stimulus![14]

Others, such as psychologist J. P. Scott, while agreeing that aggression is rooted in a physiological process and that it needs to be activated by external stimuli, would argue that aggression does not ever need to be manifested. Since the release of aggression must be stimulated by an outside trigger, if that trigger is missing, aggression will not occur.[15] If Scott's more optimistic view is correct, mankind is not doomed by its genetic inheritance; violence is avoidable.

An idea dear to the heart of ethologists is *territoriality* and the relationship between territory and aggression. For instance, Ardrey suggests that man's genetic inheritance has provided him with the same territorial instincts as his lower relations. Ardrey relies on the work of F. F. Darling, who suggested that the motivation for territorial behavior in animals was psychological, rather than physiological—arising from the dual "needs" for security and stimulation. To these two needs Ardrey adds a third need found in higher animals: identity.[16]

Ardrey suggests that territory satisfies the three basic needs. Territory defines who one is: "we" are the ones who live together in the territory; "they" are outsiders. Whether in human or animal communities, the distinction is important. Identity within the territory is also based on status ranking or "pecking orders" which apply only to members of the territory. Territory also provides security. This is the function of the center of the territory, the place where the ability of the group to protect itself is strongest and also where the willingness of the intruder to challenge territorial rights is the weakest. Territory also provides the function of stimulation. This is the function of the periphery of the territory. Here members of the territorial group come into contact with other members of the same species in neighboring territories, creating a wealth of excitement. Ardrey recounts a study of the callicebus monkey by William Mason:

> The principal area of Mason's study has been a twenty acre grove containing nine family territories. Every family knows its boundaries to the last inch: a broken branch here, an isolated bush there, a slanted tree trunk across the way. . . . [The callicebus] knows like a peasant every inch of his domain. And its periphery, as Darling suggested, respresents his fun in life. . . .
>
> I find that one of the most touching qualities in the callicebus monkey is its willingness to sacrifice a heavy breakfast for a hearty periphery. . . . The little family makes no compromises with principle, but bright and early is on duty at the border, only partly fed, hankering for action, waiting for the arrival of neighbors to be angry at. . . . Not one foot will the family place on the neighbors' domain unless neighbors are present to make intrusion worthwhile. But let their neighbors appear, having had their dew and their scanty snack, and callicebus hell will break loose.
>
> . . . There is a deal of screeching to begin with. Then father intrudes. The opposing father chases him back and intrudes in turn. Now family is after family. Mothers put aside all grace and give themselves over to lifetime grudges. . . . Bedlam and bellicosity rule for half an hour or so, then someone recalls there is another boundary undefended and unexploited. The family withdraws. The family across the way recalls that it too has another border, another enemy to become enraged at. No cards or apologies are exchanged, for the rules of the game are too well understood. . . .
>
> On other boundaries other contestants will oppose other rivals. Vast must be the satisfaction of such engagements. Blood pressures rise, tissues expand, brains roil with conventional angers. Then just about nine o'clock in the morning, after a couple of hours of emotional daily dozens, it will occur to someone that somebody is hungry. That will be the end of the day's hostilities as all take their ravenous appetites to the breakfast trees.[17]

Assuming that human behavior parallels that of its ancestral cousins, all of this would, of course, go very much against Freud's notion that human behavior is aimed at tension reduction. Indeed, a variety of research performed with animals indicates just the opposite: organisms frequently go out of their way to obtain stimulation from the external environment.[18] What is true for animals seems to be equally true for man. Estelle Ramey, a physiologist and biophysicist who has studied boredom, contends that every laboratory experiment on the pathological effects of boredom, not to mention the reports of men stationed in Antarctic outposts, prisoners of war, long-haul truck drivers, and airplane pilots, supports the notion that stimulation is an important need.[19] As F. H. Knight once observed, "What people really want is trouble, and if they do not have enough of it, they will create it artificially, the institution of sport being proof."[20]

Ardrey, of course, maintains that war also satisfies the three basic needs for identification, security, and stimulation. First, identification is provided through military rank, through membership in platoons, squadrons, corps, battalions, divisions, and armies in association with other soldiers. Glory in war is also capable of providing a kind of personal identification for soldiers. Second, war is widely presumed to be fought for the purpose of security—either to create it where it does not exist, to enhance it, or to maintain it. Third, war also provides more than enough stimulation for most men—especially for those who actually combat. Thus, it seems to Ardrey that war is a more or less perfect institution to satisfy the basic needs of man.

Recent Ethological Studies

While the works of Lorenz and other scholars of the first wave of ethological studies in the 1960s and early 1970s focused primarily on the behavior of fish and birds, a second wave of scholarship by ethologists has taught us much more about the behavior of man's closest biological relatives—chimpanzees and gorillas.[21] Since chimpanzees are closer to humans physiologically and genetically than any other creature—in their DNA structures, the two species vary by just over one percent—evidence concerning the aggressive nature of chimps would seem to be crucial to the ethological argument.

In her thirty years at Gombe, Goodall observed many behaviors that have shattered our preconceptions of man's evolutionary cousins. For instance, she discovered that chimps are not only tool users, but also tool makers. Perhaps the most startling revelations, however, deal with intercommunal violence. While violent conflict associated with the determination of dominance among males is quite ritualized and struggles to the death do not occur, contestants frequently receive severe physical punishment during dominance struggles. Goodall and her associates also observed aggressive territoriality among chimps, though encounters between members of different territorial groups typically became dangerous only for unprotected female intruders. Goodall also observed a four-year "war" between rival communities. When the chimp community she was observing divided into two separate territorial groups, the members of the original community totally eliminated the members of the break-away group one by one over a four-year period. Each of the "secessionists" was brutally beaten to death by former friends. Instances of cannibalism sometimes accompanied this warfare.[22]

Critique of Ethology

Lorenz and his followers have been criticized both for their methods and for the validity of their results. The substantive evidence seems to be extremely weak and based primarily on extrapolating disputed evidence from the behavior of certain animal species to human beings. A few specific criticisms should give the reader some of the flavor of the debate.

1. *Is aggression really an instinct?* Since individuals begin to learn from their environments at very early ages, it is very difficult to scientifically ascertain whether a particular behavior has resulted from preexisting instinct or has been learned. Owing to this difficulty in distinguishing learning from instinct, many scholars have begun to abandon the term "instinct" altogether.[23] Some, such as Ashley Montagu, suggest that where Lorenz and the ethologists err is that man is man precisely because he has no instincts, at least beyond the reaction of infants to sudden loud noises or to the sudden withdrawal of support.[24]

2. *Man is different from other animals.* Lorenz's primary failing would seem to be that he fails to recognize that man is substantially different from other animals, because of the enlarged brain he has developed. This makes him able to adapt and respond to his environment and to think. It ultimately means that generalizations based on observations of the behavior of lower animals ought not to be assumed true of humans. Generally speaking, the more advanced the species, the less genetics determine behavior.

3. *Monocausal explanation.* Lorenz's theory fails to explain all aggressive behaviors because it ignores other variables that may play a role in determing whether aggression takes place—such as the presence of frustration, the character of the sociopolitical environment, or the ability of man to reason and to learn.

4. *Methodology.* Lorenz doesn't form operational hypotheses that can be empirically tested. Instead, he relies on reasoning through the use of metaphor, analogy, and cross-species extrapolation. For instance, Lorenz argues that the cause of aggression in birds and fish is essentially the same as the causes of animal aggression, just as the cause of animal aggression is essentially the cause of human aggression. In addition, the cause of interindividual aggression is presumed to be the same as that of intergroup aggression and of interstate war. This is simply sloppy science. One should not use observations of the behavior of one species to explain the behavior of other species. Neither should one use observations of individuals to explain the collective behavior of groups. Thus, Lorenz compounds problems interspecies analogies with level of analysis problems. Attempts to apply the theory of instinctual aggression to the systemic level of states and the international system should be treated with caution.

5. *The drive-discharge model.* If there really is an accumulation of aggressive "energy" that accumulates until it is released through aggressive behavior, we should be able to find some physical evidence of this—presumably in the brain. However, there is no neurophysiological evidence for the existence of any kind of energy accumulation in the brain that impels

a spontaneous discharge. Unlike the internal changes (the change in blood sugar, for instance) that accompany the onset of hunger, no internal changes develop that precede the onset of aggression.[25] This is not to say that aggression itself is without neurological effects. Scientists have identified certain centers within the brain associated with different kinds of aggressive responses. (The hypothalmus seems to be the center for the emotion of anger, for instance.) Aggression has also been experimentally manipulated in subjects through hormone treatment and brain stimulation. But the brain centers most involved in aggression respond primarily to signals given *after* some external stimulus is interpreted, and endocrine levels in the body are typically affected in response as well. In other words, the physiological correlates of aggression are brought about by the individual's response to perceptions of the external environment rather than from within.[26]

6. *Crowding and territoriality.* It has been demonstrated that when overcrowding occurs in certain territorial species, a pathological breakdown in the normal social interactions of the species takes place and violence often occurs. However, athough territoriality occurs only in higher animals (vertebrates and anthropods), critics argue that man's nearest relatives among the primates (savannah monkeys, chimpanzees, and gorillas) do not show much territorial behavior—either collectively or individually.[27] We know nothing about the territorial behavior of precultural man, but anthropologists note that the institutions of territory and private property vary greatly in modern man. Scott cites as an example that in none of the Eskimo societies except the Aleut was there anything such as defense of territory.[28] Neither does it seem that crowding necessarily causes hostility and aggression. Man's behavior under crowded conditions varies substantially depending on crowdings's interaction with several other variables. Crowding per se, in the absence of variables such as income level, malnutrition, noise, filth, and other variables, seems to have no great impact on things such as crime, competitiveness, and aggressiveness.[29] Territoriality may have a cultural basis instead of a biological one.

In the final analysis, the substantive evidence for an ethological theory of aggression is weak. There appears to be no single instigation to aggression even among lower animals; instead, there are several kinds of aggression, and patterns of aggression vary from species to species and even within species. Samuel Kim argues that as we climb the evolutionary ladder, aggression becomes less common, and when it does occur its causes are more complex, more numerous, less rigidly programmed by the genotype, and more influenced by ecological and experiential factors.[30] Lorenz's characterization of primates as "irascible" is not accepted by many primatologists, who see them rather as generally peaceful and cooperative. Even Goodall argues that extreme violence is a rarity among chimps.

Because violent and brutal behavior is vivid and attention-catching, it is easy to get the impression that chimpanzees are more aggressive than they really are. In fact, peaceful interactions are far more frequent than aggressive ones; mild threats are more common than vigorous ones; threats per se are much more frequent than fights; and serious, wounding conflicts are rare compared to brief, relatively mild ones. Moreover, chimpanzees have a rich repertoire of behaviors that serve to maintain or restore social harmony and promote cohesion among community members.[31]

Nature: Sociobiology

With the publication in 1975 of Edward O. Wilson's *Sociobiology: The New Synthesis*, the new science of sociobiology was born.[32] This new approach is labeled by its author as an effort to place all of the social sciences within a biological framework constructed not just upon ethological studies of animal behavior, but on the study of evolution, genetics, population biology, psychology, and anthropology as well. Although Wilson argues that human behavior has been programmed to a substantial degree by natural selection, he doesn't claim that genetics are the sole cause of behavior. Instead, his theory recognizes the interaction of genes with the cultural environment. Nevertheless, Wilson's emphasis is on the genetic determinants of human behavior and human culture.

How do we know that human behavior has a genetic base? First, the social cultures of man and chimpanzees, man's closest relatives anatomically and physiologically, are similar. But second, says Wilson, human behavior is also distinct from the behavior of our evolutionary relatives in ways that can only be accounted for by a unique set of human genes. Virtually every human culture known shows these distinct characteristics; wherever they are, humans act similarly. For example, every human culture would seem to have these characteristics in common: athletic sports, community organization, cooperative labor, division of labor, education, ethics, etiquette, funeral rites, gift giving, government, hospitality, inheritance rules, kinship nomenclature, language, law, marriage, penal sanctions, population policy, property rights, religious ritual, residence rules, sexual restrictions, status differentiation, and trade, among others.[33] This could not have happened randomly; it must be genetic. How else could so many human societies have developed the same patterns of behavior?

The concept of *adaptiveness* provides a key to understanding how this has happened. Behavioral traits of human nature were "adaptive" during the time that human behavior evolved, and genes consequently spread through the population that predisposed their carriers to develop these traits. Adaptiveness means that if an individual displays these traits, he stands a better chance of having his genes represented in the next generation than if he did not. This advantage is called *genetic fitness*. Wilson contends that the greatest part of genetic evolution occurred over five million years ago, prior to civilization. There has been some evolution since then, but not enough to affect a large number of traits.

Cooperation and altruism are innate traits, presumably because they add to genetic fitness. That is the good news; the bad news is that humans are also innately aggressive. This genetic/biological disposition is necessarily reflected in human social and cultural institutions. Wilson sees organized warfare as endemic to every form of society, from hunter-gatherers to the modern urban-industrial. Like Lorenz, Wilson argues that man's aggressiveness has added to his genetic fitness through preservation of the territorial balance, defense of the young, and mating and survival of the fittest. Because aggressiveness has added to genetic fitness, there is a fairly high probability that the trait will develop in a specific set of environments, but there is no certainty that the trait would develop in *all* environments. One should not expect, therefore, that all societies will be aggressive.[34]

Aggression is seen as genetic, at least "in the sense that its components have a high degree of heritability and are therefore subject to continuing evolution" and in the sense that aggressive responses of some species are "specialized, stereotyped, and highly predictable in the presence of certain very general stimuli."[35] Even though aggression is seen as genetic, Wilson is reluctant to define aggression as an instinct. Neither does he see it as an inborn drive that builds up pressure until it bursts the dam of inhibition. Wilson maintains that there is no general instinct for aggression, only particular patterns of aggressive behvior that different species have found to be adaptive for their environment. Aggression is sort of like a "genetic contingency plan—a set of complex responses of the organism's endocrine and nervous systems, programmed to be summoned up in time of stress."[36] Out of a large variety of possible violent behaviors, man exhibits only a small range. Particular forms of organized warfare are not inherited; no genes differentiate between head hunting or cannibalism, between dueling or genocide. Man inherits a wide variety of possible behaviors. Which behavior particular human beings display depends on cultural differences. Each culture gives a specific form to aggression. In turn, the cultural evolution of aggression would seem to be guided by (a) the genetic predisposition toward learning some form of communal aggression, (b) the necessities imposed by the environment, and (c) the previous history of the group, which biases it toward the adoption of one cultural innovation as opposed to another.[37]

Biology is responsible for the initial evolution of organized aggression, but whether this behavior is maintained will be determined more by a cultural process under the control of rational thought. In other words, even though warfare may have a genetic basis, the evolution of warfare can be reversed—an example being the Maoris of New Zealand.[38]

However, the bottom line for Wilson is that man is "predisposed to slide into deep, irrational hostility under certain definable conditions."[39]

Our brains do appear to be programmed to the following extent: we are inclined to partition other people into friends and aliens. . . . we tend to fear deeply the actions of strangers and to solve conflict by aggression. These learning rules are most likely to have evolved during the past hundreds of thousands of years of human evolution and, thus, to have conferred a biological advantage on those who conformed to them with the greatest fidelity.[40]

Critiques of Sociobiology

Many of the criticisms of sociobiology have been generated by anthropologists, and thus our discussion of the critiques of that discipline will serve as an introduction to the nurture side of the debate about the causes of human aggression.

Wilson says much with which anthropologists can agree; indeed, there seems to be substantial common ground. Most anthropologists agree that there is no doubt that much of human behavior has a genetic basis, but that this is different from saying, as Wilson does, that such behavior is genetically determined. Although Wilson recognizes in turn the importance of culture, environment, and learning in determining aggression, he generally tends to give more weight to the genetic influences than anthropologists believe they merit.

For instance, Wilson argues that the reproductive efficiency of the group or its chances of survival are increased by the altruistic acts of its members. Natural selection thus selects favorably for altruism, but does that mean that genes "determine" altruistic acts? Montagu doubts this. Mankind displays great variety in altruism. Montagu also cites the study by Harlow in which monkeys which are isolated or inadequately socialized are unable to act altruistically later in life. He argues the same is true of humans. Altruism may have a genetic basis, but environmental factors play the decisive role in determining whether such behavior will be developed or not.[41] The same is true with aggression.

Critics also attack the historical basis of Wilson's reasoning. Wilson argues that the "tendency under certain circumstances to indulge in warfare against competing groups may well be in our genes, having been advantagous to our Neolithic ancestors."[42] Anthropologist Ashley Montagu disputes Wilson's implication that warfare first appeared among Neolithic communities, saying there is no unambiguous evidence of such behavior. Neolithic man had tools that *might* have been used in warfare, but they most probably had other uses as well, and we have no direct evidence of their use in war.[43] Additionally, hunter-gatherer people never achieved a Neolithic stage of development; neither did they develop warfare. Is it more reasonable to assume that they did not inherit the aggressive genes Wilson talks about, or is it more logical that warfare was absent from these groups for reasons having to do with culture and environment rather than genetics? Montagu opts for the second explanation; hunter-gatherer peoples did not engage in warfare because they had no environmental or cultural reason to. Alternatively, if Wilson is correct and evidence of warfare does first appear among Neolithic communities, then one ought to examine the particular social and environmental conditions of such communities that led to the arrival of warfare.[44]

Finally, Wilson has failed to build a convincing case for his general proposition that social behavior is determined to a large extent by heredity. His evidence for this is that man shares several similar modes of social behavior with his nearest animal relatives: the size of adult groupings is in the range of ten to one hundred, not smaller; there is a relatively long period of social training of the young; the institution of play, and so on. Likewise, all human groups share similar social behaviors (mentioned above), such as athletic sports, division of labor, education, funeral rites, gift giving, marriage, status differentiation, and so forth. The reaction of anthropologists to this is simply the common environmental influences in man are likely to produce common forms of social behavior. Faced with similar problems and similar tasks, various human groups throughout the world constructed similar institutions to resolve these problems and solve these tasks. Since Wilson can provide no genetic evidence for the claims he makes, the claims of the anthropologists are just as likely to be true.[45]

Ethology, Sociobiology, and War?

One general comment would seem to be in order now concerning the theories of human aggression we discussed above. If war is seen as being derived from an innate aggressiveness that is a part of the nature of mankind, then warfare should be a relatively constant state of affairs. Yet we know that war and aggression are not constant in time or space. Why are some nations peaceful? Why are some nations peaceful at some times, but aggressive at others? Theories that focus on the general aggressive nature of mankind are unable to provide the answers to these questions. To the extent that ethology and sociobiology accurately explain human aggression, and this is far from clear, they are still inadequate to the needs of an empirical theory of interstate war. Since they are unable to address the *variability* of war, they are essentially dead ends. A look at the nurture side of the debate should provide greater insight regarding the variation in human aggression.

Nurture

Different historical periods have witnessed different amounts of war, and within these periods different states have experienced varying amounts of war. Not only has the frequency of war varied, but the goals of war, the rules for conducting warfare, and the reasons and justifications for it have varied from time to time and place to place.[46] All of this suggests to some observers that war is not as culturally acceptable in some times and places as in others.[47] War exists within a general political culture, which is an important factor in determining whether conflicts are pursued through warfare or through less violent methods.

The flip side of the nature argument is therefore the argument of "nurture": aggression is culturally determined, not biologically determined. Man learns aggression from his cultural environment. Just as aggression is learned, peaceful, cooperative attitudes toward conflict resolution may also be learned. Aggressive behavior is not inevitable. While aggression may exist on a macro level, it is not universal; rather, it is culturally specific and culturally derived.

Those on the nurture side of the dispute, primarily behavioral psychologists and anthropologists, make several arguments. (1) Since man varies greatly in his behavior of aggression, different cultures are a good place to look for an explanation of the differences in aggression. (2) Peaceful societies do in fact exist, dispelling the myth that all men are aggressive. (3) The experimental evidence is fairly clear that aggression is greatly influenced by learning. Aggression can be taught; it can also be modified, reduced, and even eliminated by learning.

Nurture: Cultural Evolution

Anthropologists frequently argue that early man was initially a peaceful animal with a nonaggressive "nature." Montagu suggests that "everything points to the non-violence of the greater part of man's early existence and to the contribution made by the increasing development of cooperative activities" such as the social process of hunting itself, the invention of speech, and the development of tools for food getting and gathering. There is no evidence, as far as Montagu is concerned, of either intragroup or intergroup hostilities in early man before the development of agricultural-pastoral communities. Such aggressive behavior would have endangered the whole population and would—in Wilson's terms—not have promoted adaptiveness.[48]

For anthropologists, an important key to aggression is the fundamental change in the social and cultural environment that confronted mankind as we progressed from the nomadic hunter-gatherer stage of development to that of settled agricultural or pastoral existence. In agricultural or herding societies, land became a valuable possession, which was for the first time owned by individuals or groups and required protection from other individuals or groups. For instance, Richard Leaky argues that

> as soon as people commit themselves to agricultural food production as against nomadic food gathering . . . they commit themselves to defending the land they farm. To run away in the face of hostility is to face certain loss: a year's labour may be invested in the fields, and that cannot be given up easily. . . .
>
> As well as land that requires defending, agriculturalists tend to acquire property, both personal and communal, that needs to be guarded.[49]

Leaky therefore suggests that the *Agricultural Revolution* constituted a major social, cultural, economic, and political change, which was followed by a substantial increase in military encounters between neighboring groups. The agricultural revolution led directly to the creation of towns, villages, and cities. These new communities depended on new forms of social organization quite different from that of nomadic bands. Principally, they required the creation of large-scale enterprises (construction of temples, palaces, walls, irrigation ditches, and canals), which in turn required centralized control. As towns and cities developed new political structures to organize and control essential community activities, they also acquired the organizational ability to create and maintain large armies. Leaky thus sees warfare as a response to the changing economic and social circumstances in which early man found himself after the agricultural revolution.[50]

Andrew Bard Schmookler adds another piece to the puzzle. In his *Parable of the Tribes*, he argues that the transition to a settled agricultural existence constituted a major turning point in human history.[51] Agricultural societies eventually encountered limits to their growth posed by the existence of other communities. This typical Malthusian problem that agricultural communities faced could be resolved either by a more intensive use of the land or by expanding one's current farming and grazing areas at the expense of one's neighbors through the use of force. With no overarching power to prevent it (that is, under the condition of anarchy), the more highly organized cities pursued the latter course. In response, peaceful societies had essentially four possible options: destruction by their neighbors, subjugation, withdrawal through migration, and imitation. Imitation proved to be the choice of most communities.

In order to survive, agrarian societies were compelled to emulate their most aggressive rivals. They built large communities through consolidation and aggregation; they constructed large-scale political organizations in order to efficiently mobilize their populations; they iniated taxation systems to make the wealth of society available to these governments; and they created military institutions to protect and extend their power. In reality, certain avenues of cultural evolution were closed off. More highly organized societies drove out the less highly organized; the large drove out the small; the more warlike cultures drove out the more peaceful cultures. *Social evolution* proceeded in only one direction—toward the creation of ever more powerful and militant societies. A process of cultural selection seems to have been at work here. The result of this process was that powerful, militaristic political units spread throughout the world, and wars between these societies became endemic.

Nurture: Peaceful Societies

Despite the general trend identified by Schmookler, peaceful societies have not only existed in the distant past, but many such societies have survived into more recent times. A great many of these are hunter-gather societies. Observation of these communities may provide some insight into the roots of aggression. David Fabbro's study of peaceful societies focused on societies that were deemed to be peaceful due to (a) the absence of wars on their territory, (b) the absence of external war involvement by the group, (c) the absence of civil war or internal collective violence, (d) the lack of a standing military-political organization, and (e) little or no interpersonal violence in the society.[52] Fabbro investigated seven societies that met these criteria: the Semai of Malaysia, the Siriono of Bolivia, the Mbuti pygmies of Zaire, the Kung Bushmen of the Kalahari, the Copper Eskimoes of northern Canada, the Hutterites of North America, and the islanders of Tristan da Cunha in the South Pacific. (Other peaceful societies might include the Zuni of the American Southwest, the Arapesh and the Fore of New Guinea, the Walbiri aborigines of Australia, the Tasaday of the Philippines, the Tahitians, the Lepchas of Sikkim, and many more.)

What are these peaceful societies like? The seven peaceful societies examined by Fabbro could all be classified as "egalitarian band societies," which generally lack patterns of ranking and stratification, place no restrictions on the number of people capable of exercising power or occupying positions of prestige, and have economies where exchange is based on generalized reciprocity.[53] All are small, face-to-face communities, a major factor contributing to their open and egalitarian decision-making process. Though the first five are hunting and gathering societies, the last two have some agricultural base. However, they all produce little or no surplus, and what is produced is distributed equally. The lack of an *economic surplus* (that is, the production of economic goods beyond what is needed for subsistence) would seem to be important. If there is no surplus, the political authorities can not confiscate or commandeer it and use the wealth derived from it as a basis for carrying on coercive activities, including the creation of a military organization.[54]

Fabbro concludes that peaceful societies are peaceful essentially because they lack some of the most important structural prerequisites for engaging in war: a coercive hierarchy and leadership and an economic surplus to support a nonproductive military organization.[55] It is important to notice that the scarcity of resources, with which most of these societies are faced, is *not* a factor that contributes to violence; quite the contrary, it is a factor that encourages close cooperation.

Many of these societies also develop cultural norms that discourage violence. The Kung disparage physical combat as a means of settling disputes. Instead, the most admired characters in the Kung folklore are those who deal with adversity through trickery and deception rather than through force.[56]

It should be mentioned, of course, that not all primitive societies have been totally nonviolent. The variability in violence among traditional societies is fairly large; violence and even warfare exist. But the central point, according to Gwynne Dyer, is that precivilized societies did not kill people *much.* Dyer notes that of the hundreds of hunter-gatherer societies which modern man has encountered, almost all have had the same attitude toward war: "it is an important ritual, an exciting and dangerous game, and perhaps even an opportunity for self-expression, but it is not about power in any recognizable modern sense of the word, and it most certainly is not about slaughter."[57] Neither is it about the conquest of territory.

Dyer contends that there is scarcely one recorded example of such tribes participating in a death struggle with its neighbors because of population pressure or economic scarcity. Although many were engaged in low-level warfare against their neighbors in their spare time, . . . nobody thought 'winning' was sufficiently important to put much thought into organizing warfare efficiently. . . ."[58] This low-level tribal warfare was limited in nature and highly ritualized. The American Plains Indians' institution of "counting coup"—whereby the adversary was not killed, but simply touched with a stick or hand—is an excellent example. The fighting often stopped for the day after a single casualty was exacted, and there were deliberate steps taken to prevent the destructiveness of the warfare. Individuals got killed, though only a few at a time, and the societies survived intact.[59]

Dyer concludes that precivilized warfare was mostly a "rough male sport for underemployed hunters, with the kinds of damage-limiting rules that all competitive sports have." On the other hand, as these people have "progressed" toward agriculture and herding, the warriors have more free time and they begin to acquire material interests to defend; the outcome is that war becomes more destructive.[60] Quincy Wright's analysis of 633 primitive cultures confirms that the collectors, lower hunters, and low-level farmers were the least warlike of these primitive peoples while the most advanced herding and farming societies were the most warlike.[61]

The conclusion of anthropologists and historians is, therefore, that a tremendous increase in violence accompanied the transition of societies from the hunter-gatherer life to the more settled, agricultural existence and the concomitant rise of towns and cities. Changes in the social, cultural, economic, and political environment associated with the agricultural revolution brought about significant changes in the behavior of many human communities. The level of violence and warfare increased substantially.

Nevertheless, it is clear that there are many nonaggressive individuals within these generally aggressive, modern communities. Most societies are filled with people who would find it very difficult to take another's life, even in anger. Even if aggression is part of the human genetic makeup, it would not seem to be enough to cause most people to be able to kill another human being. Werner Levi, in his much quoted analysis of the causes of war, notes that there never seem to be enough "aggressive" men flocking to the recruiting stations during war, so that everywhere men are drafted to perform such services. Once drafted into the military, they need a heavy dose of indoctrination to turn them into killers. It takes a great deal of conditioning to prepare them for face-to-face combat. Even so, in some armies more than half of the men who were supposed to fight did not pull the trigger.[62] They were willing to die for their countries, but they were not willing to kill for them. Environmental factors would seem to have been at least somewhat successful in suppressing whatever genetic impulses man has toward aggression.

Nurture: Social Learning Theory

Clearly, violent behavior varies greatly between individuals and groups. What might account for this? One answer is that the differences may be accounted for by different learning experiences.

Behavioral psychologists have shown that aggression can be modified through the learning of peaceful or cooperative responses, and experimental research in the laboratory has indicated the power of conditioning to change the behavior of animals. For instance, Scott reports that male mice have been trained to be completely peaceful.[63] It is also apparent that many societies have "learned" to be nonaggressive. Aggression is almost totally absent in some cultures, even as a response to frustration. Even when aggression is present, vastly different patterns exist. (In some societies, such as the Eskimos, there is some individual aggressiveness, but there is no group welfare, while in Pueblo Indian societies individuals are not pugnacious but there is group warfare.) These circumstances tend to indicate that both individual aggressiveness and group aggressiveness must be learned, and learned separately.[64]

Albert Bandura, a proponent of *social learning theory*, maintains that aggression is learned in large part from the social environment.[65] Aggression is very much influenced by the socialization process that almost all youngsters encounter—in the home, among family members, with peers, in school, and in religious groups—as a natural part of growing up and becoming familiar with societal norms. (There is a sizable amount of information, for instance, that more aggressive individuals come from homes where corporal punishment is used, and that criminals have been abused as children.)[66] The form that aggression takes, the situations in which it occurs, its frequency and intensity, and the targets against which it is demonstrated are largely determined by social experience. The socialization process is instrumental in determining the contexts in which aggression is permitted (if any) and the targets (if any) that are permissible for individuals occupying particular roles in society.

Aggression, like any other behavior, can be learned through direct experience or by observing the behavior of others. Individuals quickly learn to anticipate the probable consequences of various behaviors through personal experience, through observing the actions of others, from communication, and so on. Once a particular behavior (aggressive or nonaggressive) is adopted, it is maintained, modified, or eliminated by positive or negative *reinforcement*. This reinforcement comes primarily in the form of the consequences that result from one's actions. Human behavior is controlled to a great extent by its consequences: responses that cause unrewarding or punishing effects are discarded, while those that produce rewarding outcomes are retained and strengthened. If aggressive responses to environmental stimuli are met with approval by peers and by dominant elders, or if those who use such behavior are met with attention and their desires are fulfilled, then aggression is reinforced. On the other hand, if aggressive tactics are met with rejection, reprimands, lack of approval or attention, or inability to attain goals, then aggression as a response to environmental stimuli will be reduced.

It might be interesting to spend a moment pondering mass culture in the United States as reflected in films. If films do indeed mirror the predominant cultural attitudes and norms of society, and if children and young adults do indeed learn attitudes and behavioral norms from such films, what does this portend for the United States? In particular, it might be interesting to reflect on the image of heroes in American film. Who are our heroes and why? From John Wayne in the 1950s to Clint Eastwood and Charles Bronson in the 1960s and 1970s, to Sly Stallone and Arnold Schwartzeneggar in the 1980s and 1990s, the male American hero has been a man of violence, a man who settled his disputes outside of the normal legal institutions, a man for whom compromise, diplomacy, mediation, arbitration, and adjudication were farces to be treated with derision or suspicion. The hero was not the man of peace who could settle disputes between his neighbors through logic and persuasion, but the man of action who settled disputes through violence and bloody retribution. In such a way do we learn violence from our culture.

A complicating factor is that individuals are subject to several learning environments. Each culture—whether it is twentieth-century American or nineteenth-century Plains Indian or tenth-century Viking—develops a general culture within which its citizens are socialized and whose cultural norms they absorb. However, most cultures—especially the more complex modern cultures—have subcultures with a set of competing values and norms. Additionally, each individual is confronted with somewhat different learning experiences in the home and in the workplace. The learning experiences at these different levels may be considerably at variance with each other. For instance, it may be that while the general culture condones and rewards violence, the family finds it repugnant and teaches cooperative, nonviolent practices. At another level, the political practitioner of international relations may find a different set of cultural norms at work in the relations among states in the international system. The behaviors for which one is rewarded in the national culture may not be the behaviors for which one is rewarded (or punished) in the international environment.

If individual behavior is the product of cultural environment, then the behavior of our rulers is probably the product of several different environments. George Bush's behavior in office will not only be the result of the American culture of his times, but it will also be the result of his particular upbringing at home and at school. It will also be influenced by the special subcultures into which he was socialized while serving in government posts such as the director of the CIA, ambassador to the United Nations, head of the U.S. liaison office in Peking, Vice President, and so on. Presumably it will also be influenced by his direct experience in international affairs and by his observation of the consequences of American action in the international arena.

In summary, social learning theory reminds us of the importance of culture as a source of violence. It admonishes us that if we seek to understand the cause of violence and aggression, we need to understand that individuals (including national leadaers) are quite frequently the products of an social and cultural environments that condone and even reward aggression and belittle peaceful cooperation. Ultimately, however, the implications of social learning theory for controlling aggression and violence are optimistic. If aggression is learned, it can be unlearned. If violence is based on cultural and environmental factors, these can be changed—albeit slowly. Cultural institutions are man-made and subject to human manipulation over time; they are dynamic rather than static. Just as certain institutions that were once thought to be "natural" in their time have now been largely eliminated in most cultures—slavery, for example—violence may also come to be condemned and eliminated in the future.

Conclusion

Before we go on to the more individualistic explanations of war, two final comments about theories of the "natural" aggressiveness of mankind are in order. First, if aggression has a genetic or instinctual basis, if it is indeed part of "human nature," then efforts to eliminate war are almost certainly doomed to failure. Logically, in order to eliminate war we would need to (1) change the nature of man, or (2) somehow place man's violent nature under severe and necessarily artificial restraints, or (3) provide outlets for man's innate aggression that are morally and culturally more acceptable and physically less damaging. We do not presently know how to do the first, and even if we did, it might not be a good idea to begin tampering with mankind through some sort of radical genetic engineering. The second and third options have been more or less continually applied throughout the ages without significant success in behavior modification.

Second, if war is derived from an innate aggressiveness that is part of the common nature of mankind, then how do we explain peace? Do men somehow "rebel" against their own nature and become peaceful? As we have stated, war and aggression are constant neither in time nor in space. Some nations are significantly more peaceful than others, and even the most warlike nations are not constantly engaged in organized warfare. Theories that attempt to explain war by reference to the reputed aggressive nature of mankind are able to give us little insight into the fairly substantial differences in the behavior of states. Since they are unble to deal with the tremendous variability in the behavior of states, theories that reduce the causes of war to innate human aggression are ultimately unsatisfing. We are much more likely to be successful in developing a theory of war if we focus, as the nurturists have done, on the factors that explain the differences in the behaviors of individuals, groups, and nations.

One explanation for the varied aggressiveness of states is that such variation is due to the individual and personal psychgological characteristics of the states' leaders. The variation in the aggressiveness of states is due to the variation in the personal psychologiocal natures of their leaders. We explore this possibility in the next chapter.

3

The Individual Level of Analysis: Psychological Explanations for War

> The common folk do not go to war of their own accord, but are driven to it by the madness of kings.
>
> —Sir Thomas More

Thus far we have been operating under the assumption that men are aggressive due to things that they have more or less in common: aggressive instincts inherited through the millennia, cultural predispositions toward violence, general psychological needs common to all members of the human species—the common "nature" of man. It is quite likely that what is more important are the differences between men rather than their similarities.

It should be apparent that not all men have the same "nature." Some men are clearly more violent than others. There are great differences in the psychological makeup of individuals, differences that are important to the understanding of conflict among men.

Consider for a moment the war between India and Pakistan in 1971. The forces of West Pakistan had invaded East Pakistan to overthrow the results of an election that would have placed an East Pakistani political leader at the head of the state. India was burdened by over ten million refugees from East Pakistan and harbored long-standing grudges against Pakistan. Finally, Prime Minister Indira Gandhi ordered Indian forces to penetrate five miles into Pakistani territory and issued an ultimatum ordering the Pakistani ruler, Yahya Khan, to withdraw from East Pakistan. Yahya Khan chose war instead, a fatal mistake since his army was quickly and decisively defeated, with East Pakistan gaining independence as Bangladesh. Why did this occur? Consider John Stoessinger's treatment of Yahya Khan's reaction to the Indian ultimatum; he maintains that the ultimatum

> was a hard blow under any circumstances, but for a man with Yahya Khan's *fragile masculine ego*, such as ultimatum from a woman was psychologi-

cally unacceptable. Thus, even though he knew that the Indian forces outnumbered his own by a ratio of five to one, the president of Pakistan ordered a massive air strike against India on December 3.[1]

The defense of Yahya Khan's male ego from intimidation by a female rival seemed to have been a decisive factor in the decision to go to war!

It is quite appropriate that we should seek the causes of war, therefore, in the individual makeup of those national leaders who are in a position to decide the fate of their states. The basic assumption at this level of analysis is that individuals do make a difference. It matters that Boris Yeltsin sits in the Kremlin instead of Josef Stalin; it makes a difference whether George Bush sits in the Oval Office instead of Jimmy Carter. It matters, presumably, because in most cases wars are precipitated by the decisions of individual leaders and their advisers. One would be hard-pressed to find examples of war that occurred without a command decision from the highest level of government authority. Thus, if we want to know what caused the outbreak of war, we need to understand the individuals who were responsible for those decisions.

On the other hand, we must be careful not to completely reduce the causes of every war to the psychological makeup of individual leaders. It is clear that the ability of any individual leader alone to determine war or peace is constrained by a great number of important factors: by the international and domestic environments, by the role of governmental bureaucracies in policy formulation and implementation, by formal and informal decision-making processes, and so on. It is also clear that there are some situations in which these constraints are less powerful and in which a single individual leader will be able to make a significant impact on national policy. In such a situation the leader's personality and psychological characteristics may be decisive.

Under what circumstances might we expect individual leaders to be able to rise above the normal organizational constraints? The obvious answer is when the decision is made at the very highest levels of the political system. The situation might be one in which only the top executives and their advisers make the decision. The higher one is in the bureaucratic hierarchy, the fewer organizational and role constraints there are to restrict the influence of one's personality on the decision. Perhaps the decision will be one in which the highest decision-maker has sole responsibility. The fewer the number of individuals involved, the more we will be able to focus on individual and personality factors instead of larger institutional factors. But when do we see decision-making at the highest-levels?[2]

Decisions are made by a small number of top level executives under a number of circumstances:

1. When formal, constitutional procedures (or informal, situational factors) demand it, owing to the type of decision involved or the structure of the situation

2. When the top leader is permitted great latitude and discretion to make decisions on his own (as in a dictatorship)
3. When the leader has a high degree of interest in the decision
4. When there is only one institution responsible for the decision, permitting a few officials in that one institution to make policy unemcumbered by opposition from other organized bureaucratic forces

Furthermore, the personal characteristics of these top leaders will be allowed greater impact on policy:

5. When the decision is a nonroutine or unanticipated situation—one for which no standard operating routines have been developed that would restrict the latitude of decision makers—as in a crisis
6. When the information concerning the situation is either extremely low or when top leaders are inundated with too much information, bringing about an information "overload"; under these conditions the situation is likely to be highly ambiguous, allowing individuals to define the situation themselves and to make decisions in accord with their own predispositions
7. When the top decision-maker has little experience or training in foreign affairs, thus vastly reducing the repertoire as possible policy choices and forcing the leader to reply more on his or her natural problem-solving predispositions
8. When the situation is accompanied by great stress

Assuming that several of these conditions are met, we may begin to examine some personal characteristics that may be crucial determinants of whether a leader will choose to take his nation to war.

Psychological Needs

Psychologists have identified a variety of *psychological needs*, some of which are relevant to politics. The need for self-affection or love, the need for self-esteem or dignity, and the need for self-actualization or fulfillment are often identified, for instance, as well as the needs for security, power, and control.[3] All individuals have the same needs; however, the importance of these needs varies. While some individuals seem to be dominated by the need for self-esteem, others seem to be dominated by the need for power or something else. Abraham Maslow hypothesizes a *hierarchy of needs*. Listed in their order of assumed priority they are:

1. Physical (biological needs)—food, water, air, sex, and so forth
2. Safety needs—the assurance of survival, security

3. Affection and belongingness needs—love
4. Esteem needs—for self-esteem and the respect of others
5. Self-actualization or self-development needs[4]

According to Maslow, these needs are both universal and instinctual; all men potentially have all these needs. Each set of goals in turn monopolizes the individual's consciousness. When the first set of needs is fairly well satisfied, the next "higher" need emerges to dominate the conscious life and serve as a central motivator of human behavior. The "higher" needs may not become activated until the "lower" needs are reasonably satisfied. For instance, if both psychological and security needs are fairly well satisfied, affection needs will become important for the individual. Thus, which needs are important to the particular individual depends on his or her prior pattern of need gratification.[5]

Particularly important is Maslow's depiction of the *self-actualizing* individual—one who has achieved satisfaction of his physical needs and for the psychological needs for security, belongingness, and self-esteem. This physical and psychological security makes it possible for the individual to have trust in his environment. Presumably, individuals with high self-esteem are not only more trusting, but also more opposed to the use of force. However, their confidence in their own abilities would probably lead them to accept greater risks than others. On the other hand, individuals with low self-esteem have been depicted as being anxious, hostile, uncooperative, tough bargainers, paranoid, nationalistic, and as having a propensity toward the use of military force. Presumably, this predeliction for aggressive behavior is the result of the individual's need to compensate (and indeed to overcompensate) for anxiety caused by low self-esteem.

One might contemplate here Henry Kissinger's observation that Soviet leaders who experienced the purges and uncertainties of the Stalinist era could not have escaped developing rather low levels of interpersonal trust. This lack of interpersonal trust and general suspicion predisposed them to be highly suspicious of the external world as well, in particular the United States.[6]

Students of politics are probably all familiar with leaders who seem to have a tremendous need for power. *Power-oriented* people tend to dominate others, to be argumentative, to be paranoid, to have very little humanitarian concern, and (perhaps, fortunately) to be hesitant to take risks. The individual's need for power is also linked to a tendency toward exploitative and conflictual behavior.[7] Power-oriented persons are frequently believed to be compensating for deprivations experienced during childhood, where their needs for security, love, achievement, and self-worth were not met.[8] Unfortunately, such individuals also tend to desire positions of leadership; indeed, this may be the defining characteristic of professional politicians! Harold Lasswell suggested many years ago that the primary motivation for political activity is emotional insecurity or low self-esteem, conditions that are compensated for by a drive for power.[9] There is even some evidence that the greater the top leader's need for power, the more aggressive his government's foreign policies.[10]

On the other hand, those individuals who are dominated more by need for *affiliation* and need for *achievement* tend to lean toward more cooperative interactions with others. Winter and Stewart's study of American presidents indicates that presidents with higher affiliation and achievement needs (as opposed to power needs) were less likely to engage in war and more likely to support arms control.[11] And Terhune's international relations simulations indicate that individuals who are achievement oriented pursue cooperative strategies at first, hoping their opponents will also be cooperative.[12]

Personality Traits

While human beings exhibit a wide variety of personality traits, some have special relevance for the topic of war. One personality type which students of international conflict might wish to watch out for is what Milton Rokeach has dubbed the *dogmatic personality*.[13] Individuals with dogmatic personalities are rather closed-minded. They find it difficult to accept and use new information that contradicts their beliefs, and they are suspicious of the sources of new information. They do not tolerate ambiguous information very well; they are unlikely to examine the full range of alternatives available; and they have a tendency to rely on stereotypes. They are generally suspicious, have high levels of anxiety, and are likely to perceive conspiracies. They are also predisposed to condone the use of force.[14] Given this unsavory set of traits, one would probably not wish someone with a dogmatic personality to occupy the driver's seat during an international crisis.

One of the most discussed set of traits belongs to individuals who may be described as *authoritarian personalities*. A famous study of T. W. Adorno and his associates identified a complex of characteristics that typefied such a personality and then developed a scale through which they could ascertain (by the use of questionnaires) whether a particular individual possessed these traits.[15] Although Adorno named his scale the F-scale for fascism, those who score high on this scale tend to have beliefs that could categorize them as members of either the extreme right (fascists) or the extreme left.

The traits involved include a preoccupation with virility and strength, a tendency to dominate subordinates, deference to superiors, the need to perceive the world in a highly structured way, uncomfortability with disorder, a preference for clear-cut choices, rigidity, and the use of stereotypes. In addition to the obvious effect such a personality would have on the ability of an individual to make rational decisions, what seems to be especially important is that authoritarians tend to be highly nationalistic and ethnocentric, characteristics that are both highly associated with support for war and aggression.[16]

Students of politics are also familiar with individuals who possess *domineering personalities*: Lyndon Johnson, Richard Nixon, and Henry Kissinger come immediately to mind. Individuals with such personality characteristics are probably plentiful on the political scene; political recruitment patterns and self-selection combine to elevate those with high dominance characteristics to high positions. Two separate studies of American presidents and their foreign policy advisers indicate that individuals who possessed the personality trait of dominance were usually much more likely to advocate the use of threats and military force and oppose conciliatory moves than those who scored lower on dominance. Indeed, based on a knowledge of the individual's personality, the authors in both studies were able to accurately predict 77% of the time whether that person would advocate the use of force or not.[17] In other words, the personality trait of dominance seemed to have been generalized from the individual's everyday life to the realm of policy. Domineering leader's tend to relate to other countries in much the same way as they relate to other individuals. This is an important finding. It would seem that decisions on the use of force at the national level are determined at least in part by the personality characteristic of dominance.

One analyst has discovered that in disagreements concerning U.S. policy toward the Soviet bloc, the more *extroverted personalities* were much more likely to advocate cooperative, inclusive policies than those who were more *introverted*. Since personality factors interact, the combination of high dominance and introversion factors would seem to create a particularly undesirable mix. Here is Lloyd Etheredge's analysis of such individuals, whom he labels "Block (Excluding) Leaders," and among whose ranks we find John Foster Dulles, Woodrow Wilson, Herbert Hoover, Charles Evans Hughes, Henry Stimson, Dean Acheson, and Cordell Hull:

> The Bloc Leaders tend to divide the world, in their thought, between the moral values they think it ought to exhibit and the forces opposed to this vision. They tend to have a strong, almost Manichaean, moral component to their views. They tend to be described as stubborn and tenacious. They seek to reshape the world in accordance with their personal vision, and their foreign policies are often characterized by the tenaciousness with which they advance one central idea.[18]

Another interesting personality trait is that of narcissism. *Narcissism* is a highly complex personality construct made up of several factors, including a disposition to exploit and manipulate others, a reveling in leadership and authority roles, attitudes of self-importance, superiority, and grandiosity, egotism, a lack of empathy for others, physical vanity, and a hypersensitivity to the evaluation of others. Strong relationships have been found between narcissism and hostility, aggression, and the need for power.[19]

At least two psychologists have concluded that Iraq's Saddam Hussein has a narcissistic personality. Saddam sees himself as a great historical figure—a world leader of the status of Nasser, Mao, or Castro. This identity is linked to dreams of glory and a messianic vision to rid the Arab world of Western influence and to unite it under a single ruler—himself. He is described as having a paranoid outlook on the world, justifying his aggression as required by threats from his enemies. He is seen as consumed by a drive for unlimited power—a drive that is unconstrained by conscience or by a concern for the suffering of others. But these dreams of glory, feelings of specialness, and messianic ambition (as well as his acts of aggression) hide underlying self-doubt and insecurity.[20]

A final personality trait also deserves mention. The individual's propensity for taking risks would seem to be a trait that may be of cardinal importance regarding decisions for war or peace. In such situations some decision makers are relatively more *risk acceptant*, while others are more *risk averse*. Given the same evaluation of the costs and benefits to be derived from war, some decision-makers may be willing to take the risk for war given a particular probability of success (say, 50%), while other decision-makers may require a greater probability of success (say, 75%). This individual difference may play an important role in the decision to go to war.[21]

The scary part of the story is that high political office seems to attract a lot of folks with strange backgrounds and fairly unattractive personality traits. Robert Isaac, in his study of eight of the major political figures of the twentieth century, finds these elements (among others) in the backgrounds and personalities of his subjects:

1. A strong ego
2. A supportive, and often religious, mother
3. A strong-willed father with whom he had conflict, but with whom he also identified
4. A restrained, redirected, or unusual sex life
5. A certain aloofness or psychological distance
6. A coherent world view
7. A tendency toward mental rigidity
8. A refusal to take existing conditions for granted
9. A disdain for bureaucracy and increasing belief in one's own willpower and inevitability[22]

Psychohistory

Anyone who has taken three final examinations on the same day is aware that there is a rather fine line between sanity and mental illness. The stresses and strains of high political office would seem to place government officials quite near the line more often than either they or we would desire. Jerome Frank maintains that as many as seventy-five chiefs of state in the last four centuries have suffered from severe mental distress while in power.[23] Hitler, Wilson, and Stalin have all been described by their biographers as having had severe psychological problems. Since these biographies combine history and psychology, they are frequently given the name "psychohistory."

Robert Tucker's biography of Stalin describes the Soviet leader as a "neurotic" personality who possessed an idealized image of himself as an heroic figure. (He also identified himself with Lenin, his own hero, according to Tucker.) Since this idealized image was combined with nagging doubts of self-worth, Stalin compulsively sought after power, position, and achievement. He used his power against his opponents—both imagined and real— and he rewrote history and constructed a cult of the personality in order to paint himself as Stalin the "Heroic Genius."[24] The clear implication is that Stalin's predeliction for the use of force in both domestic and international affairs was associated with a subconscious inner compulsion.

The classic study of personality and politics is probably Alexander and Juliet George's *Woodrow Wilson and Colonel House—A Personality Study*.[25] It might be helpful to examine in some detail the Georges' work to give the reader a feel for the kind of analysis done by psychohistorians. George and George examine Wilson's handling of his three major executive office roles: President of Princeton, Governor of New Jersey, and President of the United States. In each office his term ended in controversy and defeat under conditions that offered a very good opportunity for success.

To account for these events, the Georges looked at Wilson's personality. Wilson's behavior was characterized by rigidity and stubbornness, by denial, self-righteousness, a refusal to compromise, and a desire to dominate. Wilson had positive traits as well. He had the ability to be highly ingratiating to those whom he disliked, and he showed remarkable political flexibility at times— illustrated by his conversion from conservatism to progressivism. The Georges find that Wilson was most flexible when seeking power and most rigid when exercising power. Once in office, his need to dominate and avoid being dominated manifested itself only with respect to issues that he believed himself to be uniquely competent to address. On other issues, he had virtually no interest and no desire to dominate. On the central issues, however, Wilson was unbending and totally unable to see any virtue in his opponents' positions. He believed that compromising on these issues was tantamount to tarnishing himself.

A special problem continually occurred. Single male adversaries were especially likely to force Wilson into an inability to compromise—even when it was both possible and rational to compromise, when the compromise required was minor (such as admitting others into the treaty-making process), and even when the compromises involved were ones he himself had advocated in the past. On such issues, disagreements over principle were tinged with clashes of personality. (Wilson's battle with Henry Cabot Lodge over the Versailles Treaty, for instance). As a result, when Wilson did not have the strength to win, he suffered not mere defeats, but crushing devastations. In short, Wilson showed a repeated pattern of self-defeating actions. As far as the Georges were concerned, this nonrational behavior strongly suggested psychological roots.

The Georges conclude that Wilson's behavior suggested a number of *ego defense mechanisms*. This requires a short refresher course in Freudian psychology. The *id* is a concept that refers to one's unchecked wants and desires. The *ego* is one's check on reality. The *superego* is one's conscience. The ego needs to defend itself against the id and superego; it needs to protect the individual's self-esteem and defend against anxiety caused by frustration. Ego defense mechanisms include:

1. Repression
2. Projection
3. Sublimation (redirection of behavior into more acceptable channels)
4. Denial
5. Reaction formation (exaggerated behavior expressing tendencies that are exactly the opposite of the individual's impulses and desires)

Ego defense detracts from mastering reality and from responding rationally to the environment; instead, it leads to responses based on internal, psychological demands. In Wilson's case, his need to dominate was a type of reaction formation in which domination protected him from low self-esteem.

The Georges conclude that Wilson suffered from neurosis, the first and lowest category of mental disorders—the other categories being personality disorder, conduct disorder, and psychosis. The origins of this neurosis date to his experience in his childhood and youth, and especially in his relationship with his father. The elder Wilson was a demanding, dominant Presbyterian minister with a sharp wit that was frequently aimed at his son. There is little doubt that young Woodrow suffered deprivation of affection from his father. His father took an extremely active role in his son's education, seeking to educate him himself. Wilson's rage and resentment of his father were almost entirely repressed, as indicated by his esteem and apparent affection for his father throughout his life. But this rage expressed itself in other ways—for instance, in Wilson's inability to read well until he reached the age of eleven (by this time out of his father's tutelage) and his extremely poor performance in his first years of school. This, from a future Ph.D. in government! His unconscious refusal to learn was a way of expressing resentment and hostility toward his learned father. Wilson's later education was supplemented by writing sermons for his father, who insisted on complete revisions, with ridicule of the originals. The result apparently was that it became crucial for Wilson later in life that his own written words be unaltered.

Wilson's early relationship with his father created a feeling of deep inferiority. Wilson's low self-esteem led to a lifelong struggle against an inner feeling of inadequacy which had to be continually disproved, and it led to the need to dominate as an ego defense mechanism. The use of power compensated for Wilson's damaged self-esteem. The other problem initiated by Wilson's relationship with his father was that dominant, authoritarian males who opposed him on important issues unconsciously became father figures for him, upon whom his repressed hostility for his own father became directed.

The bottom line here is that Wilson thought and behaved normally under most circumstances. He was usually an able and astute politician who understood politics and the necessity for compromise. However, compromise was in reality difficult for Wilson in certain situations in which opposition by a single, dominant man on crucial issues triggered his unconscious problem with his father.

Wilson is not the only American President in whom psychologists have shown an interest. Calvin Coolidge suffered severe depression as an adolescent, and Warren Harding suffered several psychological breakdowns before the age of thirty-five, one of which required hospitalization. Lincoln experienced suicidal depression two decades before attaining the presidency, and according to some experts, Lincoln, both Roosevelts, and Lyndon Johnson were probably all manic depressives, with Johnson manifesting signs of paranoia and delusion.[26]

Richard Nixon has also fascinated psychologists and psychohistorians. Numerous studies of his personality have been published; all, needless to say, without the cooperation of the subject.[27] Many of these studies paint Nixon as an introverted loner: suspicious, devious, secretive, compulsive, with a divided, ambivalent personality. Most of them point to a tremendous insecurity, a fear of failure and of being unloved, and to feelings of inferiority. This feeling of inferiority was related to a need for power and the use of defense mechanisms such as the need to exert control over himself, others, and his environment, a great capacity for denial, and even (according to Fawn Brodie) a compulsion to lie. Prior to his resignation from office, Nixon's psychological condition was so abnormal that his Chief of Staff, Alexander Haig, had performed his own analysis of the President and concluded he was "suicidal." Nixon's condition so alarmed Secretary of Defense James Schlesinger, who concluded that the President was too impaired to function, that he gave orders to the military to disregard any order from the President unless it was countersigned by the Secretary of Defense![28]

Critique of Psychohistory

Although psychobiographies play an important role in alerting us to the importance of individual personalities in domestic and international politics, one must be careful in assessing their value. The main thing that separates psychohistory from the work of regular psychoanalysts is that the latter have the advantage of actually working with and interviewing their subjects; historians work one or two steps removed from this. Politicians are notoriously secretive about their personal lives, and none of the psychohistorians mentioned was able to actually interview his or her subject. Instead, they had to rely on already published biographical material, speeches, letters, diaries, and interviews with relatives and associates. Second, one often wonders about the objectivity of these studies. Biographers are usually not drawn to their subjects because they are neutral toward them; they are usually attracted to them as heroes or repulsed by them as villains. Finally, psychohistorians may be guilty of the sin of reductionism, reducing (in the most extreme form) the nation's foreign policy to the toilet training of the president. One must be careful not to focus entirely on early childhood conflicts and related pathologies as a cause of later behavior without concern for the social and political environments of the time.

Perhaps Herbert Kelman has put this in perspective best. He has argued that there can be no really autonomous psychological theory of war and international relations, only a general theory of international relations in which psychology plays a role.[29]

Stress

As if it weren't enough that we have to worry about leaders whose personality disorders interfere with their ability to make rational decisions, we must also be aware that even "normal" individuals have difficulties making rational decisions under conditions of stress.

Part of man's evolutionary heritage is a cluster of hormonal and metabolic changes that take place in the human body during times of stress. Adrenalin is secreted; stored carbohydrates begin flooding into the blood with sugar, mobilizing the body's energy reserves and alleviating the effects of muscular fatigue; the blood becomes more coagulable; the heart beats faster; breathing patterns are altered. These changes prepare man for some type of extraordinary physical exertion—for the classic alternatives of "fight or flight." However, since in modern times the circumstances that stimulate these bodily changes infrequently lead to the actual expenditures of physical energy, the individual is often left in a frustrated, disturbed, and debilitated state. These ancient mechanisms developed to prepare us for stressful encounters may actually detract from our ability to deal with stressful situations.[30]

Consider, for example, the following events. In July 1988 the U.S.S. *Vincennes*, an Aegis cruiser sent to help guard U.S.-flagged tankers in the Persian Gulf during the Iran-Iraq War, erroneously shot down a commercial airliner flying from Iran to Dubai. It had been a stressful day for the captain and crew; U.S. ships in the Gulf had just finished a skirmish with Iranian boats, sinking two, when radar reported a plane taking off from Bandar Abbas airfield in Iran. Information regarding this plane from radar and electronic intelligence sources was ambiguous, and the captain and crew had only a scant few minutes to determine what to do before the plane would be within range to launch an air-to-sea torpedo at the *Vincennes*. In an attempt to determine whether the plane might be a commercial airliner, one crew member was given the task of checking the airliner guide for flights from Bandar Abbas; the crewman hurriedly thumbed through the guide and missed the flight (which was seventeen minutes late). Another crewman incorrectly recalled the plane's altitude from the screen, leading all concerned to believe the plane to be descending toward the *Vincennes* rather than ascending. Independent psychologists who reviewed the incident concluded that the mistakes were due to combination of stress, information overload, and a breakdown in communication among the *Vincennes*' staff in the Combat Information Center.[31]

Incidents such as these sometimes provide the spark from which wars

Table 3–1
The Debilitating Effects of Stress on Individual Decision-Makers

Increase in	*Decrease in*
Misperception	Analytical thinking
Premature cognitive closure	Creative thinking
Rigidity	Cognitive flexibility
Selective Perception	Tolerance for ambiguity
Stereotyping	Ability to keep an open mind
Ethnocentric, "we–they" thinking	Ability to survey alternative courses of action
Scapegoating, projection of hostility	Ability to discriminate the important from the trivial
Reliance on habit to solve problems	Ability to focus attention
Tunnel vision, loss of perspective	Work efficiency
Oversimplifiction	
Denial	
Group Conformity	
Extreme behavior (from withdrawal to impulsiveness)	

explode, either because they are used by governments as an excuse for initiating a war that has been long desired, or because the incident genuinely arouses a passion for retribution that can seemingly be met in no other way. In this particular case, war between the United States and Iran was avoided, but nations are not always this fortunate.

Experimental simulations and the study of individuals under real conditions of stress both conclude that stress has some rather debilitating effects on the ability of individuals to react rationally to their environment. Table 3.1 provides a short list of the possible effects of stress.[32]

Ole Holsti sums up very nicely our knowledge of the nasty effects of stress:

> The conclusion is sobering: men rarely perform at their best under intense stress. The most probable casualties of high stress are the very abilities which distinguish men from other species: to establish logical links between present action and future goals; to create novel responses to new circumstances; to communicate complex ideas; to deal with abstractions; to perceive not only blacks and whites, but also the many shades of grey which fall in between; to distinguish valid analogies from false ones, and the sense of nonsense; and, perhaps most important of all, to enter into the frames of reference of others. With respect to these precious attributes, the law of supply and demand seems to operate in a perverse manner; as crisis increases the need for them, it also appears to diminish the supply.[33]

Not only is decision-making ability impaired, but the presence of stress may in fact cause physical illness and mental disorder—which might further decrease decision-making ability. Hugh L'Etang's investigation of prominent twentieth-century leaders suggests that acute stress has often led to the development of severe physical illnesses that impaired the ability for rational thought by national leaders.[34] The effects of stress differ, however, with an individual's personality and with physical factors such as age, health, and fatigue. But since national leaders tend to arrive in office in their more mature years (this is being charitable: some arrive well past their prime), the news is not all that wonderful. Increased age is associated with an increased susceptibility to illness and fatigue and with a decreased ability to cope with stress. While it would be nice to be able to create a stress-free environment for our political leaders (and make sure they get plenty of rest), it would appear that stress, unfortunately, is just one of those things that "comes with the territory."

Psychological Factors and War: Implications

At any rate, if psychological and personality factors are the problem, what is the answer? If psychological factors really are that important, one implication might be that selection for high office ought to be conditional upon passing a rigorous psychological examination. And frequent psychological checkups for the political elite ought to be instituted just as often as physical checkups. Unfortunately, political candidates are about as likely to submit to observation and testing by professional psychiatrists as they are to refuse campaign contributions from wealthy admirers. In the final analysis, states are probably best served simply by developing procedural checks on decision-making so that single leaders—whether or not they suffer from psychological or emotional dysfunctions—cannot on their own make the momentous decision of war and peace.

Images, Perceptions, and Misperception

Not only do individuals have different psychological makeups, they also have different images and perceptions of the world. They perceive things in different ways.

Let us start by defining an image. *Images* are organized representations of certain attributes in an individual's mind about objects, events, people, nations, and policies. They are mental pictures of the social and political environment in which we live. Images contain not only our knowledge about these things, but also our evaluations of them—good, bad, neutral—and our attitudes toward them. An image is, of necessity, a simplification of reality. We keep in our mind only certain images of the events, politics, or people we think about. A great deal of information is lost.

These separate images are organized into a more or less coherent and integrated whole—into a kind of *belief system* or "world view"—which contains beliefs, explanations, hypotheses, feelings, predispositions, attitudes, and so on. The belief system orients an individual to his environment, identifying its most important characteristics to him, acting as a set of lenses through which information about the environment passes, organizing perceptions into a coherent guide for action, and establishing goals and preferences.[35] As Ole Holsti has stated: ". . . our beliefs provide us with a more or less coherent code by which we organize and make sense out of what would otherwise be a confusing array of signals picked up from the environment by our senses."[36] A significant part of this general belief system has to do with politics.

We all presume that our images and perceptions of the world—its events, its nations, and its leaders—are true representations, accurately corresponding to reality. Unfortunately, this is infrequently the case. Our perceptions of events and actions in the international environment are of necessity filtered through our present images of the world. These images, which are more or less kept on file in our minds, are used to help us interpret the "real world." However, these images are a source of bias that may seriously hamper our ability to create a realistic picture of our surroundings. Just as an individual's personality predisposes him to respond to certain situations in certain ways, so do his images and his belief system.[37] For a variety of reasons, which we will explore in this section, our images of the world around us may be seriously distorted.

This is important because political leaders act on their individual images and perceptions of the world rather than on objective reality. For all practical purposes, the image *is* the reality. Two pioneers of international relations, Harold and Margaret Sprout, long ago made the important distinction between the *psychological milieu* (the world as perceived by the decision maker) and the *operational milieu* (the world as it really is, and the world in which politics must be carried out). They argued that decision-makers act on their knowledge of the former rather than the latter.[38] We can only hope that the images and perceptions used by national policy makers are accurate, but we know that this is not always the case.

The Content of Images and Belief Systems: Operational Codes

One of the most important areas of investigation is that of the content of a person's image of the world or belief system. Although several concepts have been used to describe the content of the belief system, the most widely used concept is that of the *operational code*. Alexander George defines an operational code as a "particularly significant portion of the actor's entire set of beliefs about political life."[39] (Although there are certainly subtle differences in definition involved, belief systems and operational codes overlap with what might be called an ideology—a coherent set of political beliefs.) Following an earlier work by Nathan Leites on the belief system of the early Bolshevik leaders in the U.S.S.R.,[40] George developed a framework for the operational code that consisted of ten questions about politics. The answers to these questions would delineate the crucial aspects of a person's political belief system. Five questions were "philosophical" and five were "instrumental," dealing with political tactics.[41]

Philosophical Questions

1. What is the "essential" nature of political life? Is the political universe essentially one of harmony or conflict? What is the fundamental character of one's political opponents?

2. What are the prospects for the eventual realization of one's fundamental political values and aspirations? Can one be optimistic or pessimistic on this matter?

3. Is the future predictable? In what sense and to what extent?
4. How much "control" or "mastery" can one have over historical development? What is the role of the individual in "moving" or "shaping" history in the desired direction?
5. What is the role of "chance" in human affairs and in historical developments?

Instrumental Questions

1. What is the best approach for selecting goals or objectives for political action? (For instance, on the basis of purely unilateral national interest or on the basis of multilateral considerations involving self-restraint?)
2. How are the goals of actions pursued most effectively? (For instance, through force or diplomacy? Unilaterally or multilaterally? Through threats or promises of reward?)
3. How are the risks of political action calculated, controlled, and accepted? (For instance, through slow escalation of one's actions or through a fait accompli?)
4. What is the best "timing" of action to advance one's interest? (What, for instance, is the utility of preemption or surprise? Should force be used simultaneously with negotiation? Should one wait until military parity has been achieved before one pushes demands upon a rival?)
5. What are the utility and role of different means for advancing one's interests?

Several political scientists have used George's framework in their research efforts. Typically, these analysts have chosen to investigate the operational codes of important national leaders or foreign policy advisers. Speeches, autobiographical material, books, and articles by the subject are studied, using a method called *content analysis* to identify the political beliefs of the subject. Once this has been done, attempts are often made to determine whether the state's actual policies have reflected the operational code of the individual policy maker.

It is not argued that the policy maker's operational code can be mechanically applied to the situation so that we will be able to reliably predict a state's policy from its chief policy maker's belief system. Rather, operational codes are seen as just one of many factors that play a role in determining policy. Sometimes they are extremely important, sometimes not.[42] What we *do* know is that the belief system will have an important effect on a policy maker's perceptions of events in the external world, that it acts as a filter between stimuli from the environment and the individual's response to those stimuli, that in situations of complexity and uncertainty decision-makers may have a tendency to fall back on their belief systems, and that the existence of belief systems may narrow the range of alternatives that decision-makers may consider during the decision process.[43]

Henry Kissinger has provided a fertile field for analysts. Having been a respected professor of international relations with numerous publications prior to his service as National Security Adviser and Secretary of State in the Nixon and Ford administrations, there were plentiful paper trails from which to map out his operational code; in fact, there was a veritable gold mine of writings waiting to be subjected to content analysis. Here was a man who developed an extremely coherent approach to international politics (based on the "realist" perspective) before he entered public service. Would this coherent world view, or operational code, have a significant impact on U.S. policy once Kissinger attained a position of authority?

A study of Kissinger's bargaining behavior in the negotiations to end the conflict in Vietnam indicates a very close relationship between Kissinger's belief system and his strategy and tactics in this particular negotiation. In fact, the author states that Kissinger's operational code was the most influential variable affecting the sequence of American actions during the spring and summer of 1972. Kissinger's goals and behaviors during the negotiations seemed to be a logical extension of his general beliefs, formulated many years prior to public service.[44] On the other hand, a study of U.S. policy toward the Soviet Union and China during the Kissinger years concluded that Kissinger's images of the U.S.S.R. and China were only indirectly related to American foreign policy behavior.[45]

The Structure of Images: Why Images Resist Change

Although the content of images and belief systems varies enormously among different individuals, the structure of these beliefs is much more regular. Certain definite patterns can be discerned in the way images are formed and maintained or changed, in the relationships among the different parts of the belief system, and in the way incoming information is dealt with. One of the most interesting aspects of the structure of images has to do with the process by which images are either changed or preserved as a result of new information.

Our images constantly shift and are reappraised as new information is received. They are constantly tested against our observations and experiences in the real world. A kind of *reality testing* is performed as we compare our current image of the world to new information about the world. (A gross inability to do this properly is one sign of mental illness.) Of course this process of reality testing is not at all simple. Most of us engage in *selective perception*. While we readily see (and mentally "register") those things we want to see, we ignore many things that do not fit very well with our existing images of the world.

Obviously, it is important for decision makers to be able to modify their images through reality testing. How images change is not entirely understood, but one important factor is the complexity of an individual's image structure. The images of the world that we have may be relatively simple or relatively complex, depending on the number of pieces of information held and the relationships among these pieces. A *complex image* structure is more easily changed. Such an image has many more dimensions, more nuance, more information. Most important, complex images contain bits of information that may be inconsistent with other bits of information that are also held in the image. Because such an image is so eclectic, diverse, and complex, its holder is more open to change.

On the other hand, a *simple image* not only contains less information, but the information is also much more consistent—it all sums up in the same direction; it is all positive or all negative. Changing such an image is more difficult. Simple images tend to be very rigid and may even be "closed." However, even complex images do not change swiftly. Images, by their very nature, seem resistant to change.

As social scientists are fond of saying, the data never speak for themselves. Faced with a new set of facts, an individual may find several explanations to be equally plausible. Preexisting images help us make sense of new information and we tend to fit incoming information into existing images. This is especially true if the information is ambiguous.[46]

However, when the new information clearly doesn't fit with the images already held, but instead challenges one's present images, a number of factors inhibit image change. Individuals seem to possess an inner striving for *"cognitive consistency."* Our normal tendency is to try to reduce the inconsistencies between our various beliefs and feelings. A discrepancy between inconsistent parts of our image of the world causes *"cognitive dissonance."*[47] We don't tolerate cognitive dissonance very well, and we may attempt to deal with it by modifying our image of the world to account for this new, discordant information: in other words, by successfully performing reality testing. More likely, however, we will try somehow to retain the original image. This is especially likely if central, core values are challenged by the new information.

Many techniques exist for retaining the original image in the face of such discordant information: (1) we may simply ignore or reject the new information; (2) we may discredit the source of the new information; (3) we may twist or distort the information or reinterpret it in a way that conforms to our present image; (4) we may search for information that *does* conform to our present image of the world; or (5) we may simply treat it as "the exception which proves the rule."[48]

Two warnings should be issued at this point. First, in spite of all we have said so far, most individuals are able to perceive reality correctly in many cases.[49] Not everything is distorted! And second, cognitive consistency is not always irrational. It may be quite logical to view incoming information as being consistent with one's current image. It has to be evaluated in *some* way, and given the complexity and uncertainty of much information, we may quite logically evaluate it in a manner consistent with our current image of the world, especially if it accords with our past experience.[50]

Although this tendency toward cognitive consistency is not always irrational, its presence does indicate a systematic bias in the way individuals process information. Incoming information is too readily assimilated to our prior images; new information is made to fit the individual's existing predispositions or hypotheses. Thus, there is a definite tendency toward refusal to change one's image. Since the various images in the belief system are highly interrelated, any major adjustment of beliefs (especially core beliefs) is likely to set off a chain reaction that would in turn place a severe burden on one's information-processing system—sort of like overloading our circuits. Stability of images is therefore preferred.[51]

The Resistance of Images to Change: Some Examples

Let's take an example of an international situation that might challenge a national leader's image of the world. Soviet General Secretary Gorbachev's foreign policy approaches in the late 1980s—making major concessions to the United States on arms control, the withdrawal of Soviet troops from Afghanistan, unilateral troop reductions in Eastern Europe, a renunciation of the Brezhnev doctrine, which in turn permitted democratic revolutions in Eastern Europe, the reduction of Soviet forces in Mongolia and along the Soviet-Chinese border, the pressure on Vietnam to remove its forces from Kampuchea, and the virtual abandonment of Marxist regimes in places like Mozambique—all these created a situation of severe cognitive dissonance for hard-line "Cold Warriors" in the United States.

Instead of changing their image of the Soviet Union, many American policy analysts in the late 1980s resorted to various techniques to preserve their already existing cognitive structures. Gorbachev's policies were at first discredited as mere public relations ploys cynically designed to change the West's image of the U.S.S.R. (The special problem of international politics is, after all, that since deception is common, actions by other states that do not conform to one's image can be easily categorized as deliberate attempts to deceive.) Alternatively, Gorbachev's policies were initially ignored as relatively meaningless gestures, or they were reinterpreted so as to be consistent with Cold War images. For instance, they were seen as simply a temporary retreat brought on by a combination of Western strength and firmness and by the horrendous condition of the Soviet economy rather than as concessions brought about by any real change in Soviet thinking. And Gorbachev himself was seen as an exception to his predecessors, and one not likely to last very long given the opposition to his policies from more hard-line members of the Soviet political elite.[52] As a result of these image-preserving techniques, U.S. leaders were rather slow to assess the real importance of Gorbachev's revolution in foreign policy.

One of the classic studies of images has to do with a very similar set of circumstances. Ole Holsti undertook to identify through content analysis the belief system of Secretary of State John Foster Dulles.[53] In particular, Holsti was interested in Dulles' image of the Soviet Union and whether Dulles was capable of changing this image if new events and information challenged it. Holsti describes Dulles as having a relatively closed, inflexible image of the Soviet Union. He had a distinct tendency to assimilate new information about the Soviets that fit his Cold War image of them, but he used a variety of techniques to resist information that contradicted his image: discrediting the source, reinterpreting it to fit his old image, and searching for information that was more consistent with his image.

Significantly, Holsti found that Dulles' general negative evaluation of the U.S.S.R. was not subject to change—even when he perceived reduced Soviet hostility. Positive Soviet actions, such as the signing of the Austrian State Treaty in 1955 (which removed the Red Army from Austria) and the reduction of the size of the Soviet army, did not change Dulles' general evaluation of the Soviet Union. Instead, these cooperative moves were credited to Soviet internal weaknesses: the result of necessity rather than good will. What is important about this is that if cooperative Soviet actions were unable to change the Secretary's basic image of the Soviet Union, then how could the Soviets reliably demonstrate to American officials their good intentions? What could the Soviets have done to indicate to Secretary Dulles their good will? The implication is that nothing short of the dismantling of their own system would have done it.

Kissinger has referred to this kind of image structure as the *inherent bad faith model*.[54] An individual who holds this type of image structure will be able to explain away virtually any sincere change in behavior by the opponent; there is virtually *nothing* the opponent can do therefore to change the original image. This kind of image structure clearly makes learning quite problematical. The problem is bad enough if leaders in one country have closed images of this nature; imagine what would happen if leaders in both countries have similar image structures!

How Images Might Be Changed

Since there seems to be a bias in favor of maintaining one's present image, what does it take to bring about a change? It appears that a change in images comes about more easily if new information descends all at once rather than piece by piece over extended periods of time.[55] Small bits of information coming at irregular intervals stretched out over time are easily discounted, assimilated, or otherwise coped with. On the other hand, dramatic pieces of conflicting information that descend in droves virtually demand that the individual take action to deal with the discrepancy. The occurrence of spectacular events, however, may not be enough to induce a major change in image. Real change may require both spectacular events and the accumulation of less impressive, long-term developments that challenge the image.[56]

President Jimmy Carter's conversion to a more hard-line, anti-Soviet world view in the wake of the Soviet intervention in Afghanistan is a case in point. Although the Soviet intervention certainly qualifies as a spectacular event, it came in the wake of other international (and domestic) events that probably had a cumulative impact on the president. Soviet activity in Angola and Ethiopia, the Soviet arms buildup, continued human rights violations by the Soviets, the toppling of the Shah of Iran by anti-American forces led by Ayatollah Khomeini, domestic opposition to Carter's foreign policies (especially SALT II), and the rising prominence within his foreign policy inner circle of National Security Adviser Zbigniev Brzezinski probably all had an effect on the president. Carter's image of the world was changed dramatically. His vision was no longer that of a benign and liberal world where nations could get along together through reason and diplomacy and law, but of a world where nations harbored aggressive intentions against each other and where one's opponents could not always be counted on to abide by laws or listen to reason—a world where force must frequently be employed instead of diplomacy.

While the natural resistance of images to change probably contributes to the stable, incremental nature of foreign policies, Jervis argues that a major change in image by a national leader always brings about a change in policy.[57] Once again, the Carter presidency is a good example. After Carter's "conversion" he swiftly initiated a new set of policies that reflected a more "hawkish" approach: he withdrew SALT II from Senate consideration, placed a grain embargo on the Soviets, began to restore a military aid to El Salvador, and increased the defense budget.

Evoked Sets

Not only is our interpretation of reality affected by our present images, but our expectations and our "evoked sets"—what we are concerned about when the information is received—also determine how we will interpret information from the environment by creating predispositions to notice certain things and to neglect others.[58] A perfect example can be found in the July crisis that preceded the outbreak of World War I. British Foreign Secretary Grey sent a note to the German government warning of dire consequences if war were to begin. Kaiser Wilhem's evaluation of this note was conditioned by the fact that he had just received information of the Russian military mobilization. The timing of these two messages predisposed him to view the British letter as part of a joint British-Russian plot against Germany. The British information was interpreted in light of the just-received Russian information. In this instance, the Kaiser's "evoked set" played a part in his (mis)perception of a combined Russian-British threat to Germany in 1914.[59]

Evoked sets certainly played a role in the U.S.S. *Vincennes'* shooting down of an Iranian airliner in 1988. The crew's expectations were affected by three situations. First, U.S. intelligence—based on intercepts of Iranian communications—had predicted a strike against an American ship in the Persian Gulf. Second, just minutes before the Iranian plane took off there was an attack: Iranian boats fired on a U.S. helicopter and U.S. ships then skirmished with a flotilla of Iranian vessels. Third, recent military reports indicated that F-14s were now stationed at Bandar Abbas airbase.[60] Thus, the American crew expected an attack; they expected aircraft in the area to be hostile; they were predisposed to see Iranian F-14s flying out of Bandar Abbas. In the light of the ambiguous information available about the plane on the radar screen, the crew's evoked set helped define (erroneously) the plane as a military F-14 rather than the civilian airbus that it was.

Images and the "Lessons of History"

Some images are especially powerful and difficult to change. Jervis emphasizes the impact of history on the creation of images of national leaders. He notes that some events, like wars and revolutions, make such an impression on individuals that it takes equally dramatic developments to nudge them aside. The result is that images of past events, like Banquo's ghost, hover over our attempts to understand the present through the use of historical analogy.[61] Analogies and simple images (such as seeing the countries of Southeast Asia as "falling dominoes") provide an "internal anchor" around which ambiguous information can be structured and given meaning. They provide the individual with an elegant method for reducing the uncertainty inherent in complex situations.[62] Reasoning by analogy may provide a shortcut to understanding, but it is also frought with danger.[63]

The *Munich Analogy* is, of course, the classic example of an all-purpose historical analogy, used as a guide by American leaders in virtually every crisis from Korea to Vietnam to Kuwait in 1991. The general axiom that appeasement of aggressors should always be rejected as a policy alternative (and that the proper response to aggression should be immediate and forceful resistance) came to be applied indiscriminantly, in a way that ruled out compromise and mutual adjustment through diplomacy. The image of Hitler's bullying of Europe was etched in the memory of those on both sides of the Atlantic who lived through the 1930s and 1940s. Truman and his advisers saw Communist activities in Greece, Turkey, and Iran after World War II as analogous to Hitler's step-by-step aggression in Europe in the 1930s. American diplomacy in the 1940s and early 1950s was aimed at preventing the recurrence of World War II. More specifically, Truman himself saw the North Korean attack on South Korea in 1950 in the light of analogies from the 1930s. The President tells in his memoirs of his thoughts on the plane from Missouri to Washington prior to his meeting with his advisers on the Korean crisis:

> I had time to think aboard the plane. In my generation this was not the first occasion when the strong had attacked the weak. I recalled some earlier instances: Manchuria, Ethiopia, Austria. I remembered how each time that the democracies failed to act it had encouraged the aggressors to keep going ahead. Communism was acting in Korea just as Hitler, Mussolini, and the Japanese had acted ten, fifteen, and twenty years earlier. . . . If this were allowed to go unchallenged it would mean a third world war, just as similar incidents had brought on a second world war.[64]

President George Bush is a veteran of World War II for whom the memories of Nazi aggression are part of the living past. It would be surprising if he did not see Iraqi President Saddam Hussein's brutal annexation of Kuwait as Nazi-like aggression and Hussein himself as Hitler. In fact, Bush was quick to make these connections and to argue that Iraqi aggression "should not stand." Iraq's aggression should be met forcefully, by war if necessary, lest Saddam Hussein's success lead him to attack Saudi Arabia or other Persian Gulf states, thus controlling the world's most important resource. Critics were quick to point out that Saddam Hussein was not Hitler, that Iraq was not Germany, and that the threat to American interests was nowhere as great as they had been in 1941. Nevertheless, what mattered was the association made between the two situations in the President's mind and the strategies that these associations triggered.

"Lessons of the past" also played a major role in the Kennedy Administration's 1961 decision to accept the recommendations of the Taylor-Rostow report and make a major commitment to prevent the fall of South Vietnam to communism—arguably the most important U.S. decision regarding that war.[65] Ernest May recounts how the Kennedy Administration rejected one set of "lessons"—those from the Korean War—and accepted another set from the Philippines and Malaysia. The lessons of Korea were twofold: the United States should never again fight a land war in Asia and the American people were unlikely to support a prolonged, limited war. In retrospect this should have been a powerful analogy, and in fact it was—for the U.S. military. Kennedy and his civilian advisers, Robert Kennedy, Dean Rusk, and Robert McNamara, preferred, however, to apply the lessons learned in Magsaysay's fight against rebels in the Phillipines and by the British in their fight against insurgents in Malaya—both examples of the successful use of specialized, small-scale military operations.

May's point is that frequently leaders apply analogies superficially, indiscriminately, and inappropriately. In fact, the U.S. army's chief of staff listed five rather impressive reasons why the Vietnamese and Malayan situations were not comparable—reasons which, in retrospect, are worth listing:

1. Malayan borders were far more controllable.
2. The racial characteristics of the Chinese insurgents in Malaya made identification and segregation a simple matter compared with the situation in Vietnam.
3. The scarcity of food in Malaya versus the relative plenty in South Vietnam made the denial of food to the guerrillas a far more important and readily usable weapon in Malaya.
4. Most important, in Malaya the British were in actual command.
5. Finally, it took the British nearly 12 years to defeat an insurgency that was less strong than the one in South Vietnam.[66]

Kennedy and his advisers also saw the situation in Vietnam as symbolically similar to that faced by the Truman administration with regard to China in 1949. Here the lesson was that if Vietnam were to go Communist, the administration on whose watch this occurred would be blamed for the "loss" and would suffer politically in a country where being "soft on communism" was the kiss of death.

Since the "lessons" of the last war play such an important role in creating images of international relations, leaders frequently believe that the next war will have the same causes as the last one. Appeasement in the 1930s was at least in part based on the notion that World War I could have been avoided by conciliatory diplomacy, while beliefs about the origin of Hitler's aggression in the 1930s predisposed the West to see the Soviet Union and China as aggressors for whom appeasement would be not only inappropriate, but also counterproductive.[67] Believing (correctly) that the United States became involved in World War I because of our desire to trade with belligerents,

Congress passed the Neutrality Acts to prevent the country from being drawn into another such war in the 1930s.[68]

The Soviet demands on Finland in 1939 for territory near Leningrad in the Baltic were based in part on lessons from the past, both general and specific. One of the most powerful "lessons of history" for Russian leaders has been that security depends on the creation of buffer states. This is a lesson learned from years of invasion—by Genghis Khan's Asian hordes, by the Swedes, Lithuanians, Teutonic knights, the Poles, the French, the Germans, and others. Each invasion taught that security depended on being able to create friendly buffer zones to keep hostile neighbors at arm's length, to create a set of more defensible borders than the Russian plains allowed, and, most important, to ensure that when war did break out, it could be fought outside the Russian homeland rather than on its soil. More specifically, incidents in the Russian civil war (1917–1921) in the Baltic had given the Soviets an inflated perception of the importance of that region. The White leader, Yudenich, and the British had both been active in the Gulf of Finland area, an area the tsars had been able to protect with their naval base at Porkkala, in what was now independent Finland.

The Finns, not having had the same historical experiences as the Russians, failed to understand the defensive motivation of the Soviets and believed instead that their demands were aimed at destroying the Finnish state.[69] Needless to say, the matter failed to be settled through negotiation. In the ensuing war the Russians were taught certain military lessons about fighting winter wars by the Finns, and the Finns were taught certain political lessons about accommodating the security interests of Great Power neighbors.

Historical lessons are most important for those who experienced them first hand and for those whose adult lives and careers were significantly affected by the original events. Jervis mentions that three of the British foreign secretaries involved in the policy of appeasing Hitler in the 1930s— Hoare, Simon, and Halifax—had made their political reputations by appeasing Indian demands for greater self-government. The lessons learned in one environment were inappropriately transferred to another.[70] The lessons learned early in one's political career, especially lessons learned from crucial early successes or failures, are naturally important aspects of one's overall image. President Reagan's first political job and his first political success came as president of the Screen Actor's Guild, where he was involved in a fight to prevent groups aligned with the Communist Party from taking over the union. His image of communists as devious and expansionistic was formed from this early experience.[71]

An additional consideration is that these historical lessons are not only important at the individual level; they can become institutionalized within government bureaucracies. Once this has occurred, they may form the basis of future planning, becoming permanent features of standard operating procedures, creating preferred frameworks for viewing events or preferred options for dealing with contingencies.[72]

National Role Conceptions

Perceptions of the historical past become linked with what K. J. Holsti calls our *national self-image* or *national role conceptions*—the way we view our own nation and its place in the world.[73] National leaders may perceive their states as world leaders, as neutral mediators and conciliators, as reliable allies, as aggrieved revolutionaries, as pillars of the international community, as protectors of the weak, and so on. Certainly, how a state's leaders view its role in the world affects its behavior.

For instance, American willingness to intervene with force around the globe stems at least in part from the tendency of American leaders to perceive the United States as a state with special responsibilities in the international system—as the leader of the free world, the defender of freedom, and the arsenal of democracy. Leaders of other nations also have special views of their states. Michael Brecher maintains that the Israeli perception of Jews as victims—the "Holocaust syndrome"—has led to an exaggerated fear for Israel's survival in the face of Arab aggression, which is seen as another attempt to impose a "final solution" upon the Jews. This is turn played a major role in the Israeli decision to go to war in 1967.[74]

Misperceptions

Misperceptions occur when an individual's perceptions of the world do not correspond to reality. As you may have already realized, misperceptions by national leaders abound in international relations. This is in part natural. Policy makers cannot ultimately know what is really going on in much of the external environment. International politics are rarely experienced directly. Instead, national leaders learn about them through second-hand reports: through the press, from cables from diplomatic stations around the world, through briefings by advisers, or through the television screen—the role of CNN in the recent Gulf War being a good example. Additionally, as we have already seen, our understanding of external events is subject to the misinterpretation that is provided by our preexisting images and belief systems. Our perceptual screens are quite capable of distorting whatever information is received from the environment.

Foreign policy decisions, including decisions about war, are often viewed from the perspective of *rational decision making*. It is assumed that national leaders accurately perceive the international situation and whatever threats and opportunities exist in that environment, and then, on the basis of a cost-benefit analysis, select those policies best suited to promote their national interests. We know, however, that many foreign policy decisions are, in fact, "nonrational." Misperceptions may be a key component in such nonrational decisions.[75] In fact, misperceptions by national leaders have frequently been cited as the immediate cause of war.

Misperceptions fall into a number of readily identifiable patterns: misperceptions of the opponent and his intentions, of the opponent's military capabilities and of the relative balance of power, of the opponent's willingness to give in to one's demands, of the risks involved in pursuing one's policies, of the intentions and capabilities of third countries, of the inevitability of war, of its eventual outcome, and of one's self.

Let us take them one at a time.

1. Misperceiving the opponent as having more hostile intentions and as undertaking more hostile activities than is actually the case. (And, conversely, failure to perceive that an opponent might view one's own activities as threatening to him).

The exaggeration of an opponent's intentions is probably one of the most common misperceptions. It is due primarily to the combined effects of trying to deduce the adversary's intentions from his military capabilities and to the related tendency to do this on the basis of "worst case analysis."

The pre–World War I international environment is probably the classic case of the overestimation of opponents' intentions, and President Theodore Roosevelt's personal notes are probably the classic statement of the predicament. TR wrote in 1904 that the Kaiser

> sincerely believes that the English are planning to attack him and smash his fleet, and perhaps join with France in a war to the death against him. As a matter of fact, the English harbour no such intentions, but are themselves in a condition of panic terror lest the Kaiser secretly intend to form an alliance against them with France or Russia, or both, to destroy their fleet and blot out the British Empire from the map! It is as funny a case as I have ever seen of mutual distrust and fear bringing two peoples to the verge of war.[76]

Overperception of threat was a major problem in the crisis that initiated World War I. Robert North's content analysis of documents from the 1914 crisis demonstrates that the perception by German leaders of the intentions of the Triple Entente was significantly more hostile than was warranted by an objective analysis of the situation.[77] The Germans therefore reciprocated the hostility they believed, erroneously, they were receiving from their opponents. (More about this later.)

John Stoessinger sums the situation up nicely: "When a leader on the brink of war believes that his adversary will strike him, the chances of war are fairly high. When both leaders share this perception about each other's intent, war becomes a virtual certainty."[78]

Jack Levy notes that there are two paths to war that may be followed owing to the exaggerated perception of an opponent's intentions. The first path is a direct one: a preemptive strike may be launched against the state that is perceived to harbor hostile intentions. The second path is an indirect one in which the perceiving state increases its military capabilities to compensate for the hostile intentions that it perceives to be held by the rival state, and the rival responds accordingly, initiating a spiral of ever-increasing hostility, which ends eventually in war.[79]

It should be noted that occasionally the opposite perceptual fault is present: the opponent is perceived as being *less* hostile than is really the case. During the appeasement of Hitler in the 1930s many political leaders in the west assumed that the German *führer* shared their objectives of limited political goals and a peaceful Europe. Richard Ned Lebow's explanation is that this misperception can be attributed to the projection of their own national values (and national self-images) onto Hitlerian Germany.[80] Knowing little about other nations, we tend to see them and their leaders as being similar to ourselves. The consequences of underestimating the opponent's hostile intentions is, of course, a false sense of security and a lack of defensive preparation.

There is reason to believe joint misperceptions played a role in the Kuwaiti War of 1990–1991. Iraqi President Saddam Hussein may have perceived a threat from Kuwait's reluctance to allow Iraq to cancel its debts and its unwillingness to pump less oil. He may even have perceived a joint American-Israeli-British conspiracy to deny Iraq the sophisticated weaponry necessary to make Iraq the dominant regional power and to install the United States as the regional hegemon. On the other hand, leaders in virtually all of the Middle East capitals underestimated the degree of threat posed by Iraq and were taken by surprise when Kuwait was invaded. Thus, while Iraqi leaders overestimated the degree of threat to their interests, their opponents underestimated the hostility of Iraq.[81]

2. Inaccurate perception of the relative balance of power between one's self and one's opponents—in particular, the perception that the opponent is weaker than is the case.

Geoffrey Blainey suggests that wars begin when leaders in different states have different perceptions about their relative strength. Conversely, wars cease because those same leaders come to share a similar perception about their relative strengths and weaknesses.[82] In a sense, the actual combat of war gives each nation involved a crash course in reality testing—the purpose of this course being to determine whose initial perceptions were correct.

Lebow discovers that in all five "brinkmanship crises" in the twentieth century that ended in war, leaders in the initiating countries grossly misjudged the military balance and were sure of victory if the crisis were to result in war. For instance, in the Middle East War of 1967 Nasser apparently became "intoxicated" with the cornucopia of weapons and men he saw during his inspections of Egyptian positions in the Sinai.[83] The Pakistani decision to pursue full-scale combat with India over the Kahmir in 1965 was due in part to the sense of overconfidence that Pakistani leaders gained from the brief border skirmish in the Rann of Kutch earlier in the year.[84] And prior to the Russo-Japanese War, the Russian perception that Japan would not risk war was based on the misperception of extreme Russian superiority—a perception that rested in part on racial stereotypes.[85]

All of the above are examples in which misperception of an opponent's capabilities created a feeling of overconfidence that heavily influenced the decision to initiate war. Clearly such misperceptions are important; after all, states rarely initiate wars they don't expect to win! In cases where the perception of the military balance is erroneous (as revealed by the state's subsequent defeat in the war it initiated), we can be fairly confident in stating that misperception was a direct cause of the war. In fact, one analyst has argued that the perception of a military advantage is probably a necessary condition for war, though it is probably not sufficient by itself, since leaders usually require that the war not only be won, but be won without prohibitive expense.[86]

An overestimation of the opponent's military power may also lead to war, though in a different way. Lebow finds that one of the most important perceptions of threat involves the perception of an impending dramatic shift in the balance of power in the adversary's favor. This was a factor in roughly half the thirteen brinkmanship crises in Lebow's study.[87] This is not only true of long-term changes in the general or regional balance, but it is also applicable to changes in short-term tactical advantage. Of course, some of these perceptions of an adverse change in the military balance were not *mis*perceptions; they were correctly perceived. Some, however, were erroneous. Nicholas II's order to mobilize Russian troops on July 30, 1914, was based on the erroneous perception that Germany had undertaken secret military preparations against Russia—preparations that would give her a decisive edge if not quickly countered by Russian action. In reality, no such secret preparations had occurred; Germany did not order premobilization until July 31, in response to the Russian mobilization. French mobilization was apparently based on similar misperception of a secret German callup of "tens of thousands" of reserves.[88]

The preceding discussion has probably already alerted the reader to the powerful multiplier effects of misperceptions. An overperception of hostility in an opponent *coupled with* a misperception of his relative military weakness would certainly be a potent combination. Unfortunately, perperceptions are rarely "only children;" they tend to be twins or triplets.

Since perceptions of strength are linked both to perceptions of intentions and to perceptions of risk, there are two corollaries to the basic misperception of relative strength:

2a. The inaccurate belief that the opponent will give in to your threats and ultimata rather than go to war.

2b. The misperception of the degree of risk one faces in initiating a conflict.

The defining characteristic of the brinkmanship crises that Lebow investigates is that the initiator fully expects the adversary to back down rather than resort to arms. In each crisis that he investigates these initial perceptions were proved to be inaccurate, and the initiator either had to back down or face actual hostilities. His findings suggest that the presence of a brinkmanship commitment by the opponent is not a precondition for brinkmanship crises; what counts is the *perception* by the initiator that a vulnerable commitment exists—a perception that was frequently erroneous.[89] Misperception thus appears to be a major cause of war in brinkmanship crises.

A good example is the misperception of Indian leaders in the 1962 crisis with China in the Himalayas. Indian leaders perceived that China would back down when confronted with India's aggressive "forward policy" of manning military posts in the disputed regions—even though China had military superiority on both fronts involved. This perception by Indian political leaders was abetted by a sycophantic military that was unwilling to challenge what they believed to be an erroneous image of Chinese behavior.[90]

Not only do different individuals have different propensities for risk taking, but they also perceive different degrees of risk in the same or similar situations. Jervis maintains that (unlike what many historians have suggested) Hitler was not reckless in his attempts to dominate Europe in the 1930s, but was merely certain the other side would back down.[91] It was not that Hitler was more willing to take risks than others, but that he believed the risks of war were slight.

A classic case of misperception of risk was the American decision to try to unify Korea after the initial task of driving back the North Korean attack on the south had succeeded. Both Chinese strength and Chinese willingness to defend North Korea were severely underrated by the American side—in particular by General MacArthur and his staff. Part of the problem was bureaucratic. Army intelligence played down the evaluation of Chinese strength both to avoid demoralizing the South Korean army and to avoid the wrath of MacArthur, whose position on Chinese strength was well known. MacArthur's staff (like the Indian military two decades later) had learned to be properly obsequious and submissive to their leader. Consequently, Mac-

Arthur was unaware of the anxiety of some of his generals because his closest subordinates had insulated him from it.[92] DeRivera suggests that that the basis for this was that MacArthur had a psychological need to be free from disagreement and be surrounded by people supportive of his own views, a need created by his own lack of security.[93]

To some extent the misperceptions about Chinese capabilities and intentions were also based on *wishful thinking* by American leaders. Though warnings abounded that the official interpretation of Chinese strength and intentions was inaccurate, U.S. leaders persisted in their adherence to the image of Chinese weakness and bluff. With Truman's popularity plunging like a pelican looking for a quick meal and with his administration being attacked by the Republicans for being soft on communism, the creation of a unified and democratic Korea would certainly have been the answer to a host of political problems for Truman and Secretary of State Acheson. On the other hand, failure to push ahead with unification would be seen as appeasement. Truman and Acheson needed a victory in North Korea; there was no acceptable alternative. In the face of information that such a victory might be complicated by Chinese entry into the war, American leaders responded by *bolstering* (a type of psychological activity designed to reinforce one's belief in the correctness of one's previous positions and actions) and with *selective attention* to information in order to dismiss Chinese threats as a bluff.[94]

3. Perception that war is inevitable.

There are two versions of this perception. The general phenomenon of war may be seen as an inevitable feature of the landscape of international relations, or specific wars may be perceived as inevitable at specific times. Each perception has an impact on the willingness of leaders to opt for war.

Evan Luard has remarked on the importance of the perception of the general acceptability of war as a feature of international relations:

> Wars are made by people—individuals within governments or other collective bodies—who decide at some point to try to secure their ends by armed force. Those decisions are determined ultimately by the beliefs they hold about war: about its usefulness, legitimacy or morality, about its value in enhancing national prestige, upholding national honor, or asserting national will; above all about its normality as a constant feature is the behavior of states.[95]

Luard traces beliefs about the normality of war in the international system from 1400 to the present. He argues that the main change is not in the degree to which war in general has been regarded as legitimate (this hasn't changed too much), but in the type of war that is seen as legitimate in successive periods.[96]

The bottom line is that while attitudes toward outright aggression may have gradually become more negative, war is still seen as an acceptable instrument of national policy under certain circumstances. And to the extent that war is perceived as a normal and acceptable feature of international relations, leaders will continue to include it in their repertoire of options for dealing with other states.

The extent to which political leaders perceive that a particular war is inevitable at a particular point in time may also be an important factor in the decision to go to war. Whether this actually constitutes a misperception is difficult to say; after all, the war actually does take place. Leaders' forecasts or predictions about future realities are substantially unlike their perceptions of a current realities; the latter can more easily be seen as accurate or inaccurate than the former.[97] Nevertheless, we shall treat such predictions as misperceptions since they are commonly treated as such in much of the writing about war.

World War I constitutes the classic example of a situation in which leaders on all sides perceived war as inevitable.[98] It should be fairly obvious that if leaders perceive that war is inevitable, they will not be inclined to vigorously pursue methods to prevent such a war. In retrospect, one of the most interesting things about the July 1914 crisis is that, while all of the European crises that immediately preceded it led to international conferences of leaders or foreign ministers, attempts to settle the Austro-Serbian crisis by means of an international conference never really got off the ground. We can speculate that it was probably seen by many as a useless waste of time, given the perception that war was inevitable.

The perception that war is inevitable, combined with the perception that the present time will be more advantageous militarily than a future time, creates an especially dangerous set of circumstances.[99] Certainly this was the case in the July 1914 crisis. Not only did German (and Austrian) leaders perceive that war was inevitable, they also perceived that the summer of 1914 might be the last opportunity to win such a war, which would come—sooner or later.[100] Russian rearmament would be completed by 1916–1917, creating a much more dangerous environment. Ironically, many British and French leaders (the French general staff in particular) also believed they were superior and that it would be best to fight Germany sooner rather than later. Similar perceptions affected French decision-making in 1870 prior to the war with Prussia and Japanese military leaders in 1903–1904, who believed they had a temporary strategic advantage vis-à-vis Russia that would be quickly lost.[101]

4. Perception that the war will be relatively inexpensive and short.

We have mentioned that it is usually not enough for decision-makers to perceive that the war they are considering be militarily winnable; the perceptions that the war will be short and will not entail prohibitive costs are perhaps just as important. It certainly makes sense that war becomes more probable if it is perceived as being both militarily and economically acceptable. Under such circumstances political leaders will be more inclined to undertake the risks of war.[102] On the other hand, if war is seen as being ruinous, political leaders will be less likely to plunge their nations into it.

The widespread belief that a war in Europe in 1914 would be a short one has been widely commented on. This misperception was based on several factors. First, there was the power of historical analogy. The shortness of the last major wars in Europe—the Franco-Prussian War and the Austro-Prussian War—led twentieth-century statesmen to expect more of the same. Second, there was the belief that no Great Power could financially sustain a long war, especially given the commercial and financial interdependence of European states. Finally, there was the factor of military strategy. European militaries emphasized the offensive side of warfare, believing offensive strategies and technologies to have a decisive advantage over the defense.[103] The presumption was therefore that someone's offense would quickly overcome an opponent placed on the defensive, thus precluding a long war.

5. Misperceptions of the intentions (and capabilities) of third states.

Blainey points out the importance of perceptions (or misperceptions) concerning the behavior of third states: who will enter the war on whose side and who will remain on the sidelines, who will honor their alliance commitments and who will welsh out.[104]

The correct perception of third-party intentions can be enormously beneficial. American leaders correctly perceived that no European nations would intervene on behalf of Mexico in 1846; European leaders correctly perceived the American Civil War would prevent the United States from aiding Mexico against their intervention in the 1860s; and Japanese leaders accurately perceived that no Great Power would intervene on China's side in her 1937 invasion of that country.

Misperceptions are just as plentiful, however. The typical misperception (which might be seen as a kind of wishful thinking) is that one's potential enemies will remain neutral while one's allies will remain faithful to their commitments. Erroneous perceptions of this sort directly affect leaders' cost-benefit analysis of the desirability of war by contributing to military overconfidence. For instance, Hitler's perception that Poland would receive no outside assistance was rudely corrected by the British and French declaration of war in 1939. In 1914 German and Austrian leaders believed the war against Serbia could be kept "localized" without outside intervention by other Great Powers. The Kaiser's initial perception that British involvement was unlikely seemed to have been a crucial factor in German calculations. While the decision of the North Korean and Soviet leadership to attack South Korea was probably based (erroneously) on the perception that the United States would not intervene, the Truman administration's decision to send U.N. troops into North Korea was based on the (equally erroneous) perception that China would remain neutral in spite of her protestations to the contrary.[105]

In the weeks preceding his attack on Kuwait, Saddam Hussein almost certainly perceived little risk that the United States would intervene to overturn Iraq's annexation of Kuwait. He was probably aided in this misperception by U.S. leaders. Just as the initial North Korean attack on South Korea may have been affected by the absence of a formal U.S. military commitment to aid South Korea (as defined by Secretary Acheson's "defense perimeter"), Saddam Hussein's decision was probably affected by statements by the U.S. State Department that the United States had no formal commitment to defend Kuwait. Additionally, at a hastily called meeting between Saddam Hussein and American Ambassador April Glaspie in Baghdad just days before the attack (as Iraqi forces were massing on the Kuwati border), the American envoy, adhering to standard policy positions, assured the Iraqi leader of the American desire for good relations and declared that the United States took no position on the dispute between Iraq and Kuwait.[106]

The perceptions that war will be economically manageable and militarily winnable and that there will be no third-party surprises all create a sense of optimism that Blainey believes is a key to the cause of war. He argues that it is exceedingly doubtful whether there has been a war since 1700 in which the initial hopes about the impending war were low on *both* sides. He concludes that ". . . optimism is a vital prelude to war. Anything which increases optimism is a cause of war. Anything which dampens that optimism is a cause of peace."[107]

6. Misperception of oneself and the opponent's image of oneself.

It is probably only natural to believe that others see us the way we see ourselves, and to expect them to respond to us accordingly. Though this may be "natural," it is frequently an inappropriate view of reality. Lebow details the distorted images of self and the perception of oneself by others in both the Sino-Indian conflict of 1962 and the Sino-American conflict in Korea in 1950. In 1950 American leaders believed the United States was linked to China through a special relationship based on a century of good will.[108] After all, from our perspective, we had fought against imperialism in China (wasn't that what the Open Door Policy was all about?); we had fought with China against the Japanese in World War II; and we had mediated between Chiang Kai-shek and the Communist Party during the Civil War in the late 1940s. Why should they harbor any hostility toward us? Additionally, since we knew that our pronouncements of nonaggressive intentions in Asia were sincere, we "naturally" believed the Chinese would feel reassured.[109]

The image that our leaders (especially Acheson) had of the situation blinded us to the reasons the Chinese were prepared to go to war against us. We were, after all, defending Mao's archenemy, Chiang Kai-shek, by sending the fleet to the Taiwan Straits; we were rebuilding Japan, the country that had spent the better part of a decade occupying Chinese territory; the United

States seemed to be taking over the Japanese role as the superpower in the Asia-Pacific region; and now the American army was invading the territory of an ally, North Korea, and marching toward the Chinese border! As Stoessinger suggests, "Truman, MacArthur and the State Department perceived a China that no longer existed."[110] As a result, the United States pursued a high-risk policy in Korea, while denying the risk existed.

Indian attitudes toward the Chinese in the early 1960s suffered from the same kind of misperceptions. The Indians, especially Prime Minister Nehru and Foreign Minister Menon, believed their altruistic foreign policy set them apart from other nations and helped to create a special relationship with China. This special bond was both political and personal. Nehru believed himself to be instrumental in gaining the world community's acceptance of the People's Republic of China and he even claimed that Chinese Premier Chou En-lai was a disciple of his. Consequently, Indian leaders felt confident that their aggressive "forward policy" along the border would not lead to war. In the end, India's position in the world (as a moral beacon, as the father of Asian nationalism, and as a leader of the Third World) would deter China from war.[111] The outcome was that the Indians pursued an aggressive and risky policy, which embroiled them in a war they didn't want.

Wishful thinking and rationalization permitted both the United States and the Indians to maintain their distorted images of the Chinese and to continue risky policies long after they should have been abandoned.

Why Misperception? Two Answers

Having illustrated that misperceptions are plentiful in international relations and that they frequently play an important role in decisions about war, we are still left with the question of why they occur so often. Lebow investigates two possible theories, the cognitive approach and the motivational approach. The *cognitive approach*, used by Jervis, "emphasizes the ways in which human cognitive limitations distort decision-making by gross simplifications in problem representation and information processing."[112] The human mind may simply not be capable of carrying out rational problem solving under complex circumstances. The chief failing, from this point of view, would seem to derive from the existence of "natural" pressures for *cognitive consistency*, which create a systematic bias in favor of information that is consistent with one's current image. This in turn affects the way individuals interpret and respond to stimuli from the environment. A related tendency, from the cognitive perspective, is *premature cognitive closure*—arriving too quickly at a single theory to interpret and explain the myriad of information that the decision-maker faces.

An alternative approach is offered by Irving Janis and Leon Mann, who argue that the primary source of perceptual distortion is *motivational*.[113] Their basic assumption is that we are all emotional beings (rather than rational calculators) with strong needs to construct and maintain positive images of ourselves and our environment.

Important decisions generate stress. Mild amounts of stress may have a positive effect on decision-making, but stress becomes more acute (and thus detrimental) if decision makers believe that the present alternatives entail great risk of failure and that no better strategies are available. Under these circumstances decision-makers have a strong need to avoid the truths that would be faced through reality testing. They may retreat therefore to a psychological state of *defensive avoidance*—characterized by efforts to avoid warnings that one's present beliefs and actions are incorrect. The acceptance of these warnings should generate more fear and more stress, creating an intolerable psychological environment. Janis and Mann identify three forms of definsive avoidance—procrastination, shifting the responsibility for the decision, and bolstering. These are all methods of coping with stress, but each leads to some kind of perceptual distortion.[114]

Lebow summarizes the difference between the cognitive approach of Jervis and the motivational approach of Janis and Mann:

> For Jervis, the starting point is the human need to develop simple rules for processing information in order to make sense of an extraordinarily complex and uncertain environment. Janis and Mann take as their fundamental assumption the human desire to avoid fear, shame, and guilt. Jervis describes cognitive consistency as the most important organizing principle of cognition. Janis and Mann contend that aversion of psychological stress is the most important drive affecting cognition. Whereas Jervis concludes that expectations condition our interpretation of events and our receptivity to information, Janis and Mann argue for the important of preferences. For Jervis, we see what we expect to see, for Janis and Mann, what we want to see.[115]

Lebow's analysis of international crises leads him to the conclusion that the motivational approach provides the better explanation for misperceptions. His study focuses on brinkmanship crises—crises in which the initiator attempts to achieve specific political goals by employing threats of force. Crisis initiators uniformly (and erroneously) expected the adversary to back down rather than resort to war. Normally, one would hypothesize that such crises would occur if there was a vulnerable commitment that could be exploited, thus providing a good opportunity for the initiator. Lebow found, however, that an "objective" good opportunity for aggression existed in only a third of the cases. In each case, however, there was a perception that an opportunity existed and there were also strong needs on the part of the initiator to pursue aggressive foreign policies. Lebow suggests that decision-makers are more responsive to internal imperatives than to external developments. Aggression would seem to be less a function of opportunity than it is a function of need.[116]

The additional problem is that to the extent that leaders perceived the need to act, they became insensitive to the interests and the commitments of others. As a result, deterrence was a manifestly ineffective policy. Decision-makers used denial, selective attention, and other techniques to dismiss indications of the adversary's resolve to act on its commitment.[117] The July 1914 crisis that led to World War I is a case in point.

Mediated Stimulus-Response Model

It should be obvious from the preceding sections that misperceptions may play a crucial role in decisions concerning war and peace. We have even recounted some rather impressionistic evidence to that effect. Now it is time to look at this more systematically. We have suggested that images and perceptions play an extremely important role in determining how the individual responds to the actions taken by other individuals and states in the international system.

To understand why individuals (particularly leaders of states) undertake certain actions, we need to know how they perceive their environment. One of the most familiar models of behavior is the *stimulus-response model* used by some psychologists. The model assumes that certain stimuli in the environment initiate, more or less automatically, certain responses from the individual.

$$S \longrightarrow R$$

Behavior by actor 1 (S) instigates behavior in response by actor 2 (R). One does not need to know how the individual perceives the stimuli or how he or she evaluates it. It is assumed that most individuals will respond similarly to the same stimuli. Therefore, any attempt to go inside the individual's mind would be a needless complication of the model. In a sense the mind of the individual is treated as a *black box*. We don't need to know what is inside.

On the other hand, we have seen in the previous sections how important it is to discover how the individual actually perceives the stimuli from the environment. Not all individuals will perceive events in the real world in the same way; as a result they will respond differently to the same stimuli, depending on their perceptions of it. In this view it is extremely important to go inside the black box—that is, to go inside the thoughts of individuals—to determine why they responded to certain stimuli in certain ways, or to predict how they will respond in the future.

Thus, for those interested in images and perceptions, the standard stimulus-response model must be reformulated to address variables that the original model neglects. The *mediated stimulus-response model* looks like this:

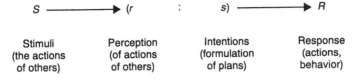

According to the mediated stimulus-response model, whatever stimuli we receive from our environment are mediated through our perceptions and images of those stimuli. Our response depends on our impressions of the stimuli, not on the stimuli themselves. And, as we have seen, these perceptions of the stimuli may be distortions of reality.

A group of researchers at Standard led by Robert North attempted to apply this model to the outbreak of World War I in order to see whether the perceptions of European leaders were an important factor in the decision to go to war. This required a massive data collection and creation effort. The most difficult part of the effort had to do with gathering data on the innards of the black box. How was the Stanford group to know how the leaders of the Great Powers perceived the events of the day? Easy. Their perceptions could be inferred from their statements, letters, diary entries, diplomatic memos, and so forth. Professor North and his colleagues used content analysis to determine the perceptions of European statesmen from their written statements. These statements could be culled for certain key phrases indicating certain categories of perceptions: hostility, anxiety, fear, threat, friendship, satisfaction, frustration, and so forth. The statements could be counted to give an indication of the importance of the perception to the individual. The perceptions could also be scaled to determine their intensity.

Likewise, the actions undertaken by the various states could be counted and scaled. For instance, actions could be scaled in terms of the degree of hostility they contained. Once the perceptual data and the action data had both been qualified, the researchers could investigate statistical correlations between S and R, between S and r, between r and R—in other words, between every link in the model, for each of the participants in the 1914 crisis.

What did the North group find? First, they found the links one would expect to find between r and s and between r and R. To the extent that national leaders see their states to be the target of the hostility of others, they reciprocate that hostility. There is a statistical correlation between the perception of hostility (r) and both the expression of hostility (s) and actual hostile actions (R) as a response.[118]

Second, German leaders perceived themselves to be relatively weak compared to the military strength of their opponents. They perceived that a war would be disastrous for Germany. Nevertheless, these perceptions of weakness and of relative inferiority were not enough to prevent a decision to go to war. Why not? The answer is that at some point in the crisis German leaders' perception of weakness were overtaken by their perceptions of fear, anxiety, threat, and injury. While all of the Great Powers felt themselves to have been injured by the actions of their opponents in the July crisis, German leaders felt the most sense of injury and threat. Thus, perceptions of weakness (and of the opponent's relative strength) don't always prevent war.[119]

Third, when comparing the action stimuli (S) with the state's actual response (R) to it, some interesting differences appeared between the two blocs—the Dual Alliance (Germany and Austria-Hungary) and the Triple Entente (Britain, France, and Russia). The Triple Entente tended to under-react to the actions of the Dual Alliance, especially early in the crisis period, when they were less directly involved. On the other hand, the Dual Alliance consistently overreacted to the actions of their opponents. Why? The answer seems to lie in the differing perceptions of the leaders of the nations involved. A close examination of the links between the actions of others (S) and the perceptions of those actions (r) indicate that German leaders especially perceived the actions of the Triple Entente to be more hostile and threatening than those actions were in the opinion of objective evaluators. As a result, the actions that Germany took, being based on these overly hostile perceptions, were themselves overly hostile. On the other hand, the leaders of the Triple Entente tended to underperceive the level of threat present in the actions of the Dual Alliance.[120] To make a long story short, the culprit in this great disaster is found inside the black box—in the minds of men.

Fourth, what we really have here is a *two-step, mediated stimulus-response model.* Not only do state A's actions (mediated by the perceptions of state B's leaders) drive the actions of state B, but in turn b's actions (mediated by the perceptions of A's leaders) drive the actions of state A. This pattern of action and reaction then continues.

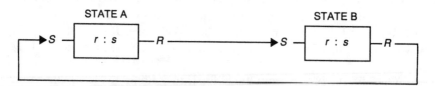

The clear implication of North's research is that perceptions (or misperceptions) may intervene in the stimulus-response process to either accelerate or decelerate a crisis. Escalation to war may occur—due to a misperception of the actions of others—even in situations where neither side desires it. One reason why the Cuban Missile Crisis was resolved successfully, according to Ole Holsti, was that leaders on both sides were able to correctly perceive the other side's moves toward deescalation and respond in like manner. Unlike the 1914 crisis, the link between S and r correspond rather closely to reality; misperception was avoided and so was a war.

Conclusion

We have seen from the ethlogists and sociobiologists that the possibility for violence exists in mankind. We have also seen that this general biological potential would seem to be inadequate for explaining war. (It is certainly not very useful in explaining peace.) Human beings are not equally violent; indeed, the behavior for individual humans seems to be endlessly variable. We have focused in this chapter, therefore, on those factors that might explain the differences in the behavior of individuals: differences in willingness to take risks, different perceptions (and misperceptions) of the environment and of one's opponents, different images of the world and operational codes, differences in ability to change or adjust present images, different psychological needs, different personality traits, and differences in ability to deal with stress.

Several points should be made in summary. First, while any of the above variables could play an important role in the initiation of a given war, they are probably not of equal theoretical importance. Misperceptions are probably the most important factor—especially misperception of the opponent's hostility, mispereption of the balance of power, and misperception of risk. Second, all these individual level variables would seem to be highly interrelated.

If, for the sake of argument, we identify a major cause of war to be an overestimation of an opponent's hostility, coupled with a predisposition (in spite of tremendous risks) to confront that opponent with hostile and confrontational actions in the hope of forcing him to back down, then there are several variables at the individual level that might interact to produce such a situation.

We have seen how psychological needs might foster misperceptions concerning the risks inherent in a crisis situation and about the relative military capabilities of the states involved. It is also likely that operational codes will influence the leader's perceptions of the opponent and of the strategies most likely to be effective in dealing with that opponent. As we will see in Chapters 6 and 7, leaders with a "Realpolitik" operational code are more likely to perceive opponents as aggressors who will back down in the face of "bullying" tactics. They therefore are predisposed to follow hard-line, brinkmanship-type tactics against others. Additionally, leaders whose personalities are characterized by power orientation are highly sensitive to the possibility of foreign threats—perceiving them in fact when they do not exist—and are quite likely to respond aggressively. Leaders whose personalities are characterized by risk acceptance or by dominance will be inclined to pursue tough, high-risk tactics vis-à-vis their international rivals. Likewise, leaders with active ego defense mechanisms are prone to discount warnings of risk in their pursuit of foreign policy. Finally, a leader's inability to change his or her incorrect image of the rival as a hostile opponent is likely to be influenced by personality varibles and psychological needs as well as cognitive variables such as image structure and the content of one's operational code.

We do not as yet have a "psychological theory of war" or a "cognitive theory of war." What we do have is a lot of evidence from case studies (though some of it is fairly unsystematic) that misperceptions have frequently accompanied decisions by national leaders to go to war. The problem in developing supporting evidence for psychological and perceptual causes of war is a daunting task. The business of determining a leader's psychological state and his or her perceptions is fraught with danger. Any such analysis should be viewed with caution. On the other hand, the evidence from an extremely large number of cases indicating that decision-making elites have been the victims of misperceptions is virtually overwhelming.

What we know from these cases is that in a sizable number of instances, elite misperceptions appear to have played a crucial role in the decision to go to war. What we *don't* know, and perhaps can't know, is why these misperceptions occurred, what would have happened if they had not (would war have been prevented?), and how widespread such misperceptions have been generally across the universe of cases of interstate war. Neither can we at this time be precise about the exact relationships between misperceptions and other individual level variables.

While it would seem that psychological and cognitive variables may not always play the vital and determining role in whether war breaks out, they are certainly quite important. As we will see in later chapters, psychological and cognitive factors are also highly interrelated with variables at other levels of analysis. This increases their importance as elements of a theory of war.

Let us switch gears for a moment. We have assumed thus far that the key element in the cause of war was the role of the individual national leader in making the decision to initiate violence and send his or her country into war. However, this may be an oversimplification. Decision-making is not always an individual process; frequently it is a collective political process. Government decisions are typically made by small groups of people. If this is the case, then the role of the individual may be less important than how the members of the decision-making group interact with each other to determine government policy. We must move on therefore to explore explanations of war at the next level of analysis—the small group.

4

Governmental Decision Making

> Madness is the exception in individuals but the rule in groups.
> —Nietzsche

> The process was the author of the policy
> —Under Secretary of State George Ball, 1962

In this chapter we explore the causes of international conflict that may be found at the small group level. The basic premise here is that war between nations involves at some point decisions by governments. Within modern governments decisions are frequently made by cabinets, "kitchen cabinets," politburos, juntas, or committees—rather than by presidents, prime ministers, or generals acting alone. Policy making is very much a group activity. Thus, our search for the causes of war leads us to an examination of the methods by which small groups of government leaders make decisions about war and peace. The central assumption at this level of analysis is that the structures and processes of decision-making, rather than the characteristics and perceptions of the individuals involved, have the decisive effect on government policies and behaviors.

Rationality and Decision Making

In the best of all possible worlds governments pursue peaceful policies rather than aggressive ones, their leaders are enlightened and humane rather than incompetent or venal, and reason and good intentions prevail over stupidity and evil. In this world of philosopher-kings and well-intentioned (and well-behaved) governments, we would expect policy to be made in a reasoned, calculated manner. Political scientists and logicians point to just such a decision-making process; it is referred to as the *syncratic model* or, more simply, the *rational actor model* (RAM).[1]

Enlightened government leaders who desire to formulate policy in the most logical manner possible can use the rational actor model by following these nine easy steps:

1. Identify and *define the problem.*
2. *Identify goals.* If there are multiple goals, then they will have to be ranked (prioritized) in order of importance.

77

3. *Gather information.* (This process is more or less continuous and may in fact start at step 1. It is included arbitrarily as step 3.)
4. *Identify alternative means* for achieving the objective(s).
5. *Analyze each possible alternative.* (You will want to examine the possible consequences of using each option, determine the relative effectiveness of each alternative means for achieving the goal(s), gauge the probability of success for each alternative, calculate the effect of each alternative on other goals, estimate the probable costs and benefits of each alternative, and so on.)
6. *Choose* the alternative best able to achieve your objectives. In other words, select your optimal strategy—the one most likely to maximize your success.
7. *Implement* the decision; that is, put it into action.
8. *Monitor and evaluate* your policy decision. Is it a success or failure? Does it have defects? Is it achieving the desired results?
9. *Terminate/alter/continue* the policy as determined by your evaluation of it in step 8.

Like all models, the rational actor model requires certain simplifying assumptions. Proponents of the RAM assume, among other things, that governments can be thought of as single, unitary actors who make rational choices from among the universe of possible options in order to maximize the probability that their goals will be realized. This, in turn, assumes that decision-makers can place a concrete and meaningful value on each outcome so that two or more outcomes can be compared. The model further assumes that decision-makers can calculate the probability that a desired action will lead to success.

A final assumption is that unwanted and unnecessary wars can be avoided if a rational decision process is adhered to. This does not, of course, preclude national leaders from pursuing "utilitarian" wars that are seen as rationally maximizing their goals. Wars often do result from careful cost-benefit analyses of alternative strategies through which to attain desired ends.[2] The assumption is only that leaders who use a rational decision process will decide in favor of war only if the expected utility of doing so is greater than the expected utility of not going to war. Wars that are in this sense irrational and unnecessary can be avoided.

Critique: Why Governments Don't Use the RAM

Obviously, we all hope our governments apply this logical process to their foreign policy problems. Unfortunately, in the "real world" it often becomes impossible for governments to use the rational actor model in making their decisions. The best methods are not always used and the best results are not always obtained. Why aren't decisions made in the most rational manner? The following is a short list of impediments to rational decision-making, some stemming from the individual level of analysis and some from the small-group level.

1. Not all decision-makers are completely rational; at least, some men are less rational than others. As we have seen, psychological factors interfere with the ability of government leaders to engage in rational problem solving. To the extent that these factors exist, decisions will be made in order to meet the subconscious needs of political leaders rather than to address legitimate national security needs.

2. As we have also seen, misperception, if not exactly rampant among policy makers, is at least pervasive. Attempts to resolve foreign policy problems require an accurate image of the situation—a condition not often met.

3. Human frailties frequently play a role. Tough policy choices are frequently accompanied by hefty amounts of stress. Stresses that can impair rationality are often abetted by lack of sleep and physical infirmities among the political elite. None of this is conductive to good decision making.

4. Decision makers may not always have the quantity or quality of information they require to make a perfectly rational decision. National security policies must frequently be made in an environment of uncertainty; information may be false, missing, contradictory, or ambiguous. The most important information—the intentions of others—is probably unknowable from normal sources of intelligence. The problem of information deficiency is often compounded by the tendency of subordinates to refrain from telling their superiors information that challenges their views. Alternatively, information may be so overwhelming in quantity that analysts are simply overloaded in their ability to make sense of the product of the intelligence services. The human mind has limited ability to process information, and these human limitations ultimately prevent governments from applying perfect rationality to political decisions.

5. The amount of time available for making the decision may be limited, thus impairing the ability of policy makers to develop and analyze options. Even if adequate time is available, leaders may choose not to take it. The use of time entails costs, and a speedy decision may be seen as preferable to a better decision that takes longer.

6. "Imperfect prognostication." Step 5 of the rational actor model requires the impossible, or at least the nearly impossible. Evaluation of policy options requires that decision makers peer into the future and predict the likely outcomes and the probability of success of pursuing particular alternatives (or a package of several alternatives). Most of us probably have

enough trouble trying to figure out the past and the present; trying to imagine the future entails more insight than we can muster.

7. Identifying all the goals the state might pursue and then prioritizing them may be beyond rational assessment.[3] The selection of goals frequently means choosing the lesser of several evils. It is often the case that the pursuit of one goal can only be achieved at the expense of others. Two goals, both cherished, may not be simultaneously pursued; indeed, they may be mutually exclusive.

8. Identifying all the possible alternatives and then subjecting them all to some kind of cost-benefit analysis is an incredibly daunting task. For practical reasons, such as lack of time and lack of human insight, the search for and analysis of options is likely to be limited. A special problem in foreign policy decisions is the perceived need for secrecy. In an attempt to prevent leaks of sensitive information, top decision-makers frequently choose to restrict the number of people consulted, thus severely limiting the range of alternatives as well as the variety of analysis. McGeorge Bundy suggests that this has been a typical problem for American decision-makers in the Cold War age, but it also has bedeviled Soviet leaders. Khrushchev, for instance, apparently consulted only one diplomat (Gromyko) for his analysis of the decision to put missiles in Cuba in 1962.[4]

Snyder and Diesing's study of decision-making in sixteen international crises discovered that most alternatives are either ignored or quickly eliminated as unfeasible or ineffective by preliminary scanning, and only a few options are really seriously considered.[5] In an extremely interesting study of the decision-making processes of the Truman, Eisenhower, and Kennedy administrations (concerning Korea, Vietnam, and the Cuban Missile Crisis), Paul Anderson finds that although decision-makers did consider a surprisingly large number of alternatives, very few of the alternatives were actually mutually inconsistent. A large number of alternatives, once proposed within the group, were simply ignored without analysis; they essentially "died for lack of a seconding motion." Additionally, when incompatible alternatives were identified, they were usually in reaction to a previous suggestion with which a member of the group disagreed, and consisted of "don't do X" rather than a separate course of action. Perhaps most important, Anderson also found a tendency to search for goals *after* alternatives had been identified and approved.[6]

Studies of corporate decision-making by Herbert Simon, James March, and Richard Cyert indicate that the number of alternatives that are considered is frequently limited by the twin processes of "*satisfycing*" and "*sequential search*."[7] Decision-makers don't really lay out all the options and assess the pro's and con's of each. Instead, the possible alternatives are examined one-by-one in a sequential manner (sequential search) until an option is discovered that meets some minimal standard of acceptability (satisfycing). The options are not ranked by the analysts from best to worst; they are simply categorized as acceptable or unacceptable. The first option discovered that fits into the "acceptable" category is the alternative that is chosen.[8] (It was this insight which earned Simon the Nobel Prize in economics in 1978.) It is quite likely that a better option could be found if the search were to continue and other options analyzed; indeed, the optimal solution may be the very next alternative. But the decision-makers will never know. The selections process ends with the choice of the "satisfactory" solution.

Why are such processes employed? Simon and March claim that satisfycing and sequential search are devices designed to simplify and expedite the decision process. Executives realize that time is short and that long decision processes are costly. Furthermore, the perfect solution may *never* be found. Since it is difficult if not impossible to compare the value of two outcomes, there is no rational process by which the "best possible" outcome can be ascertained.[9] Under these circumstances, it is better to seek a solution that is merely acceptable, rather than engage in a drawn-out process that may become a wild goose chase.

We have some indications that government policy making has in fact followed these practices. Anderson's study of the Korean War, Vietnam War, and the Cuban Missile Crisis concludes that American decision-makers did not consider each alternative (or each subset of alternatives) before making a final decision, but considered alternatives sequentially, making a yes-no decision about accepting each alternative in turn.[10]

9. Most important for this level of analysis, it is quite possible that one individual's rationality is not the same as another's. If several individuals were to go through our rational process model with regard to a particular policy problem, each would probably select a different optimal solution. Different individuals or subgroups within the decision-making body will rank goals differently, will prefer different outcomes, and will support different policy options.

Here we return to the central assumption of the small group level of analysis: *governmental decision making is usually a group sport rather than an individual activity.* There will inevitably be disagreements between cabinet ministers about the best possible solution to the problem and the best policy to pursue. There may be even more fundamental differences over the correct goals to pursue, leaving aside the methods by which these goals are to be met. The bottom line is that decisions require bargaining and compromise between the members of the group. Policy making is ultimately a political process rather than a cognitive, rational process. And, to the extent that decisions are political, the probability of poor (that is to say, nonrational) decisions increases.

In conclusion, we must be skeptical of the ability of governments to make good, rational, reasonable decisions. We must admit that lousy decisions get made, that nonrational decision-making processes abound, and that every once in a while governments will bring themselves closer to war because the decision process failed and the policy factory turned out a real lemon.

If government decisions are not made in a rational manner, we will need to discuss how governments *do* make decisions. This is the task of the remainder of this chapter. Two theories constitute the primary alternatives to the RAM—bureaucratic politics and groupthink. However, before we investigate these two theories, it might be useful to investigate some insights from two other approaches—incrementalism and the organizational process model.

Incrementalism

A quarter century ago David Braybrooke and Charles Lindblom made a major impact on political thinking with their analysis of how political decisions were made.[11] For many of the reasons we have already cited (lack of information, lack of agreement on goals and means, limitations of time and resources, limits on individual problem solving ability, etc.), decision makers rarely use the RAM. Instead, they attempt to simplify the process. As a result, political decisions are typically made through an incremental process. Not all alternatives are analyzed thoroughly. Only those options which differ in relatively small degrees from the present policy are fully scrutinized. Major changes and comprehensive reforms are usually not discussed. The result is that most policies vary only marginally (incrementally) from the previous policy. This can be shown schematically in Figure 4.1.

The policy options that are likely to be given the most serious consideration will usually be those that differ from the present policy in only marginal ways. Policy options A and Z, and even G and T, are unlikely to be evaluated. Instead, policy makers will most likely look closely at only K, L, N, and O. These options will result in policies not too much different from the present policy.

Why is this method used rather than the synoptic method? First, this method is less complex. Decision-makers only need to analyze the differences between the old policy and a few new ones. Presumably, they know—roughly—how the present policy functions, what its results are, to what

Alternative policies   Alternative policies
                              Present
                              Policy
←A _____ G _____ K _ L _   **(M)**   _ N _ O _____ T _____ Z→

Figure 4–1. The Incremental Model of Policy Choices.

degree it is successful, and what its defects are. In other words, they *understand* the consequences of the present policy. Comparing the present policy to alternative policies that are only slightly different makes it possible for analysts to be more confident in their predictions about how the new policy might work. They don't have to reinvent the wheel every time a decision needs to be made. Since they know how the present policy works, and since option L (or N) is only marginally different from the present policy, its consequences will be only marginally different. In a sense incremental decision-makers are acting "rationally"; they acknowledge their understanding of the problem is limited and they act to limit the damage that low understanding might have on policy making.

This brings a second benefit; major mistakes can be avoided—at least in principle. By making incremental choices, policy makers can be reasonably sure they are not choosing a policy that will be a serious blunder. On the other hand, they would feel much less confident that any predictions they would make about options A or Z (or G or T) would come true. Policy makers recognize that unanticipated consequences will always turn up and that these are more likely when the policy chosen is dramatically different from the present policy. The selection of A or Z might lead to a monumental disaster! It is also true that the selection of A or Z might turn out to be the best choice that could possibly be made. The problem is that one can't be absolutely sure, since adopting such a policy would constitute a major change. Braybrooke and Lindblom imply that policy makers are motivated more by avoiding policy disasters than by achieving policy successes.[12] As a result, incrementalism can be seen as a "damage limitation" approach to policy making or as a "muddling through" strategy. Government policies are continuously made and remade by successive marginal adjustments in an endless series of trial-and-error experiments.[13]

Braybrooke and Lindblom, like Simon and March, are suggesting that in the real world decision-makers make concessions to reality. They realize that they probably cannot make the absolutely perfect decision; they therefore take shortcuts to simplify the process. The result is that they end up with decisions that are less than perfect.

The third reason for the popularity of incrementalism has to do with the nature of politics. The choosing of alternatives by groups demands that accommodation, compromise, and coalition building take place. It is not likely that too many coalitions will be built around alternatives (like A or Z) that require radical changes in present policy; neither are these options likely to be selected as compromise choices. It is much easier to build broad-based support for options that resemble the current policy; just about everyone can agree that L or N represents a good compromise position between keeping the present policy and making a major change. In other words, incremental decisions are politically easy. Choosing nonincremental policies usually requires overturning a previous incremental decision based on some carefully crafted package of political compromises. Nonincremental choices are therefore politically difficult.

The result is that "nonoptimum" decisions are being made. Policy makers are not necessarily seeking the *best* choice; they are instead pursuing the *safest* choice. It might be suggested that this is not at all bad. After all, we certainly prefer that our governments do not rush hastily into conflict through rash judgments. The implication here is that when faced with a decision that might result in war, political leaders ought to be wary of choosing options that might have unforseen or unintended consequences; they ought to stick to the safe path and proceed incrementally.

On the other hand, Baybrooke and Lindblom argue that policy areas such as wars and revolutions fall outside of the types of decisions that are made incrementally. By their very nature they entail changes that are quite large and important; thus, they are not susceptible to incremental decision-making.

Incrementalism and Vietnam

The American involvement in Vietnam is frequently depicted as having come about through incremental decisions by several successive administrations. In these analyses, incremental decision-making is seen at best as inappropriate, and at worst as the source of disaster. Leslie Gelb and Richard Betts, in their iconoclastic *The Irony of Vietnam: the System Worked*,[14] argue that decisions by each administration concerning the American involvement in Vietnam were highly incremental. U.S. involvement increased step by step as each decision deepened American commitment and increased the ante of money, material, and manpower. (The most important decisions included the Truman administration's decision to support with military assistance the French effort to retain Vietnam as a part of the French colonial empire against the nationalist Vietminh; the Eisenhower administration's decision, after the end of French rule, to support the newly created South Vietnamese government against the rebellious Vietcong; the Kennedy administration's decision to vastly increase the number of U.S. military advisers to South Vietnam; and the Johnson administration's decisions to begin an aerial bombing campaign against North Vietnam, to send U.S. combat troops to fight in Vietnam, and to steadily increase the numbers of these troops.)

Gelb and Betts describe American strategy as "doing what was minimally necessary not to lose" until 1965 and then "doing the maximum feasible to win within certain domestic and international constraints" after that.[15] Over the course of time the floor on the minimum necessary was raised by conditions in Vietnam; later, domestic and international constraints were increasingly discarded to stave off defeat. The result was an incremental escalation of the war effort. What was responsible for the incremental nature of these decisions?

First, U.S. presidents understood that incrementalism would preserve their flexibility by keeping their options open. A major jump in U.S. commitment would reduce the number of future choices available to the president, whereas incremental policies would give the president something to do next time.

Second, incremental choices were also compromise choices. Especially for Johnson, who desired consensus from his advisers, compromises were politically pragmatic; they represented a way to avoid political defections and to minimize the intensity of dissent. Each president chose middle-ground solutions between positions of more hawkish and dovish advisers. Incremental, middle-of-the-road policies kept both extremes on board: "The Right was to be given escalation. The Left was to be given occasional peace overtures. The middle would not be asked to pay for the war."[16] The middle ground was politically safe and smart. A small step that maintained momentum toward the final goal gave each president the best chance to gather more political support before going forward.

Third, incremental choices were pragmatic, a way of playing safe. They gave the appearance of minimizing possible mistakes. Incremental escalation represented the middle of the road between the high-risk alternatives of losing the war or doing what was really necessary to win.

Gelb and Betts believe that the decision-making system at the top of the American government worked: the series of decisions on Vietnam were rational rather than irrational. Political leaders were not fooling themselves; this was not a case in which American leaders believed that each small step would be the last one necessary to gain victory.[17] Gelb and Betts argue that American leaders were not overly optimistic and were not deluded by reports of progress—as some have suggested. The United States did not march into a quagmire because its leaders were unaware that there was any muck in the area; we *knew* it was a quagmire. The escalation was not a blind slide down a "slippery slope"; instead, American escalation was a rational response to the progressive escalation of the minimum price of keeping our commitment.

In other words, American decision-makers understood that they were operating in a policy area of high uncertainty and low understanding, and that in those situations it was quite rational to use an incremental decision style. If one takes as a given the U.S. commitment to prevent a Communist victory in South Vietnam (and this is a big given), then the incremental policies designed to attain this goal may be seen as logical and appropriate responses to changing national and international conditions.

The Organizational Process Model

An important contribution to our understanding of government decision-making was put forward by Graham Allison in his famous analysis of the Cuban Missile Crisis, *Essence of Decision*.[18] Allison suggested three possible explanations of the American decision in that crisis by offering three competing frameworks from which to view the decision. The first framework was our old friend the *rational actor model*, the second he called the *organizational process model* (OPM), and the third—and the one that Allison claimed best described the process by which government decisions are actually made—was termed the *governmental politics model*. More recently, models II and III have been seen by their creator as complementary rather than separate and competing models, and insights from the two have been combined and are popularly refered to as the *bureaucratic politics model* (BPM).[19] Nevertheless, because some of the insights of model II are analytically distinct from those of model III, let us take a brief look at the organizational process model before investigating its more famous sibling.

Allison's organizational process model, drawing on organizational theories of large firms, sees governments as conglomerates of largely autonomous, "semi-feudal, loosely allied organizations." Government decision-makers "can substantially disturb, but not substantially control, the behavior of these organizations" which is determined largely by standard operating procedures.[20] Model II focuses on the methods devised by large organizations to deal with decisions that must be made under the uncertain conditions of limited time, resources, and information. Given this situation, shortcuts around the syncratic model are taken. Problems are typically "factored" or split into different segments and parceled out to subunits with specific roles and missions that deal with only a particular aspect of the problem. Coordination by top leaders is sporadic, and subunits attempt to deal with their problems in isolation from other subunits, devising solutions and then implementing them in a relatively independent manner.

Governmental subunits function according to *standard operating procedures* (SOPs), which can, in turn, have a significant impact on policies. Government activity consists largely of organizations searching for routines to deal with immediate problems. The options available to decision-makers are primarily those that are currently present in some organization's repertoire of contingency plans. For instance, when President Kennedy's "Ex-Com" was summoned to devise tactics to remove Soviet missiles from Cuba, the Pentagon called up its "organizational memory" and responded with a plan to overthrow Castro left over from 1961. No contingency plan existed for destroying Cuban missiles because no such missiles had previously existed, but there was an invasion plan and its organizational sponsors were still in office.[21]

Thus, existing SOPs help determine which routines are actually identified as policy options, which may be actually chosen, and how the options—
once chosen—are put into effect. The imperatives of organizational routines
may therefore severely limit flexibility in decision-making and decision
implementation. Not suprisingly, the process is characterized by sequential
search, satisfycing, and incrementalism, as well as by the lack of flexibility
and imagination.

The effects of these processes are relevant for our discussion of the
causes of war. First, because the search for alternatives is limited to those
options available in the organization's repertoire of contingency plans, the
choices are probably narrower than necessary. Options that might prevent
conflict may be missed because they are not included in any organization's
package of routines.

Second, organizations that operate according to the OPM are subject to
bureaucratic inertia and are slow to respond to major changes in the
environment. Model II processes call for incremental "patches" to be placed
on failing policies. Rather than undertaking a wholesale reassessment of the
policy and devising major changes, a "cybernetic" damage-limitation process is followed. As John Steinbruner explains, organizations attempt to
reduce complexity. They do not monitor all aspects of the present policy; this
would be impossible. Instead, a few simple, critical factors are monitored and
there is an attempt to keep these variables with a tolerable range. If these
variables for any reason exceed the acceptable limits, corrective procedures
and adjustments are triggered. At this point decision-makers proceed routinely through SOPs designed to restore the critical factor to within the range
of tolerance. The policy then persists until the next instance of trouble. Such
cybernetic procedures lead to an incremental "tinkering" with policy, but
not to a total reassessment.[22]

Third, SOPs determine how policies, once decided upon, are actually put
into practice. Policy makers who are unaware of the procedures by which the
policy will be implemented may be surprised to see that the actions being
taken are significantly different from those they originally contemplated.
Allison's classic example concerns President Kennedy's decision to blockade
Cuba. The U.S. Navy implemented the blockade according to standard
procedures, which placed the U.S. fleet as far as possible from Cuban jets, but
far closer to Soviet ships approaching Cuba than was desirable if Kremlin
leaders were to have a chance to deliberate without haste. Although the
implementation of the blockade decision was monitored by political
decision-makers and the Navy was ordered to move the blockade closer to
Cuban shores, Allison argues that in fact the Navy did not follow the
president's orders and intercepted the first Soviet ship along the original line.
President Kennedy was forced to compensate for Navy intransigence by
letting one or several Soviet ships through the blockade in order to increase
the Kremlin's decision time.[23]

The Organizational Process Model and World War I

Jack Levy's review of the pre–World War I crisis suggests that organizational routines—specifically, the war mobilization plans of the great powers—were a major factor (though not the only factor) in the cause of that war.[24] The rigidity of the mobilization routines made changing or even modifying mobilization plans extremely difficult, if not impossible. The German response to the crisis in the Balkans between Austria and Serbia (and Serbia's protector, Russia) was to implement the Schlieffen Plan—which called for the invasion of France through neutral Belgium! The Germans were unable to change the mobilization plan to one that mobilized troops for an offensive in the east, thus ensuring both French and British participation against Germany and a two-front war.

The Austrians were likewise unable to change their plans so that they could accept a political compromise and temporarily occupy Belgrade (the Serbian capital); Austrian troops were not positioned to march on Belgrade because their mobilization plan called for them to prepare for war against the Russians. Austria thus turned down the diplomatic compromise that might have kept the conflict localized. Similarly, Russia found itself unable to carry out a partial mobilization in the south against Austria; its only plan called for complete mobilization against both Austria *and* Germany, and modifications could not be made on the spur of the moment without disastrous military consequences.

Though military routines alone did not cause the war, they contributed to its outbreak in conjunction with certain other factors, some of which also operate at the level of small groups of organizational subunits. For instance, the natural rigidity of mobilization plans was compounded by the tendency of organizations and individuals who had a vested interest in the mobilization policy (because they devised it and were responsible for it) to resist any change in the plan—a tendency consistent with the bureaucratic politics model. For instance, Moltke's resistance to the Kaiser's attempts to alter the Schlieffen Plan are well known.

Second, the rigidity of mobilization plans in Germany was abetted by the fact that German war plans were constructed without consultation with political authorities and in disregard of political considerations—illustrating the tendency of large organizations to "factor" problems. Thus, political leaders were largely ignorant of the mobilization plans and their consequences. While mobilization in reality meant preparation for an immediate war, the political leaders were more likely to see it merely as a tool of coercive diplomacy that might have a salutory deterrent effect on opponents. They were unaware that once begun, military logic required that mobilizations be carried forward toward their intended conclusion—the initiation of war!

In this respect it is interesting to reflect on the very significant effect that the mobilization and deployment of 425,000 U.S. active duty and reserve forces in the Persian Gulf had on the ability of the United States to choose a course other than war in January 1991. It was widely believed to be impossible—for political, economic, cultural, and logistical reasons—to keep such a large force at the front for an extended period of time while permitting economic sanctions to force the Iraqi military out of Kuwait. The mobilization created a "use them or retreat" situation, which was extremely difficult for civilian opponents of the use of force to challenge.

Third, the fact that militaries possess mobilization plans places them in a good internal bargaining position vis-à-vis those who oppose mobilization but who have no alternative plans to offer. Militaries own several built-in bargaining advantages over other institutions on issues of national security: they are perceived as having a legitimate place in the debate; they control sizable resources germane to the problem; they may have the ability to mobilize public support on behalf of their preferred solutions; and civilian officials are usually dependent on their sources of information.[25]

Finally, organizational interests may have been responsible for the creation of the offensive military doctrines upon which the mobilization plans of Germany and other states were based. Levy argues that the offensive doctrines were probably not based on rational strategic calculations, since the technology of warfare at the time actually favored the defense over the offense. It is more likely that the organizational interests of the militaries dictated an offensive doctrine. Offensive strategies would increase the size and resources of the military (offensive forces require greater personnel and weaponry than defensive); offensive doctrines enhance military morale and prestige (who wants to stand behind barricades when you could be in on the charge?); and offensive doctrines require a large standing army rather than a system of reservists.

Levy sees two paths connecting organizational routines to war. Wars may be attributed to the rigid implementation of mobilization plans—owing to the inherent inflexibility of those plans and to bureaucratic factors that assist the military in resisting changes in those plans. Alternatively (or simultaneously), wars may develop because organizational interests dictate the formation of offensive military doctrines, which in turn increase the incentive for preemption by all concerned.

The Bureaucratic Politics Model

The model that Professor Allison believes best explains how governments really make decisions is his model III, the bureaucratic politics model (BPM). Allison starts by assuming that governments are not single, rationally calculating units. Instead, they are made up of organizations and individual actors who hold differing opinions about government policy options and who compete with each other to influence decisions.[26] Decision-making in the governmental arena (actually, in the executive branch in the United States, since this is Allison's focus) involves considerable conflict between disparate "players" who have different responsibilities, resources, and sources of information, who have different perceptions and operational codes, see different sides of each issue, and have different "stakes" in the outcome. Most important, governmental actors have different interests and different goals. Because they have dissimilar institutional and personal interests, their views of the national interest are correspondingly dissimilar as well. They therefore prefer different solutions to policy questions.

It is assumed that no individual or organization has preponderant power. The president, if he is involved, is merely one participant among many. Although his influence may be strong, he is far from omnipotent. His preferences are not always the ones chosen, and even if he were to exercise his authority, his decisions are not always binding. They can be reversed, ignored, or emasculated through the mischief of those in charge of implementation. The BPM implies a kind of "bureaucratic captivity" of the president (or of the central decision-maker in other countries), who is seen as heavily reliant on the bureaucracy for information, for identification and definion of problems, for identification and analysis of alternatives, for the advocacy of solutions, and for policy implementation.

One of the most important propositions of the BPM is encapsulated in the famous phrase "where you stand depends on where you sit." This means that the stand a particular participant takes on an issue depends on what organization he or she represents. This is not a new idea, but one that has been borrowed from *role theory*, a basic staple in sociology departments for years. It is assumed that each organization—the foreign ministry, the defense ministry, the intelligence agencies, and so forth—has its own well-defined interests. For instance, each organization has certain institutional goals that are important to it: more missions, greater autonomy from outside interference, greater influence within the government, greater capabilities, resources, and personnel, and, of course, a larger budget. It is also assumed that individuals who represent these organizations see most issues through the institutional perspective of their own organizations. "Parochial" organizational interests shape the participants' goals, priorities, interests, and perceptions. They examine policy proposals to determine what effect they might have on their organization's interests, and they tend to equate the national interest with their institutional interests.[27]

The reasons for this parochialism are primarily sociological. Leaders within an organization share a similar set of values and assumptions because individuals select (and are selected by) organizations whose values are compatible with their own. Additionally, the process of *institutional socialization*, which takes place once an individual joins an organization, helps to inoculate the individual with the official perspective of his or her institution. A certain amount of attitudinal conformity comes with employment in large organizations.

Each role (or position) occupied by government policy makers entails certain expectations about how it should be performed and is encumbered with certain obligations and duties. These *role expectations* are pressures that encourage the individual to modify his or her attitudes and behaviors to accord with the perceived requirements of the position. Presumably, all those occupying a particular role will act similarly. Hence, we would expect government actions and policies to remain fairly stable, regardless of changes in personnel. It is assumed that a new role player's position on basic issues will tend to be the same as his or her predecessor's.[28]

The most famous story concerning the effect of roles on behavior is that of Henry II of England and Thomas Beckett. As Chancellor, Beckett was Henry's most loyal and aggressive supporter. Henry reasoned that if he made Beckett the Archbishop of Canterbury, he would have an ally who would help him tame the power of the church—an ally who would assert the prerogatives of the king over the religious realm. But once Beckett became the Archbishop, he became a defender of religious authority and Henry's mortal enemy! The role had transformed the man. A similar phenomenon seems to have occurred in recent American politics. As George Shultz's second-in-command at the Office of Management and Budget (OMB), Casper Weinberger had been called "Cap the Knife" for his willingness to slash federal programs in order to keep the United States within budgetary contraints. It was assumed that when he was named Secretary of Defense by President Reagan, the Pentagon would at last have a boss who would ride herd over its runaway budgets. Instead, Weinberger became an extremely effective supporter of military spending and played no small part in helping the United States pile up the largest budget deficits in history!

On the other hand, it must be recognized that individuals do have the capacity to transcend their roles. Some actors may actually remake the role, thus turning the proposition of role theory—that the role makes the individual—on its head. A strong player may redefine the interests of the organization he or she leads. Changes in policy may therefore be initiated by role transformations.[29]

Politics, Conflict, and the BPM

Because individuals and organizations have different goals and interests and because they differ over the best methods of implementing them, policy making involves conflict and competition. Political elites struggle among themselves to exert power over the making of policy. The occasion for a decision mobilizes a wide variety of political forces (both inside and outside the government) to join in the political struggle. This is essentially a *pluralist* model of policy making—many political actors and organizations are presumed to be involved in making the decision.[30]

Policy options are linked to institutional interests. Options are not likely to be put forward nor supported unless they reflect some institutional preference.[31] But because foreign policies ususally require the support (or at least the neutrality) of several different organizations, and because it is unlikely that a single, powerful individual can simply decide for everyone, players must negotiate with each other or risk deadlock.[32] The issue is not so much which position is best, but how to reconcile all the conflicting views over what constitutes the best policy.

Decisions are the result of bargaining, compromise, logrolling, "pulling and hauling," coalition building, competition, and conflict among individuals positioned hierarchically in roles. (Not all actors are equal in rank.) In other words, decisions are determined through a *political* process rather than a logical, intellectual process.[33] Decisions depend not just on the reasons or rationales used to support a course of action, but also on the relative power and skill of proponents and opponents.[34]

Presumably, bureaucratic politics results in compromise.[35] This compromise could be based on an option constructed to contain some aspects preferred by each of the major contenders or on a "brokered" solution that splits the difference. Or it could represent the lowest common denominator—a solution that is the least intolerable for all sides. It is quite possible, in fact, that the solution chosen would actually please *none* of the players nor be very effective in achieving their preferred goals. This phenomenon is called "Arrow's Paradox" after its discoverer, Kenneth Arrow, another Nobel Prize–winning economist.[36] By their very nature, political compromises usually turn out to be suboptimal in achieving objectives.[37]

Aside from compromise, there is another possibility, however. A majority coalition may be able to force its will on the minority.[38] Inducements (which may take the form of compromises) may be given to coalition partners to attain their support. But whatever the process of coalition building, the result is victory for one side rather than compromise. In fact, Snyder and Diesing's analysis of international crises reveals that decisions are more frequently constructed through creating winning coalitions than through compromise. They found decision-making to be decidedly less pluralistic than BPM would predict. Domestic coalitions were able to exclude certain points of view and/or participants from the decision process, thus limiting the number of options placed under consideration.[39]

A final proposition of the BPM is that there is considerable slippage between decisions and implementation. How the decision is carried out depends on standard operating procedures and on the political and organizational interests of those in charge of implementation. The latter may carry out the policy in ways totally unanticipated by the policy makers; they may consciously choose to make minor alterations in the policy or even totally subvert the policy with major changes; or they may simply refuse to carry out the orders at all.

Players who are opposed to the policy imposed by the winning coalition may attempt to sabotage its implementation. Sometimes this has a direct effect on situations of war and peace. For instance, Paleologue, the French Ambassador to Russia, ignored orders from his government to pressure the Czarist government against taking risky action during the July 1914 crisis. Instead, he urged mobilization of Russian forces, pledging unqualified French backing![40] As it turned out, Russian mobilization was a key factor leading to German mobilization and World War I. Such insubordination is carried out not only by major individual players, but also by midlevel officials. President Roosevelt's 1940 export orders permitted licensing of low-grade gasoline and crude oil exports to Japan, but hard-liners in the State Department who were in charge of implementation turned this into an all-out embargo—making the Japanese economic plight more desparate and increasing Japanese hostility toward the United States.[41] And at the very apex of the Cuban Missile Crisis in 1962, when tensions were at their highest levels, a local Soviet commander on the island gave orders that led to the shooting down of an American U-2 spy plane in violation of standing orders from Moscow not to fire on U.S. aircraft.[42] Fortunately, this last example of insubordination did not trigger hostilities that might have ignited World War III.

Consequences of Using the BPM

If the BPM is an accurate reflection of how governments make decisions, then there would seem to be several important consequences.

1. Domestic interests can be expected to predominate over national and international interests. Political leaders rise and fall depending primarily on whether they satisfy domestic needs, and organizations prosper or decline depending on the degree of domestic support they can generate. Furthermore, certain institutions (the White House staff in the United States, for example) are very much attuned to the domestic political climate and see their function as protecting the power of top office holders from domestic political repercussions of policy.

2. Policies will be fragmented. States seldom have a single, integrated foreign policy; they are more likely to have several competing "mini policies" made by different organizations or tailored together by different coalitions, which change over time. Policies may be uncoordinated and only loosely connected; they may even be incoherent and contradictory, with different agencies pursuing different goals. For instance, while the National Security

Council Staff and the White House were negotiating with "moderate forces" in Iran for the release of U.S. hostages in Lebanon, the State Department was pressuring U.S. allies to refrain from negotiating with hostage takers. And in 1960 the State Department and the CIA apparently even gave assistance to opposing armies in Laos![43]

3. There should be a tendency toward middle-of-the-road, incrementalist policies. Political allies must be kept on board and temporary opponents appeased, and this requires moderation and compromise. Incremental choices avoid offending major political constituencies. Furthermore, if government policy is significantly influenced by standard operating procedures, as the BPM implies, then the government's behavior at time t will probably be only incrementally different at $t + 1$. Bureaucratic elites are stifled by organizational inertia: policies at rest tend to stay at rest. Decisive and innovative policies are discouraged and incremental ones are preferred because of the preference of career officials to "go along to get along." The competition for political power and for influence over policy does not necessarily lead to risk taking.[44]

4. Few decisions will be either decisive or final.[45] Government decisions are likely to be the result of unstable, internally inconsistent compromises. Actors who have been defeated in early rounds of policy struggles will try to win support from other players in an attempt to reverse the policy in succeeding rounds. What one political coalition decides is a reasonable solution to a conflict may be abandoned or overturned by the next governing coalition, especially if the continuation of the conflict serves the vital interests of some group. This may help to explain the existence of protracted conflicts and enmities in international relations.[46]

5. Decisions are likely to be nonrational and nonoptimal. Policy makers do not seek the best solution to a problem, but the one that satisfies the most important and powerful political actors on this issue. Alternatively, decisions may represent the lowest common denominator.

Before we proceed, several important questions need to be answered concerning the BPM. First, is it an accurate reflection of the way decisions are made in the U.S. government? Second, is it useful as a *general* model of decision-making? That is, can it be accurately applied to countries other than the United States? Third, does it help us to understand why governments make decisions for war? Fourth, is the BPM a good theory?

Does the BPM Accurately Depict Decision-Making in the United States?

There are essentially three issues concerning the validity of the BPM. Are organizational interests the most important determinant of the stands taken by political elites? Does the BPM accurately depict the role of the president in the decision-making process? Under what circumstances should we expect decisions to be made according to the BPM?

Do Organizational Interests Predominate?

Research by political scientists yields only mixed support for the proposition of "where you stand depends on where you sit." Support comes from the often-quoted study by Robert Axelrod of interdepartmental groups in the American government. Axelrod found that the participants in these groups could accurately and reliably predict the stand of other group members on any issue on the basis of agency affiliation, independent of the personality of the particular individual involved.[47] Individuals didn't matter; organizational affiliation did. The results of Andrew Semmel's study of U.S. State Department officers' attitudes toward multilateral diplomacy are also consistent with Allison's proposition. However, Semmel's study suggests that players' stands depend less on their affiliation with the larger bureaucratic entity that employs them than on the immediate position within a departmental subunit. Large organizations like the State Department are best seen as several interacting subcultures rather than as a single monolithic culture.[48]

On the other hand, Allison's own analysis of the Cuban Missile Crisis indicates that institutional perspectives had little relationship to the policy positions taken by major players. For instance, the Secretary of Defense initially saw *no* major threat to U.S. security from the missiles in Cuba and opposed a full military option. Several other players had no bureaucratic role to defend; they were "wise men" trundled in from the cold. And some "ExCom" members, such as Robert Kennedy and Ted Sorenson, were more loyal to the president than to any bureaucratic fiefdom.[49]

Anderson's study of three foreign policy decisions from three administrations indicates that major foreign policy actors were almost as likely (43.8% of the time) to suggest alternatives outside of their institutional/organizational domains—such as a military staff member suggesting diplomatic action—as they were to suggest alternatives relevant to their own institutions (56.2%).[50] Similarly, Graham Shepard's analysis of top "players" in the national security bureaucracy of the United States from 1969 to 1984 indicates that at least when it came to secretaries of state and defense, it was difficult to determine the effect of their roles on positions they took on issues concerning the use of force.[51]

A popular assumption (and one tested by Shepard) is that players who represent military organizations are more likely to advocate the use of force than other actors. Another is that the military will have a unified position on the use of force. Neither of these propositions is consistently true. General Ridgeway, the Army Chief of Staff, successfully led the political coalition that opposed direct U.S. military action to rescue the French war effort in

Vietnam at the time of the Battle of Dienbienphu in 1954, while top civilian officials such as Vice President Nixon and Secretary of State John Foster Dulles joined Admiral Radford, the Chairman of the Joint Chiefs of Staff, in supporting the proposal.[52] In the Vietnam discussions in 1966 and 1967, Secretary of Defense McNamara advocated diplomacy while Secretary of State Rusk supported the position of the military in favor of escalation.[53] Likewise, we know now that the Soviet military leadership (including Marshal Nikolai Ogarkov, the Chief of Staff, and his principal deputy, Marshal Sergei Akhromeyev) opposed intervention in Afghanistan, but were essentially overruled by a coalition of powerful civilian leaders led by General Secretary Brezhnev and Defense Minister Ustinov.[54]

Richard Betts' analysis of the influence of American military advisers on decisions to use force in Cold War crises concludes that military advisers were neither more nor less aggressive than their civilian counterparts on intervention decisions. In fact, the advice of the Joint Chiefs of Staff was similar to that of the civilian advisers more than half the time. In addition, there was frequent disagreement among military advisers; the armed forces were usually divided on recommendations to commit U.S. forces to action. (The Army chiefs were the most cautious, and Navy chiefs were the most aggressive.) Betts discovers that the Joint Chiefs were more influential when they *opposed* intervention than when they supported it. Presidents and civilian advisers were not persuaded to use force by the military, though they could be persuaded against it if the military thought the use of force unwise.[55]

Other analysts come to very similar conclusions. Snyder and Diesing, in their study of decision-making in sixteen international crises in the nineteenth and twentieth centuries, find that military representatives supported accommodation as often as or more often than they supported a firm stand. Their preference, however, was usually based on estimates of military preparedness rather than personal bias. Role influences, although generally less important than personal values, were seen most often among military players. The military aside, however, they conclude that the stances taken by policy makers are based primarily on personal values and cognitive "mindsets" rather than on role or bureaucratic positions.[56]

These findings indicate that one of the most distinctive propositions of the BPM is frequently found wanting for support. Where one sits does not always indicate the stand one will take on policy alternatives. Even BPM supporters such as Morton Halperin and Arnold Kantor recognize that some actors are less prone to represent narrow, parochial institutional perspectives than others. They make a distinction between "organizational participants," whose stands can be predicted with high reliability from their organizational affiliation, and "players"—those for whom institutional membership is not a good predictor of policy stands. They hypothesize that the higher one's formal position, the less likely one is to be affected by parochial institutional interests.[57]

Is the President Really an Equal Player?

Many of the critiques of the BPM are centered on the role of the president.[58] Remember that Allison sees the president as only one of many central decision-makers. However, if the political system has a chief decision-maker—such as the American president, the British prime minister, the Soviet general secretary—then it is quite possible that decisions are made through a personal, individual process rather than a group process. Even though each of these top leaders has council of advisers of some sort, the decisions process may in fact revolve around the individual dispositions of the top leader. In that case, the bargaining, coalition building, and logrolling among the members of the leadership group may have a relatively insignificant effect on policy selection.

Critics of the BPM argue that the fact that cabinet members are hired (and may be fired) by the president means that they cannot be entirely independent of him. As Amos Perlmutter puts it: "How powerful is a group which can be dismissed at the President's whim?"[59] If a secretary of defense as powerful as Robert McNamara can be forced out once he begins to oppose the president's policy on Vietnam, then it is fairly clear where the balance of power lies. Cabinet heads are tied to the president every bit as much as they are tied to their departments. In fact, one critic suggests that Allison's famous dictum ought to be rephrased as "Where you stand depends upon where the President stands."[60] The president not only appoints the heads of bureaucracies, he also sets the rules of the game, determining which actors will participate in which policy decisions and who will have access to him. The search for, and evaluation of, options may be greatly affected by presidential preference.[61]

Even in Allison's own analysis of the Cuban Missile Crisis decision, many of the options are immediately foreclosed ("do nothing" and "make a diplomatic protest") not by deliberation of the group, but because the president (for domestic political reasons) was not interested in them.[62] Even in the central debate between proponents of an air strike and a naval quarantine, some supporters of the former understood that making arguments for the air attack was probably an exercise in futility, given the well-known support of the Kennedy brothers and Secretary McNamara for the quarantine.[63]

Finally, critics argue that it is inaccurate to depict the president as the captive of a bureaucratic consensus. Even a total negative consensus against the president may not dissuade him from pursuing the option he prefers. In the Missile Crisis when the ExCom did agree on a decision (to bomb a SAM base after a U-2 spy plane had been shot down), the President vetoed it!

Critics admit that on certain occasions bureaucratic interests are decisive in the formulation of policy; some policy options never get presented owing to bureaucratic imperatives, and frequently the president fails to seek out options other than those presented to him by the bureaucracies. But this all depends on presidential interest. When presidents are uninterested, when they fail to assert control, or when they delegate authority, they take themselves out of the equation and reduce their role to that of merely being first among equals; but they have the power to rise above this if they wish. The president can be an omnipotent player if he so desires. The ability of bureaucracies to independently establish policies on their own is a function of presidential attention—a fact that is acknowledged even by advocates of BPM.[64]

When Does the BPM Apply?

Whether governments are actually operating according to the dictates of the bureaucratic politics model at any given time is open to question. Advocates of the model concede that government decisions are not always made according to BPM procedures; other models of decision-making may more accurately describe the policy process, depending on the issues. For instance, Wilfred Kohl's investigation of foreign policy decisions in the Nixon administration finds that in only two of the eleven cases—international monetary policy and the international economic crisis of 1971—does the BPM provide the most satisfactory explanation of the policy. On some issues the "Royal Court" model—which emphasizes the personality and operating style of the top decision-maker—provides the best explanation, and bureaucratic politics plays no role at all. On other issues several models together are needed to provide a satisfactory explanation of the decision.[65]

Certainly, a theory of bureaucratic politics must set out the circumstances under which the model can be expected to be used by policy makers and when it will not be used. The bureaucratic politics model is most likely to be in operation when the following conditions are met.

1. The number of actors and organizations that might be "legitimately" involved in the issue is fairly large. In order for a decision to be made by the bureaucratic politics process, a minimum number of three individuals or organizations probably need to be involved; one or two decision makers is not enough.[66] Essentially, BPM processes require committee decision-making of some sort, or at least a central decision-maker who must consult with a circle of advisers. The more individuals or groups involved in the decision, the more likely the BPM will be used. "Intermestic issues," which cross boundaries of domestic and foreign policy issues, are particularly susceptible to bureaucratic politics—international economic issues being a prime example.[67]

2. The group that decides the issue is fairly heterogeneous and socially-culturally-institutionally lacking in cohesion. For reasons we will examine later, the less intragroup cohesion there is, the more conflict one can expect.

3. Members of the group should be relatively equal in power. Bureaucratic politics doesn't require complete equality of participants, but it cannot operate when one member exercises decisively more power than others. Bureaucratic politics is most likely if the top leader is either absent from the process or is part of a truly collegial leadership group. If there is a strong leader, then he or she is in a position to push the decision toward his or her own preferred solution.[68] Especially if the top decision-maker is actively involved in the issue, the result tends to be a personal decision rather than a group decision, and therefore the leader's personality, perceptions, images, operational code, and world view play the dominant role.

4. The primary loyalty of the decision-makers is to their own institution rather than to the decision unit.[69] This ensures institutional competition instead of consensus.

5. There must be sufficient time for members of various institutions to organize their attempts to influence the decision process. The longer the time available for decisions, the greater the possibility that interested actors and organizations will be able to insinuate themselves into the policy-making process and mobilize support for their positions. Decisions with short time frames are not conducive to bureaucratic politics. Therefore, true crises probably are not handled through the BPM.

6. The more open the process, the more likely bureaucratic politics will develop. Obviously, a closed decision process that prevents interested actors and organizations from participating is not likely to be in accordance with bureaucratic politics procedures. Bureaucratic politics, though it does not require popular participation and democratic institutions, does require a degree of openness to input from a variety of institutional actors.

Do these conditions eliminate issues of peace and war from consideration through the BPM? Probably not. Not all decisions on war and peace are made in the midst of a crisis that limits the amount of time available. The Soviet decisions on Czechoslovakia and Afghanistan and the American decision to use force against Iraq, though they certainly operated under some time constraints, could in no way be called quick decisions. Neither could U.S. decisions on Vietnam. Likewise, issues of war and peace are so important that actors and institutions that might normally play only limited roles in foreign policy issues could legitimately participate. Also, while the chief decision maker would certainly be keenly involved in such an issue, he or she would not be likely to want to carry the ball alone on this one. On issues of such momentous import, top decision makers want to have a lot of political padding if they stumble; this requires the support of a wide spectrum of political elites.

Is the BPM Applicable to Governments Other Than the United States?

Since the BPM has been developed largely by studying U.S. foreign policy and its use has been confined almost exclusively to case studies of U.S. government decisions, one has to question its generalizability to other states. On this score, Snyder and Diesing see the BPM as actually less relevant to the United States, where the president holds the ultimate power of decision in foreign policy, than to other regimes where responsibility for foreign policy decision-making is shared.[70] For example, it has been argued that the BPM is applicable to British-style parliamentary systems. The same kind of parochial concerns motivate policy makers in these systems as in presidential systems— the major difference in Westminster systems being the concentration of authority in the cabinet, where "ministry is set against ministry."[71]

It would seem that the BPM would be applicable in many regimes where there was a collective leadership body of elites, including even the (former) Soviet Union with its ruling Politburo. In fact, the BPM does have stiking similarities to Kremlinological studies of Soviet decision-making. Several "models" used by specialists to describe the decision-making system in the Soviet Union focus on the conflict between elites representing institutional interest groups.[72] One Kremlinologist, Jiri Valenta, argues that while the BPM must be modified somewhat to take into consideration the distinctive features of the Soviet system, the approach is nevertheless useful in explaining Soviet foreign policy decisions.

> Soviet foreign policy actions, like those of other states, do not result from a single actor (the government) rationally maximizing national security or any other value. Instead, actions result from a process of political interaction ("pulling and hauling") among several actors—in this case, the senior decisionmakers and the heads of several bureaucratic organizations, the members of the Politburo, and the bureaucratic elites at the Central Committee level. Bureaucratic politics is seen as based upon and reflecting the division of labor and responsibility for various areas of policy among the Politburo members. . . . Soviet foreign policy decision-making is affected by a number of constraints, among them shared images of national security, organizational interests, domestic interests, various personal interests and ideosyncracies, the rules of the game and the sets of participants, and internal bargaining and manuevering.[73]

What has made the Soviet system essentially a bureaucratic politics system is that decisions in the post-Stalinist era have been made by a collective body—the Politburo. In the last four decades, Soviet leaders have rarely possessed enough power to make decisions individually on foreign policy matters. Compared to the American president, the general secretary of the Communist Party of the Soviet Union (CPSU) has probably enjoyed more limited power in making decisions. His power within his own "cabinet"—if we wish to see the Politburo in these terms—has certainly been less dominant. He typically has been *primus inter pares* (first among equals), while the president dominates his cabinet. Lincoln's famous quip about the cabinet vote in which all members voted against his proposal and he alone voted in favor was that the "Ayes have it!"

The situation for the Soviet leader has been somewhat different. According to Dennis Ross, the ending of the use of terror against the party elite after Stalin's death and the "palace coup" in which the Politburo ousted Khrushchev in 1964 institutionalized a collective leadership based on multiple power centers.[74] Khrushchev's demise symbolized the fact that the general secretary could not run roughshod over the interests of major political players and over the institutional prerogatives of essential organizations. If the general secretary could be removed by a majority faction within the Politburo, he could not be considered an ultimate authority; he must rule through his ability to create either a consensus or, at least, a majority coalition. The general secretary was forced to become primarily a "broker" of the interests of various factions within the Politburo rather than an "initiator." This was especially true of the Brezhnev period. Brezhnev's consensus building kept his colleagues happy, while simultaneously ensuring that any mistakes or failures were collective ones and could not be pinned easily on him alone.[75]

Creating a consensus for policy has required at least the acquiescence, if not the approval, of a majority of senior leaders within the Politburo, and perhaps a wide body of supporters within the larger Central Committee as well. This frequently has made necessary such tactics as internal bargaining, compromise, and logrolling. It has also involved the mobilization of various relevant pressure groups, the changing and rearranging of personnel who might make up the decision team, attempts to manage information, the use of the press to try to influence the debate, and the persuading of uncommitted leaders—all techniques familiar to those who use the BPM to study the American political system!

The result was a system that can be described, according to Ross, as a "pluralism of elites" or an oligarchy. Policy making increasingly became rule by committee in which the most powerful institutional interests in the country were mediated. The principle of weighing all major interests became a "central norm" of the process.[76]

The most important factor in this process has been *coalition maintenance.* This was in large part compelled by the key ideological myth of party unity, which denied the possibility of conflict among the party elite. But the fear that the ruling coalition would break up, possibly ending the political careers of some members, was an equally strong incentive to resolve internal policy conflicts in a way that maintained the coalition. The system was characterized therefore by a willingness of political actors to compromise, by a lowest common denominator approach to policy making, and by incrementalism—all the marks of a bureaucratic politics system.

This "muddling through" style has also meant that Soviet decision-makers were likely to avoid rash decisions. Soviet elites were extremely cautious anyway, but they have been especially sensitive to the high political costs of failure. Policy failure constituted the paramount basis on which individual members of the elite could be successfully challenged and relieved of their positions by their political enemies. However, Ross concludes that even though the system was structured to avoid risks internally, the Soviets might still run risks externally, especially if their internal positions depended on it.

Is the BPM Useful in Explaining the Cause of War?

It would seem that a BPM explanation of the cause of war would require that (1) the decision for war be made in a situation where numerous individuals, organizations, and governmental institutions that have differing interests are competing to have their versions of governmental policy adopted; (2) the decision for war is the result of either bargaining or compromise or power struggle between these various political factions in which a balance of power within the government favors the initiation of war; and (3) the decision for war is seen by one or more of the groups as promoting its organizational or political interests (or the decision to forgo war is seen as detrimental to its interests) or maintaining a particular coalition in power.

Advocates of the BPM have used it to explain a variety of different national security policy decisions, which—in addition to the Cuban Missile Crisis—include decisions about procurement of weapons systems, international economic policy, arms control policy, and alliance politics.[77] A small number of case studies have actually investigated the decision to use force from a bureaucratic politics perspective; they focus on two very different political systems, the United States and the (former) Soviet Union.

Bureaucratic Politics and Soviet Involvement in War

Perhaps the most interesting of these studies is Jiri Valenta's *Soviet Intervention in Czechoslovakia, 1968: Anatomy of a Decision*.[78] As the Czech government under Alexander Dubcek began to implement a variety of liberal economic, political, and social reforms in 1968, the Soviet Union was faced with a serious foreign policy crisis. A brief summary of Valenta's analysis of the Soviet response to the Czech reforms might prove useful at this point to give the reader an idea of how the BPM can be used to explain decisions to go to war.

Soviet officials saw somewhat different sides of the problem and identified somewhat different stakes for themselves and their organizations. In effect, they defined Soviet national interests differently, depending on their instituional responsibilities. Although virtually all Soviet leaders saw the Czech reforms as a threat, there was division about how to respond to the threat. Two rather informal coalitions began to form early in the crisis—prointerventionists and anti-interventionists—with some members uncommitted.

Prointerventionists

1. Party bureaucrats in the non-Russian Republics such as Pyotr Shelest, a Politburo member and First Secretary for the Ukrainian Republic, were concerned about the "spillover" of reformist ideas from Eastern Europe into the nearby Soviet Republics. Shelest's concerns were echoed by P. M. Masherov, the First Secretary of the Belorussian Republic and a candidate Politburo member.

2. Central Committee bureaucrats charged with ideological supervision and indoctrination were concerned about the spread of "revisionist" ideas from Czechoslovakia and the likely effect on their ability to contain dissidents within the Soviet Union. These men included A. Pel'she, a Politburo member and head of the Party Control Commission; P. N. Demichev, a candidate Politburo member and Central Committee Secretary responsible for the Ideological Committee; and S. P. Trapeznikov, the head of the Central Committee Department of Science and Education. Party officials in large cities, such as Moscow Party First Secretary Grishin, who had to deal with large numbers of vocal dissidents in the urban intellectual and literary communities, also perceived the need to stiffle Czech reformist experiments.

3. The KGB and the Department of Main Political Administration (in charge of ideological and political supervision of the army and led by General Yepishev) perceived that the new political winds in Czechoslovakia were a threat to the morale and discipline of Eastern Europe forces in the Warsaw Pact. Soviet generals responsible for Warsaw Pact forces, including the Pact's commander-in-chief, General I. Jakubovsky, certainly perceived the Czech reforms as a threat to the organizational mission of the Warsaw Pact forces. The KGB had additional reasons for wanting to reverse the tide of reform in Czecholovakia; Czech officials had dismissed many of their most trusted men from positions of responsibility in the Czech Ministry of the Interior. The KGB's organizational mission inside Czechoslovakia was therefore at stake. A similar problem probably confronted the military's Chief Intelligence

Directorate (GRU), as GRU collaborators within the Czech Army were also being dismissed.

4. East German and Polish party leaders Walter Ulbricht and Wladyskaw Gomulka, respectively, feared the spread of liberal reforms to their countries and attempted to influence the Soviet decision in favor of intervention.

Anti-Intervention Coalition

1. Mikhail Suslov, the Politburo's leading ideologist and the man responsible for the coordination of Soviet policies in the international communist movement, emerged as the spokesman for the noninterventionists. Suslov and Boris Ponomarev, the Central Committee Secretary for the International Department, were concerned that a Soviet military intervention would undermine their organizational mission—maintenance of good ties with Communist parties in the West and "progressive" forces in the Third World. Intervention would also jeopardize the World Communist Conference scheduled for November 1968 and organized by Suslov. Finally, the use of force would jeopardize the strategy of a rapprochement with West Germany and a united front with West European social democratic parties.

2. Premier Anatoly Kosygin, presumably the number two man in the Politburo and responsible for government diplomacy at the time, feared that an intervention would jeopardize the desired goals of concluding a nonproliferation treaty and an early beginning of SALT negotiations. Kosygin's personal power and prestige were also at stake because of the similarity of some of the criticized Czech economic reforms to those advocated by him for the Soviet Union.

3. Bureaucrats in the Foreign Ministry and the Central Committee International Department who had responsibility for Soviet relations with the West clearly felt intervention would adversely affect Soviet interests.

4. Dubcek supporters in Eastern Europe, such as Hungarian leader Janos Kadar, Yugoslavia's Tito, and Rumania's Ceausescu, feared that Soviet intervention against Czech reform would threaten their own reforms.

Fence Sitters

General Secretary Brezhnev is the only major player identified by Valenta as an "uncommitted thinker," one who sees many sides of the issue, though there were assuredly others as well. Brezhnev wavered between the two coalitions until the very end, acting as a broker between the two factions, but also trying to identify himself with the winning coalition. The position of Brezhnev was crucial in this case, not just because he was the general secretary, but because the Soviet leadership were divided on the proper policy to follow. Neither of the coalitions had a strong enough majority to force its will on the other. Thus, a change in the position of any major uncommitted player might tip the balance.

Negotiations between the Soviets and the Czechs took place at Cierna and Bratislava in late July and early August. The immediate result was a policy of compromise—both a compromise among members of the Soviet leadership and a compromise between Soviet and Czech leaders. The Czechs provided assurances of their loyalty to the Warsaw Pact and COMECON, agreed to control their news media more effectively, promised to prevent the creation of political parties, and agreed to purge certain leaders from high office. For their part the Soviets agreed to withdraw all troops from Czech territory (they had been there on Warsaw Pact maneuvers) and to approve the September Congress of the Czech party. Nevertheless, only seventeen days after the final meeting, Czechoslovakia was subjected to a military intervention. Why did this reversal occur?

The action revolved around trying to create enough political converts that a winning coalition could be created in favor of overturning the Cierna-Bratislava compromise and launching a military intervention. The normal techniques of persuasion were attempted, including the use of the press by various factions to try to mobilize support. The KGB and the Soviet Ambassador to Czechoslovakia, S. V. Chervonenko, also attempted to distort information and analysis to lend credence to their preferred course of action. The KGB's primary motivation was the continuing purge of Soviet agents by the Czech government. Chervonenko's motives were more personal. Having been the Soviet Ambassador to China when the Sino-Soviet split erupted, he did not desire to be tagged with the loss of another Socialist state on his watch. He advised his colleagues in Moscow that although the situation in Prague was getting worse and that a "second Hungary" was possible, the Dubcek faction was a minority within the Czech Politburo, lacked support among the masses, and could easily be replaced by "healthy elements" if the Soviets intervened.

According to Valenta, the *modus vivendi* with the Czechs began to come apart when segments of the Soviet military elite who were dissatisfied with the compromise began to press the political leadership for a reversal. We have mentioned that Warsaw Pact commander Jakubovsky viewed the Czech reforms as undermining discipline in East Euopean forces. Other Soviet military leaders, especially General Pavlovsky of the newly restored Ground Forces Command, were dissatisfied with the absence of Soviet armed forces from Czech soil. Given the growing loss of confidence in Czech forces, forward deployment of Soviet Ground Forces on Czech soil was no doubt seen as essential to carry out Soviet military doctrine in Europe. A military operation against Czechoslovakia would, of course, coincidentally improve the role and prestige of the Ground Forces Command! This is not to say that the Warsaw Pact generals were all in favor of intervention. General

Kazakov, chief of staff of the Warsaw Pact forces and a participant in the Soviet intervention in Hungary in 1956, was apparently very skeptical of Soviet intervention in Czechoslovakia. He was unexpectedly replaced after the Cierna-Bratislava Conferences, however, by General Shtemenko, described by Valenta as a "Ground Forces lobbyist."

The military and their allies had another argument that was becoming increasingly more relevant—logistics. Not only were regular units involved in the Soviet troop buildup and maneuvers in Czechoslovakia, but thousands of reservists had been called up and thousands of motor vehicles had been requisitioned from the civilian sector in eastern Russia. A shortage of civilian manpower and trucks was beginning to have a detrimental effect on the 1968 harvest, and this effect could only worsen. The Soviets would have to move quickly, or dismantle the whole military effort. The implementation of organizational routines for military maneuvers had a substantial effect on the options available to Soviet decision-makers.

At this point Ukrainian Party Secretary Shelest mounted a prointervention campaign. We have already mentioned Shelest's concern over Czech reforms infecting the Ukraine. Shelest was probably also motivated by considerations of his own political position—after all, he had been on the losing side at Cierna and Bratislava; his prestige and position within the Politburo were at stake. Simultaneously, renewed pressure was applied by party bureaucrats responsible for ideological issues and concerned about the failure of the Czechs to reinstate censorship of the media. Polish and East German leaders also opened up a new political offensive aimed at overturning the accords. Gomulka (and to some extent Ulbricht) felt threatened internally by the compromise with Czech reformers; their domestic opponents would draw strength from Soviet willingness to permit reform in Prague. Thus, renewed pressure was placed on wavering Politburo and Central Committee members to overturn the Czech compromise.

Finally, anti-Dubcek forces in Czechoslovakia mounted a desparate last-ditch attempt to save their political skins. Their communications to Moscow signaled to the Soviets that the political situation was deteriorating in Prague. Intelligence reports, skewed by the personal and institutional interest of the senders, permitted the Soviets to believe that a military operation would involve low risks and would have a high probability of success.

The combined pressure of the military, the KGB, the regional secretaries in the U.S.S.R.'s Western republics, party bureaucrats dealing with ideological affairs, and their allies in East Germany, Poland, and Czechoslovakia turned the tide in the internal debate. Those who had sat on the fence in the past, and even some who had previously supported diplomatic compromise, now gave their support to military intervention. Perhaps there was a fear of being in the minority on an issue of such momentous importance. Forced resignations could be the penalty for being on the wrong side on major policy questions. Noninterventionists like Suslov, Kosygin, and Ponomarev were already being criticized in reports to the party organization and in the press for their failure to understand the dangers of the Czech reforms. Savvy political observers could tell that the wind was now blowing in a different direction.

Brezhnev himself now supported intervention. Domestic political considerations were probably paramount in Brezhnev's analysis of the situation according to Valenta. The fact that the Cierna-Bratislava accords had not been well received by certain political and military elites certainly did not enhance Brezhnev's political position. The General Secretary came to see Soviet intervention as required both by Soviet national interests and by his own political interests.

It might be noted that political analysts have provided BPM explanations for other Soviet decisions as well. Dina Rome Spechler traces the change in Soviet policy toward the Middle East in 1973, and in particular the decisions to permit Egyptian purchases of Soviet military equipment and to give a green light for a military confrontation with Israel, to a change in the relative balance of power among elite factions within the Politburo. It would seem that those who held a "competitive" image of Soviet-American relations (led by Prime Minister Kosygin and including officials in state administration and those with responsibility for consumer goods and technological development) shifted their support from those who held a "cooperative" image of Soviet-American relations (led by General Secretary Brezhnev) to those who held an "antagonistic" image (including Minister of Defence Grechko, Admiral Gorchkov, party ideologist Suslov, KGB Chairman Andropov, Trade Union Secretary Shelepin, and others.[79] In this case, pressure for the shift came from events in the external environment, such as the Egyptian expulsion of Soviet advisers in 1972.

Max Jacobson's analysis of the Soviet decision to use force to obtain territory from Finland in 1939, though not a BPM analysis, indicates that a coalition of three Soviet officials provided the bureaucratic impetus for putting the issue on the agenda and for convincing a more reluctant Stalin (the final arbiter) to go along.[80] The three each had institutional and personal political reasons that undoubtedly led them to view Soviet national security as requiring the acquisition of Finnish territory. Andrei Zhdanov, the Party Secretary of the Leningrad region, was responsible for the defense of Leningrad and would benefit from the expansion of his territorial base; Otto Kuusinen was an ethnic Finn who would become the leader of any Finnish territory that would become Communist; and Admiral V. F. Tributs, the commander in chief of the Baltic Fleet, was of course worried about the security of the Soviet fleet, and his organization would stand to gain from the acquisition of Finnish naval bases in the Baltic.[81]

Bureaucratic Politics and Vietnam

The American involvement in Vietnam has become something of a cottage industry for those who use a bureaucratic politics perspective. The most explicit attempt to explain U.S. decisions in Southeast Asia using the BPM is Robert Gallucci's *Neither Peace nor Honor*.[82] Gallucci focuses specifically on the Kennedy administration's decision (1961–1963) to send military advisers and President Johnson's decision to begin the aerial bombing campaign and to development of the ground war between 1965 and 1967.

Gallucci's thesis is that in the early (1961–1963) period the policy process was essentially open and competitive. As a result, dissent from the State Department led to a policy of moderation and compromise and prevented the administration from accepting proposals for gradual increments of military force. Cautionary input from the State Department permitted the president the necessary flexibility to resist more activist elements in the executive branch. In these early years there were a substantial number of bureaucratic battles, and the moderation of U.S. policy reflected that bureaucratic division. The absence of comparable dissenting opinion in later years is likewise reflected in the increasing activism of American policy after 1963.

After President Kennedy's death, the State Department's contribution diminished and the focus of policy making shifted to the Defense Department. Later, the process became even more closed as significant decisions in the Johnson administration were relegated primarily to the top-level Tuesday Lunch Group.[83] In part this was due to President Johnson's changes in the policy-making process, but it was also due to a change in the cast of characters at State, as dissenters were forced out or "domesticated"— formally tolerated, but informally ignored. The domestication of dissenters was enhanced by the "effectiveness trap"—in which participants, in order to maintain their influence and effectiveness, decided not to fight strongly on certain issues in order to retain some influence and effectiveness on issues that might arise later. Domestication of dissenters was also furthered by the nature of the American political system. Unlike cabinet officials in parliamentary systems, American cabinet officers have no safe political offices (such as a backbench parliamentary seat) to which to return if they wish to resign in protest over policy issues. Hence, they tend to stay on and mute their own dissent.[84]

Early in the Johnson administration a consensus developed to try to defeat the insurgency in the south by direct military pressure on North Vietnam. The 1965 decision to begin bombing the North was arguably the single most important decision made about American policy in Vietnam. It developed from a fragile bureaucratic consensus in which the participants supported the decision for a variety of different reasons, with a variety of different hopes about what the policy would achieve, and with dissimilar positions on the costs and risks they were willing to absorb to continue the program.

Air Force officers were, not surprisingly, the most ardent supporters of the bombing policy. The effectiveness of conventional air power was at stake in Vietnam.

> The air force, like no other advocate, was fighting for the credibility of a part of its organizational identity and the preservation of primary missions by arguing that bombing would "work" in Viet-Nam before it was begun, maintaining that it was effective after it was started, and protesting that it could not produce victory unless it was conducted with more vigor after it appeared to fail.[85]

Obviously, reporting about the air war, once begun, would be affected by institutional biases in the Air Force. Since the Air Force's *raison d'être* was to fight in the air or bomb, and since promotion depended on evaluation by one's superiors, it would be unlikely for subordinates to tell the general in charge that the air strike he had ordered was a failure. To criticize the bombing was to harm one's own organization as well as one's own career.[86]

The other services also viewed the bombing policy in light of its effects on their own roles. In 1965 they supported the bombing proposal because it was seen as a way to increase the general American commitment to military force in Vietnam. The bombing was seen by the Army and the Marines as a means of ensuring their own continued involvement in the war; its use increased the probability of a larger American military commitment.[87] The Navy, with its own air component, naturally shared the Air Force's interest in bombing. As a result, the US military services each found organizational reasons to support the air war.

The President's chief civilian advisers supported the bombing, but had quite different ideas about what objectives the air war would promote. Walt Rostow, counselor for the State Department and perhaps the most aggressive civilian advocate of aerial bombing, believed that bombing of key industrial targets in the North could force Hanoi to end its support for the insurgents. Maxwell Taylor, the ambassador to South Vietnam, supported the policy because he believed bombing the North would weaken morale in the North and improve it in the South, as well as reduce the North's ability to support the insurgency. McGeorge Bundy, the President's national security adviser, supported the policy because he believed it would have a positive effect on our allies in the South while having a sobering effect on the Vietcong. Under secretary of State George Ball, although he generally opposed aerial bombing and believed it would be ineffective, supported the consensus because he saw the bombing policy as a substitute for the use of ground troops, an eventuality he saw as a far greater evil.

Secretary of State Dean Rusk, Secretary of Defense Robert McNamara, and President Lyndon Johnson all had their doubts about the effectiveness of a bombing policy, but hoped it would work and felt obliged to support it. It was a course less risky and less costly than a resort to ground troops. The President especially saw the policy in light of the domestic political necessity not to appear soft on communism.

In the final analysis, Gallucci sees a significant amount of "tugging and hauling" in the decision to begin aerial bombing—the tugging for a more aggressive policy from Taylor, CINCPAC, the Air Force, and the JCS, and the resistance from the President and his Secretaries of State and Defense.

In conclusion, early in the Johnson administration the bounds of legitimate debate were set rather narrowly, and little fundamental dissent took place (except for the domesticated and formal dissent of George Ball). President Johnson skillfully removed the most dovish opposition players. Undersecretary of State for Political Affairs Averill Harriman, Assistant Secretary of State for Far Eastern Affairs Roger Hilsman, Hilsman's staff specialist on Asia, Michael Forrestal, and Attorney General Robert Kennedy were all pressured to resign in one way or another. Undersecretary of State George Ball was "domesticated"—permitted to stay and dissent as the "house dove"—and National Security Adviser McGeorge Bundy was gradually won over to a more hawkish position.[88] Expulsion of dissenters was essential to the building of a majority coalition in support of the bombing and then the introduction of combat troops. The typical pattern was that in the absence of real civilian dissent, the military pushed policy along, the civilians more or less following reluctantly, and the president chose from among the very limited options presented to him.

Of course, it would be foolish to take the position that bureaucratic politics alone was responsible for U.S. actions in Vietnam, and Gallucci recognizes this. Certainly other factors were important as well. There were certainly shared images of the situation held by most policy makers, and the personality of various presidents—especially Johnson—played a role as well. In addition, external factors in the international arena cannot be dismissed. But the BPM may be a good starting place if one wishes to investigate the reasons for the American decisions in Vietnam.

BPM as a Theory

At the outset perhaps we ought to state that it is not entirely clear whether the BPM is a theory or something less. In Allison and Halperin's reformulation of the BPM, they label their combination of the organizational process model and the governmental process model a "paradigm" rather than a theory, making more modest claims for it.[89] Keeping this in mind, let us examine the theoretical assets and liabilities of the BPM.

What does the BPM attempt to explain and how is this explanation achieved? What is the dependent variable and which independent variables are supposed to "cause" it? The dependent variable that the theory purports to explain is government "action." The independent variables are things such as the players, their positions and roles, their motivations, their organizational and political interests, the bargaining process, and the regularized procedures through which the policy is made. The relationship between these variables and their relative importance is unclear, and probably varies from case to case. Operationalization of these variables, not to mention their measurement, presents the researcher with considerable difficulties.

This is all pretty messy. The BPM is an extremely complex and nonparsimonious theory. The result is that BPM explanations tend to be rather complex as well. Such explanations require a substantial narrative, much like an historical explanation of the decision process, which focuses on those concepts or variables identified in the model.

This presents several problems. A BPM explanation requires access to a quantity and quality of data that most researchers are unlikely to find readily available. After all, the most reliable information would be notes of Cabinet meetings, Politburo meetings, National Security Council meetings, or their equivalent. Objectivity is also a problem. As one critic notes, "given the often ambiguous data they have to work with, bureaucratic politics analysts run the danger of imposing their theory on the data, rather than testing their theory on the basis of the data."[90] If one is looking for evidence of bureaucratic politics at work, one is likely to find it.

Another problem with the BPM as a theory is that it has generated a paucity of specific hypotheses that can be tested to assess the validity of the theory itself. With the exception of the hypothesis that "where you stand depends on where you sit," one is hard pressed to find another. And as we have stated, this crucial hypothesis seems to be incorrect as often as it is valid. The difficulty of testing specific hypotheses is related to a more general problem. What constitutes proof of the existence of bureaucratic politics? And, what evidence is necessary to prove that the decision in question was the result of the bureaucratic politics process? The developers of the model have left us without clear answers to these questions.

This is not to say that the BPM is without merit; it is just extremely difficult to employ. And while the kind of evidence used to provide a BPM explanation of war is not of the statistical or correlational sort with which political scientists feel comfortable, there is certainly more than one way of assessing the validity of empirical theories.[91] It is virtually impossible at this point to determine the extent to which bureaucratic politics has played a role in war initiation. But even if we find that it is useful in explaining only a relatively small percent of cases of war, the BPM still provides the theorist with several important insights on the causes of war which should not be discarded. And in some cases bureaucratic politics may in fact provide a more satisfying explanation than rival theories.

Groupthink

The final theory we will examine at the small-group level of analysis is *groupthink*, developed by Irving Janis, a social psychologist who is interested in international affairs. Janis describes "groupthink" as set of decision-making problems (a syndrome) that afflict policy makers. In a nutshell, groupthink refers to a deterioration of critical thinking, mental efficiency, reality testing, and moral judgment that results "when the group members' striving for unanimity override their motivation to realistically appraise alternative courses of action."[92] The decision-making group seeks conformity, harmony, and consensus at the expense of sound policy making.

Following is a list of the dominant characteristics of the groupthink syndrome:

1. Members of the group consider loyalty to the group to be the most important objective.

2. Group members seek to foster and maintain consensus, harmony, and unity.

3. Group loyalty requires each member to avoid raising controversial questions, challenging weak arguments made by other members, or criticizing the opinion of the majority. Personal doubts are voluntarily suppressed. As a result, the consensus that seemingly appears is actually an illusion.

4. Dissent is seen as disloyalty to the group.

5. Nonconformists are excluded from the group and some group members act as "mindguards" to pressure possible nonconformists to withhold their objections or mute their criticisms.

6. Group members hold the conviction that the policy positions of the group are moral.

7. Group members hold "hard-headed" attitudes toward out-groups, believing for instance that the opponent is "fiendishly evil" (but also weak and stupid). Stereotyped thinking about outgroups abounds.

8. The attitude of the group is generally characterized by overoptimism, a sense of false security, and invincibility. There is a belief that a group made up of such good and intelligent individuals can do no wrong.

As you can imagine, such a situation might lead to serious distortions in the group's ability to perform rational problem solving. For instance, Janis identifies the following flaws in decision-making which may result from groupthink:

1. There is little or no attempt to gain information from experts, seriously impairing the information-gathering process and casting doubt on the objective nature of the search.
2. There is a selective bias toward facts and judgments.
3. Discussions of the group are limited to a few alternative courses of action.
4. There is an incomplete survey of objectives.
5. The group fails to reexamine its preferred solution in order to assess its risks and flaws. The group coalesces around an alternative that is uncritically accepted.
6. Assumptions shared by group members are never examined; misconceptions are never corrected.
7. The group neglects to examine fully those courses of action that were initially evaluated as unsatisfactory.
8. Little time is spent examining how the plan might fail; contingency plans are rarely developed.
9. There is a lack of vigilance and sensitivity to the threat of failure.
10. Past decisions that have ended in failure are rationalized.

Whereas Allison starts from the proposition that governmental decisions made by groups have a character all their own owing to the political nature of actors representing different institutional interests and different constituencies, Janis starts from the proposition that decisions made by groups are different than decisions made by individuals owing to the social nature of the decision-making process. Specifically, small groups—under certain circumstances—have a tendency to seek conformity.

Sociologists have long known of the strong pressures for conformity that exist within social groups, and the greater the cohesiveness of the group, the more pressure for conformity. Pressures for conformity come in part from the simple desire to get along with one's co-workers. Additionally, many individuals fear that if they voice dissent too often, they will lose their "effectiveness" or their chance for further promotion. Pressures for conformity also arise due to the need for "social comparison." Individuals strive to find out whether their opinions (about the best policy to pursue, for instance) are correct. When objective means are unavailable, we evaluate our opinions by comparing them to the opinions of others. If the opinions of the other members of the group coalesce around an opinion different from our own, there is tremendous pressure to write off our opinion as faulty and accept that of our peers.

Most important, highly cohesive in-groups constitute a source of security for their members, which serves to reduce anxiety and to heighten self-esteem. This mechanism is even more heavily needed and relied on in time of stress, because stress increases self-doubt and insecurity. It should come as no surprise that in-group solidarity increases when clashes arise with out-groups.

Janis has been careful to point out that not all decision-making groups are subject to the groupthink syndrome. Groupthink can be avoided and often is. We need to know, therefore, what conditions lead to its presence. Janis points out several antecedent conditions that give rise to groupthink; some have to do with the nature of the group and others with the nature of the situation. It might be speculated that the psychological attributes of the individuals within the group would be a factor. For instance, individuals with strong affiliative needs or individuals who are most fearful of disapproval and rejection might be particularly susceptible to groupthink. Although this may be true, Janis contends that all decision makers, even those with high self-esteem, may be vulnerable to groupthink under certain conditions.[93]

The most important antecedent condition for groupthink is the presence of a cohesive in-group—a group whose members are socially compatible, who get along well, who respect and admire each other, who are loyal to each other, and who value the group's compatibility and its *esprit de corps*. Indeed "Janis' Law" is that the more amicability and *esprit de corps* among members of the group, the greater is the danger that independent, critical thought will be replaced by groupthink.[94]

Group cohesiveness is a necessary condition for the appearance of groupthink, but it is not a sufficient condition, according to Janis; not all cohesive groups experience groupthink. Other conditions must be present as well. (Indeed, group cohesiveness may actually lead to better decisions if individuals feel secure enough in the confines of the group to voice critical viewpoints. On the other hand, noncohesive groups make poor decisions also—though not because of groupthink. Too much conflict between group members may turn the decision process into a power struggle. Thus, cohesiveness is a two-edged sword; too little cohesiveness and the group degenerates into endless squabbling, too much and groupthink takes over.)

Certain structural factors enhance the probability that groupthink will arise. First, a group that is insulated from the input of others is more susceptible to groupthink than one that is open. Second, a group that lacks impartial leadership is more likely to succumb to groupthink. The group leader, rather than refraining from trying to influence the group, uses his or her position to steer the decision in a certain way as an advocate. Subordinates find it very difficult to challenge the leader's ideas, and prefer to defer, thereby limiting a really critical analysis of the problem. Third, a group that lacks norms of methodical decision-making is more likely to develop groupthink than one that adheres to more rigorous procedures. Fourth, a group whose members share similar social and cultural backgrounds is more prone to groupthink than a socially and culturally diverse body.

Finally, certain situational factors also contribute to the presence of groupthink. Typically, groupthink develops when group members are under a high degree of stress from an external threat. Additionally, group members may suffer from low self-esteem brought about by a recent policy failure, by the recognition that the decision they face may be beyond their competence, or by the fact that they face a difficult moral dilemma. Group members find psychological security and mutual support in the company of like-minded colleagues who agree among themselves that the policies they have devised to deal with a crisis will work. The cohesive interaction of the group preserves each member's self esteem. Janis sums up by saying that this concurrence seeking within the group is:

> a mutual effort to maintain emotional equanimity in the face of external and internal sources of stress arising when they share responsibility for making vital decisions that pose threats of failure, social disapproval, and self-disapproval.[95]

Without the illusion of unanimity brought about by groupthink,

> the sense of group unity would be lost, gnawing doubts would start to grow, confidence in the group's problem-solving capacity would shrink, and soon the full emotional impact of all the internal and external sources of stress generated by making a difficult decision would be aroused.[96]

When a group is moderately or highly cohesive, the more of these antecedent conditions that are present, then the greater the chance that groupthink will occur, leading to a faulty decision. And, of course, the more frequently a group displays the symptoms of groupthink, the worse will be the quality of decision-making—on the average. (Janis also recognizes, of course, that the decision-making flaws he identifies don't have to be caused by groupthink; they can be created by other factors as well. Just because sloppy decision-making is taking place doesn't mean groupthink is responsible.)

Groupthink in American Foreign Policy

Having outlined his theory, Janis then proceeds to illustrate it with several examples from American foreign policy. He identifies the Kennedy administration's decision to carry out the Bay of Pigs invasion of Cuba in 1961 as the classic case of groupthink—one that resulted in "a perfect failure." He also builds convincing arguments that groupthink played a major role in the faulty decisions surrounding three other cases: the Truman administration's decision to send United Nations troops into North Korea despite Chinese warnings of intervention, the lack of preparation by the U.S. military in Pearl Harbor prior to the Japanese attack in December 1941, and the escalation of the war in Vietnam. In each case he identifies the symptoms of groupthink within the decision-making unit, the antecedent conditions that might have given rise to groupthink, the resulting flaws in the decision-making process, and the errors in policy that flowed from them.

Janis balances these failures by citing how the Truman and Kennedy administrations were able to avoid the pitfalls of groupthink and produce good results during the planning for the Marshall Plan and the Cuban Missile Crisis. The latter is especially significant because the very same decision-makers who participated in the Bay of Pigs fiasco learned from their mistakes and took conscious steps to avoid the problem-solving errors of the previous year, illustrating that it is possible for cohesive in-groups to avoid groupthink.

Can the Groupthink Theory Be Applied Cross-culturally to Government Policy-making Groups in Other Countries?

Although one could find cultural reasons why groupthink might not be prevalent in certain cultures—if, for instance, the culture valued argumentation rather than harmony—it is quite likely that groupthink applies to a good many cultures. Janis identifies the signs of groupthink in decisions by several different countries. He singles out the Nasser government's provocations that led to the outbreak of the Six Day War of 1967, the Pakistani government's actions that led to war with India in 1971, and the Israeli government's lack of preparation for the Yom Kippur War of 1973 as prime candidates for groupthink. His most interesting analysis of a non-American decision is his explanation of the British government's decisions to pursue a policy of appeasement in the 1930s vis-à-vis Hitler—a policy that led to failure and war. While many in the West simplistically refer to appeasement as Prime Minister Chamberlain's policy, Chamberlain was not alone; he received political and social-psychological support for his policies from his "inner cabinet." Consequently, the British government pursued this policy long after it should have been clear that it contained serious flaws.

Does Groupthink Have Direct Relevance to the Causes of War?

Groupthink would seem to be linked to war in two ways. First, and most directly, to the extent that government decisions to go to war are arrived at through a groupthink process, we can say that the process itself was at least in part a cause of the war. The nature of social interactions within the group was responsible for a decision-making process that deviated significantly from rational problem solving. A better (and presumably more peaceful or less risky) solution could have been devised through a more rational process. Especially important in this regard would seem to be the interrelated patterns of lack of critical analysis, lack of vigilance concerning risk and error, and feelings of overoptimism.

The second contribution of groupthink to war may be through the "risky shift" phenomenon—a concept touched on by Janis, but explored more deeply by others. The risky shift has less to do with the breakdown of rational problem solving within a group than the ability of a group situation to induce individuals to take greater risks than if they were acting (or deciding) alone. Although it would not be true that all groupthink decisions lead to militant or risky decisions, Janis does point to a tendency of group members to view outgroups stereotypically as enemies who are intractable and evil and deserving of punishment. There is a tendency therefore for groupthink decisions to be "hardheaded" toward outgroups. Janis also sees a propensity for group members to take stances of "virility."[97] Others have referred to this phenomenon as the "hairy chest syndrome." Richard Barnett, for instance, gives this picture of American policy makers:

> One of the first lessons a national security manager learns . . . is that toughness is the most highly prized virtue. The man who is ready to recommend using violence against foreigners, even where he is overruled, does not damage his reputation for prudence, soundness, or imagination, but the man who recommends putting an issue to the U.N., seeking negotiations, or, horror of horror, "doing nothing," quickly becomes known as "soft."[98]

The hairy chest syndrome is somewhat similar to the concept of the risky shift developed by social psychologists. In the early 1960s researchers accumulated a sizable amount of evidence that indicated that while individuals in their own problem-solving experiences would choose more conservative, risk-averse solutions, when they were asked to make decisions as part of a group, they tended to support much more risky solutions to the same problems.[99] This conclusion has more recently been modified as a result of further research. The "choice shift" may proceed in either direction—toward more risky or more conservative solutions.[100] The evidence now points to a *group polarization* tendency in which the group decision enhances whichever point of view—risk acceptant or risk averse—is initially dominant within the group.[101] The effect of the group is to make the solution more extreme (in either direction) than the one preferred by separate individuals, since group members are prone to reinforce each other's extreme positions.

To the extent that a shift to a riskier position takes place within the group, several overlapping explanations have been put forward.[102] First, a risky shift could be attributed to the psychological bolstering and peer pressure that is part of the groupthink syndrome. This is consistent with Janis' view that group members tend to seek and maintain group cohesion, and one way to do this is to support the prevailing view—even if that view is extreme—rather than to challenge it. The *espirit de corps* that is so central to Janis' theory of groupthink may encourage, among other things, a shift toward the acceptance of riskier alternatives. Second, a risky shift might be attributed to the recognition that group decisions relieve individuals of direct personal responsibility for risky courses of action; the risks are shared, making individual acceptance of them easier. Third, strong, confident leaders who are risk acceptant may, through the process of group interaction, be able to pull along more recalictrant, undecided members. Fourth, the shift may simply represent an intensification or strengthening of the initial predispositions of individuals through their association with the group.

The makeup of the group may have an effect on the direction of the choice shift. Semmel used simulations of different national security crisis scenarios to study the shift in choices between individual and group recommendations. He used three different sets of groups: university students, U.S. Army officers, and ROTC cadets. All of the Army officer groups shifted to riskier recommendations, almost always recommending the use or threat of force. Almost all of the ROTC groups shifted to to more extreme options as well. But most of the student groups shifted to a milder set of preferences, generally preferring negotiations.[103] The clear implication is that higher-quality decisions are more likely when the group is composed of a heterogeneous mix of individuals recruited from different organizational subunits, a conclusion with which Janis would concur.[104]

Although the risky shift is not part of Janis' groupthink theory, it does share some interesting similarities with it. It is possible that the need for group security, the consensus seeking, and the general deterioration of decision-making skills that Janis describes as groupthink may lead to a shift by the group to riskier actions than the same individuals would ordinarily choose if deciding by themselves.

Groupthink as a Theory

Groupthink has some of the same theoretical defects as the BPM. It requires a great deal of the sort of information that is difficult to come by—such as minutes of cabinet or politburo meetings—making replicability a problem. Groupthink explanations also require a rather long narrative, though this narrative can be more precisely organized than in the BPM, thanks to Janis' precision in laying out the theory. And like bureaucratic politics, groupthink is a fairly complex theory, though the relationships between the variables are more clearcut than in the BPM.

On the positive side, Janis has given great care to developing groupthink as an empirical theory. He has attempted to specify how the theory can be tested (and falsified) against real-world conditions. To this end he has been fairly specific about defining the concept of groupthink and providing empirical referents so that other researchers may be able to identify its presence or absence. He has also delineated quite specifically the conditions under which groupthink should arise—again in a way that is observable.

The theory charts a clear causal path between the presence of certain *antecedent conditions* (including one necessary condition, a cohesive in-group), the *independent variable* (the presence of observable groupthink symptoms), and the *dependent variable* (the observable symptoms of defective decision-making). The links between antecedent conditions, independent variables, and dependent variables are stated in a probablistic, if . . . then, manner. If a group is modestly or highly cohesive, then the more of the antecedent conditions that are present, the greater the chance that the group will experience groupthink. The more numerous the symptoms of groupthink, then the more likely that the decision will be defective. The more defects in the decision-making process, the lower the probability that the policy will be a success. Case studies have been developed to confirm the existence of groupthink in foreign policy decisions of the American government, though these in no way indicate how widespread the groupthink phenomenon may be.

More recently, Janis and his associates have studied the relationship between the quality of decision-making procedures and foreign policy outcomes. Their investigation of American decision-making in nineteen post World War II crises reveals that high-quality (synoptic) decision procedures are associated with better outcomes, while defective decision procedures are associated with outcomes that have more adverse effects on American interests and are more likely to increase international conflict.[105]

Janis recognizes the problems associated with a single-factor theory of behavior and is therefore careful to note that other variables that are not part of the groupthink syndrome can cause defective decision-making. As he points out, "blunders have all sorts of causes—some, like informational overload, being magnified by groupthink; others, like sheer incompetence or ignorance, having nothing at all to do with groupthink."[106] Janis sees the groupthink syndrome as likely to be a contributing cause that augments the influence of other sources of error, though it can sometimes be the primary cause.[107]

Comparison of Groupthink and the Bureaucratic Politics Model

It should be borne in mind that both groupthink and the bureaucratic politics model are empirical theories. Each attempts to explain the way decisions are made and why they are made that way. Neither groupthink theorists nor BPM theorists advocate that policies *should* be made through the groupthink or BPM method; they only state that policies *are* in fact made that way, whether we like it or not. They both depict policy making as nonrational and suggest that governments frequently fail to make the best decisions in international affairs.

Both theories deal with decision making by small groups—politburos, cabinets, juntas, interagency committees, and so on. Each suggests that a certain set of group dynamics has a negative effect on decision-making—though for different reasons. Both recognize that conflicts and disagreements over policy are likely within groups, but in the groupthink syndrome policy makers try to avoid conflict by seeking group cohesion, while conflict is managed in the bureaucratic politics process by bargaining and other political maneuvers among players.[108]

The major difference between the theories is that groupthink envisions a decision process in which group cohesiveness, unity, and harmony are paramount, while BPM theorists see group dissension, division, and conflict as predominant. (This being the case, it is pretty much logically impossible that the two processes would occur at the same time in the same group.) Charles Hermann sees the pivotal difference as the fact that in groupthink the individuals attach their primary loyalty to the decision-making group itself, while in bureaucratic politics most of the players owe their primarily allegiances to the outside groups they represent.[109] This factor appears decisive in determining whether consensual or conflictual politics are pursued.

Finally, neither theory is specifically a theory of war; both are general theories of decision-making that can be applied to decisions about war. Neither claims even to be able to explain all decisions made by governments, let alone all decision for war. While both theories are rather complex and difficult to apply, and while they are most likely to provide only subsidiary explanations for most cases of war, both may occasionally provide important insights into the initiation of particular wars.

Prescriptions

If flawed and irrational government decision-making processes do in fact play a major role in causing war, what is the solution? Presumably, we should be able to find and implement better methods of decision-making. Whether the problem is bureaucratic politics or groupthink, the solution might be to devise a policy-making process which approximates as closely as possible the rational actor model.[110] Janis offers several solutions to deal with the problems associated with the groupthink syndrome.

1. The leader should assign each group member the role of critical evaluator and encourage all group members to air their objections and doubts.

2. Leaders should remain impartial and refrain from staking out their initial preferences so as not to influence other group members.

3. Several independent policy-planning and evaluation groups might be set up on each policy question.

4. The group should occasionally divide into two or more subgroups under different chairmen to reduce the possibility that the entire group will develop a concurrence-seeking norm.

5. Each group member should discuss the group's deliberations with associates in his/her department or agency and report back their reactions.

6. Outside experts who are not core members should be invited to each meeting on a staggered basis and encouraged to challenge the views of the core group.

7. At least one member of the group should be assigned the role of a devil's advocate at each meeting.

8. Group members should set aside a block of time to survey all warning signals from rival states and construct alternative scenarios of the rival's intentions. An outsider might be enlisted as a "Cassandra's advocate" to call attention to alarming possibilities that might otherwise be overlooked.

9. After a preliminary consensus is reached, the group should hold a "second chance" meeting at which members would be expected to express whatever residual doubts they might have and to generally rethink the entire issue.

Alexander George has also put forward a highly developed decision-making scheme designed to address the problems that develop out of bureaucratic politics.[111] His approach, which he calls "multiple advocacy," is a normative (prescriptive) theory of decision-making intended to give guidance to those practitioners who actually make government decisions.

George realizes that in spite of its well-documented defects, the bureaucratic politics process also has positive components. After all, bureaucratic politics is pluralistic, and therefore it is a process in which different positions will be put forward and (presumably) taken into consideration. It therefore avoids the problem of artificial consensus that one finds in groupthink. Pluralistic procedures in which different groups compete to influence policy can potentially be quite healthy for the decision-making process, and a certain degree of conflict is beneficial in problem solving—if the conflict can be managed and resolved properly. Unfortunately, conflict is handled in an unstructured and uregulated manner. The policy options that are put forward in this process are quite limited. Unpopular viewpoints that do not represent the "mainstream" opinion of any particular agency or department are given little attention. Furthermore, the most powerful actors or coalitions—not necessarily those who argue for the best solution—win the policy battle. Institutional and personal interests make it difficult for detatched political analysis and logic to prevail.

George's multiple advocacy approach calls for a balanced, open, and managed process of debate centered around an institutionalized system of advocates, each of whom would make the best case for a particular option, ensuring that a wide range of options would be addressed by the group. A top government official (probably the President's Adviser for National Security Affairs in the United States) would play the role of a *custodian manager.* This official would be an honest broker of ideas, a coordinator who would ensure fair competition. He would see that all the options were represented by an advocate and that all advocates had equal resources—such as influence, competence, information, analytical resources, and bargaining and communication skills. He would make sure that time was scheduled for adequate debate and discussion. He would coordinate the independent analysis of options and objectives and monitor the policy-making process for malfunctions. The manager would refrain from being either an advocate himself or an adviser to the leader or a spokesman for the administration. The leader would listen to the presentation of the options and to the debate that followed. The leader asks questions, evaluates alternatives, and then chooses among the options.

If this sounds too good to be true, it probably is. Multiple advocacy is certainly not without its flaws. The process may create greater variety, ambiguity, and complexity than is necessary for a good decision. Confronted with all the argumentation the system would spew forth, the leader may be less able to decide which option is best than if he were given fewer alternatives to choose from. One critic points out,

> in the context of data overload, uncertainty and time constraints, multiple advocacy may in effect give all of the various viewpoints an aura of empirical respectability and allow a leader to choose whichever accords with his predisposition.[112]

A warning label should be issued for the use of the remedies prescribed by Dr. Janis and Dr. George. Both recognize the rather hardy resistance of small groups to rational procedures, and then blithely recommend that the groups should try harder to be more rational, as if this were only a matter of recognizing flaws and correcting them. After presenting marvelous arguments explaining why the RAM is unlikely to work in the real world, they base their antidotes squarely upon it! As Richard Ned Lebow points out, their prescriptions are based on the assumption that leaders will be willing to make a serious effort to structure the decision-making process so as to encourage and enhance critical thinking and dissent. But this may be totally unrealistic. Most leaders dislike criticism and dissent; it threatens their authority (or at least they think it does), it loosens their control over the decision process, and it may be interpreted by their opponents as a sign of weakness. Thus, leaders may be both psychologically and politically unwilling to accept even the soundest criticism.[113]

The impediments to rational decision making are strong and pervasive. Though the policy process may be structured to eliminate faulty decisions, flaws are likely to remain. Nonrational decision making seems to be very much a part of the territory of government policy making.

Conclusion

Let us end this chapter by noting that decision-making processes at the small-group level are linked to, and interrelated with, individual level factors. Whether the decision process develops along the lines of the rational actor model, the bureaucratic politics model, or groupthink and whether risky or incremental policies are selected by group decision-makers depend at least in part on the individual characteristics of the key players.

Certainly the psychological traits possessed by the group leader will be important. For instance, we might hypothesize that groups headed by authoritarian, domineering, or power-oriented chief executives are more likely to develop along groupthink lines than along the lines of bureaucratic politics.[114] On the other hand, groups led by open, nonauthoritarian leaders are more likely to develop syncratic or bureaucratic politics processes.

Of course, the leader alone cannot determine the character of group processes; the personal characteristics of the group members are also important. For instance, what if our group consisted of a room full of self-confident political leaders characterized by the psychological traits of antagonism and extroversion and motivated by needs for power and dominance? Certainly the tendency would be for group members to interact with each other through rough-and-tumble bureaucratic politics processes rather than the cooperative and consensual processes described by the groupthink model. Conversely, if the group consisted largely of political leaders characterized by the traits of agreeability and introversion who were motivated by needs for achievement and affiliation, one would bet that groupthink would develop. And if this latter group were headed by the domineering, power-oriented authoritarian figure mentioned earlier, then groupthink might be virtually assured.

5

The State and International Conflict

Since most international relations scholars see states as the primary actors in international politics, it should come as no surprise that many theorists of international conflict focus on the nature of the state as the primary determinant of war. The underlying assumption of most of the theories at this level of analysis is that a certain national attribute (or some combination of attributes) influences the way in which states behave. States with similar characteristics act in a similar manner. Personality variables and the psychological makeup of national leaders are relatively unimportant since attributes of the state itself "compel" decision makers to act in certain ways.[1]

One of the most interesting discoveries of the research on war is that states are not equally violent; great variation in conflict activity exists among the states of the world. Dina Zinnes, summarizing from many statistical studies of war, concludes,

> International violence is a widespread phenomenon not confined to a few states; at one time or another almost all states have engaged in this type of activity. However, some nations seem more prone to engage in this type of behavior than others.[2]

Similarly, J. David Singer and Melvin Small conclude from their study of nineteenth- and twentieth-century wars that "most of the war in the system has been accounted for by a small fraction of nations."[3] Indeed, data from Singer and Small's "Correlates of War" Project indicate that of the 176 members of the interstate system from 1816 to 1980, ninety-four states (53.4%) have never participated in international war.

If states vary considerably in their war experience, perhaps this has something to do with some fundamental differences in the attributes that states possess. The question becomes "what makes some states more warlike than others?" As usual there is no lack of competition for answers. International relations theorists have emphasized five general factors that might have a bearing on this question: (1) the type of government the state has, (2) the type of economic system the state has, or certain economic factors that are present in the state, (3) certain demographic, cultural, physical, or geographic attributes of the state, (4) the degree of political instability that exists in the state, and (5) the state's previous war involvement. The purpose of this chapter is to investigate these theories.

Type of Government

In a world of simple explanations (in which we, unfortunately, do not live) states can be divided into two categories—good, peaceful states and bad, aggressive states. Who are the good guys and who are the bad guys? The most often heard argument is that *democratic* states are peaceful and that *authoritarian* states are aggressive. This is essentially a "liberal" theory based on the assumption that mankind is basically peaceful, rational, and cooperative and that relations among states are therefore generally harmonious and cooperative as well. It is argued that since humankind is essentially peaceful, this desire for peace will be reflected in the policies of governments, especially if they are democratic. Democratic governments, being democratic, represent the wishes of their peaceful citizens (or at least they represent the will of the peaceful majority). By giving prospective soldiers and their families the chance to share in the decision to go to war, the probability of war is reduced. Few people will vote for an unnecessary war that might mean the destruction of their property, the reduction of their standard of living, and the death of themselves or their loved ones.

A narrow (and, I think, correct) reading of this theory would predict that democracies should be less inclined to initiate wars against others. Conflicts initiated by a popular clamor for war should be extremely rare. (Though this has in fact been the traditional interpretation for President McKinley's decision to ask Congress to declare war on Spain in 1898.) On the other hand, the theory does not necessarily state that democracies are less likely to be the targets of other states' aggression. In fact, the opposite might be the case if the general unwillingness of democracies to use force undermines their ability to deter the aggression of others.

In nondemocratic countries, on the other hand, it is assumed that the leadership is bound neither by the popular will nor by constitutional restraints on central power. Leaders of autocratic governments will therefore be more likely to initiate hostilities. The existence of autocracies therefore endangers world peace. In short, wars occur because some states are bad.

If the view of the liberals is correct, how is war prevented? Obviously, the long-term solution will have to be the creation of a world of democratic states. The more important question is how is this to be achieved? The answer comes in two varieties—active and passive.[4]

American *isolationists* have been typical proponents of the passive policy. They argued that the United States should lead other countries along the enlightened path to democracy and peace through example. The United States should function as a beacon—a "shining city on the hill"—to all those who would follow. Since democracy was quite obviously the best system of government, reason dictated that eventually most nations would become democratic and peace would be the result. Direct intervention was therefore unnecessary.

To others, serving passively as a model would not be enough. One could not be a force for peace by standing by while bad states attacked good; eventually, one's own state might be attacked! Thus, proponents of a more activist (or *interventionist*) policy argued that it might become necessary for democratic states to intervene in the affairs of authoritarian states to make them more democratic. As Edmund Burke, one of the founders of modern conservatism, remarked, "all that is necessary for the triumph of evil is that all good men do nothing."[5] Thus, Woodrow Wilson (a liberal) sent the Marines to Mexico to "teach them to elect good governments" and sent American forces to Europe to "fight for democracy," while Presidents Reagan and Bush (both conservatives) sent troops to Grenada and Panama to "restore" democracy.

The problem with this approach should be readily apparent. War is seen as the way to create peace. Furthermore, wars waged for such universal principles tend to become unlimited. As A. J. P. Taylor stated, "Bismark fought 'necessary' wars and killed thousands; the idealists of the twentieth century fought 'just' wars and killed millions."[6]

War and Democracy: Empirical Evidence

Is there any evidence that the liberal theory of war is valid? Are democracies more peaceful than autocracies? If ever there was a good theory mugged by a gang of facts, I suppose this is the one. However plausible it may seem, and however much our democratic values predispose us to cheer for this theory, there nonetheless seems to be little evidence to support it.

Quincy Wright, in his mammoth work *A Study of War*, builds elaborate theoretical explanations for the proposition that democracies should be more peaceful than absolutist autocracies. The power of their central governments is limited by constitutional restrictions; dispersed by the principles of federalism and separation of power; restrained by widespread political participation, procedural deliberations, and freedom of criticism; and ultimately subjected to majority rule. Political accountability requires that government elites in democracies maintain public support for their continuance in office. Unpopular policies (such as war) will be avoided out of fear of electoral punishment. When Wright looks at the historical record, however, he is forced to conclude that democracies seem to be highly involved in war—and not just because they are forced to defend themselves against the attack by others! There just doesn't seem to be much difference in the war activity of different kinds of political systems.[7]

The work of Singer and Small on the Correlates of War (COW) project at the University of Michigan has yielded similar results. Investigating wars occurring between 1861 and 1965, they discovered no difference between democracies and nondemocracies in terms of either their war participation or war initiation.[8] The heavy war involvement of democracies was not due to their selection as defenseless victims by others; they seemed to be just as involved in the aggressive use of force as nondemocratic states. Russett and Monsen also found that the type of political system a state possesses has little effect on its war proneness; size seems to be a much more important predictor. Large polyarchies (representative democracies) have been involved in more wars than either small polyarchies or nonpolyarchies of any size.[9]

As we have seen, however, nothing is completely cut and dried in conflict research. Some contradictory evidence has emerged. Michael Haas grouped nations into three categories: constitutional, authoritarian, and totalitarian. When these three types of government were run against foreign conflict data from the late 1950s, Haas found that authoritarian regimes exhibited the most foreign conflict behavior, constitutional governments the least, and totalitarian governments fell in between. None of the statistical links were very strong, however.[10] Moreover, Haas' study suffers from certain limitations. First, it examines a very limited period of time (1955–1960) compared to COW's; second, it doesn't directly look at war involvement, but examines instead general conflict behavior (which includes not only war but several nonwar measure of conflict such as diplomatic protests, sanctions, etc.); and third, its statistical results are meager.

Two other studies, by Wilkenfeld and Zinnes and by Salmore and Hermann, also indicated a difference in the conflict participation activities of democracies and autocracies.[11] As in the study by Haas, the statistical results were not very strong and war was lumped together with other kinds of conflict behavior. The findings of these last three studies were consistent, but they were also consistently weak. Thus, the first wave of research on this topic rather consistently failed to find a strong relationship between democratic government and peace. Nevertheless, the ideological attractiveness of a theory linking democracy and peace propelled further research.

The debate was revived in the 1980s when a study by R. J. Rummel found substantial support for the theory.[12] For the years 1976–1980, Rummel found that the more *libertarian* or free the state, the less its foreign violence, and the less free a state, the more its violence. This appeared to be true whether the dependent variable was a scale of foreign conflict intensity or war data only. When the traditional operationalization of free states was expanded from the presence of political rights and civil liberties to include economic freedom (free markets) as well, the relationship appeared even stronger.

Other scholars begged to differ, noting several problems with Rummel's research. Steve Chan's analysis of the 1816–1980 period, an expanded retesting of the older Singer and Small study, once again found no strong relationship between government type and war involvement.[13] Democracy did not significantly inhibit states from initiating wars or from siding with those who did. Most important, however, Chan discovered a significant difference in war behavior after 1973. From 1816 to 1972 he found a positive relationship between democracy and war; democracy and war were highly correlated—just the opposite from what the theory predicts! But this relationship was reversed in the 1973–1980 period. Erich Weede's investigation of the 1960–1980 period produces somewhat similar results. Generally, no strong relationship seemed to exist between war involvement and the type of government; however, the 1960–1974 period was different from the 1975–1980 period. These results both suggest that Rummel's use of the 1976–1980 period may have been responsible for his results. The more recent time period appears to be atypcial when compared to previous periods. Weede concludes, "At most, Rummel's new evidence seems to support the idea that democracies were less often involved in war in the late seventies."[14]

Morgan and Campbell's analysis of militarized disputes between 1816 and 1976 adds further evidence. Instead of focusing on democracies per se, they emphasize the presence (or absence) of structural constraints on the ability of a government to make decisions for war. Such political constraints include the accountability of the leader to a selection process, the presence of political competition, and institutional power sharing on decisions of war and peace. They find that the probability of war does decrease slightly as the constraints on government decision-making increase, but the relationship is hardly significant. They conclude that structural constraints are not an important determinant of whether militarized disputes escalate to war.[15] Thus, a number of recent studies refute Rummel's contention and back the traditional view that the type of government a state possesses has little effect on a nation's propensity for war.

However, one finding of Rummel's has received no challenge. His *Joint*

Freedom Proposition—that libertarian (democratic) systems mutually preclude violence, or that violence will occur between states only if one is nonlibertarian—seems to have garnered overwhelming support among scholars.[16] For the five years between 1976 and 1980, Rummel finds no instance of violence between politically free states or between states that he terms "free"—that is, both politically free and economically free.[17] His analysis also demonstrates that this is not simply due to the lack of geographic contiguity between libertarian states. Similarly, the Singer and Small study, which examined fifty cases of interstate wars between 1816 and 1965, found only two "marginal" instances of war between democratic states: Finland's joining with Germany to fight the U.S.S.R. and the democratic Allies in World War II and "an emphemeral republican France attacking an ephemeral republican Rome in 1849."[18] Marginal exceptions aside, there has not been a real war between democracies in over a century and a half.[19] Indeed, one analyst concludes that the lack of war between democracies is the closest thing we have to an *empirical law* in the field of international relations![20]

Exactly why this should be so is not entirely clear. Expectations of war and threats of war between democracies are almost certainly reduced by the presence of a common political culture, by a mutual identity and sympathy, by stronger people-to-people and elite-to-elite bonds, by the ability of interest groups within these countries to form transnational coalitions, by more frequent communication, and by more positive mutual perceptions.

At any rate, the validation of the joint freedom proposition leads to the suggestion that it is not the type of political system per se that inhibits or causes war. (Democratic and nondemocratic states are almost equally aggressive.) Instead, the important factor appears to be *political distance*. The propensity of two states to fight each other may be linked to the degree of difference *between* their two political systems. This takes us to a different level of analysis. The joint freedom proposition predicts the mutual behavior of a pair of states; it operates at the dyadic interaction level, not at the nation-state level.

The Economic System: Capitalism and Imperialism

John Hobson, the British economist, was intrigued by exactly the problem we have been discussing. Being a believer in democracy, he was forced to address why democratic countries, especially his own Britain, engaged in imperialism—aggressive expansion aimed at the establishment of foreign colonies. His answer was that although Britain's political system was democratic, its economic system was *capitalist*.[21] The problem, then, was to be found not in the nature of the state's political system, but in the nature of the its economic system.

For Hobson, imperialism resulted from a "maladjustment" in the capitalist system. Capitalist countries seemed to suffer chronically from the unhealthy syndrome of overproduction, unequal distribution of economic wealth, underconsumption, surplus capital, and periodic depression. The wheels of production turned apace, but the vast majority of people—their wages having been held down by the capitalists' desire for increased profits—lacked the ability to purchase goods. Supply exceeded demand and surplus capital existed in the hands of the factory owners.

These problems could be remedied in several ways. The economic elite could choose to redistribute wealth through higher wages, or the government could redistribute income through its taxing and spending policies, thereby raising the standard of living and creating greater consumer demand. Instead, the capitalists chose to invest their surplus capital abroad, chose to carve out new foreign markets in which to sell their surplus production, chose to make use of cheaper foreign labor to further reduce production costs, and chose to dominate foreign lands in hope of securing necessary raw materials. As governments found it difficult not to help the elites in these economic endeavors, the result was the policy of imperialism.[22]

Hobson produced data to show that imperialism had been largely unprofitable for the economy in general. It entailed high costs and high risks, while generating low returns. In fact, it was bad business policy. If this was the case, why was imperialism the order of the day? Because, said Hobson, it benefited a few powerful and well-placed groups: ship builders, export industries, international bankers, investors, and arms merchants—those elites whom President Eisenhower, twenty years after Hobson's death, would describe as the "military-industrial complex." These elites were able to induce the government to pursue colonial policies to benefit the few. The policy of imperialism was essentially "a vast system of outdoor relief for the upper classes."[23] The elites in capitalist states turned democracy into a sham. Minority interests dominated the general will.

All of this begs the question of what imperialism and colonialism have to do with interstate war. The answer is nothing—if the world is made up of relatively few, well-behaved capitalist states, each with plentiful opportunities for overseas investment and trade. Otherwise, quite a lot. In a world of many capitalist countries imperialism means economic competition between rival states. Each state strives to gain exclusive control over markets, raw materials, sources of cheap labor, naval bases, and investment opportunities. At some point these can only be gained at the expense of other capitalist states. Economic conflict eventually leads to military conflict.

Since the problem, according to Hobson, lies in the nature of the economic system (and its effects on the political system), the logical solution is to change the economic system. Hobson argued that with the advent of socialism (achieved through an evolutionary and parliamentary process), imperialism could be ended and wars avoided. And as the economic system became more egalitarian, the political system would become more democratic. The ability of certain strategically placed economic elites to control government policy would be greatly curtailed and the need for foreign investment would decrease as the domestic market expanded. Once true democracy was achieved, reason and peaceful cooperation could be pursued.

Vladimir Illych Ulyanov, better known as Lenin, embraced Hobson's ideas and (drawing as well on Marxist writers such as Hilferding, Kautsky, and Bukharin) set out his own theory of international conflict in *Imperialism: The Highest Stage of Capitalism* in 1916.[24] While Hobson believed that imperialism was due to a maladjustment in the capitalist system and that it was possible for imperialist wars to be prevented, Lenin argued that imperialism was an inevitable by-product of the final stage of capitalist development.

Lenin believed that the capitalist economic system must expand or die. Falling rates of profit required economic expansion, which sooner or later (through the process described earlier by Hobson) required war. Foreign economic expansion is not a matter of choice; it is a necessity. When the state pursues a policy of imperialism, it is only doing what it must to deal with the inevitable crises capitalism engenders.

Lenin's explanation for war was not too dissimilar from Hobson's. The root cause lay in the crisis of the capitalist economy: surplus production and underconsumption. Lenin argued that the final years of capitalism as a state of history would be characterized by "finance capitalism" or "*monopoly capitalism.*" In this situation the control of the economy becomes increasingly concentrated in the hands of a smaller and smaller group of owners. The most important of these corporate oligarchies are the financial and banking institutions; this paralleled Lenin's belief that further economic growth would depend on the export of surplus capital (that is, foreign investment). As monopoly capitalism progresses, giant corporations begin to divide up the world. Owing to the "fusion of state and capital," the government becomes the agent of the capitalist class.

One thing leads to another and—given the simultaneous existence of many states in the late stages of capitalism—it eventually becomes necessary for the capitalist states to fight each other over increasingly limited overseas markets, materials, and investment opportunities. International economic relations becomes a *zero-sum game*—a game in which the winners win only what the losers lose. The world becomes like a pie of a fixed size; it contains only so many areas usable for colonial expansion. Once the pie has been initially divided among the competitors, a state that desires to expand (that is, to increase its portion of the pie) can do so only at the expense of another state's portion.

Since capitalist states develop at different rates of growth and from different starting points, some of them will inevitably be economically (and therefore militarily) superior to others. This is the *law of uneven capitalist development*. Economic competition naturally leads the more powerful capitalist states to exploit weaker capitalist states. The result, of course, is war. This conclusion is inevitable from Lenin's point of view. The logic of monopoly capitalism—that capitalist states must continually expand or collapse—leads to imperialism and thus to wars between imperialists.

Lenin's solution was significantly different from that of Hobson. Peace could be secured only by the abolition of capitalist states and the creation of a world of socialist states. However, the transition from capitalism to socialism would not come about peacefully through elections; rather, socialist revolutions would be the agent of this change. However, as Kenneth Waltz has indicated, there is some confusion here about what actually brings about peace. Is it the destruction of capitalism or the destruction of states?[25] The two are linked in Marxist theory because socialism, the economic phase of history that replaces capitalism, will eventually develop into true communism—a stage of development in which the state "withers away." As Michael Haas points out:

> The most peaceful political system turns out to be the one with no visible government at all. There will be no elites to compel men to fight, and there will be no states to attack or defend.[26]

Critiques of Theories of Imperialism

How well have the theories of Hobson and Lenin held up? Is there any evidence that capitalist countries are more warlike than socialist countries? Several observations must be made.

First, the essence of the theory is that domestic underconsumption and the lure of higher profits through foreign investment cause imperialism (and thus war). But there exist several other ways to cure the economic problems, as Hobson points out: for instance, pumping up domestic demand by redistributing wealth so that the masses would have more purchasing power. Determining among the several policy options is a matter of government policy. As Kenneth Waltz points out, the economic conditions aren't sufficient to bring about the result. Political conditions, not economic ones, are dominant.[27]

Second, contrary to the contention of Lenin, capitalism should require a policy of peace. War upsets economic planning; destroys land, labor, and capital; makes profits uncertain; hinders trade; and uses up scarce resources in the process. War is therefore counterproductive and one should therefore expect it to be opposed by business elites. If it is equally plausible that A (in this case capitalism) leads to B (war) and that A also leads to C (peace), it is probably true that neither relationship is valid as a general rule.

Third, although most capitalist nations did pursue imperialist policies in the late nineteenth century, some did not produce any surplus capital and many that did exported very little to their own colonies. As D. K. Fieldhouse points out, Hobson and Lenin were "entirely wrong in assuming that any large proportion of British overseas investment went to those underdeveloped parts of Africa and Asia which were annexed during the 'imperialist' grab after 1870."[28] England invested half of its capital outside the colonies, primarily to the United States, and France consistently ranked only second or third in investment in her own colonies![29]

Since most of the capital investment during the age of colonialism was in other capitalist nations (just as it is now) rather than in colonies, and since most capitalist trade was with other capitalist states, it seems appropriate to conclude that colonies were a relatively unimportant factor in the economic growth of the capitalist mother country. If this is true, it would be illogical for the great powers to fight over them. Indeed, colonial competition did not usually end in war but in accommodation and the negotiation of spheres of influence. With the exception of the Boer War, almost all colonial conflicts were settled with diplomacy.[30]

Fourth, although many capitalist states were engaged in imperialism, some were not. How does one account for the peacefulness of capitalist Sweden and Switzerland? On the other hand, some important imperialist states were neither capitalist nor surplus producing, for example Japan and Russia.[31] We have a situation here where not all capitalist states were imperialistic and not all imperialist states were capitalistic. One should logically conclude from this that capitalism is neither a necessary condition for imperialism, nor is it a sufficient condition.

Fifth, socialist states have themselves exhibited aggressive tendencies. The last half century has witnessed the Soviet invasion of the Baltic countries (1939), Finland (1939), Hungary (1956), Czechoslovakia (1968), and Afghanistan (1979); China has attacked Tibet (1956), India (1962), and Vietnam (1979); Vietnam has attacked Cambodia (1975); the Soviets and the Chinese have fought several border clashes; North Korea has invaded South Korea (1950); and the Ethiopians and the Somalis have fought over the Ogaden (1977). Of sixty-one international conflicts of the 1945–1967 period, socialist systems participated in fifteen—roughly 25%. This is compared to the fact that only approximately 15% of all countries had socialist economies.

Sixth, it should be obvious that imperialism and war both occurred before the age of capitalism and that the feudal, agricultural status of many states, past and present, has not prevented them from pursuing aggressive policies of expansion. Imperialism is older than capitalism, a situation that prompts Waltz to reflect that we have a unique (and totally unsatisfying) situation here of a theory whose cause (capitalism) is much younger than its effects (imperialism and war).[32]

Seventh, there is no doubt that capitalist states have been highly involved in warfare in the nineteenth and twentieth centuries, but the fact that such states have engaged in expansion and war does not mean that they have done so *because* they were capitalist. Capitalism may not require economic expansion or growth in order to survive. What may be more likely, as William Appleman Williams, a founder of the revisionist school of American history, argues, is that political and economic leaders in capitalist countries *believe* that capitalist economic systems require growth and act accordingly.[33] Notice, however, that this explanation takes us back to the individual level of analysis.

Also, as Waltz, suggests, since most advanced nations practiced imperialism, we should ask ourselves whether advanced states are imperialist because they are capitalist, or rather because they are technologically advanced Great Powers? Is imperialism caused by advanced capitalism, or are capitalism and imperialism both simply manifestations of advanced development?[34]

The Business Cycle: Good Times and Bad Times

One commonly held belief has been that nations tend to go to war during times of economic distress and depression. The explanation for this reputed phenomenon comes in several varieties. First, some theorists suggest that economic hard times create pressure on political leaders to expand the economy through searched for greater markets for their products and investments or for access to more productive resources—a process that eventually leads to war. Iraq's attack on Kuwait in order to control its oil reserves and to relieve itself of its debt to Kuwait is only the most recent example of war based on such motives. Second, it is also argued that national leaders seek war in the belief that this will stimulate the economy through the creation of more products and jobs. In other words, war itself is believed to have a beneficial impact on the economy. Third, during economic hard times political elites may seek war as a method of diverting the attention of the public from internal woes. Severe economic conditions in Argentina certainly led to the decision to invade the Falkland/Malvina Islands in 1982. (This last explanation, the scapegoat theory, will be taken up later in the chapter.) Finally, it is also possible that political leaders are more willing to take risks during periods of sudden economic distress.[35]

It might be argued that industrial democracies should be especially affected by situations of economic distress. For instance, the vulnerability of

American presidents to electoral punishment during times of economic adversity is well known. It is also understood that the president's domestic popularity may be increased by forceful actions toward rival states. Ostom and Job point out that in the post–World War II era, the international use of force by presidents has been especially common during lean economic times (as indicated by the "misery index," which combines data on unemployment and inflation).[36] Research by Bruce Russett indicates that there is some reason to believe there is a relationship in the nineteenth and twentieth centuries between economic downturns and American participation in "militarized disputes." The combination of poor economic performance with U.S. presidential election years is an even better predictor of involvement in international disputes. However, there does not appear to be a relationship between weak economic conditions and interstate war per se.[37]

Several scholars argue the opposite point of view—that the depths of the economic cycle do not instigate international conflict but serve instead to constrain the pursuit of war. Blainey cites this as a major factor in preventing Austria from attempting to recapture Silesia in 1749 and for delaying the Japanese invasion of Korea in 1873.[38] In fact, several analysts suggest that it isn't depression that leads to war, but economic *recovery*! In other words, it is the up side of the business cycle, not the down side, that is most frequently associated with war. The most famous argument is probably that of A. L. Macfie, who published in 1938 a study of the effects of the British business cycle on twelve wars from 1850 to 1914. (The British themselves were only involved in three of these wars, but it is assumed that the fluctuations present in the British economy reflected a truly international business cycle, thus justifying the use of British economic statistics with the war behavior of several countries.) Matching annual statistics on employment against the onset of war, he concluded that wars were most likely when an economic recovery was in its later stages.[39]

A recent study of global economic cycles (called "long cycles") and war from 1495 to 1975 by Joshua Goldstein finds a strong and consistent correlation between the severity of war and economic upswings.[40] Although wars have occurred in roughly equal numbers throughout history in the upswing and downswing phases, the most severe wars have taken place in upswing phases. From 1495 until 1918 each peak in war severity occurred near the end of an upswing phase.

Why should economic recoveries be related to war? It could be that the underlying cause of hostilities had been present for many years, but that governments practiced restraint during the period of economic distress. War was undertaken only when the economic upswing made it financially feasible for them to engage in military action. Goldstein suggests that major wars occur only when nations can afford them—that is, after a sustained period of stable economic growth.[41] It should be noted that in this explanation, economic upturns are not cited as the actual cause of war, but as a factor that enables wars to occur. The historical association of wars with economic upswings may therefore actually obscure the real causes of war, which might be found in the preceding period of economic decline.[42]

A psychological explanation for the relationship between war and economic upturns is also frequently made. Indeed, both Macfie and Blainey, as well as Goldstein, suggest that economic recoveries are associated with a general mood of *optimism*, which is the real cause of war. Blainey argues,

> When trade is deteriorating and when unemployment is increasing the mood of governments tend to be cautious and apprehensive. Dwindling revenues and soaring claims for the state's aid aggravate the mood. On the other hand, when prosperity is high—and this time is the most dangerous to peace—there comes a sense of mastery of the environment.[43]

Blainey is describing here a collective national mood. This general feeling of optimism and confidence colors the judgment of both political leaders and common people.[44] Blainey believes such a feeling of optimism and mastery was evident on the eve of the Crimean War, the Franco-Prussian War, the Boer War, and others.[45]

Dexter Perkins finds the American experience fits this general pattern. He contends that belligerent, prowar feelings in the United States coincided with recoveries from economic downswings. The War of 1812 followed hard on the heels of a commercial upturn; the Mexican War occurred after the depression of 1837–1842; the Spanish-American War took place after the return to prosperity following the depression of 1893; World War I followed the economic decline of 1913–1914; and World War II took place during the recovery from the Great Depression of the 1930s.[46]

William Thompson looks at business cycle data for Great Britain, France, Germany, and the Unites States from the nineteenth and twentieth centuries in an effort to test the Macfie/Blainey hypothesis that war should be positively associated with economic recovery. (Macfie suggests war is associated specifically with the *last* phase of the recovery, Blainey with *any* phase of the recovery.) Thompson finds that support for Macfie's hypothesis is confined to Britain's nineteenth-century colonial wars. Support for Blainey's more general thesis is found only in the American experience—validating Perkins' observations. With the exception of the Boxer Rebellion, all the American wars examined were begun during an expansionary (upward) phase of the business cycle.[47] Britain and France had some warfare in every phase of the cycle.

Probably the most we can say about the business cycle is that it may play a role in the development of war, but its effects are less than clear. Some wars have broken out in hard times, others have occurred in good times. Neither economic weakness nor prosperity seem to prevent war.

Power, Size, and Development

An argument quite frequently made by "realists" is that large, powerful states (regardless of the nature of their political or economic systems) tend to be perpetrators of war rather than small states.[48] This would seem to make intuitive sense. It is more likely that large states would pick on small states than vice versa. In a world of rational calculation, the larger, more powerful states are more likely to win and this enters its leaders' calculations of the costs and benefits of war and of the probable outcome. Also, larger states would seem to be more likely to get involved in conflicts simply because they are more involved in international affairs in general. They have more interests, are participants in more international organizations and alliances, have more international commitments, and have greater capacity to act in international affairs than smaller states. Additionally, they are more likely to feel a responsibility to take action in the international arena—to rectify the international balance of power, for instance. Leaders of large states are also more likely to hold *national role conceptions*, which picture their states as responsible for protecting allies, defending the international status quo, and ensuring world order.

A sizable amount of empirical evidence tends to support the thesis outlined above. In their study of wars from 1815 to 1965 Singer and Small found that the larger, more powerful nations seemed to be the most warlike. Eleven nations—Britain, France, Russia, Turkey, China, Spain, Germany, Italy, the United States, Japan, and Austria-Hungary—accounted for 90% of all battle deaths and 60% of all nation-months of war. At least one of these eleven states was involved in 71% of the wars in the period studied.[49] The Great Powers were clearly disproportionately involved in war. During the same period 77 of the 144 smaller powers were able to escape war entirely.[50] A post–World War II listing of states highly involved in war would not only include the five Great Power members of the United Nations Security Council, but would also include a conflict-ridden group from the Middle East and South Asia: India, Pakistan, Israel, Egypt, and Syria.

Stuart Bremer ranked members of the international system from 1620 to 1964 according to a composite index of demographic, economic, and military power. He discovered what appeared to be a strong linear relationship between power rank and war involvement. The states with the greatest capabilities were involved in the most wars and also initiated more wars than the less powerful states; the less powerful a state, the less likely it was to be involved in war. The states occupying ranks 1–5 averaged war once every ten years; states ranked 41–45 and 46–50 averaged a war once in every one hundred years.[51]

Michael Haas used United Nations dues to divide nations into four categories based on wealth. (U.N. financial assessments are based on a state's ability to pay and thus give a good ranking of a state's financial status.) The results indicate that the richest nations rank highest in significant foreign conflict, and the amount of foreign conflict a nation experiences drops consistently with its level of wealth. Since wealthy states are frequently also militarily strong states, this is a good test of the relationship of power and conflict.[52]

It would be unusual in the field of international relations theory to finds results that are totally one-sided. The research on the relationship between national capabilities and war is no exception.[53] R. J. Rummel's Dimensionality of Nations (DON) project, which studied international affairs in the 1955–1957 period, in fact finds no relationship between characteristics such as the size and military capabilities of a nation on the one hand and foreign conflict behavior (a variety of conflictual actions, both military and nonmilitary) on the other.[54] Several other studies of the post–World War II era indicate that while larger, more developed nations have more total acts of conflict behavior (this would include verbal as well as nonverbal action) than other nations, this is because they are generally more involved in international affairs and are involved in more total international actions. When the total number of actions is controlled for, larger, more developed states actually have a slightly higher percentage of cooperative actions than smaller, developing states. Also, the conflictual acts of developed states are slightly more likely to be verbal and less coercive than the conflict behavior of less developed states.[55]

It seems, however, that the preponderance of evidence in this debate favors those who find an association between power capabilities and war. Much of the contrary evidence is from studies that examine an extremely limited period of time or examine the more general concept of "conflict behavior" rather than war per se.

A large amount of the globe's warlike behavior is accounted for by a small number of states. Great Powers seem to be quite heavily involved, with the distinction that (at least in the post–World War II era) they rarely seem to be directly involved against each other. Of the roughly eighteen interstate wars from 1945 to 1980, only one (Korea) involved forces of the Great Powers arrayed against each other.

If we assume that larger, more developed (and therefore, more powerful) states are indeed the most war prone. How could the threat of war be lessened? Presumably, the answer lies in creating a world of small, weak states. Certainly, however, there is no great movement calling for a slow-down of modernization and development, especially in the underdeveloped world. And while political theorists from Plato to Rousseau to Dahl have trumpeted the peaceful virtues of small societies, until recently there has been little evidence of the willingness of modern states to participate in their own fragmentation into smaller societies. The recent disintegration of the U.S.S.R. into independent states and the fragmentation of Yugoslavia into smaller ethnic units may presage an incipient international trend, but one cannot be encouraged by the violence with which this has taken place, especially in the former Yugoslavia. Finally, even if it were possible to create an international society of small states, the history of small city-states is not at all encouraging: witness the Peloponnesian Wars or the wars of the Italian city-states.

The problem is, perhaps, that power, wealth, and development are not absolute concepts; they are relative ones. Even in a world of small states, some will be relatively larger, wealthier, and stronger than others. The difference is based on mutual comparison. This discovery takes us to a different level of analysis—away from the nature of the state and toward the power disparities between them, or to the individual level of analysis and perceptions of threat based on comparisons of relative power.

If it is the relative power of nations that is at fault, or the perception of power disparity, then it would seem that war will last as long as men are organized into entities (states or cities or whatever) whose power disparity can become a cause of alarm to others.

Population I: Lebensraum

One interesting state characteristic often discussed as a cause of war is that of overcrowding caused by population growth. This, of course, is the *lebensraum* theory of war. Lebensraum, or the state's need for "living space," was closely associated with the development of the discipline of geopolitics in Germany in the late nineteenth and early twentieth centuries.[56] German political geographers like Friedrich Ratzel saw states as much like living organisms and with similar life cycles: they occupy space, they grow, they contract, and they eventually die. Ratzel and the Swedish geographer Rudolf Kjellen contended that states, like men, were involved in a continuous struggle for living space and survival, thus introducing concepts from Social Darwinism into geopolitical theory. The chief proponent of these ideas in the interwar years was General Karl Haushofer, a professor of geopolitics at the University of Munich and a mentor of Rudolf Hess—who introduced his ideas to Adolf Hitler.[57] Many of these themes eventually found expression in Hitler's *Mein Kampf*.

The thrust of German geopolitics from Ratzel to Haushofer was that Great Powers needed to achieve population growth, needed to enlarge their boundaries to obtain lebensraum, and needed to achieve economic self-sufficiency. Japan's successful imperial expansion in the 1930s was taken as proof of the desirability of following such geopolitical strategies.[58]

It is important to note that the lebensraum theory had both empirical and normative aspects. It was the normative side that Hitler emphasized. If one believed that states either increased their populations and their territories or they died, then it becomes a matter of compelling national interest that the policy of the government should be one of expansion. Hitler believed the German or Aryan race must expand at the expense of Slavic peoples in Eastern Europe. As he stated in *Mein Kampf*, "nature has not reserved this soil [Europe] for the future possession of any particular nation or race; on the contrary, this soil exists for the people which possesses the force to take it."[59]

Of course, one does not have to view the lebensraum theory only in terms of its German, fascist, and racist backround. More generally, the lebensraum theory of war simply states that if population pressures within a country become extreme, the government will be faced with a number of related problems. There will be a greater demand for many kinds of resources (including land) as the population grows and consumes resources at a faster rate. And there will be a greater demand for the provision of government services—demands to relieve the situations of mass misery, poverty, and unemployment caused by rapid population increases. Government leaders may seek to address these demands through the expansion of their national territory at the expense of their neighbors.

The implications of this theory for conflict in the modern world are staggering and obvious. The soaring growth rates in Third World countries must be seen as a dangerous development in international relations. There is no doubt that rapid population growth has already caused severe economic (and therefore political) distress in many countries. It would seem to be simply a matter of time before the governments in the most severely affected countries initiate conflict with their neighbors as a way out of this dilemma. Before we get carried away with forecasts of dire events, however, let's turn to some empirical studies of the lebensraum theory.

J. David Singer and his associates in the Correlates of War project studied wars between 1816 and 1965 to determine whether overcrowding (as indicated by population density and by changes in population density) has had any effect on the incidence of war. As it turned out, no such relationship could be found.[60] As a general rule, population growth does not seem to induce warlike behavior. Indeed, there are important instances in which international conflict was precipitated by states experiencing a relative decline in population. Quincy Wright relates that one of the causes of French bellicosity in the late nineteenth century was that its population was declining relative to that of Germany.[61]

Population II: Lateral Pressure

In their *Nations in Conflict*, Nazli Choucri and Robert North developed a more complex version of the old lebensraum theory and attempted to evaluate its ability to explain the occurrence of World War I.[62] To greatly oversimplify their argument, they contend that it is not just population growth alone that is the root cause of war, but the combination of population growth with technological growth that is the source of conflict. The crux of the problem is that a growing population leads to increased demands for resources, while simultaneous technological growth means that resources are actually used at an increased rate. Resources are needed in greater variety and in larger quantities. These two simultaneous developments lead to rising demands.

When existing domestic capabilities are insufficient to meet demand, new capabilities have to be developed. Demand leads therefore to *lateral pressure*—the expansion of activities beyond the state's borders by private citizens, corporations, and governments. This can take a variety of forms: foreign investment, trade, acquisition of spheres of influence or colonies, the dispatch of troops to foreign areas, the establishment of military bases in foreign lands, and so on. A national policy of expansion becomes institutionalized. The state develops a "stake" in external growth, and lateral expansion is increasingly seen as a national interest that must be protected.

This process of lateral expansion caused by population and technological growth leads to war when the external interests of two or more Great Powers "intersect" or come into conflict. The stronger a country's lateral pressure, the greater the likelihood of intensification of competition, and the more intense the competition, the greater the likelihood it will lead to arms races, crises, and war. Choucri and North argue that lateral pressure itself rarely triggers war. Indeed, if the only form that lateral pressure takes is trade, the result may be that countries develop closer relations with each other. Intersections are most likely to develop into war when relations are already hostile or when at least one of the parties perceives the actions taken toward them by the other to be "dangerously competitive, threatening, coercive, menacing, or overtly violent."[63]

Choucri and North's theory of lateral expansion may sound like those of Hobson and Lenin. But whereas all these theorists trace the cause of war backward to economic competition between the Great Powers, Hobson and Lenin pinpoint the presence of capitalist economic institutions as the cause of such competition, while Choucri and North argue that the type of economic system is irrelevant. What matters is the simultaneous presence of population and technological growth, regardless of the type of economy.

Choucri and North subject their theory to statistical analysis using data from 1870 to 1914. What they find only partly supports their theory. While simultaneous population and technoblogical growth did seem to stimulate colonial expansion by the Great Powers prior to World War I, colonial competition and intersections did not seem to be very strongly linked to the outbreak of violence. Thus, a direct path from domestic growth to lateral pressure to colonial competition to war was not found.[64] Attempts to apply lateral pressure theory to the more recent actions of the United States, the (former) Soviet Union, and the Peoples' Republic of China have proved equally disappointing. There appears to be little relationship between measures of lateral pressure and conflict.[65]

The more recent work of Choucri and North has been in the development of country "profiles" based on lateral pressure theory. *Alpha* countries are states with large and growing populations, with advanced technologies, and with access to plentiful resources. Alphas are high-lateral-pressure states. *Beta* countries have large populations relative to their territory, are advancing technologically, but have impeded access to resources. Rising demands in these states lead to pressure to expand through increased territory or trade. *Gamma* states have a limited resource base, but have a high degree of access to resources through an extensive trade network (present-day Britain and Japan). Choucri and North claim that high-lateral-pressure countries (Alphas, Betas, and Gammas) fight more wars per country than developing nations (Epsilons, Zetas, and Etas), though most wars tend to be fought in the developing regions of the world rather than in the industrialized portion. High-technology, low-population countries (*Delta* states, such as Norway) seem to fight the fewest wars, and when they are involved in wars, it tends to be as victims, rather than as initiators.[66]

Choucri and North's analysis of country profiles, as well as the studies mentioned previously on the close relationship between power capabilities and war, indicate much the same phenomenon. Strong, developed countries with growing needs are prone to international conflict. The national attributes at issue here are part of the fundamental makeup of the state. To the extent that these attributes are important, the implications for reducing international conflict are fairly pessimistic. As Choucri and North admit, a conscious attempt to change one's profile as a method of reducing one's chances of conflict is not likely to work. These attributes are highly resistant to change in the short term and difficult to alter even in the long term. Nevertheless, Choucri and North suggest that population management programs might be helpful in reducing these long-term pressures for expansion, if combined with a more even diffusion of technology and a more equitable access to global resources.[67]

Boundaries

Another geopolitical factor often mentioned as a cause of war is the territorial dispute.[68] While territorial disputes were once one of the chief reasons for war, strictly territorial conflicts seem to have declined as a major motivation for war in the nineteenth and twentieth centuries, especially after World War II.[69] Nevertheless, wars do continue to be fought because of differing territorial claims. In modern times these tend to be conflicts over the precise boundary between states—the Iran-Iraq conflict over the Shatt-al-Arab waterway and the Soviet-Chinese dispute over the boundaries along the

Amur and Ussuri Rivers, for example—rather than disputes over the possession of entire areas. However, even wars belonging to the latter category may be found in recent times—Somalia's war with Ethiopia over the latter's Ogaden region and Iraq's war to possess Kuwait, for instance.

Oddly enough, research on border wars has been rather limited, and the results of these efforts are somewhat contradictory. As one might imagine, states that have border conflicts are more likely to go to war than states without such conflicts.[70] Which border disputes are most likely to lead to the use of war as a method of settlement? A study of border conflicts between 1945 and 1974 by Mandel discovered that wars over borders are most likely to occur between states that are relatively equal in power and are technologically less advanced.[71] On the other hand, Diehl and Goertz's examination of territorial changes from 1816 to 1980 suggests that Mandel's finding is not representative of the broader span of history. They conclude that violence is most likely to be used to transfer territory when the gaining state is a major power and the losing state in a minor power. Diehl and Goertz also find that the more important an area is in terms of geographic size or population, the more likely that a territorial transfer involving that area is to involve violence. Transfers of territory involving "home areas" were the most violent, while transfers involving colonial territory were the least likely to be violent. Finally, violent transfers were more likely when the territory in question was contiguous to both sides rather than to just one or neither of the disputants.[72]

Most research on the link between territory and war has focused on borders as a conditioning variable, rather than as a direct source or cause of war. In other words, borders are seen as an attribute of states that might increase the war proneness of states, though not necessarily because of disputes about these borders per se. Research by social scientists into the relationship between borders and war appears to have produced mixed results. While some studies find little relationship between the number of borders a state has and the number of wars in which it engages, this seems to be the minority view.[73]

Lewis Richardson's study of 33 states for the period of 1825–1946 revealed a positive correlation between the number of wars a country had and the number of frontiers it shared with other states. The greater the number of boundaries a state possessed, the greater the number of wars it participated in. This general conclusion has been confirmed by more recent investigations by others.[74] When one moves beyond simply counting the number of shared frontiers a country has and takes into consideration the importance of these borders to the state (as measured by the length of these borders and the population density on each side), the correlation with war is even more startling.[75] Additionally, once wars begin, common borders seem to stimulate the spread of war. The tendency of wars to become contagious and to spread to nearby states is supported by an abundance of research and is related logically to the number of borders with adjacent states.[76]

In an interesting study of "militarized disputes" between major world powers from 1816 to 1980, Paul Diehl finds a statistically significant relationship between contiguous borders and the escalation of a Great Power disputes to war.[77] Of the thirteen wars in the sample, twelve (92%) began with a dispute involving an area that was geographically contiguous to one or both of the rival states. On the other hand, only 2% (one of fifty-four) of the disputes that did not involve contiguous territory escalated to war. Clearly, if a dispute was contiguous (by land) to one of the rivals, the probability of escalation to war increased; the probability increased even more if both countries were contiguous to the site of the dispute.[78] Of course, even when both Great Powers were contiguous to the site of the confrontation, over two-thirds of the disputes did not end in war, illustrating that borders are unable to supply the total explanation for war; they merely contribute more fuel to the fire. Nevertheless, the data strongly indicate that "the absence of contiguity virtually assures that escalation to war will not occur."[79]

It is fairly clear from the statistical evidence that a relationship exists between the number of borders a state has and its war frequency. What is not clear is *why* the relationship exists. Do nations fight because they share common borders? Or does geographical proximity simply makes it easier to engage in hostilities? Bruce Russett sums up his answer as follows:

> Except in some sense for border disputes, countries do not fight each other because they are physically close; they merely have the *opportunity* to fight because they are close. Proximity becomes the catalyst.[80]

States that border each other are more likely to go to war with each other than they are with noncontiguous states; they simply have more opportunity. After all, we would not expect China, for instance, to be involved in wars with, say, Tunisia or Paraguay, but we would not be surprised to find her at war with Russia, India, or Vietnam. Richardson explains this as being much like domestic violence.[81] Nationals tend to slay each other rather than foreigners. This is simply because most people have few contacts with foreigners. Likewise, murders are most frequently committed by friends and relatives of the victim because these are the people with the most interaction with the victims and therefore with the most opportunities to kill them.

Another facet of "opportunity" has to do with military logistics. As Kenneth Boulding's concept of the *loss of strength gradient* reminds us, the ability of a state to use its military power declines with geographic distance from its home base; thus, relatively fewer wars are fought between noncontiguous countries because neither is able to easily mobilize its military capabilities for effective action. Proximity makes the fighting of war logistically feasible.[82]

However, proximity not only produces opportunities for violence, but it also creates opportunities for cooperation. Common borders may lead to enhanced economic cooperation and trade, increased communication, cultural and diplomatic exchange, and joint membership in regional and international organizations and even in alliances. And, as the European Community has shown, shared borders may even lead to opportunities for increased political integration.[83]

Since proximity alone seems insufficient, what additional theories might explain the relationship between borders and war? Starr and Most suggest several ideas.[84] First, not only do nations with many borders have many targets and opportunities for aggression (if they are so inclined), they also have many potential dangers and problems. States with multiple borders are "confronted with great risks because they must protect and defend themselves against many proximate potential aggressors whose power is not offset by distance."[85]

This is similar to the reasoning of Midlarsky, who hypothesizes that borders are a source of uncertainty for nations—they represent factors that lie outside a nation's control. Since nations tend to go to war to reduce uncertainty (according to Midlarsky), and since the more borders a state has, the less control it has over its environment and the more uncertainty it faces, it would seem logical that the more borders a state has, the greater its chances of going to war.[86]

Second, contiguity is related to a state's "willingness" to go to war. Certainly, conflicts related to areas that are geographically close are viewed by national leaders to be more important, more threatening, more urgent, more closely related to vital national interests, and therefore more worth risking war over than issues concerning distant lands.[87]

Third, certain types of borders might be conducive to peaceful relations while other types of borders may stimulate violence. K. J. Holsti demonstrates that "strategic" territories and borders—those areas possessing notable economic or strategic value—are significantly different from other territories and borders. While territorial and border issues in general have declined substantially as a source of war, "strategic" territories have continued as root cause of war.[88]

Perhaps it is appropriate to conclude, as Starr and Most do, that "borders may not cause wars, but it seems reasonable to suggest that they create certain structures of risks and opportunities in which war is likely."[89]

Internal Conflict: The Scapegoat Theory

One of the most persistent theories of conflict is that there is an important relationship between internal conflict and external conflict. One explanation of this relationship has been called the *scapegoat theory* or, alternatively, the *diversionary war theory*. Specifically, it is believed that when states are beset with deteriorating economic conditions, ethnic divisions, increasing political opposition, or civil strife and rebellion, their leaders will seek to end these internal woes by initiating conflict with an external foe. Presumably, war is undertaken in the belief that it will rally the masses around the flag in the face of a "foreign threat," and that a healthy dose of patriotism is the best medicine for the internal problems facing the government. The external foe, then, becomes a scapegoat. Internal problems are either blamed (unjustly) on the external opponent and victory over the scapegoat is touted as essential to reverse the wretched internal situation, or the war is simply used by the government to divert the attention of citizens from the internal situation. Whether the use of war actually alleviates the internal situation is, of course, another question.

It is also an open question as to whether autocratic regimes or democratic regimes are more susceptible to scapegoating. Autocratic governments are less constrained in their ability to go to war, but democratic regimes are more dependent on the necessity of popular support and therefore perhaps more inclined to use foreign adventures to affect the domestic political situation. We have already mentioned the propensity for the United States to become involved in "militarized international disputes" during election years, especially if this coincides with a period of economic stagnation.[90] Richard Rosecrance's classic study of international instability within nine different European systems from 1740 to 1960 discovered that the domestic insecurity of political elites was one of the most important causes of Major Power war. However, the type of political system did not seem to matter; elites in democratic and nondemocratic systems alike sought relief from internal troubles through war.[91]

Finally, Richard Ned Lebow's investigation of "brinkmanship crises" in the twentieth century also underscored the importance of domestic political uncertainty. Ten of the thirteen crises were initiated by leaders who perceived their rule to be vulnerable to domestic opponents; in four of these ten cases, the political system itself was weak and unstable.[92]

Historians have frequently made scapegoat arguments for the French decisions for war in 1792 and in the Crimean War, for the Russian provocations that led to the Russo-Japanese War, and for the Austrian and German decisions for World War I.[93] More recently, scapegoat arguments were commonplace in journalistic attempts to fathom the Argentine government's decision to wrest the Falkland Islands from Britain by force of arms in 1982. Severe economic problems in both Argentina and Britain had led to increased political opposition to both the Galtieri and Thatcher governments, thus providing the former with a strong incentive to take the Malvinas by force and the latter with an equally strong reason to reverse the situation through war.[94]

Internal Conflict: "Kick Them While They're Down" Wars

In *The Causes of War* historian Geoffrey Blainey investigates this relationship between internal conflict and war. It seems clear to Blainey that internal conflict is not the only key to the puzzle of the causes of war. After all, not all wars were preceded by civil strife, and civil strife has not always led to war. Nevertheless, in the 125-year period he examined (1815–1939), Blainey discovered that at least thirty-one wars (representing just over 50% of all wars during the period) were immediately preceded by civil conflict in one of the belligerent nations.[95] An important relationship clearly exists between internal and external conflict. But what theory might explain this relationship?

Blainey argues that the explanation provided by the scapegoat theory is unproven and probably wrong. He examines and refutes evidence offered by historians to prove that the Crimean War, the Russo-Japanese War, and World War I were scapegoat wars. For instance, the evidence that the Russians were seeking a scapegoat in the 1905 war is usually based on a statement by Russian Minister of the Interior Plehve early in the Russo-Japanese War that "[w]e need a little victorious war to stem the tide of revolution"—a statement later recalled by Plehve's political opponent, Minister of Finance Witte. This may be interesting for its illumination of Plehve's view, but it in no way links his view to the decisions made within the Russian government prior to the outbreak of the war. Blainey notes that other scapegoat theory explanations are frequently of a similar nature: no "smoking gun" is cited that connects the view to the deed. In addition, the authors of scapegoat explanations frequently have axes to grind. Their explanations usually place blame for the war either on their domestic political rivals or on leaders of foreign countries.[96]

More important, Blainey argues that another theory is supported more abundantly by the facts and provides a more logical explanation of the relationship between internal and external conflict. In those thirty-one wars in which civil unrest preceded external conflict, war was not usually initiated by the strife-torn state. Instead, most of the wars were initiated by outside powers, with the internally troubled state in the role of the victim.

Blainey argues effectively that nations do not generally start wars to quell their own internal revolts. Instead, wars occur because internal conflicts change the balance of power between states. Internal strife in stronger countries lowers their margin of superiority and tempts other nations to strike at the most opportune moment. This could be described as the "Kick Them While They're Down" theory of war. (Blainey uses the term "Death Watch Wars" to describe situations in which foreign leaders sit—rather like vultures in trees—waiting for monarchs in the target state to die and bring on political uncertainty.) Iraq's decision to attack Iran during the domestic upheavals associated with that country's revolution can certainly be placed in this category.

On the other hand, if the internal conflict occurs in a relatively weak nation, peace is more likely to be preserved. The internal strife simply confirms the assessment of inferiority; the balance of power is not altered.[97] It should be noted here that the "Kick Them While They're Down" theory essentially concludes that domestic conflict in state A provides the *opportunity* for state B to attack, but it does not address the underlying *cause* of state B's attack on state A. In other words, this theory doesn't help explain *why* B attacks A, only why B attacks A *now*.

At any rate, the "Kick Them While They're Down" theory makes intuitive sense. Governments with internal conflicts aren't likely to attack foreign states; instead, they attack the rebels within. If the disorder isn't serious, the government doesn't need to seek war with outsiders. If the situation is extreme, government leaders will be much more inclined to seek peaceful relations externally in order to devote their attention and their resources to internal problems. Additionally, serious internal dissent reduces the political reliability of the military as well as the internal political cohesion necessary to pursue an external war. Indeed, most nations involved in war at the same time as they were beset by unrest at home have been anxious to seek external peace: Russia in 1905 and 1917, Germany at the end of World War I, the United States during the later stages of the Vietnam War.[98]

The above arguments suggest a modification of the scapegoat theory. The relationship between internal and external conflict may well be curvilinear. Wars should be unlikely during either extremely low levels of internal conflict or extremely high levels of internal conflict. However, moderate levels of internal conflict might be conducive to diversionary war. However, it is still possible, as Jack Levy contends, that during extremely high levels of internal conflict, elites will not behave rationally, but will instead develop a "fortress mentality" and become more risk-acceptant. The stress that accompanies such internal strife may lead both to greater chances of misperception and to greater psychological need to attain foreign policy successes, even if these entail enormous risks.[99]

We have stated that the most likely relationship between external and internal conflict is that nations weakened by internal strife are attacked by their rivals. And we have stated that scapegoat wars may exist under certain conditions. However, these two patterns are not the only possible explanations of the link between internal and external conflict. The *internationalization of civil wars* is another. Internal revolutionary groups engaged in civil wars frequently forge strong ties with foreign governments to assist their revolt, and the government itself also forms ties with external powers to assist it internally against the rebels. Such ties between rebels and foreign governments were present in twenty-six of the thirty-one wars studied by

Blainey. Modern examples of civil wars that have become internationalized are abundant: Vietnam, Angola, El Salvador, Chad, Afghanistan. Thus, civil wars show a penchant for becoming international wars through two different paths: a direct external attack on a government weakened by internal strife or through aid to rebel groups fighting against the government.

Internal Conflict: Revolutionary States

A fascinating study by Zeev Maoz offers another look at the link between internal and external conflict.[100] Maoz suggests that an important consideration in the explanation of international conflict is its link to two kinds of revolutionary changes: the birth of new states out of revolutionary or violent struggles and the revolutionary transformation of older political systems.

States emerging from revolutionary births or midlife transformations are likely to receive a chilly welcome into the club of nations, and political elites within these revolutionary states may perceive the international environment to be hostile. Political elites in the older, more established states in the system may perceive the goals and ambitions of these new states as a threat to themselves and to the current international order. And indeed, states that have gone through revolutionary beginnings or transformations may harbor quite different conceptions of world order. Thus, the political transformation of states through revolutionary means creates mutual distrust between old and new states in the system which can lead to violent conflict. Since this mistrust is mutual, the initiator may be either the newly transformed state (the Wars of the French Revolution and Russia's war against Poland in 1919–1920) or members of the old order (the War of the First Coalition against France from 1792 to 1798 and Iraq's attack on revolutionary Iran in 1980).

Using data on militarized state disputes from 1816 to 1976, Maoz confirmed that both new and old revolutionary states were involved in a larger number of militarized disputes (uses of force, displays of force, and threats of force) than new or old states whose political development was more evolutionary. Thus, Maoz finds that revolutionary change within states increases the likelihood that they will experience subsequent militarized conflicts—either as initiators or as victims.[101]

Empirical Studies of the Internal-External Conflict Link

Before this discussion goes too far, we should note that there are some scholars who question whether there is any empirical link at all between internal and external conflict. Several studies, in fact, cast doubt on this central proposition.

Michael Haas examined the link between social stresses and strains in a society (as indicated by levels of unemployment, industrialization, suicides, and homicides) and the state's foreign aggressiveness (as indicated by its military expenditures and its war frequency). He examined data from 1900 to 1960 for ten countries, almost all Western and/or industrialized, and found that there was only a slight relationship between these stress factors and the nation's foreign conflict.[102]

Rummel investigated data from 80 countries for the years 1955–1957 to see whether nations with high levels of domestic conflict behavior (as indicated by assassinations, purges, strikes, riots, coups, demonstrations, etc.) also exhibited high levels of foreign conflict behavior (including wars, sanctions, troop movements, expulsions, and verbal protests and threats). Using the technique of factor analysis, Rummel found three distinct dimensions of foreign conflict (war, diplomacy, and belligerency) and three different dimensions of domestic conflict (turmoil, revolution, and subversion). He further discovered that the various dimensions (or factors) of foreign conflict behavior were almost completely independent of the various domestic dimensions. That is, nations with high scores on any of the three domestic conflict factors did not necessarily have high scores on any of the foreign conflict factors. Unrest at home was not necessarily linked to foreign conflict.[103]

In a later study Rummel found foreign conflict to be inversely related to one of the three domestic conflict dimensions—subversion. States that experience subversion at home are less likely to be involved in conflict with other states.[104] This would seem to buttress at least part of Blainey's argument about the link between internal and external conflict.[105] In general, however, Rummel's conclusion that internal and external conflict are not related is supported by similar factor analysis studies by several others.[106]

Jonathan Wilkenfeld hypothesized that lack of a relationship between internal and external conflict in these studies was because Rummel and his followers had grouped together different kinds of political systems in their analyses. Perhaps if one looked at political systems separately, clearer patterns would emerge. He reanalyzed the data, but divided the countries into three groups—personalist (primarily Latin American states), centrist (primarily communist states and some Middle Eastern states), and polyarchies (democracies). He discovered different internal-external conflict patterns for different types of states. For instance, centrist states manifested a positive relationship between revolutionary unrest and war. (Positive relationships also appeared between turmoil and both belligerency and diplomatic conflict for the centrist group.) For the polyarchies relationships appeared between turmoil and war and also between revolutionary unrest and belligerency.[107] As you can tell, these results represent a fairly mixed bag, and interpreting these results is a hazardous task at best.

Summing up the Internal-External Conflict Relationship

While a substantial body of opinion (Rummel, Haas, and others) seems to indicate that internal conflict is not very strongly related to external conflict, this seems to run counter to both common sense and historical example. While not all wars are preceded by internal unrest and not all domestic conflicts result in war, still there are enough historical examples of these for the theorist to be able to conclude that there is something important here. The conflict between the historical evidence and cross-national evidence compiled by political scientists such as Rummel may be due to certain methodological peculiarities of the latter's research. Most of these studies are based on data reported for only a small number of years (between 1955 and 1960), which may comprise an unrepresentative time sample. Moreover, the conflict variable in these studies is frequently a composite of several different kinds of foreign conflict, rather than purely war. Finally, these studies are primarily descriptive studies of internal and external conflict and are not designed to test a particular theory of war. As such, they do not address two fundamental questions of causality: What is the direction of the relationship? That is, which variable (internal conflict or external conflict) is supposed to cause which? And what is the timing of such a relationship? As a result, it is difficult to use these studies as evidence to either confirm or disconfirm a theory that domestic conflict causes external conflict.[108]

While a relationship probably exists between internal and external conflict, it is obscured somewhat because several different causal mechanisms are needed to explain this association. Through the scapegoat mechanism, states torn by moderate civil strife seek foreign conflicts to solve domestic problems; through the death watch mechanism, states experiencing serious internal weakness or conflict are attacked as easy prey by their opponents; through the internationalization of civil wars, rebels and governments alike may attain external allies and turn domestic conflicts into international wars; and finally, through the process by which revolutionary regimes are brought into existence, interstate conflict may be precipitated between the supporters of the old international order and the new revolutionary states.[109]

Internal-External Conflict: Implications

The existence of a direct relationship between internal and external conflict implies that the world would be a much more peaceful place if states themselves were more peaceful places to live. International conflict could be substantially reduced if internal conflicts could be reduced or eliminated.

This, of course, raises the question of just how internal conflicts might be diminished. It also raises the question of whether the leaders of the world community can bring about a reduction of internal conflict in turbulent states by way of policies and programs applied from the outside or whether this is a matter that can only be addressed and solved internally.

To some extent, U.S. foreign policy in the post–World War II era has been predicted on just such a presumed link between the reduction of internal conflict and prevention of external conflict. The general purpose of American foreign aid—whether Marshall Plan aid to western Europe, Alliance for Progress aid to Latin America, or Caribbean basin aid—has been to prevent internal disturbances in the receiving countries that might make those states fertile grounds for Communist revolution or attractive targets for aggression. The rationale for foreign aid programs has been that economic unrest leads to internal political unrest, which leads to external (communist) subversion or assault. There is, of course, a second set of assumptions as well: that economic aid will bring about economic growth and development, that such growth will result in stable social and political conditions, and that this will prevent the rise of strong, left-wing radical groups. Quite a few social scientists, however, would argue that economic growth and the process of development—especially if the growth is rapid—bring about social and political *instability* rather than stability. Development aid might be instrumental in fostering the very conditions of instability that the aid was designed to prevent! Since the resolution of this debate is beyond the scope of this inquiry, let us agree to leave this question uresolved and move on to other theories of war at the nation-state level.

War Weariness

In the ninth volume of Arnold Toynbee's *A Study of History* the British historian claimed to have identified a cycle of peace and war. The one-hundred-year cycle, repeated over the centuries, consisted of the following sequence. A general war was followed by a period of peace, then by a cluster of small wars, a second period of peace, and finally by another general war.

Toynbee's tentative theoretical explanation was that war made a deep psychological impression on those who lived through it, and these men and women were hesitant to have their children's lives disrupted by similar experiences. A whole generation of leaders whose lives had been molded during wartime were determined to keep the peace as long as they ruled. Eventually, however, a new generation would come to power. Never having experienced firsthand the horrors of war, they were much more inclined than their elders to test the waters of combat. The result would be a series of small wars—larger wars presumably still being avoided due to the aversion to such things handed down to them by the previous generation. The period of peace following these small wars would finally be shattered by another great war—a war that would come about only when the last memories of the first great war had been erased by the death of the wartime generation.[110] Then, of course, the cycle would start over again. Toynbee's one-hundred-year cycle was almost a perfect fit when matched with the period between the Napoleonic Wars of the early nineteenth century and World War I.

The explanation given by Toynbee for this cycle of war and peace is generally referred to as the *war weariness theory*. It predicts that nations that have recently experienced a long and costly war should be the most peaceful—at least in the short term. Conversely, states that have endured long periods of peace are probably most likely to experience war in the near future. As Blainey observes, the theory ironically implies that we should beware Sweden and the Canary Islands.[111]

More specifically, why and how is war weariness supposed to lead to peace? To some extent the war weariness theory draws on psychological arguments. It maintains that political leaders who have directly experienced the devastation of war are deeply touched by the experience—presumably at a conscious level, but perhaps unconsciously as well. The experience of war results in a strong aversion to war, and this war wariness affects these leaders' personalities, their operational codes, their images of the world, and their value preferences. This explanation operates at the individual level of analysis.

The war weariness theory also operates at the level of the nation-state. Here the theory implies that the common experience of a severe and destructive war has made an impression on the *collective* psyche of the nation. War weariness becomes part of the "collective national consciousness" or part of the "national character" or the "political culture." In other words, there is a collective psychological phenomenon that is shared by the population. War weariness is not a personal characteristic as much as it is a national attribute.

A complete theory of war weariness would have to specify the link between the war weariness of society as a whole (or certain groups within society) and political decision-makers. The presence of popular aversion to war implies that, at least in a democracy, people will make known to the government their predisposition for peace and that government policy will reflect the wishes of the people. Even in authoritarian countries this collective support for peace cannot be discounted entirely; dictators, too, must take into consideration such widely held sentiments. Consequently, other state-level attributes may not matter greatly; states with similar histories of war experience should act similarly in the future.[112]

War weariness has relevance for war *initiation* but not necessarily for war *involvement*. It is concerned with the effect of a costly previous war on a nation's desire to start a new war. However, if a nation is attacked, war weariness will count for little. War weariness is not likely to prevent a nation from participating in a war if it has been attacked. One might in fact hypothesize that nations that have recently experienced war are more likely to be attacked than other nations. Opponents may sense the spirit of war weariness in such a nation and see this as a sign of weakness. Similarly, a state weakened by a costly previous war might be seen as an easy target by other states.

As you have probably already noticed, war weariness has much in common with the concepts of disease and immunity. As Richardson has suggested, war resembles a disease. One possible cure for this disease is, ironically, a potent dose of war itself. The actual experience of war constitutes a kind of immunization against future war. Unfortunately, like a tetanus shot, the effects of the inoculation don't last and the nation's immunity fades.[113]

If the war weariness theory is true, wars are caused by states whose immunity to war—generated by the devastation and death of a previous conflict—has begun to lose its potency over the course of time. The implications of this theory are fairly pessimistic. There is good news and bad news. The good news is that wars can be prevented. The bad news is that the only way to prevent them in the future is to fight them in the present—and even this won't prevent war indefinitely.

Before we go further, certain factual and theoretical problems must be addressed. First, the war weariness theory does a lousy job of explaining the outbreak of World War II, a major war that occurred just two decades after the end of World War I. Leaders of the nations of Europe were all part of the generation whose lives were molded by the what had been the most horrible war in history. Surely, if any generation were to be war weary, this would have been the one.[114] Certainly, our confidence in the war weariness theory must be reduced by such a glaring example of events that run counter to the theory.

Second, although the war weariness theory might be applied to any participant in a recent war, whether on the victorious side or the vanquished, in reality whether a nation wins or loses a war will have an important effect on its future policy. We can surmise that victory might make the winner more likely to engage in war in the future. Certainly, this would be consistent with the logic of the war weariness theory. In most cases, winning states experience a lesser degree of devastation and suffering than losers; thus, they should be less war weary. Coincidentally, winning a war might increase a state's propensity for future aggression. The winning state's physical capabilities might be enhanced as the result of victory; victory might raise levels of nationalistic fervor and create a climate of optimism about war; it might solidify in power (or bring to power) a "hawkish" political faction identified with the success of the war; or it might reinforce a cultural norm of aggression.[115]

It could be argued that a defeat in a long and destructive war would be the situation most likely to bring about the war weariness syndrome. As we have suggested, it can usually be assumed that the greatest devastation of the war will be borne by the loser. The greater the devastation and loss of life and the harsher the war, the greater the resultant war weariness and (presumably) the greater the immunity to future war initiation. Thus, it could logically be expected that war weariness would have a greater impact on countries that have been defeated in the previous war, rather than on those that have been victorious.

This argument is not foolproof, however. It could just as easily be argued that nations that have suffered on the losing side might in some cases be the most likely to take up arms again in the near future. Certainly, the desire for revenge would be a strong motivating factor, as would be the associated desires to regain lost territories, peoples, and resources. It is frequently asserted, for instance, that Germany's desire for revenge following its defeat in World War I was a major cause of its aggression in World War II.

If it is equally plausible that A (a costly defeat) causes B (peace) and that A also causes C (initiation of future wars), then neither proposition is likely to be true as a general rule. Theoretical arguments that war could logically lead to periods of peace as well as to future war are equally plausible and, of course, incompatible. Herein lies perhaps the greatest weakness of war weariness as a general theory of war and peace. Previous wars may be *negatively contagious* (inhibitory) or *positively contagious* (contributory) to future wars; if so, the negative and positive effects will tend to cancel each other out.

Third, regardless of whether a country has been defeated or victorious in a previous war, it might be argued that the mere experience of war is a factor enhancing the possibility of a more warlike rather than a more peaceful future. For instance, Karsten argues that war accustoms individuals to military attitudes and values—attitudes and values that are spread by returning veterans.[116] Of course, not all veterans have militaristic attitudes, but veterans frequently return home with new or reinforced attitudes toward military virtues and the use of force.[117] A kind of "reverse war weariness" may in fact occur, as the military way of life is glorified. Veterans organizations, whose ranks would be swelled by the war, may become important institutional factors influencing governments toward more aggressive policies. In addition to the creation of a large number of veterans and veterans organizations, wars lead to the creation of large military establishments with equipment, personnel, bases, budgets, bureaucracies, and general staffs, not to mention the various industrial manufacturers involved in military production. All of these may be difficult to reduce in size and political power after the end of the war. In other words, wars lead to the establishment of "military-industrial complexes." It is the opinion of many that such institutions are factors that increase the probability of future war rather than factors that serve to decrease that probability.[118]

Fourth, even if it is true that wars are followed by sustained periods of peace, war weariness may not be the only (let alone the best) explanation for this. It may be that a decisive end to the war has resolved all outstanding issues, removing the political causes for future wars. It may be that a nation's resources have been so depleted that is is physically unable to pursue war. Similarly, a decisive victory by one side may have created a balance of power so lopsided that those who have grievances are nonetheless deterred from redressing these grievances through force.[119] Therefore, an empirical link between war and subsequent periods of prolonged peace does not necessarily confirm the hypothesis.

War Weariness: Empirical Studies

Empirical studies of the war weariness hypotheses have once again produced a mixed bag of results. Some studies have produced limited support. In their analysis of wars from 1816 to 1965, Singer and Small conclude that neither initiators nor defenders were very likely to initiate war within a decade, though winners were far more likely to initiate subsequent wars than losers. Both results are consistent with the war weariness theory. However, the authors emphasize the preliminary nature of their study, arguing that evidence for confirmation of the theory is far from complete.[120]

A later study by Singer and Cusack focuses on war participation rather than war initiation. Their general conclusion is that prior war experience seems to have had little effect on the propensity of states to become involved in subsequent wars. Winners of previous wars have a slight tendency toward early reentry into war, but so do defeated states. In fact, the average time interval to the next war is even shorter for defeated states. Although the difference between defeated states and winning states is not statistically significant, the finding points toward the the revenge motive and away from the war weariness theory.[121] On the other hand, Singer and Cusack conclude that defeated states that have fought costly wars (wars with high fatalities) do seem to be inhibited from participating in wars too soon after their defeat. The combination of defeat and high cost would seem to be much more important than either of these factors alone in explaining why states returned to war so soon after their experiences in previous war.[122]

Other studies find virtually no support for the war weariness hypotheses. In his analysis of great power wars from 1816 to 1965, David Garnham finds victorious major powers are no more likely than losers to initiate a future war, nor does he find any relationship between the cost of war and the elapsed time until the next war. He also investigates the classic proposition of Immanuel Kant that democratic states ought to be more susceptible to the war weariness phenomenon than nondemocratic states. He finds no evidence that war weariness has constrained the behavior of the major democracies of the nineteenth and twentieth centuries—Britain, France, and the United States.[123]

Finally, Levy and Morgan study the involvement of great powers in wars between 1500 and 1975. They discover many more instances of nations reengaging in wars in a relatively short period of time than should be expected. In fact, out of 115 cases of wars that were begun after a previous great power war, ninety-one wars were begun within ten years of a previous great power conflict. Sixteen were begun between ten and twenty years later; five were begun in the next ten years, two in the next decade, and only one in the fifth decade following a Great Power war. The war weariness hypothesis would predict very few cases of war should begin in the first decade, with the chances of war increasing over time as the immunizing effects of war weariness began to wear off. Levy and Morgan's research indicates almost exactly the opposite of this hypothesis![124]

When Levy and Morgan shift their attention to the hypothesis that the more serious the war, the greater the length of time between wars, the results are similarly disappointing. Using duration of war, the number of participating countries, battle deaths, and a battle death/war duration ratio as indicators of the seriousness of war, they find only weak correlations between these measures of the independent variable and the dependent variable (elapsed time until the next war). Neither are they able to confirm that inhibition to war is brought on by a series of wars instead of a single previous war. In short, they are neither able to confirm any of the war weariness hypotheses nor find any distinctive or consistent patterns with regard to the effect of previous wars on subsequent war participation.[125]

It should be noted, however, that since Levy and Morgan investigate the propensity of war weary states merely to become involved in subsequent wars rather than to initiate them, it is not particularly odd that they fail to find support for the theory. They have imposed a stricter test than is warranted by the logic of the theory. Nevertheless, we must conclude that the evidence supporting the war weariness theory is considerably less than compelling.

Conclusion

What shall we make of all this research on the connection between national characteristics and war? Its hard to escape the conclusion that national attribute theories have done a relatively poor job in explaining the incidence of war. The only proposition that seems to have been consistently supported is that the size and power of a nation are directly related to the probability that it will be involved in war. It appears that the presence of contiguous borders with the rival disputant may be a contributory factor. And internal conflict does seem associated with interstate war, though there seem to be multiple paths from the former to the latter. Beyond these findings, it would be difficult to build a comprehensive profile of war-prone states based on any other set of factors. Neither the type of government a state has nor its economic institutions, its economic well-being, its population growth rate, or its previous involvement in war seems to matter much.

Before we move on to the next chapter, let us return momentarily to the "man-milieu" hypothesis of Harold and Margaret Sprout, which was discussed earlier. The Sprouts reject the idea that the behavior of nations is determined directly by objective environmental factors such as a state's size, geographical position, or type of government. They argue instead that the environment can only affect the behavior of states in two ways. First, environmental factors can influence the decisions of leaders only if they actually perceive such elements in the environment. The environment affects decisions only indirectly—through the perceptions of individuals. Second, environmental factors can limit, restrain, and control the outcomes of decisions made by government leaders. That is, the reality of certain factors (geographical proximity, economic weakness, etc.) will directly affect the decisions as they are put into practice.[126]

The Sprouts' theory suggests that theories of conflict at the nation-state level must be seen in a different light. For instance, it may not be that capitalist states are inherently aggressive because capitalist economies are by nature expansionistic. The more important point may be that leaders of capitalist states *think* that the economic system requires continuous expansion. Similarly, it may not be true that states with rapid population and technological growth pursue expansionist policies in a manner determined by these attributes. It may be more important that the leaders of these states *perceive* that they must pursue an expansionistic foreign policy because of their growth. Likewise, it may not be the power of nations that is important in and of itself as an explanation of war. What may instead be more important is the perception of leaders of powerful states concerning what great powers can and must do, and of the proper role of great powers in the international system. What all of this suggests, of course, is that theories that emphasize the nation-state level are all barking up the wrong tree.

The position of the Sprouts is, however, somewhat extreme. Instead of saying that state-level theories are totally negated or invalidated by individual level perceptual factors, this analyst prefers to see factors at these levels as linked. A comprehensive theory of war will require variables at several different levels of analysis. In this case, certain nation-state–level variables, such as size and power, may be thought of as important underlying conditions that cause war, but individual-level variables, such as perceptions and national role conceptions, operate as the mechanisms through which these underlying conditions lead to war.

*   *   *

There are plenty of trees in the theoretical forest, however. Before we pass judgment on which contain the best fruit, it would be wise to explore the woods a little more. We will now proceed to a higher level of analysis, one that examines the relationships *between* states rather than looking at the attributes of a single state. In a sense, we have been looking thus far at individual trees, or at least individual types of trees—capitalist trees, democratic trees, authoritarian trees, strong trees, rapidly growing trees, weary trees, and so forth. We will now turn our attention to the forest (or at least parts of the forest) and look at the interrelationship between some of the trees.

6

International Interaction: Stimulus-Response Theory and Arms Races

> Eye for eye, tooth for tooth. . . .
> —Exod. 21:24

> If thine enemy hunger, feed him; if he thirst, give him drink. . . .
> Be not overcome of evil; but overcome evil with good.
> —Rom. 12:20, 21

> Absolute security for one power means absolute insecurity of all others.
> —Henry Kissinger

Imagine a pair of eight-year-old boys making a wreck in the recreation room. Their mothers, having been interrupted from a quiet afternoon of tea and soaps, race off to quell the disturbance. As the mothers enter the room, little Johnny is about to crown little Sammy over the head with his G.I. Joe machine gun.

"What's going on here? Why are you fighting?"

"Johnny won't let me play with his tank."

"But Sammy won't let me use his Astro Blaster and it's my turn. I'm not going to share if he's not."

"Well, Johnny started it. He refuses to die when I shoot him. He's not playing fair."

"Yeah, well he started it. He always has to be the good guy."

Sound familiar? From time to time we have all been reminded how the actions of states are not unlike those of small children. The above scenario illustrates a common conflict spiral. One individual responds to actions by a second, who in turn responds to those of the first. Each reacts to the prior behavior of the other. The interaction becomes conflictual, the conflict escalates, and fighting breaks out.

Many analysts argue that nations go to war because of previous actions directed against them by others. State A is simply responding to the hostile acts of state B. Aha, you say, then what about state B? Same answer. State B's

160

action was prompted by an earlier action by state A. And so it goes. The beginnings of this process of interaction between the two states may be shrouded in history. We may never know who did what to whom first. Ultimately, it doesn't matter.

Stimulus-Response Theory

As an explanation of national behavior, the stimulus-response (or action-reaction) theory of international relations mirrors the stimulus-response theory of individual behavior, which has been a staple of the "behaviorist" school of psychology. According to these theories, most actions are a response by the actor to a stimulus (or a set of stimuli) in the environment. The behavior of individuals can be explained largely on the basis of the stimuli that impinge on them in their surroundings. States are not alone in the world; their actions are in large part responses to the behaviors of other states (and nonstate actors) that also participate in the international system. What one state does has a bearing on what the others do. The political actions of nations are interdependent with each other.

At this level of analysis the emphasis is on the interaction of states and on the structure and process of these interdependent actions. It is unimportant what individual political leaders think, what their personalities are like, what their perceptions are, what the decision-making process is, and what domestic policy considerations exist. As J. David Singer has suggested, these variables can all be thought of as being within a *black box*.[1] We don't need to know them. We don't need to understand them. We can assume that most states react in the same way to the same stimuli—regardless of their particular national attributes or the personal characteristics of their leaders. Certain actions seem to engender certain kinds of reactions. If we can identify and understand this process of action and counteraction, we can perhaps learn to avoid dangerous sequences of events that lead to war.

It is possible that a *dyadic* (bilateral, involving two actors) action-reaction process might proceed in a number of different ways, as illustrated in Table 6.1. One possible pattern would be that as conflict develops between a pair of states they begin to develop a tit-for-tat relationship. Each state responds to the other with actions that are similar in type and magnitude. The response of each to the behavior of the other is proportionate to the preceding act of the other. We might call this pattern the *reciprocity/symmetry* pattern. This particular pattern indicates a stable relationship in which the level of conflict/cooperation remains constant, neither escalating nor deescalating. An example of such an interaction pattern might be twentieth-century Canadian-American relations or North Korean-South Korean relations since the Korean War.

The second possible interaction pattern is an escalation process, one that

Anatol Rapoport has also labeled as a "fight" process.[2] The *escalation/fight* pattern describes a situation in which each adversary in a conflict responds to the actions of the other with somewhat bolder, more hostile reactions. This is not the "eye for an eye" approach described above, but more like "two eyes and a thumb for an eye." Leng and Goodsell have described it as a pattern of "self-aggravating feedback."[3] The behavior of the states becomes increasingly threatening and aggressive, creating a *conflict spiral*. Unless this escalatory cycle is broken, the level of violence will eventually reach that of all-out war. One example of such a pattern might be Sino-Soviet relations during the late 1950s and early 1960s, an era of mutual recriminations and general nastiness that culminated in armed border clashes between the two leaders of the Communist world.

Why the escalation/fight pattern should occur rather than the reciprocity/symmetry pattern is, of course, a crucial theoretical question. Several possibilities exist. (Some of which require skipping to another level of analysis.) Leng and Goodsell suggest that escalation occurs because one side in the conflict uses a threat of military violence. In their analysis of five interstate conflicts between 1850 and 1965, they discover that conflicts are more likely to escalate when one adversary uses such a threat.[4] Threats of military violence may represent a kind of threshold. Once that threshold has been exceeded by one side, the symmetry process is replaced by the escalation process.

This may very well be true, but it begs the question of why one side decides to increase the level of hostility by using military threats in the first place. An answer consistent with our examination of the individual level of analysis is simply that individual leaders in one of the countries misperceive the level of hostility directed at them and thus respond at a higher level of hostility, even though they believe themselves to be returning it in a proportionate, reciprocal way. Another possibility is that the operational codes of leaders involved require a kind of "one-upmanship" response to the unfriendly behaviors of rival.

An *asymmetrical escalation* pattern is also possible. It is conceivable that in a conflict between a pair of states, one of the states will engage in escalation while the other is content to merely reciprocate. The relationship between Germany and her rivals in the Triple Entente in the weeks prior to the outbreak of World War I is often seen in this light, with Germany in the escalatory role, overreacting to the behavior of Britain, France, and Russia.

A fourth interaction pattern is also feasible. This is a pattern of deescalation. Each of the states in the *deescalation* pattern reacts to the behavior of the other by responding with actions that are more cooperative and less hostile. Thus, the behavior of the states becomes increasingly more cooperative and harmonious as time goes by. (This process can be either symmetrical or asymmetrical. For simplicity's sake, it is represented below as symmetrical.) Instead of a conflict spiral, there is a peace spiral. American

Table 6–1
Four Typical Conflict Interaction Patterns
(using a nine point hostility scale with 9 as maximum hostility)

	Reciprocity/symmetry			*Escalation/fight*	
Time	A's hostility Level	B's hostility Level	Time	A's level	B's level
T	5		T	4	
T +1		5	T +1		5
T +2	5		T +2	6	
T +3		5	T +3		7
T +4	5		T +4	8	
T +5		5	T +5		9

	Asymmetrical escalation			*Deescalation*	
Time	A's level	B's level	Time	A's level	B's level
T	5		T	6	
T +1		6	T +1		5
T +2	6		T +2	4	
T +3		7	T +3		3
T +4	7		T +4	2	
T +5		8	T +5		1

relations with the Chinese in the early 1970s and with the Soviets in the immediate aftermath of the Cuban Missile Crisis (the period of the "Kennedy experiment") as well as the detente period of the early 1970s all illustrate this type of relationship. (Soviet-American and Soviet-Chinese relations in the Gorbachev era are probably best characterized as asymmetrical deescalation, with the Soviets in the role of the chief deescalator.)[5]

In summary, the stimulus-response theory of international conflict suggests that a state's behavior depends on the actions directed against it by other states. The classic formulation of the stimulus-response theory is that the actions of any state tend to be similar in type and magnitude to the actions directed at it by others. The interaction pattern may be relatively stable or it may involve either the escalation or deescalation of conflict as states respond to each other's moves.

Stimulus-Response Theory: Liberal and Conservative Views

Politicians and academics in the United States in the post–World War II era have engaged in a major debate that has bearing on this theory. Liberals have argued that tough, militaristic actions by the United States led inevitably to

tough, militaristic reactions by the former Soviet Union. Friendly, cooperative actions by the United States should lead to friendly, cooperative reactions by the U.S.S.R. Superpower interaction was believed to be based on the
norm of reciprocity. This is the classic formulation of the action-reaction
theory: violence begets violence and cooperation begets cooperation. The
implication for U.S. foreign policy is that the best way to bring about Soviet
cooperation is to treat them with conciliatory and cooperative actions.

Conservatives argued just the opposite. They maintained the Soviets
acted inversely rather than reciprocally. Cooperative actions by the United
States produced only uncompromising, aggressive acts by the Soviet Union,
while tough, strong actions by the United States were the most likely to
produce cooperative actions by the U.S.S.R. The implication was that
"bullying" the Soviets was the approach most likely to produce the desired
results.

What accounts for this divergence of opinion between liberals and
conservatives? To a large extent the difference must be traced to their
divergent views on the nature of states in general and to their view of the
nature of the (former) Soviet state in particular. Liberals view all states as
essentially cooperative and peaceful. States (that is, their leaders) are motivated more by fear of others than by any evil intentions to destroy others or
to take their property. Conservatives are generally more skeptical of the
intentions of states, and they saw the Soviet state (or any Communist state,
for that matter) as being radically different from democratic states. Since the
nature of the state was different, its goal—the creation of a Communist
world empire—was different. Thus, the Soviet Union would not respond to
the cooperative acts of others with cooperation of its own. Its leaders
perceived cooperation as a sign of weakness in its enemies and thus reacted
aggressively.

How Do We Know?

Which theory correctly explains U.S.-Soviet interaction? How will we know?
The obvious answer is that we must observe U.S.-Soviet behavior (or the
behavior of other pairs of states) on a day-to-day basis or a week-to-week
basis. We will want to determine what kinds of actions by each state led to
what kinds of reactions by the other. It would also be useful to be able to
discern to what extent each action is cooperative or hostile. These are
certainly polar opposites, but many actions will lie between these poles and
we will want to be able to categorize these actions as well. A useful way to
start is to place actions on a scale, say a nine-point scale, from actions that are
the most cooperative (at the low end) to those that are the most hostile (at the
high end of the scale). The scale might look something like the one in Table
6.2. (Notice that this scale was used in Table 6.1 to help depict conflict
interaction patterns.)

Table 6–2
Nine-Point Cooperation–Hostility Scale[6]

1. Most cooperative—Signing of cooperative agreements, treaties, and alliances
2. Granting of foreign economic aid or military assistance
3. Reception of political, economic, or military delegations
4. Exchange of cultural delegations
5. Neutral
6. Verbal denunciations or accusations, formal protests, propaganda attacks
7. Economic or diplomatic sanctions, military show of force, troop movements
8. Mobilization or alert of armed forces, issuance of military threat or ultimatum
9. Most hostile—War

The hard part, of course, is to gather information on all the possible actions taken by the two countries over a particular period of time. This will have to be done by combing a variety of daily news reports for evidence of specific actions. Once these actions have been identified, then each will have to be placed into its proper category and awarded a numerical value according to our scale of hostility. After each event or action has been assigned a numerical value, charts and graphs can be constructed to depict the interactions of states, and a number of statistical tests can be performed to help us investigate the relationship between the actions of state A and state B.

Empirical Evidence of Reciprocity

Several studies have used variations of this *Event-interaction* approach to examine patterns of conflict interaction between the United States and the Soviet Union. Russell Leng examines data on the bargaining interaction between the two superpowers during three periods of crisis: the Berlin Blockade of 1948–1949, the Berlin Crisis of 1961, and the Cuban Missile Crisis of 1962. He is specifically interested in the rival liberal and conservative hypotheses discussed above. Leng reports that the weight of historical evidence overwhelmingly supports the liberal contention. The Soviets were far more likely to be accommodative in response to positive American acts than to American threats. The most effective American influence technique, however, used both carrot and stick—combining threats and positive inducements.[7]

William Gamson and Andre Modigliani studied interaction between the Western and Eastern Bloc nations during the Cold War period between 1946 and 1963. Their findings also support the notion that cooperation begets cooperation and hostility and begets hostility. They conclude that belligerent activity of one side (it doesn't matter which) was most likely to generate belligerent activity by the other. Likewise, actions of accommodation were most likely to prompt a conciliatory response by the other.[8]

Other studies reach similar conclusions concerning Soviet-American relations. Jan Triska and David Finley, two experts on Soviet foreign policy, discover pronounced patterns of reciprocity in Soviet-American relations throughout the Cold War period.[9] Ole Holsti also finds that during the Cuban Missile Crisis between the United States and the U.S.S.R. the level of hostility on each side was largely based on the other's hostility in the immediately preceding time period.[10] More recent event-interaction studies consistently confirm the reciprocal nature of U.S.-Soviet interactions.[11] And Soviet-Chinese relations fit the same pattern.[12]

Goldstein and Freeman's analysis of U.S.-Soviet-Chinese relations from three major events–interaction data sets (COPDAB, WEIS-X, and ASHLEY), which collectively cover the period between 1948 and 1989, concludes that bilateral reciprocity is the norm in all three sides of the strategic triangle. Responses of all three nations to actions of the others are almost universally reciprocal in nature, though not necessarily completely symmetrical. The United States, the Soviets, and the Chinese each reciprocate each other's actions on a short-term basis. In none of the interaction patterns is there any evidence of inverse response. None of the superpowers showed any signs of opportunistically exploiting the cooperation of others. Nor did any of the three show signs of backing down when faced with hostility from the others. In sum, Goldstein and Freeman find no evidence of nations behaving the way conservatives hypothesize that they should.[13]

Events data from the interactions among diverse nations in several time periods show remarkable similarity. Robert North's research group at Stanford studied conflict interaction during the 1914 crisis preceding World War I. A major conclusion was that hostility level of both the Triple Entente and the Dual Alliance powers was based primarily on the hostility targeted at them by the other bloc.[14] Leng and Goodsell investigated interaction patterns in five dyadic conflicts between 1864 and 1962: the Schleswig-Holstein conflict between Germany and Denmark (1864–66), the Moroccan Crisis between France and Germany (1904–1906), the Austrian-Serbia conflict on the eve of World War I (1914), the Suez crisis involving Britain and Egypt (1956–1957), and the Cuban Missile Crisis between the United States and the U.S.S.R. (1962). The authors found that the conflict behavior of all the nations involved was remarkably symmetrical. The negative acts of the pairs of states paralleled each other in typical stimulus-response fashion. Additionally, they discovered that as the amount of interaction increased, the behavior of the two nations became more and more similar.[15] As the quantity of actions the two nations direct at each other increased, they seemed to become more aware of their mutual relations and their interactions began to become more directly responsive to each other. The actions of each nation became, in a sense, more finely tuned to the actions of the other.

The Middle East has become a much studied area of the world, and analyses of prewar interaction in this region bolster the validity of the stimulus-response process. Jeffrey Milstein's study of Arab-Israeli violence in the Middle East from 1948–1969 indicates a high correlation between Israeli actions and the actions of Arab states. The violent actions of each country could best be explained by the violent actions of its opponent.[16] Burrowes and Garriga-Pico examined interactions between the Middle East nations for the two and a half years prior to the Six Day War in 1967 and found support for the stimulus-response model.[17] McCormick explicitly tested the stimulus-response model in contrast to the bureaucratic inertia model in explaining the behavior of Middle East states in the Suez Crisis and the Six Day War. He found the stimulus-response model to be superior—especially in the most intense periods of the crises.[18]

Another interesting analysis of Middle East relations also supports the stimulus-response theory. Wilkenfeld, Lussier, and Tahtinen examined events data from June 1949 to June 1967 for the states of Egypt, Iraq, Israel, Jordan, Lebanon, and Syria.[19] Their test was specifically designed to determine whether domestic factors or the actions of other nations were more important in determining the behavior of states. Two domestic factors were chosen. The first was the presence of internal conflict. The importance of this variable, of course, derives from its links to the scapegoat theory, a previous acquaintance from the nation-state level of analysis. The second domestic factor selected was bureaucratic inertia—the tendency for the behavior of nations to echo their past foreign policy behaviors. This is more or less a test of two theories from the small–group level of analysis—incrementalism and organizational politics. The researchers made use of multiple regression analysis to test the effects of these several independent variables on the dependent variable—foreign policy behavior. Multiple regression is a statistical technique that enables the researcher to determine the degree to which each independent variable contributes to the explanation of the dependent variable. For each nation a standard formula was devised and tested. For instance, the behavior of each nation was assumed to be accounted for by the following formula (using Egypt as an example):

$$EG_{fcn} = \text{(Egypt's foreign conflict at time } n \text{ equals)}$$
$$a \text{ (an unknown constant, representing policy inertia) +}$$
$$b_1 EG_{dc\ n-1} \text{ (Egypt's previous domestic conflict) +}$$
$$b_2 EG_{fc\ n-1} \text{ (Egypt's external conflict vs. others) +}$$
$$b_3 IRAQ_{fc>EG} \text{ (Iraq's conflict toward Egypt) +}$$
$$b_4 ISR_{fc>EG} \text{ (Israel's conflict toward Egypt) +}$$
$$b_5 JOR_{fc>EG} \text{ (Jordan's conflict toward Egypt) +}$$

$b_6\text{LEB}_{fc>EG}$ (Lebanon's conflict toward Egypt) +
$b_7\text{SYR}_{fc>EG}$ (Syria's conflict toward Egypt)

The results of the statistical test will then indicate how well the model applies to the real world. In other words, can the behavior of Egypt (or of any of the other states) be accounted for by these variables or are there other (missing) variables that are needed to explain Egypt's actions? And, of the variables in the equation, which are the most important determinant of the state's behavior?

The results indicated that in fourteen of the fifteen equations tested, the strongest predictor of one nation's actions was the action directed at it by others during the same time period.[20] The actions of others seemed far more important than domestic factors in explaining foreign policy behavior. For instance, the best explanation of Israel's active hostility (that is, her hostility short of military actions in war) was the combination of Egyptian and Iraqi active hostility. The best explanation of Israel's military action was the combined military actions of Jordan, Egypt, and Syria. Egypt's active hostility was almost solely a function of Israel's hostility directed at Egypt, and the most powerful predictors of her military action was Israeli military action and her own military action in the previous period.

Since replication is one of the hallmarks of the scientific method of theory testing, Wilkenfeld later repeated his study using more refined techniques and discovered remarkably similar results. In each case the level of conflict received by a state was the crucial explanatory variable. Of course, conflict received could not totally explain *all* of a state's behavior. Virtually all the equations for the Arab states also indicated a significant carryover effect of past policy on future policy, though this was not at all important in determining Israeli policy. On the other hand, the effects of domestic conflict on the behavior of Middle Eastern states seemed rather minimal.[21]

Michael Ward has also used regression techniques to test the relative importance of bureaucratic inertia (which he calls short-term memory) and international interaction on a country's foreign behavior. He looked at five cases of long-term interaction from 1948 to 1977: U.S.-U.S.S.R., U.S.-France, U.S.-Japan, U.S.-Israel, and Israel–United Arab Republic. He concluded that bureaucratic inertia plays only a minor role in determining a state's behavior, while reaction to the behavior of others seems to be crucial. He discovered a reciprocal, action-reaction process in each of the five relationships: conflictual behavior by one state leads to conflictual behavior in another, and cooperative behavior by one begets cooperative behavior in others. Ward discovered, however, that the action-reaction process is not always symmetrical. For instance, he discovered that the Soviets reacted to U.S. conflict behavior twice as strongly as the United States did to Soviet conflict behavior.[22]

Empirical Evidence: Stimulus-Response and War

We have seen that the behavior of states is largely reciprocal. But can we find any more direct evidence that tough behavior leads to war initiation by one's rivals? In a study of twenty serious disputes in the present century, Leng and Hugh Wheeler discovered that the use of bullying tactics is associated with disputes that escalate to war, while the use of a reciprocating strategy is associated with the avoidance of war. In fact, a reciprocating strategy was found to be the only strategy able to successfully counter a bullying strategy. All attempts to counter bullying strategies with bullying led to war.[23] Leng's analysis of a sample of 14 serious bilateral disputes between 1850 and 1965 produced similar results. Although Leng found some support for the "realist" proposition that threats are (modestly) more successful than promises in gaining compliance, it was also true that the use of threats was a highly risky strategy. Weaker nations might occasionally be bullied into compliance, but when the states were evenly matched, the situation became much more dangerous. Negative inducements (threats) increased the probability of defiant responses, and this was particularly true between states with relatively even capabilities. Influence attempts that involve threats of military violence seemed to produce extreme responses—either abject compliance or counterthreats and punishments, which in turn were associated with war. There was no positive association between the frequency of the use of threats and the outbreak of war, but there was an association between defiant responses to threats and war.[24]

Leng and Gochman's investigation of thirty militarized dyadic disputes between 1816 and 1975 also produced some interesting results. They investigated the effects of three aspects of behavioral interaction in disputes: militarization of the dispute, escalation of the dispute, and the degree of reciprocity by the disputants. As predicted, conflict interactions characterized by a high degree of militarization, escalation, and reciprocity were the most likely to result in war. (Five of six such interactions ended in war.) Interaction characterized by low militarization, nonescalation, and low reciprocity—a pattern called "prudence"—were the least prone to war (zero of four). Generally speaking, when bargaining behavior is highly militarized and highly escalatory, the probability of war is high (eight of twelve), but when behavior is militarized but nonescalatory, war is less probable (three of nine).[25] Once again, the use of bullying strategies to deter or coerce an opponent appears to be a risky proposition.

Leng also discovers an interesting pattern that arises out of continued and repeated confrontations between pairs of states. He argues that statesmen tend to be guided by conservative "Realpolitik" assumptions about bargaining that prescribe strategies which demonstrate power and resolve. (It might be best to think of "Realpolitik assumptions" as an operational code or a world view.) Leaders with such a view tend to believe that failure in previous crises was due to insufficient demonstration of toughness, and therefore they adopt a more coercive strategy in the next confrontation with the rival than in the last crisis. On the other hand, the state that was victorious "learns" that bullying has worked and continues its past reliance on coercive interaction techniques. Thus, both states become locked into coercive strategies and the two rivals escalate the level of coercion in each successive encounter. Leng finds that war becomes likely by the third dispute (if it has not already occurred).[26]

Finally, we need to return to Choucri and North's study of the roots of World War I and their theory of lateral pressure—a topic we discussed at the nation-state level of analysis. Choucri and North's *Nations in Conflict* is a unique attempt to blend theories from the nation-state level with theories from the interaction level of analysis.[27] Before describing the portion of their analysis that is relevant to our discussion of the action-reaction theory, we should briefly review their theory of lateral pressure.

Choucri and North posit that the root cause of international conflict is the combination of rapid population growth and technological growth, which increases the demand of resources within the state. The search for resources leads the state to undertake an expansionary process beyond its own borders. This process of external expansion, which Choucri and North call lateral pressure, may be manifested in a variety of ways—including the expansion of trade or the acquisition of colonies.

This lateral pressure brings a state into conflict with other nations that are undergoing a similar process of growth and expansion. "Intersections" develop—areas where the lateral pressures of two or more nations overlap with each other, bringing competition and conflict. The more intense the competition between states, the greater the likelihood of war.

Here we begin to enter the realm of interaction processes. Once lateral pressure has placed states in competition with each other, they begin to respond to the actions of their rivals. Choucri and North single out the formation of alliances and arms buildups as important actions that may cause reciprocal behaviors by the other side. Additionally, violence by one side will lead to violence by the other. War may be the result. Schematically, Choucri and North's ideas can be illustrated by Figure 6.1, which indicates the hypothesized links between the variables in their theory.

The theory was tested using data for the six major European nations beginning in 1871 and ending with the outbreak World War I in 1914. Statistical analysis led Choucri and North to conclude that war (violence behavior) has a number of different roots and can be reached by following several different paths. One pattern seems particularly strong. Colonial expansion is stimulated by population growth and by technological advance. Colonial expansion generally leads to increased intensity of intersection as the national interests of various countries begin to conflict over colonial area.

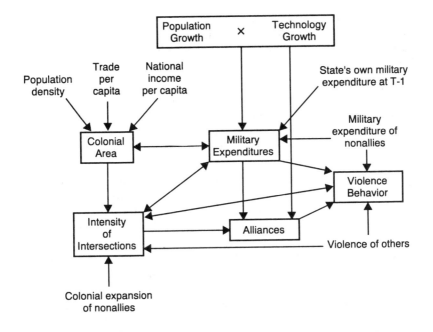

Figure 6–1. Choucri and North's Conceptual Model.

Source: Adapted from Nazli Choucri and Robert C. North, *Nations in Conflict: National Growth and International Violence* (San Fransisco: W. H. Freeman, 1975), p. 245

Simultaneously, military buildups (and, to some extent, alliances) are also stimulated by population and technological growth and by the incremental momentum present in defense bureaucracies. The growth of a nation's defense capabilities (its military expenditures and its alliances) then evokes hostile behavior from other nations, and the violence of others evokes further violence. Thus, Choucri and North conclude that although violence has its roots in the domestic, socioeconomic process of growth, it is primarily a reactive process; violence is for the most part a response to external factors such as the military expenditures of other states and the hostile behavior of other states.[28]

Stimulus-Response: Summary

Although these studies of the conflict interaction process that we have just discussed constitute impressive evidence of the validity of the stimulus-response theory, they have not gone unchallenged by conflicting evidence. Three studies of conflict interaction have often been cited as producing evidence contrary to that presented above. Each study was designed to explicitly test the relative potency of the stimulus-response model versus the bureaucratic inertia model (hypothesizing that a nation's present policy is based primarily on its past policy). Raymond Tanter's study of NATO–Warsaw Pact interaction in the Berlin Crisis of 1961 and Duncan and Siverson's analysis of Sino-Indian interaction between 1959 and 1964 provide only modest support for either model, but conclude that of the two, the stimulus-response model is the weaker.[29] Gordon Hilton's analysis of pre–World War I interaction shows that previous hostility expressed is the strongest factor in determining a country's subsequent expression of hostility.[30]

Despite these dissenting studies, we seem to have rather uniform support for the stimulus-response theory of conflict. A sizable accumulation of evidence supports the notion that countries seem to act the way they are treated. Most of the time they reciprocate the behavior of others. Hostile behavior received leads to hostile behavior sent. Cooperative behavior received leads to cooperative behavior sent. Just as important, when the causal effect of other states' behavior is examined in conjunction with other potential influences, the former are fairly consistently found to be more powerful than the latter.[31] Not only does the evidence strongly support the proposition that the behavior of states conforms generally to the norm of reciprocity, it also strongly suggests that war is derived from the reaction of one state to the hostile and belligerent actions of another.

It would seem that any comprehensive theory of interstate war would have to take these findings into account. While there may be many paths to war, the path of reciprocal escalation of hostilities by states pursuing "bullying" tactics appears to be an important piece of the theoretical puzzle. Let us now explore a different aspect of the stimulus-response theory—arms races.

Arms Races

Arms races have been identified by many as a particular class of international behavior that exhibits an action-reaction pattern. The concept of an arms race is one of those slippery terms like power; everyone seems to have his or her own definition of the term. One of the most quoted definitions is that of Samuel Huntington, who has defined an arms race as "a progressive, competitive peacetime increase in armaments by two states or coalitions of states resulting from conflicting purposes and mutual fears."[32] Even though the exact wording of definitions varies tremendously when other authors are consulted, several common elements in definitions can be identified:

1. Arms races develop out of a conscious awareness by each nation of the dependence of its own arms policies on those of another nation. They

result from external, competitive impulses. The arms buildups of two nations are simultaneous and interdependent.

2. Arms races consist of rapid increases in arms accumulation which constitute an "abnormal" rate of growth in military procurement.

3. Arms races are best thought of as occurring in times of peace; arms accumulations during war do not count.

4. The weapons involved in the arms race are designed to combat each other in some way. They are either similar (tanks versus tanks) or they are complementary (anti-tank weapons versus tanks).

Do Arms Races Follow a Stimulus-Response Pattern of Interaction?

Several attempts have been undertaken to determine to what extent arms races are in fact propelled by an interactive, stimulus-response process. The most famous formulation is that of Lewis Richardson, who surmised that the rate of change in any nation's increase in arms was a function of several factors: (1) the opponent's level of military strength, (2) a state's own willingness to accumulate arms because of its opponent's strength and his fear of that strength, (3) the negative factors of fatigue and cost involved in increasing one's arms levels, and (4) the general level of grievance against the opponent—a kind of hostility or revenge factor. Richardson then constructed a mathematical formula (model) based on these factors.[33] Although the military policies of other nations are not the only determinant of a state's decision to accumulate arms, Richardson's formula nevertheless suggests that the rate at which a state's arms procurement increases is to a large extent dependent on the actions of rivals.

Richardson's own analysis of nineteenth- and twentieth-century defense spending data concluded that military spending tended greatly to be a reciprocal process. Oddly enough, efforts to reproduce Richardson's findings have met with only meager success. Indeed, there seems to be a large amount of evidence that nations involved in mutual arms buildups are not reacting primarily to the behavior of others. Increases in military outlays on one side don't necessarily lead to increases on the other.

A variety of studies suggest that, contrary to popular opinion, neither Soviet nor American arms accumulations in the post–World War II era can be characterized as an action-reaction phenomenon.[34] Indeed, some even question whether the term "arms race" can even be applied to the Soviet and American arms accumulation processes. While both superpowers certainly sustained long-term military buildups in the postwar years, neither buildup represented really "abnormal" rates of growth in military spending.[35] Additional research indicates that not only are Soviet and American arms build-ups not interactive, but neither is the Chinese arms buildup.[36]

Several statistical studies of the military buildups of the two superpowers and their allies in the post–World War II era suggest that bureaucratic momentum (as indicated by past levels of military spending) and other domestic processes have a greater impact on a country's level of weapons spending than does the military expenditure of its rivals. For instance, Rattinger finds this to be true of arms procurements of NATO and Warsaw Pact countries in the 1950s and 1960s. This conclusion is supported by several studies of American and Soviet arms policies.[37]

Choucri and North investigated the arms races between various European states as part of their comprehensive analysis of the long-terms causes of World War I.[38] They hypothesized that several factors might plausibly be related to a nation's military expenditure decisions. First, the general socio-economic dynamics of population and technological growth might play a role. Arms expenditures might be a function of the overall growth rate of a nation. Second, a state's own military expenditures in the preceding time period might play a role. This would provide evidence of another domestic factor at work—bureaucratic momentum. Third, a state's colonial expansion and its intersections with other nations' colonial interests might have effects on military expenditures. As a nation expands its activities outward and becomes involved in international trade and in the development of a colonial empire, it would need a larger military presence to protect its new colonial territory and its sea lanes. Finally, military expenditures could be a function of the military expenditures of one's rivals. Thus, Choucri and North include in their analysis both internal and external factors. Their test produced interesting, but mixed, results. (What did you expect?)

The authors reviewed specifically the Anglo-German naval race of 1871–1914, in part, to see whether Richardson's interactive process was in effect. The judgment of historians seemed to affirm that it was. German colonial expansion had created a desire for a larger merchant marine and navy, and German leaders considered a strong navy to be essential for the defense of its colonies and its international commerce.[39] The German navy was to be constructed in specific relation to that of the British. Admiral Tirpitz's "Risk Policy" consisted of trying to build a German navy which—although numerically smaller than the British fleet—would be sizable enough to present a risk to the British navy. The British would be deterred from an attack on Germany by the knowledge that an Anglo-German naval confrontation would pose the risk that a severely weakened (though victorious) British fleet might fall prey to a hostile third power. On the other hand, British policy had consistently been one of building and maintaining naval superiority. Her arms accumulation strategy was based on the rule that the British navy ought to be superior to any two powers combined and have a

10% margin for safety. The policies of both states clearly mandated a close watch on the building programs of rivals.

There is much historical evidence that British leaders perceived the German naval buildup as a threat, and we know that both German and British leaders watched each other's buildup closely. Indeed, in the years prior to the outreak of the war, Winston Churchill, as First Lord of the Admiralty, repeatedly quoted the most recent German Naval Law to Parliament to justify British naval procurements. Britain's yearly naval construction was thus in part dictated by German building.[40] France and Russia were also extremely interested in Germany's military buildup, and the reverse was equally true.

The question was to what extent these trends in military growth could be accounted for by domestic factors and to what extent by external, interaction factors. Choucri and North discovered that Germany's buildup from 1871 to 1914 could be explained much more effectively by internal processes such as population and technological growth and by bureaucratic momentum in arms procurement than by the action-reaction process. This was also true for Britain in the period between 1871 and 1890, but not for the 1890–1914 period. By 1890 Britain seemed to become much more responsive to German moves, though military expansion continued to be influenced by bureaucratic factors. A shift in the dynamics of British arms procurements had apparently taken place as the arms race heated up and as general hostility increased.

Additionally, French, Russian, and (especially) Italian military expenditures seemed to be accounted for primarily by domestic factors. The authors report that each nation's military spending at time T-1 (the bureaucratic momentum factor) was a major factor in determining the level of arms expenditure. Arms buildups (we may or may not be able to call them arms races) seem to have internal roots.[41] Choucri and North conclude:

> The primary importance of domestic factors . . . does not preclude the reality of arms competition. Two countries whose military establishments are expanding largely for domestic reasons can, and indeed almost certainly will, become acutely aware of each other's spending. Thereafter, although spending may continue to be powerfully influenced by domestic factors, deliberate military competition may increase and even take the form of an arms race (although the race may be over specific military features and may be a very small portion of total military spending).[42]

We should probably not be too surprised at these findings that arms races are more strongly influenced by domestic factors than by interaction with rivals. Arms expenditures would seem to be perfect candidates for government decisions arrived at through bureaucratic and incremental processes. They are long-term, noncrisis, budgetary decisions that ordinarily involve a large number of interested domestic actors—especially in Western democratic countries: legislators, political officials in the executive branch, civilian defense officials, military officers in various rival services, manufacturers of weapons and their subcontractors, citizens groups, and so on. Political leaders may be aware of military procurement increases in a rival country, but this awareness must be filtered through a vast web of domestic constituencies before the final decision is made.

Lloyd Jensen has suggested several reasons why action-reaction models of arms races do not adequately explain real-world decisions to accumulate arms. First, arms expenditures are subject to severe domestic pressures emanating from the military-industrial complex. Second, there is probably a tendency for arms races to reflect past spending levels because of the general tendency of military programs to expand in order to absorb whatever dollars are available. For instance, the end of the war in Vietnam did not produce a decrease in U.S. military spending, but instead facilitated the continuation of huge military budgets in peacetime. Third, defense spending may be less than responsive to military programs of rivals because of misperception and miscalculation of the rival's capabilities and intentions. Fourth, in the real world a nation's arms decisions are made not on the basis of simple bilateral relations, but on the basis of third-party military threats as well. Fifth, it may be that lowered arms levels by rivals actually increase the incentive for a state to add to its military capabilities instead of the reverse.[43]

It might be added that a final reason why researchers have failed to validate an action-reaction process for arms races may be methodological. By concentrating on total yearly defense budgets, researchers may not be adequately capturing the arms race phenomenon that is taking place in the development and deployment of particular weapons systems.[44] A state may greatly increase the size of its army (or its supply of particular weapons) in response to developments on the other side, but the effect of this action on the overall defense budget may not be noticeable. If, for instance, the United States races with the U.S.S.R. in the buildup of atomic warheads and simultaneously reduces its troop levels, the overall effect on the defense budget is likely to be a net decrease—even though an intense race is taking place in particular sector of the total defense program. This actually happened in the 1950s as the United States rearranged its defense priorities in order to get "more bang for the buck." It is quite possible, then, that the failure to discover evidence of an interactive U.S.-Soviet arms race is due to the use of yearly defense budget figures as indicators of a buildup rather than the actual accumulation of arms themselves. Indeed, Michael Don Ward demonstrates that when data on actual military stockpiless are included in the arms race equation along with figures for defense expenditures, the U.S.-Soviet arms race appears much more reactive.[45]

Arms Races and War: Theory

So far we have been discussing the arms accumulation process, but we have not mentioned war. One of the reasons that there has been so much study of arms races is the belief that arms races somehow play a role in the outbreak of war. If arms races are seen as one manifestation of a generally hostile and reciprocal interaction process between nations (or coalitions), then it is reasonable to assume that arms races may accelerate and intensify the conflict spiral and eventually lead to war. Let us examine the connection between arms races and war in more detail.

The hypothesis that arms races are positively related to war can be derived deductively from the general stimulus-response theory of conflict. If it is true that nations act toward others as they are treated, and if it is true that an arms buildup by one side is seen as a sign of hostility by rival states, then we can expect nations to reciprocate this hostility with hostile actions of their own—not just with the accumulation of more weapons, but with other kinds of hostile actions as well. Thus, an arms buildup by one side should lead to increased hostility by the other. As we have seen, it is possible for this general conflict interaction to increase in intensity and "get out of hand." The *conflict spiral* might end in war. This, of course, leads to the conclusion that a rapid accumulation of arms might lead not to greater security for a country, but to increased hostile activity by rivals. This would seem to flatly contradict the ancient maxim attributed to the Roman military writer, Flavius Vegetius Renatus, "Si vis pacem, para bellum," if you desire peace, prepare for war. We will have more to say about this later.

A classic article by Samuel Huntington attempted to discover just how often arms races have led to war and under what circumstances.[46] It seemed clear to Huntington that while some arms races ended in war, not all did. Arms races could also end in an informal mutual agreement to call off the competition or in a "victory" for one state over the other. The question therefore becomes: under what circumstances are these alternatives likely to occur?

Huntington suggested that a crucial point may come in the early phases of an arms race. After the challenger makes its initial move to alter the military status quo, the challenged state may choose one of several possible responses. First, it might seek a diplomatic counterbalance through an alliance with a third state or through an arms treaty with the challenger. Second, it might increase its own level of arms—setting the stage perhaps for a series of interdependent arms increases by both sides. Third, it might attempt a preemptive military action while still relatively strong, attacking the challenger while the balance of power is still in its favor. Fourth, the challenged state may take no immediate action. The challenger thereby achieves its goal. If the challenged state then makes a belated, last-ditch effort to catch up and redress the balance of power, war may result from the challenger's reaction.

Thus, Huntington argues that there are two danger points that occur at the beginning of an arms race. The first point is the response of the challenged state to the initial increase in arms of the challenger. The second point is the reaction of the challenger (which has been initially successful in its goal) to the frantic and belated efforts of the challenged state to retrieve its former position. Huntington offers as an example of the first danger point the Israeli decision to attack Egypt in 1956 after that nation had been supplied with Soviet bloc weapons. Huntington argues that the French (and British) reaction to German rearmament in the 1930s constituties a good example of the second pattern. Although the French defense budget remained fairly constant between 1933 and 1936, and then increased somewhat in the next two years, the real reaction didn't begin until 1939 when France proposed to spend more on arms than in the last five years combined![47] By the end of the year France and Germany were at war. Huntington concludes that the likelihood of war increases just prior to a change in the military superiority. At this point there would seem to be both great uncertainty and tremendous instability.

The good news is that the probability of war varies inversely with the length of the arms race. Huntington contends that as an arms race continues, the interaction pattern between the states tends to become more predictable, more stable and regularized. A situation of "dynamic equilibrium" is produced. Each state continues to increase its arms, but the relative balance remains the same. The two nations will probably by this time have come to a tacit, mutual understanding, in which both accept the relative balance. Huntington concludes that a sustained arms race is much more likely to have a peaceful ending than a bloody one.[48]

As one critic points out, much of Huntington's argument about the relative dangers of short- and long-term arms races depends on his initial selection of arms races and the determination of their length.[49] For instance, Huntington decides that the Anglo-German naval race ended in 1912 (with German acceptance of inferiority). If we instead place the end of the arms race two years forward in time, to 1914, it becomes a prime example of a lengthy (sixteen-year) arms race that ends in war instead of peace!

Another factor that Huntington identifies as important is whether the arms race is qualitative or quantitative. The latter appears to him to be much more dangerous. A *quantitative arms race* refers to the addition of larger numbers of men and weapons to one's military machine. In such an arms race superiority is likely—owing to unequal resources and determination. Thus, quantitative races tend to be settled one way or another. Huntington argues that quantitative races impose greater and greater burdens on those nations involved in them. Meanwhile, governments must mobilize popular support for the sacrifices required by an arms buildup, generating in the process suspicion, fear, and hostility toward the potential opponent.

> Eventually a time is reached when the increasing costs and tensions of a continued arms race seem worse than the costs and the risks of war. Public opinion once aroused can't be quieted. . . . Prolonged sufficiently, a quantitative race must necessarily reach a point where opinion in one country or the other will demand that it be ended, if not by negotiation, then by war.[50]

This does not exactly square with his earlier proposition that the probability of war varies inversely with the length of the arms race, but it may explain why some long arms races end in war.

On the other hand, *qualitative arms races*—races involving decisions to introduce new weapons systems through technological innovation—involve less risk of war, according to Huntington. Unlike quantitative races, they do not necessarily increase arms budgets. They represent a competition of elite technicians in weapons laboratories, not a competition of masses, and therefore impose no great burden on the general public. Additionally, qualitative races tend toward equality, owing to the tendency for simultaneous invention of parallel military technology. Historically, technological breakthroughs in military weaponry have not resulted in a lasting edge for the innovator.[51] Qualitative arms races are therefore more stable and thus more peaceful than quantitative races.

One might wish to add to Huntington's general argument about the relative stability of qualitative arms races a certain qualification. It would appear that a danger point is reached when a qualitative jump in weaponry is about to be made by a challenger. Frequently, the challenged state will not wish the challenger to cross a certain *qualitative threshold*. This threshold may be nuclear weapons, chemical or biological weapons, or some other category of weapons. But at the point at which the challenger is perceived to be about to cross that particular threshold, a resort to arms is sometimes contemplated.

In September 1969, as the Chinese had completed several nuclear tests, and as they were preparing to launch their first earth satellite (demonstrating their ability to deliver nuclear weapons with ballistic missiles), the Soviet Union apparently considered the possibility of a preemptive surgical strike on Chinese nuclear installations.[52] When it appeared that the Libyan government was nearing completion of a chemical weapons plant in late 1988, the U.S. government contemplated military action to destroy this capability.[53] When the Osirak nuclear research reactor neared completion, providing Iraq with the possibility of making weapons-grade plutonium, the Israeli government undertook an air strike to destroy this facility. And certainly Iraq's continued search for nuclear weapons technologies was a factor in the decision by the Bush administration to send U.S. forces to liberate Kuwait from Iraqi control in 1991. Thus, it would appear that the breakthrough phase of a qualitative arms race is just as dangerous as the early phase of a quantitative arms race.

Arms Races and War: Empirical Evidence

Numerous statistical studies have addressed the relationship between arms races and war. The results offer mixed results, as usual. In a much-reported study, Michael Wallace used Correlates of War Project data to investigate great power disputes between 1816 and 1965. His research question was this: "Do serious disputes between nations engaged in an arms race have a significantly greater probability of resulting in all-out war than those between nations exhibiting normal patterns of military competition?"[54] Having identified almost 100 instances of serious disputes between pairs of major powers, he found only twenty-six disputes that resulted in full-scale war. Of these twenty-six wars, twenty-three were preceded by arms races. Of the seventy-three disputes that did not lead to war, only five were preceded by arms races. Wallace concludes that the presence or absence of an arms race between rival nations correctly predicted war (or no war) in over 90% of the disputes.[55] Arms races seemed to make a substantial difference in whether a dispute escalated into war or not.

It should be recognized that Wallace did not address head-on the question of whether arms races cause wars; instead, he was investigating a somewhat narrower proposition, which has been called the *tinderbox hypothesis*. The tinderbox hypothesis suggests that while arms races don't necessarily lead to wars directly, they may play an important intervening role in the escalation of disputes to war. That is, arms races do not directly initiate conflagrations, but they do create a flammable condition between racing states in which a small spark that settles down in an atmosphere of preexisting tension and hostility might ignite a firestorm.

Wallace's methods have been attacked, however, as loading the dice in favor of his hypothesis. Several researchers have taken issue with Wallace's arms race index, the device he uses to determine whether the level of arms expenditure in a pair of nations was great enough to conclude that an arms race was in fact present. The index is obtained by multiplying the arms expenditure scores of two nations together. Thus, it is possible for one nation to have a very high arms score and the second nation to have a moderately low score and the product be high enough to determine that the pair was in an arms race. This means that some arms races identified by Wallace were not really *mutual* races but situations where only one state was actually rapidly increasing its defense expenditures.[56]

Altfeld reanalyzes Wallace's data using a stricter standard for the presence of arms races. He finds that all arms races thus categorized led to war! On the other hand, many other wars broke out without being preceded by arms races.[57]

A second problem is that Wallace chose to treat all arms races and all wars as dyadic (bilateral). This meant that instead of having World War I represented by a single case it was represented by nine disputes, and instead of World War II being represented by two cases it was represented by seven disputes. Overall, twenty-six distinct wars were created where only seven or eight integrated wars occurred.[58] The effect of this was to vastly overemphasize the statistical importance of the arms races that preceded the two world wars in the twentieth century. To correct this problem, Erich Weede reconstructed Wallace's table, but grouped together all dyads that resulted in a single war (while keeping the European and Pacific theaters of World War II separate). This weakens the association between arms races and wars somewhat, but the percent of arms races that escalate to war is still 55%, while the percent of disputes not involving arms races that escalate to war is only 3%.[59]

Further refinements, however, have led to a further weakening of Wallace's original results. Paul Diehl also retested Wallace's work using stricter assumptions and conditions. He devised a new arms race index based on the average rate of change in defense expenditures; he required arms races to consist of mutual buildups in which both sides increase their expenditures at a rate of 8% or more for three years; and he treated disputes as multilateral rather than bilateral where this corresponded to reality. After reanalyzing

Table 6–3.
A Comparison of the Relationship Between Arms Races and Wars

	Wallace '79		Weede '80		Wallace '82		Diehl '83		Altfeld '83	
	War	No war	War	No war	War	No war	War	No War	War	No war
Arms race	23	3	6	5	11	2	3	9	11	0
No arms race	5	68	2	68	4	63	10	64	15	73

Sources: Wallace, "Arms Races and Escalation," *Journal of Conflict Resolution* 23 (1) (March 1979), p. 15. Weede, "Arms Races and Escalation: Some persisting Doubts," *Journal of Conflict Resolution* 24 (2), (June 1980), p. 286. Wallace, "Armaments and Escalation: Two Competing Hypotheses," *International Studies Quarterly* 26 (1), (March 1982), p. 46. Diehl, "Arms Races and Escalation: A Closer Look," *Journal of Peace Research* 20 (3), 1983, p. 208. Altfeld, "Arms Races?—and Escalation?: A Comment on Wallace," *International Studies Quarterly* 27 (2), (June 1983), p. 226.

Wallace's data, he concluded that no meaningful covariation existed between arms races and war. The presence or absence of an arms race had no effect on the presence or absence of war.[60] Table 6.3 illustrates the findings of these researchers.

Most analysts agree that not even a majority of arms race disputes lead to war. Using data from six different collections, James Morrow produces a list of thirty-five Great Power disputes in the nineteenth and twentieth centuries that were preceded by mutual military buildups. Of the seventeen disputes that were found in all six data sets, only four ended in war (and only five of the total thirty-five).[61]

That arms races have been a preliminary to war is clear. The major wars of our century—World Wars I and II—have each been preceded by arms races. But just as clearly, many wars have not been preceded by such mutual arms buildups, and many arms races never end in war.[62] Just how many wars are preceded by arms races depends on the operational criteria one uses to determine their existence. We must conclude that while the final evidence is not yet in, it is likely that arms races play only a modest, subsidiary role in the general causation of war. As one analyst put it: "Disputes preceded by arms races do escalate to war more often than other disputes, but they do not overwhelmingly escalate to war."[63] They are neither a necessary nor a sufficient condition for the outbreak of hostilities. Nevertheless, it is probably true that arms races do make it somewhat more likely that a serious dispute will escalate to war.

Since some arms races lead to war and some do not, it is appropriate that we ask (as Huntington did) what kind of arms races are most likely to lead to war and under what conditions. As Morrow suggests, some tinderboxes are more flammable than others.[64] There has been some research on these topics, but the answers are far from clear.[65] Several rival theses have been developed. Arms races lead to war: (a) if the arms race leads to a change in the dyadic balance of power, (b) if a "revolutionary" power is winning the arms race, rather than a "status quo" power, (c) if the arms race is unable to attain an equilibrium.

Using expected utility theory to analyze a nation's motivation for war, James Morrow argues that arms races that simply lead to the continuous matching of a rival's capabilities do not alter the relative balance of capabilities and thus do not change either's calculations of the probability of success in war. Most arms races, however, result in neither continuous nor instantaneous equilibria. Different rates of arming result in temporary swings in the relative balance. When a state holds a temporary military advantage, its calculations about probable success in war are favorably altered, and it is at this point that disputes are most likely to escalate to overt conflict. The larger the swing in military superiority, the greater the likelihood of war. Fighting a war becomes more attractive—at least momentarily, since this "window of opportunity" will most likely close later as the rival catches up. Using data from seventeen cases from the nineteenth and twentieth centuries in which major power disputes were preceded by military buildups, Morrow confirms that escalation of disputes to war becomes more likely as the "amplitude" of the arms race increases.[66]

Research by other scholars seems to point in the same direction. Paul Diehl looks at arms races in twenty-two enduring Great Power rivalries between 1816 and 1976. He finds that war occurs rather late in these rivalries, usually after two prior militarized disputes. He concludes that military buildups have little direct effect on the escalation of rivalries to war, but that they were dangerous under two conditions: (a) the buildup is unilateral or asymmetrical and (b) the buildup leads to a power shift toward parity (in the nineteenth century) or toward military preponderance (in the twentieth century).[67]

Writers in the realist tradition argue that arms races are dangerous when they lead to a change in the relative balance of military power between rivals, but that this is not the complete story. What is most important is which states are being relatively advantaged or disadvantaged by this shift. The presumption is that the most dangerous situation occurs if the shift in power is in favor of a *revisionsist state* that is dissatisfied with the current international system and is to the detriment of a *status quo state*—an idea similar to the power transition theory, which we will discuss in Chapter 8. Wallace finds, however, that neither gains in the relative balance by revisionist states nor revisionist state and superiority in the balance is related to the outbreak of war.[68]

Another contender for the title of the most war-prone class of arms race comes from the father of arms race theory, Lewis Fry Richardson. In Richardson's formulation, "unstable" races—those that fail to reach a point of stability where no further changes take place but instead exhibit greater and greater activity and tend toward ever-increasing arms expenditures without meaningful restraint—were most likely to exacerbate international tension and incite violence.[69] Theresa Clair Smith uses data from major and minor power arms races to investigate the presumed relationship between unstable arms races and war. Her results suggest that unstable races are indeed more prone to war than stable races. Of particular interest is the finding that arms races that begin intensely tend to quickly reach political and economic limits, and thus level off, reaching a stable (and peaceful) equilibrium. On the other hand, races that begin slowly have a tendency to intensify over time and escalate to war.[70] These findings are almost diametrically opposed to Huntington's earlier contention that the longer an arms race, the greater the chance that it will end in peace.

Thus, the available (though meager) evidence suggests that long-term arms races that have unstable or asymmetrical characteristics tend to be most likely to end in war. This makes a great deal of intuitive sense. In these races temporary swings in arms accumulation take place that grant to one side or the other an advantage which had not previously existed. The arms race "leader" now has a temporary advantage that permits it to contemplate military actions. For the "loser," the military gap that has recently opened may engender a new and profound fear of the opponent. Under these conditions, either state might consider taking more extreme actions.

In conclusion, a more fundamental question needs to be asked: Do arms races lead to war? Or do expectations of war lead to arms races? It may be that men do not fight because they have arms, but rather they have arms because they believe it is necessary to fight. These questions imply that arms races ought not to be considered as root causes of war, but rather as manifestations of other underlying causes of war.[71] Arms races increase the chance of war simply because they increase the amount of tension and hostility and the perceptions of threat that probably already exist between nations. To be fair, of course, stimulus-response theory does not argue that arms races are root causes of war, only that they are part of an overall environment of reciprocated tension and hostility between nations and that they play a role in the more general conflict escalation process which leads to war.

Implications for Policy: The Security Dilemma

In summary, we can conclude that a large array of scientific studies provide evidence to support a stimulus-response theory of international conflict. Whether it is Soviet-American relations or NATO-WTO interaction, whether it is countries in the Middle East or Asia, similar patterns of interaction have been found. Nations seem to respond to others in the same manner as they are treated. Cooperation begets cooperation; hostility begets hostility. As the level of hostility escalates, conflict spirals develop that may eventuate in war. Arms races may be an important factor in the escalation of this action-reaction pattern toward war, although the evidence is less clear on this point.

Before continuing, we ought to contemplate the implications this theory has for conflict and cooperation in the real world. If the stimulus-response theory of conflict is true, it provides a clear, unambiguous challenge to some strongly held ideas of international relations. One of these is the notion that security lies in strength and that the best way to ensure peace is to prepare for war. (This idea and those associated with it have been referred to as the conservative or "realist" view of international relations.) Related to this notion is the belief that other nations will back down from the pursuit of their interests when faced with threats. Saber rattling will deter aggression and bring peace. Conversely, conciliatory acts will have the effect of leading one's rivals to believe that you will not defend your interests. Conservatives draw on the "Munich analogy" here, arguing that the appeasement policies of

France and Britain in the 1930s merely whetted Hitler's appetite for more territory and convinced him the West would not fight. It is argued that a policy of threats backed up by strong actions would have kept Hitler in his place. Conservatives then generalize from this experience and apply the "lesson of Munich"—never appease an opponent—to international politics in general. (We will pick up on this theme in the next chapter when we examine deterrence theory.)

The fly in the ointment is that if the stimulus-response theory is correct, then threats, bullying behavior, and arms buildups by nation A will produce parallel behavior by nation B. Saber rattling may scare the other side, but not into backing down.

Robert Jervis suggests that the central theme of international relations is not evil, but tragedy.[72] The tragedy revolves around what political scientists call the *security dilemma*. The dilemma is that in seeking to enhance its own security a nation takes actions that unwittingly stimulate in its rival exactly the kind of behavior it wanted to prevent. Attempts to create greater security for oneself may, unfortunately, result in even less security. The defense policies of nations are interdependent; greater security for one nation may mean relatively less security for others. The problem, as Jervis puts it, is that "most means of self-protection simultaneously menace others."[73] He explains as follows:

> When states seek the ability to defend themselves, they get too much and too little—too much because they gain the ability to carry out aggression; too little because others, being menaced, will increase their own arms and so reduce the first state's security. Unless the requirements for offense and defense differ in kind or amount, a status quo power will desire a military posture that resembles that of an aggressor. For this reason others cannot infer from its military forces and preparations whether the state is aggressive. States therefore tend to assume the worst.[74]

The result of attempts by each state to create greater security for itself is that no one is more secure. Indeed, the result may be a spiral of ever-increasing levels of belligerence as nations try to respond to the prior actions of others. Eventually, this attempt to gain greater security may end in war. The French philosopher Rousseau long ago explained the tragic logic of this unfortunate train of events:

> It is quite true that it would be much better for all men to remain always at peace. But so long as there is no security for this, everyone, having no guarantee that he can avoid war, is anxious to begin it at the moment which suits his own interest and so forestall a neighbor . . . so that many wars, even offensive wars, are rather in the nature of unjust precautions for the protection of the assailant's own possessions than a device for seizing those of others.[75]

Notice that Rousseau (and the advocates of the stimulus-response model) are in a sense describing a kind of "no fault war." No state desires war, and none seeks territorial gains; the chief motivation is not self-aggrandizement but fear. Nations initiate wars because they believe others will soon begin them, and in such circumstances prudence requires that the best defense is a good offense. A sequence of hostile actions and reactions among nations convinces each of the hostile intentions of its rivals; the *conflict spiral* increases in intensity as each responds to the provocations of the other. At some point the threshold of military combat is crossed and war breaks out. No one wanted it. No state can be blamed as having started it. No one is more responsible than any other. It just happened!

Implications for Policy: GRIT

The implications of stimulus-response theory, the conflict spiral, and the security dilemma are fairly obvious. A clear-cut strategy for peace can be derived logically from them. If war is the result of an reactive process that spirals upward, then it is necessary to intervene in some way in the conflict process to reverse the escalatory spiral. While the bad news is that aggression, violence, and hostility and reciprocated by others, the good news is that so are cooperative and conciliatory actions. All that is required is for one nation to take the initiative. Instead of returning an eye for an eye, it must turn its cheek and even act charitably toward its antagonist.

Charles Osgood devised just such a strategy for reducing the hostility that existed between the United States and Soviet Union. He calls his strategy GRIT—graduated and reciprocated initiatives in tension reduction.[76] Osgood suggests that unilateral actions, coupled with clear verbal statements, can be used to initiate a reciprocal deescalatory spiral. By communicating through deeds as well as words, states can learn mutual trust and can reduce the level of tension and hostility that exists between them. Osgood offers several guidelines for the application of this strategy.[77]

1. All unilateral actions should be announced publicly prior to their execution and should be specifically identified as part of a deliberate policy of reducing tensions. This enlists world public opinion and augments pressure for reciprocation.

2. The announcement should clearly state an explicit invitation to the rival to reciprocate the initial action with a unilateral response of his own choosing. Reciprocity need not be in the same form as the original act or equal in quantity, but it must be made clear that some form of reciprocity is expected.

3. In order to convey a real commitment to the reduction of tension,

unilateral actions that have been announced must be executed on schedule even if the rival does not immediately signal a willingness to reciprocate.

4. Unilateral actions should be in the form of overt deeds rather than positive or negative sanctions. While sanctions are contingent on some prior action of others, Osgood prefers that GRIT actions be deeds that are immediate rather than contingent. The actions should be visible, unambiguous, and clearly verifiable. Overt actions are in this sense also better than nonactions such as test bans.

5. Unilateral actions should be planned and arranged in a graduated series—from least important (and least risky) to most important (and most risky). Osgood suggests that unilateral actions should start out on a small scale and progress from there. As the initator's actions are reciprocated, more far-reaching policy actions can be contemplated.

6. It is probably best to begin GRIT with actions that are not in the military/disarmament sphere, but move to these areas later in the process after trust has been built up through reciprocating actions in other areas. Initially, unilateral actions should be designed not to reduce a nation's ability to deter aggression. GRIT should not involve taking risks that would leave the nation vulnerable to its enemies. The lower the reciprocity, the less risky the actions that should be contemplated.

7. Unilateral actions should be diversified so as not to weaken a nation in any one sphere. Tension reduction can be cumulative over a range of actions in different fields: economic, diplomatic, cultural, and military.

8. Unilateral actions should be continued over a considerable period of time regardless of immediate reciprocity or the lack thereof. In the early phases of the strategy, reciprocation may not be forthcoming, but it is important to continue on one's schedule of unilateral, tension-reducing actions nevertheless. This is necessary because one's initial acts may be regarded by the rival as mere tricks or ploys for purposes of propaganda. The genuineness of the acts and the intention of the initiator will become certain to the rival only over a period of time. In essence, GRIT entails a learning process. The initiator must teach his rival that he really wants cooperation and he must provide an environment in which this message can be learned. On the other hand, the rival will eventually have to teach the initator that he, too, is interested in cooperation rather than taking advanatage of the initiator's acts of generosity.

9. If "encroachment" occurs (that is, if the rival takes advantage of your unilateral concessions to do you harm), it must be resisted firmly. The resistance should be targeted exclusively in the area of the encroachment; tension-reducing moves should be continued in other areas. In other words, there should be no linkage between an isolated incident of "bad behavior" in one area and continued progress in another area.

10. GRIT is a flexible, self-regulating policy. The two sides constantly monitor each other's actions and communicate through deeds. If reciprocity

is not attained, the policy can eventually be abandoned without harm to the initiator.

GRIT: Evaluation

The major problem in implementing GRIT seems to be in initiating the first move. Unilateral concessions are about as popular with world leaders as blind dates are with undergraduates. In both cases a tremendous amount of courage is required to take the first step. Once a nation has undertaken a GRIT policy, however, there are some fairly powerful inducements for its rival to play along. GRIT will, of course, be a very controversial policy within the initiating country. The only way to contain the domestic opposition will be to attain success—the quicker the better. Leaders in the rival states will, of course, understand that if they fail to reciprocate, they risk strengthening domestic forces in the initiating state that are more antagonistic toward them. The two sides are therefore mutually dependent on each other for success.

A second type of problem with GRIT should also be identified. A policy based on GRIT requires a tad more flexibility and maneuverability in policy making than most governments can muster. Domestic considerations and the vicissitudes of factional, organizational, and bureaucratic politics may place serious limits on the abilities of governments to pursue a GRIT strategy.[78]

Your reaction to GRIT may be that it is a rather risky experiment designed to test a hair-brained, academic theory of international relations using the real world as a giant laboratory. Clearly, leaders should not subject their citizens to dangerous experiments, but experiments per se cannot be entirely avoided. In a sense, all government policies are experiments based on implicit theories of how the world works.

Obviously, a test of GRIT in the real world would be difficult to arrange. Tests of GRIT have occurred primarily through simulation and gaming. For instance, experimental gaming studies carried out by a team of psychologists led by Svenn Lindskold at Ohio University have concluded that GRIT is an effective strategy for fostering trust and cooperation. Furthermore, GRIT is effective in inducing cooperation for both men and women, for both individuals and groups, whether the choices are made sequentially or simultaneously.[79]

One real-world situation is frequently referred to as an example of a GRIT-like approach to international relations. The so-called "Kennedy experiment" began in June 1963 when President Kennedy announced a unilateral ending to nuclear tests in the atmosphere, stating that the United States would not resume such tests unless another nation did. The Soviet Union reciprocated. Khrushchev then took the next step a few days later by announcing a halt in the production of strategic bombers. A series of unilateral conciliatory moves ensued, leading to a number of arms control agreements. The deescalatory cycle ended when the Soviets resumed testing in response to nuclear testing by the French government.

In their study of U.S.-Soviet-Chinese interaction from 1948 to 1989, Goldstein and Freeman examine six cases of cooperative initiatives, one by each of the superpowers toward each of the others.[80] They find that five of the six attempts were successful in creating cooperative bilateral reciprocity. (The one failure was Gorbachev's unilateral nuclear testing moratorium aimed at the Reagan administration.) In virtually all cases, the initiator had to overcome significant policy inertia in the target state. As a result, success in gaining reciprocal cooperation depended on the willingness of the initiator to persevere after initially disappointing responses. This suggested to Goldstein and Freeman that an "extended" GRIT policy (or EGRIT), in which the initiator makes sporadic (rather than continuous) unilateral gestures over an extended period of time might be the best policy to gain mutual cooperation.

Goldstein and Freeman performed computer simulations on their Soviet-American interaction data in order to test the effectiveness of several different strategies in inducing cooperation. The strategies were (1) TIT-FOR TAT (TFT), which involves a single initial cooperative move and then simply reciprocates the rival's previous move; (2) EGRIT; (3) progressive GRIT (PGRIT), which is essentially the GRIT strategy outlined above, which starts with limited initiatives and progressively moves on to actions of greater and greater importance; and (4) a standard GRIT strategy in which the unilateral initiatives do not progress from minor to major, but instead remain constant at an intermediate level.

Once again, the results indicate the superior properties of "soft-line" strategies. Although all the strategies were somewhat effective in eliciting some cooperation, EGRIT and PGRIT were the best strategies. Mutual cooperation lasted longest when EGRIT was used, while PGRIT produced higher levels of cooperation. No strategy was successful in the simulation in maintaining cooperation over the long term, however; Soviet-American relations returned eventually to their "steady state" of hostility—an effect the authors maintain is due to policy inertia in both states.[81]

Goldstein and Freeman conclude that the best strategy to induce cooperation might be a "super-GRIT" policy, which would essentially be a policy of permanent EGRIT in which unilateral initiatives would be pursued at a level that could be sustained over a number of years.[82] In fact, the authors argue that Soviet President Gorbachev followed just such a policy in his "new thinking" approach to foreign policy beginning in 1985. Unilateral concessions were made in order to induce cooperation from both the Chinese and the Americans. With regard to the Chinese, Gorbachev's Vladivostok speech in 1986, announcing Soviet willingness to meet long-standing Chinese conditions for better relations, resulted in "normalization" of Soviet-Chinese relations.

Winning cooperation with the United States was not as easy. A number of Soviet unilateral undertakings were initiated without significant recipocation: the Soviet nuclear test moratorium of July 1985; the Soviet military withdrawal from Afghanistan in December 1988; Gobachev's United Nations speech (December 1988) announcing a unilateral Soviet decision to cut the Soviet military by 500,000 troops over two years and to remove or destroy substantial numbers of tanks, artillery, and aircraft; and the May 1989 promise to unilaterally withdraw 500 nuclear weapons from Europe. Until the end of 1989, according to Goldstein and Freeman, the Soviets seemed to be doing the initiating *and* the reciprocating, while the United States rarely initiated and reciprocated only weakly. Improvements in Soviet-American relations took place primarily because of Soviet willingness to persist in making concessions even though the American response had been meager. By the end of 1988 all the Soviets had to show for their efforts was the INF (intermediate range nuclear forces) agreement, a treaty made possible primarily by Soviet willingness to make significant substantive concession to the United States.

The next two years changed all that. A series of spectacular events transformed U.S.-Soviet relations (and international relations in general) in a shockingly brief period of time. The fall of communism in the six former Soviet bloc states in eastern Europe in the last four months of 1989 was made possible by Gorbachev's willingess to abandon the Brezhnev Doctrine and allow peaceful transitions. The unification of the two Germanies in October 1990 under Western terms, which maintained German membership in NATO, was also made possible by Soviet concessions. These events were followed logically by the demise of the Warsaw Pact (and COMECON) in April 1991 and the process of removing all Soviet forces from Hungary, Poland, Czechoslovakia, and Germany. In the meantime, the Soviet Union had begun to transform itself from one-party Communist state to a fledgling democracy experimenting with market capitalism.

These events led to a virtual landslide of reciprocity by the west. The CFE (conventional forces in Europe) Treaty was signed by the NATO and WTO states in November 1990, and the Soviets and Americans signed the START (strategic arms reduction) Treaty in July 1991. Numerous bilateral and multilateral trade and aid agreements were signed between the Soviets and Western states. Bilateral and multilateral summits proliferated.

Then in September 1991, in the aftermath of the abortive coup that had attempted to remove Gorbachev from power, President Bush made a startling television speech. He announced a package of American unilateral actions, which included, among other things: (a) the withdrawal of all U.S. tactical nuclear weapons from Europe, (b) elimination of nuclear cruise missiles from certain types of naval vessels, (c) the removal of U.S. bombers from alert status, and (d) the termination of U.S. mobile ICBM programs. The president asserted that these steps would be implemented with or without reciprocation from the Soviets, but he challenged the Soviets to join the United States in taking equally bold and concrete steps. The American president had adopted the language and the strategy of GRIT!

This is the most direct use of the GRIT strategy ever used by a world leader. Gorbachev's earlier unilateral initiatives were accompanied neither by unambiguous communications about Soviet expectations nor by clear invitations to the United States to reciprocate Soviet actions in an open-ended way. At most, the United States was invited to reciprocate a single specific act, such as the nuclear test moratorium, and this request was not put in the context of further Soviet gestures if the United States reciprocated.

The Soviet response to President Bush's speech was not long in coming. Approximately a week later, Gorbachev announced his own unilateral actions. He directly reciprocated most of the American cuts and then went several steps further by once again suspending Soviet nuclear tests and by pledging that the Soviet strategic arsenal would be kept at a level of 1,000 warheads below the American arsenal. He then proposed the two nations agree on a further 50% cut in strategic weapons

Within months a second round of GRIT proposals was underway. In his State of the Union address in January 1992, President Bush presented a package that included unilateral defense initiatives (some old, some new) and challenged the new Russian government of Boris Yeltsin to reciprocate. Yeltsin's reciprocation was virtually simultaneous. (The joint announcements had obviously been worked out in advance—a new twist on GRIT strategy.)

It is clear that a number of significant changes had taken place between 1985 and 1991, which had made possible the successful use of GRIT strategies by the two superpowers. In large part, Gorbachev's continuous unilateral initiatives and his willingness to make concessions were able, over a period of years, to teach the leaders in the United States (and China) that their previous impressions of the Soviet state needed to be changed and that Soviet desire for cooperation was not just a ploy, but was sincere. Trust had begun to replace suspicion in the relationship between the former enemies. Of course, the fact that the democratic experiment in the U.S.S.R. had led to the demise of Communist control not only in that country but in all of eastern Europe also played a role in creating a totally different international environment. Neither should one discount the fact that on both sides of what had once been the Iron Curtain budgetary crises impelled drastic cuts in defense. Regardless of the exact causes, the Cold War climate of mutual hostility, suspicion, and tension had given way to the realization by both sides that cooperation in the pursuit of mutual interests was possible. Under these circumstances, the American president was essentially freed from the domestic political constraints that had bound foreign policy making for decades. He could, for the first time, undertake unilateral military cutbacks without fear of a conservative political backlash leading to defeat at the polls. A "soft line" was at last acceptable.

Goldstein and Freeman, whose analysis ended in 1989, argued that decision-makers in the three superpowers have operated over the last several decades in an environment of "limited reciprocity" in which limited cooperative reciprocity was present, but was made difficult by the existence of high levels of policy inertia in all three states.[83] The current environment is one in which this policy inertia (at least for the Americans and the Soviets) has given way to a rush toward cooperation.

Onward

We shall return later to more discussion about GRIT, but now let us go on to the next chapter for an examination of two other theories of international interaction: game theory and deterrence theory. Since we remain at the dyadic interaction level, you will notice a number of distinct similarities in the themes that are examined. Indeed, we will revisit many of the major concepts introduced in this chapter—conflict spirals, the security dilemma, arms races, the strategies of peace through strength and peace through conciliation and cooperation—providing alternative perspectives on each.

7

International Interaction: Game Theory and Deterrence Theory

Game Theory

Interaction between nations can be seen as a game in the sense that nations compete with each other to attain certain rewards. In some types of games only one winner can attain the reward; in other games there can be multiple winners or losers. The essential element of politics as a game, however, is that the strategies followed by each player (nation) are interdependent. Each player has to take his opponent's interests and strategies into account. The best course of action for each player will depend on what he expects the other to do.[1]

Game theory has been developed from the disciplines of logic and mathematics to provide a way of understanding certain types of gamelike situations and to assist in the development of strategies for making actual decisions. Its purposes are twofold. One is practical and *normative*—to help decision-makers cope with certain situations in the real world by developing strategies for rational behavior. The other is theoretical and *empirical*—to help explain why certain actions occur in certain situations. Game theory might be useful in helping us understand a variety of international interactions in which strategies are developed by one side to counter the actions and strategies of others: crisis interactions, diplomatic bargaining, arms races, deterrence, prewar mobilizations, colonial competition, and many others.

Game theory, like all social science theories, is based on certain simplifying assumptions. The most important assumptions of game theory are these:

1. Mankind is rational (or at least most men are rational most of the time), and governments may be thought of as single, rationally calculating entities. Rationality in this sense means that each party seeks to maximize his or her own interests.

2. The utility (worth or payoff) of each outcome can be calculated and quantified on either an interval scale or an ordinal scale of relative desirability. This provides a standard by which strategies can be rationally compared according to their ability to contribute to the maximization of one's interests.

Game theorists frequently use a game matrix to illustrate the choices facing each player and the payoffs that can be expected for each possible outcome. A typical game matrix is displayed in Game Matrix 7.1.

Each player has two strategies. Player I has strategies A and B; player II has strategies C and D. The strategy options may be the same for each player or they may be different. In this example they are different. Since each player has two strategies, four possible outcomes are depicted by the four cells of the matrix. (If there were more players or more strategy options, there would be more cells.) The numbers inside each cell indicate the payoffs (utilities) for each player for each of the four possible outcomes. The utilities for player I (the row or horizontal player) are always designated first and the payoffs for player II (the column or vertical player) are placed second, in parentheses. The choices are usually assumed to be made simultaneously, and the outcome depends on the mix of strategies chosen.

Notice that this particular game is a game of pure conflict. One player always wins and the other player always loses. There are no chances for mutual gain or mutual loss. Further, what one player wins corresponds exactly to what the other player loses, and the sum of the numbers in each cell is therefore zero. This type of game is called a *zero-sum game*.

The game depicted in Game Matrix 7.1 is a two-person, zero-sum game

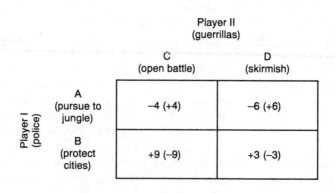

Game Matrix 7–1: Guerrilla Warfare

that has been made famous by Martin Shubik, a pioneer in game theory.[2] Player I is a police force and player II is a rebel guerrilla unit. The police can choose either (A) to enter the jungle in pursuit of the rebels, a dangerous strategy since this is the rebels' home territory, or (B) to protect the cities, areas where they presumably have more support. The guerrillas have a choice of (C) full-scale, open battles or (D) small-scale skirmishes fought with unorthodox techniques. From the perspective of the police, city protection is the preferred strategy. If they pursue the rebels into the jungle, they lose— whether in open battle or in skirmishes—it's just a question of how much. The guerrillas also have a dominant strategy. Whether in the jungle or in the cities, they stand to win more and lose less if they restrict the battle to skirmishes. Thus, both sides have a dominant strategy—a strategy that they should try to play consistently given the structure of the situation, the choices available to them, and the payoffs. The interests of each side therefore converge in the cell B,D in the lower right quadrant. The police will stay at home and protect the cities and the rebels will attack with skirmish techniques.

This solution represents a *saddlepoint*, an equilibrium point at which the strategies of each side logically converge. If a game has a saddlepoint (not all do), it usually denotes a *minimax* (or maximin) solution. A minimax solution represents the best each player can do against a fully rational opponent. It is also a solution in which each player attempts to minimize his losses if the other does his worst. Knowing that the police are not foolish enough to enter the jungle but will protect cities instead, it is rational for the rebels to choose to lose only three by engaging in skirmishes instead of losing nine, which would be the outcome if they chose to attack in open battle. It is a general axiom in two-person zero-sum games that the best strategy for each is based on the minimax principle: each player should try to maximize his minimum gain or minimize his maximum loss. This is a conservative strategy and applies only to zero-sum games.[3]

Chicken

Not all situations are zero sum in nature; in fact, most political situations include elements of cooperation as well as conflict. Players may seek mutual gains or may suffer mutual losses. Players have common interests as well as an interest in besting the other. Some common interests among nations might include the avoidance of mutual negative payoffs (such as nuclear annihilation and the cost of an arms race) as well as the achievement of mutual benefits (such as increased trade and mutual access to the wealth of the seabed). Let us look at some non-zero-sum games, games in which the sum of the payoffs in each cell do not add up to zero. Game Matrix 7.2 is illustrative of a game commonly called *chicken*.[4]

Each player has a choice of the same two moves: to drive one's car straight down the center line of the road at high speed against the on-rushing machine of one's rival or to swerve to avoid hitting the other car (thus "chickening out"). If both refuse to swerve, the result is a cataclysmic clash of chrome and steel with the high probability of injury and death for both drivers. The payoff for this mutual disaster has arbitrarily been set at –20; it could just as easily have been set at –50 or –100. The specific value doesn't matter as much as the fact that it is a number significantly greater than the next worst payoff. If one driver swerves while the other does not (cells B,C or A,D), then the swerver suffers the indignation of being called a chicken (–5), and his opponent wins the admiration of the crowd (+5). If both swerve, they suffer mild humiliation, but since they share the dubious distinction of both being chicken, the blame is somewhat reduced (–2) for each and, of course, both live to blaze down the highways another day.

The minimax strategy here dictates that if you assume the other driver will do his worst, the better part of valor is to swerve, suffer brief humiliation, and wake up alive the next day, thus minimizing your losses. Given the high cost of guessing wrong, you would probably not want to take the chance that the other player will swerve; it is much more prudent to assume he or she will not. On the other hand, believing that your opponent is a logical and prudent person, one might seek to take advantage of his or her prudence, but this is risky business. Nevertheless, if your goal is to win rather than to just cope with a bad situation, game theory provides some clues.

In order to have a chance of winning a chickenlike confrontation, you must pursue a strategy designed to ensure that your opponent will believe beyond a doubt that you will not swerve and that therefore the only logical action for your adversary is to get out of your way. A winning strategy therefore depends on your establishing your credibility. Winners of the game of chicken are successful because they succeed in conning their opponents into believing they are committed to a strategy of suicide and that they are absolutely inflexible in this strategy. In a sense, success depends on demon-

		Player II	
		C (drive straight)	D (swerve)
Player I	A (drive straight)	–20 (–20)	+5 (–5)
	B (swerve)	–5 (+5)	–2 (–2)

Game Matrix 7.2: Chicken

strating that you are not rational, but irrational—that death (−20) is more preferable to you than humiliation (−5). If this belief can be generated, then the choice is purely up to your opponent to choose life or death for both of you.

The success of this strategy depends on two things. First, you must establish your credibility. That is, you must make your opponent believe that you will do precisely what you have threatened to do. This can be done (in terms of the example) by visibly locking the wheel so that it is incapable of movement from side to side. Alternatively, you might stick your hands out the window, indicating that you will not be able to get them back on the wheel in time to turn. Both these actions indicate to the other driver that you have no alternative but to continue straight ahead. Second, you must establish your credibility *before* your adversary steals your strategy and does exactly the same thing. The first one to adopt this strategy has the advantage because the burden of choosing life or death is placed on the opponent.

The central problem here is that what's good for the goose is good for the gander. If the best way to win a crisis confrontation is to make an iron-clad commitment and charge ahead, then it is reasonable to assume that this posture will be adopted simultaneously by *both* sides! The strategy then becomes an iron-clad rush to destruction. Snyder and Diesing find that coercive (competitive) tactics are frequently effective in real-world chicken situations among nations, especially against weaker opponents. But such tactics run serious risks against rivals with relatively equal capabilities and interests.[5]

In continuous or indefinitely repeated (iterated) chicken games, each driver may choose to drive straight (defect) rather than swerve (cooperate) on the assumption that this will coerce the adversary into swerving in the future. Each may seek to acquire a reputation as a hard-charging, nonswerving player.[6]

Chicken games have been seen as applicable to deterrence relationships and to crisis confrontations, including "brinkmanship" crises. We have seen previously that such confrontations frequently lead to war, especially if leaders in one state perceive the rival's no-swerve strategy to be a bluff rather than a real commitment. In such cases the saddle point of swerve/swerve cannot be reached owing to a misperception of the opponent's commitment. Of course, the saddlepoint may also be unattainable if one side sees the payoffs for swerving to be so severe that humiliation is seen as equal or preferable to death.

It might be argued that some of the interactions between the United States and Soviet Union during the Cuban Missile Crisis took on aspects of a chicken game. The United States signaled that it was willing to use force (including the use of nuclear weapons) against the Soviet Union if the latter's missiles were not removed from Cuba, thus establishing a firm no-swerve position. The Soviets could choose to proceed full steam ahead, but the

United States had already demonstrated the credibility of its willingness to act rashly if pushed. This credibility had been conveyed through words (Kennedy's public statements) and deeds (the naval blockade of Cuba and the alert of U.S. forces). Although American credibility to fight over the issue had been established, Soviet credibility to fight on behalf of her Cuban ally was lacking, and the Soviets probably realized this. The best they could do was to minimize their loss and retreat gracefully.

Kennedy's promise to refrain from attacking Cuba, along with the possibility of American missiles being removed from Turkey, made the payoff for backing down (swerving) more palatable than it would otherwise have been and serves as a good example of how changing the payoffs for the other side can help one side achieve its goals.

Prisoners' Dilemma

Let us turn now to the most analyzed non-zero-sum game of all, *prisoners' dilemma*, as depicted in Game Matrix 7.3. Two suspects are apprehended by the police and charged with a crime. A wily district attorney devises an ingenious scheme. He refuses to allow either suspect to communicate with the other, locking them in separate cells, and has them interrogated separately. Each is offered the following deal:

1. If you both refuse to confess, you will get off with 90 days for vagrancy (+10 each).
2. If only one confesses, implicating the other, the informant is freed and his partner gets life in prison (+20, −20).
3. If you both confess to the crime, you will both receive five years in jail (−10 each).

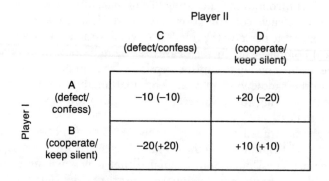

Game Matrix 7–3: Prisoners' Dilemma

What should you do? As always it depends on what you think the other prisoner will do. If you are player #1 and you think #2 will cooperate with you, you can join in an effort to fool the police and get off with a vagrancy charge, or you can defect and go free—leaving your buddy to rot. Purely in terms of individual interests, it pays to defect if you think the other suspect will cooperate (keep silent). On the other hand, player #2 may decide to confess. If he talks, it would be foolish of you to remain silent and earn a life sentence in jail. If you also defect, you only get five years. So it pays to defect regardless of whether you think the other player will defect or cooperate. No matter what he does, your best response is to defect and assure yourself of the higher payoff. The other player, not being a complete dunce, will undoubtedly come to the same realization as you. He will also defect (confess). Defection is thus the dominant strategy for each player. The resulting solution is a saddlepoint at A,C (–10, –10) in the upper left quadrant, representing mutual defection.

The interesting thing about this game is that each could do better. Through mutual cooperation both could arrive at a satisfactory solution. By refusing to rat on the other, each could achieve +10, representing the relative good fortune of a ninety-day vagrancy sentence. This is each player's second choice (its payoff is the second highest possible), while the saddlepoint is in fact each player's third choice! Certainly, each players prefers +10 to –10. The dilemma is that by choosing what appears to be a safer course and one that maximizes individual utility, each contributes to an outcome relatively less satisfactory for both than is possible to attain.

Why are mutual cooperation and mutual gain so difficult to achieve? First, to achieve mutual cooperation each player has to renounce the higher payoff he can attain by unilateral defection. Although there are rewards for mutual cooperation in the game of prisoners' dilemma, unilateral noncooperation gives the highest reward. Second, the players have no advance knowledge of the other's choice; they cannot communicate prior to their decision. This makes it extremely difficult to forge a mutual strategy of cooperation. Third, trust, an important ingredient for mutual cooperation, is presumed to be absent. Thus, in the absence of trust and in the absence of communication that might generate such trust, each party is compelled to act in a manner injurious to both.

Finally, the ability to cooperate depends on the number of times the game will be played. In the classic example the two suspects will get only one chance to play. However, in an *interated game*, in which play is continuous, competitors are able to learn from each other's moves. If the game is only played once, players don't have to worry about which option their rivals will choose the next time. But the knowledge that numerous interactions will appear between them in the future will quickly make them realize that neither has anything to gain from continued noncooperation. Realizing that the choices one makes today will influence one's rival's moves tomorrow, players learn to signal their willingness to cooperate through their moves. A cooperative choice in the present may induce reciprocal cooperation in the future.[7]

Prisoners' Dilemma Games Applied to International Relations

Prisoners' dilemma games are widely applicable to all sorts of situations in international relations. For instance, prisoners' dilemma might be applied to the prewar mobilization of armies, to the formation of alliances, to imperialistic competition for colonies, or to free trade versus protectionist policies. The structure of these situations is analogous to prisoners' dilemma games in that they are all situations where mutual restraint is preferable, but where the best policy is to forgo restraint and avoid being a sucker if others refuse to restrain themselves. Robert Axelrod identifies another interesting prisoners' dilemma example. He claims that soldiers in World War I developed a tacit "live and let live" policy in the trenches in western Europe. Army battalions avoided action to damage the enemy under certain circumstances in return for mutual restraint. The important point for Axelrod is that in trench warfare:

> . . . small units faced each other in immobile sectors for extended periods of time. This changed the game from a one move prisoners' dilemma in which defection is the dominant choice, to an iterated prisoners' dilemma in which conditional strategies are possible.[8]

The result of sustained interaction between units was that mutual cooperation based on reciprocity was possible. Soldiers understood that their actions had indirect consequences: providing discomfort for the enemy was but a roundabout way of providing it for themselves.[9] While artillery barrages against enemy positions would inevitably produce incoming fire, restraint was also likely to be reciprocated.

Finally, arms control would seem to be the classic case of prisoners' dilemma. Let's look at Game Matrix 7.4.

The scenario might go something like this. At the height of the Cold War the American president and the Soviet president gather their top strategic and political advisers together to discuss recent developments. In each nation scientists have determined that a new, highly sophisticated strategic weapon is now possible. The cost, however, will be tremendous. The intelligence community in each nation has also discovered that the other superpower is also at a similar technological point; they may also decide to build and deploy this new weapon. It is also understood that the decision of each country may be influenced by their evaluation of what the other may do. Although mutual

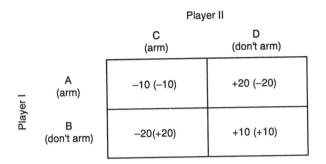

Game Matrix 7–4: Arms Control

benefits (slowing the arms race, easing the domestic economic burden associated with that race, and decreasing world tension) could be derived from mutual restraint, the greatest fear for both would be to scrap the program and find out that the other had begun to deploy it. Thus, any desire to foster mutual cooperation must take into consideration the possibility that one's rival might build unilaterally, taking advantage of your naiveté. On the other hand, you could attain military superiority by building while the other pursued a policy of unilateral restraint. Of course, if both choose to build, no one would be better off, great expenses would have been incurred, and resources that could have been put to better use would have been squandered in another round of a futile arms race.

Unfortunately, the decision to build tends to be impelled by the structure of the situation. Not being able to trust the other side, you build—a choice that minimizes the possibility of great loss and has the added benefit of giving you military superiority if the other side exercises self-restraint. The pursuit of individual interests leads, however, to mutual disaster. Arming is the dominant strategy for both sides.

Luckily, arms acquisition processes are not constrained by the formal restraints placed on prisoners' dilemma games. Real-world players may communicate with each other with words and deeds; this greatly improves their understanding of the future moves of their rivals. Second, arms races are not "one-shot" games. Instead, they are made up of a series of many decisions over many years—decisions about testing, research and development, and deployment of many different weapons systems and modifications of those systems. In a sense, it is a continuous game with an infinite number of interactions, that is, an "iterated" game. Knowledge that the "game" will continue indefinitely has a significant impact on the way in which players approach the game.[10]

In such situations both parties have knowledge of their adversary's past behavior and understand that their own present behavior will affect the future behavior of their rival. This makes it possible for players (states) to learn to cooperate. The question is, of course, what strategy is best for attaining mutual cooperation, and how can you prevent yourself from being taken advantage of if your rival is aware of your desire for cooperation?

Solving the Prisoners' Dilemma: TIT-FOR-TAT

Robert Axelrod devised a unique way to test various strategies for playing iterated prisoners' dilemma games. He decided to hold a computer tournament. Game theorists from many countries and from a variety of academic disciplines were invited to submit "decision rules"—computer programs that embody a strategy or rule that determines which move to make in each successive turn of the game. Each entry was paired against every other entry (as well as with itself and with a program representing a random series of choices). The winner would be the decision rule with the most total points accumulated in all the matches.[11]

Two computer tournaments were held. The same program won both tournaments, TIT-FOR-TAT, a rule submitted by Anatol Rapoport. TIT-FOR-TAT (TFT) is a very simple rule. Its first move is to cooperate, and thereafter it does exactly what the other player did on the previous round. It rewards cooperative behavior and punishes antagonistic behavior. What makes TFT so successful? Axelrod has suggested that TFT and the other successful tournament rules had several similar properties.[12]

First, it paid to be *nice*. A nice rule is one that will never be the first to defect. Nice rules did very well in both tournaments.

Second, the best rules were also *provocable*. That is, they immediately punished rivals after an uncalled-for defection. Provocable rules immediately defect after the defection of an opponent. If a rule does not retaliate in this manner, it will frequently be taken advantage of by rules that are not nice. It pays to be nice, but it doesn't pay to be too nice.

Third, the best rules were also *forgiving*—defined as the propensity of the rule to cooperate in the moves after the other defected. If the other program resumes cooperation after its defection, TFT is willing to let bygones by bygones and will immediately resume cooperation in response. In other words, it engages in short-term punishment, but is willing to return to cooperation if this is signaled by the opponent. TIT-FOR-TAT represents a perfect illustration of the concepts of niceness, forgiveness, and provocability. "It is never the first to defect, it forgives an isolated defection after a single response, but it is always provoked by a defection no matter how good the interaction has been so far."[13]

Fourth, TFT benefits from its own *simplicity* and clarity. It is easily recognized by its opponents. It is usually quite clear early in the encounter that TFT is offering cooperation in return for reciprocity, but will also reciprocate defection. Since TFT's strategy is clear, it is evident to the opponent that the best way to respond to TFT is with mutual cooperation. TIT-FOR-TAT represents a good strategy for dealing with iterated prisoners' dilemmas because, as Axelrod states, "Its niceness prevents it from getting into unnecessary trouble. Its provocability discourages the other side from persisting whenever defection is tried. Its forgiveness helps restore mutual cooperation. And its clarity makes it intelligible to the other player, thereby eliciting long-term cooperation."[14]

It might be added that not only has TFT produced good results when subjected to computer simulation, but game simulation experiments with human subjects have also indicated that the TIT-FOR-TAT strategy elicits a good deal of cooperation from rival competitors.[15] Perhaps most important, analyses of adversarial relationships between states in the international arena suggest that reciprocating strategies generally produce better results than alternative strategies—especially if the states are evenly matched. For instance, Leng and Wheeler find that a reciprocating strategy is especially effective against opponents who use a bullying strategy.[16]

Although TFT is generally recognized as the single best strategy for playing iterated games of prisoners' dilemma,[17] it is probably applicable as well to iterated chicken games. For instance, Kenneth Oye notes that a strategy of reciprocity in such situations can offset the perverse effects of no-swerve strategies designed to establish reputations for toughness.[18]

Of course, TFT is not a perfect strategy. Perhaps the single most important problem with TFT is that it may prove ineffective in getting reciprocal cooperation stated in the midst of a long-standing dispute. In the real world most relationships are *in medias res*; they are ongoing. If the other side has just undertaken a noncooperative action, TFT calls for reciprocal noncooperation. The two sides may then become "locked in" to repetitive competition. Strategists playing TFT must then wait for the adversary to initiate cooperation. In other words, TFT may not be forgiving enough to induce cooperation.[19]

It is possible to modify TFT somewhat to reduce this propensity for "locking in" to reciprocal hostility. If we assume that players are not faced with the two extreme choices of cooperate or defect, but with gradations of each, players might have a continuum of choices, ranging from total cooperation to total defection. A strategy sometimes called *tFT* (small tit-for-tat) responds to the opponent's defection by retaliation one degree less than the opponent's original move. In fact, this modified strategy won a computer tournament constructed by Theodore To, with TFT coming in second.[20] A tFT strategy permits opponents to get away with a little more defection, but it prevents the escalation of punishment that leads to a locking in of mutually competitive moves. It is therefore better able to restore mutual cooperation when the interactions begin with mutual noncooperation. Other researchers also find that when an adversary attempts exploitation, the most effective method of inducing cooperation is the use of *mild* retaliation rather than strong retaliation or no retaliation.[21] These experimental findings lend support to Axelrod's recommendation to reciprocate "only nine-tenths of a tit for a tat."[22]

There are other problems with a TIT-FOR-TAT strategy, which should be briefly mentioned. Roy Behr points out that TIT-FOR-TAT may be an inappropriate strategy for some goals. For instance, the goal in Axelrod's tournaments was to score as many points as possible; TFT did this admirably. But if the goal is changed to *winning* against as many opponents as possible, TFT fails miserably. In a tournament of this type staged by Behr, TFT was unable to win over *any* opposing strategy.[23] The winners were FELD and JOSS, two strategies that were not nice—they attempted to exploit the opposition through unprovoked defections a certain percent of the time. Clearly, in order to score more points than the opponent, one must be willing to defect more than the opponent; TFT can therefore never win in this sense. (And, of course, a strategy that defects in every round can never lose in this sense.) Behr's point is that there are times when defeating an opponent is more important than maximizing one's own payoff, and TFT is inappropriate for these situations.

The success of a TFT strategy is also affected by the values in the payoff matrix.[24] At a minimum, for TFT to work the payoffs to each side must be greater when they cooperate than when they both choose noncooperation (defect), and they must forsee further interactions in the future.[25] If the penalty (or perceived penalty) for mutual defection is reduced, then we could expect that winners in computer tournaments as well as in real life would be less likely to initiate cooperation, less likely to respond to cooperation with cooperation, and more likely to respond to the opponent's defections.

Steven Van Evera illustrates this point by showing how misperceptions among European leaders in the 1914 crisis twisted the payoff structures so perversely that a TIT-FOR-TAT strategy would not have worked to prevent World War I.[26] Generally, beliefs of European leaders about the effectiveness of bullying strategies to get others to back down, beliefs about the necessity of rapid mobilization and of the necessity of offensive strategies, beliefs about the positive benefits of war, and perceptions of the hostility of others resulted in a payoff matrix unlikely to induce cooperation. Specifically,

(a) by enlarging the rewards of Defect/Cooperate outcomes and the penalties of a Cooperate/Defect outcome, the attractiveness of opportunistic defection and defensive defection were increased;

(b) by narrowing the difference between Cooperate/Cooperate and Defect/Defect outcomes, the attractiveness of Cooperate/Cooperate was diminished;

(c) by raising fear that Cooperation would be answered by Defection, a greater incentive was given to Defection; and

(d) by raising hopes that Defection would be answered by Cooperation, they made Defection more attractive.[27]

Under such conditions, the price of using a nice strategy was too high, and it would probably have been incapable of eliciting cooperative behavior from the opponent as well.

TIT-FOR-TAT and GRIT Compared

It might be argued that the attributers that make TFT a success—niceness, provocability, forgiveness, and clarity—also describe the strategy of GRIT. In fact, TIT-FOR-TAT and GRIT constitute similar strategies for dealing with prisoners' dilemma situations. Both are designed to induce cooperative behavior through the communication of conciliatory intentions. Both combine a carrot-and-stick approach to reward cooperation and punish defection. There are, however, several important differences between them.

First, while TFT relies on nonverbal communication, GRIT has the advantage of being able to use explicit communication in attempting to induce cooperation.

Second, aside from the cooperative cue that it gives on the first move, TFT lets the other party take the initiative and simply follows suit. However, players using the GRIT strategy take the initiative themselves. Leng and Wheeler found that the most successful strategies used by international rivals were not ones of pure reciprocity, such as TFT, but ones that included unilateral initiatives of conciliation.[28]

Third, both TFT and GRIT retaliate in response to defection. However, GRIT players always take the lead in returning to cooperation, while the TFT strategy requires defection as long as the opponent defects, leading to the possibility of a prolonged retaliatory spiral.

Fourth, in GRIT the initial reciprocation is not expected immediately. The initiator must be prepared to risk some exploitation without retaliating. TFT, on the other hand, lets no defection go without retaliation.

Fifth, the GRIT strategy is basically for games involving sequential choice by rivals. TFT is usually seen as applicable to games involving simultaneous choice. GRIT thus probably reflects more precisely the real world of political decision making.

Several tests of the comparative effectiveness of TFT and GRIT have been performed. In experimental simulations with human subjects, GRIT has proved to be more effective in eliciting cooperation that TFT. The ability of GRIT players to use explicit verbal communication accounts for much of GRIT's superiority over the TFT strategy in such experiments.[29] Goldstein and Freeman performed computer simulations on four decades of Soviet-American interaction data to test the relative effectiveness of TFT and three versions of GRIT in inducing reciprocal cooperation. They conclude that while all four strategies were somewhat successful, TFT was the least effective. Progressive GRIT (PGRIT) and extended GRIT (EGRIT) were the most successful.[30] The potency of these strategies was due to their willingness to persist in continued unilateral concessions without reciprocation as a way of inducing mutual cooperation. Since the TFT strategy calls for only one such unilateral initiative, it was less able to overcome the reluctance of the target to cooperate.

Critique of Game Theory

Before we end our discussion of game theory, it might be wise to mention a few of its defects. First, one might question the assumptions on which the theory is based. As we have seen from the literature on decision-making, it is questionable whether policy makers are capable of engaging in rational decision processes all the time. It is also questionable whether meaningful values can be placed on alternative sets of goals and whether hypothetical outcomes can be assigned precise numerical weights according to their desirability. It is especially difficult to try to guess the opponent's evaluation of the expected outcomes, given the general difficulty of reading others' minds as well as the common problems of misperception of the opponent's goals and strategies.

Second, and most important, it is debatable whether game theory can be said to actually "explain" why certain events and behaviors occur—whether it is actually capable of explaining the *cause* of behavior. For instance, it is probably stretching game theory too far to say that arms races occur *because* the structure of the situation two nations find themselves in is a prisoners' dilemma structure. Likewise, it would be difficult to say that wars are caused because of the chickenlike situations that may precede them. For this reason, there is no "game theory of war" in international relations.

Perhaps game theory is best seen as a *heuristic device* rather than an empirical theory. Heuristic devices are merely analytical methods that provide us with insights and analogies that help us to understand why things happen, but do not actually point to causal relationships between variables.[31] Even in this limited role, however, game theory can be a useful guide to policy makers, helping them to clarify their thoughts about possible alternative courses of action and assisting them in developing optimal strategies for attaining their objectives.

Deterrence Theory

The stimulus-response theory and the GRIT and TFT strategies all suggest that the way to bring about peace is through a willingness to initiate cooperation and to persevere in this. An alternative theory has previously been mentioned. It is encapsulated in the Latin phrase *si vis pacem, para bellum*. If you seek peace, prepare for war. This is the essence of deterrence theory.

The concept of deterrence refers to one's ability to prevent another person or country from doing something that is undesirable or harmful to one's own interests.[32] For instance, you don't want another person to steal your property and you don't want another country to attack you or your allies. There are typically two ways to prevent this from happening—defense and deterrence.

Let's consider *defense* first. Suppose you own a collection of rare jewels. To prevent them from being stolen you might consider hiring some muscular Rambo types with heavy artillery to protect your goods twenty-four hours a day. (If this were a movie you might hire a modern-day "Magnificent Seven" made up of Clint Eastwood, Arnold Schwartzenegger, Jean-Claude Van Damme, Sylvester Stallone, Danny Glover, Mel Gibson, and Sigourney Weaver to do the job.) Presumably, this would make it physically impossible for any thief to steal your treasure. Your possessions are defended by making it physically difficult, if not impossible, for the opponent to achieve his goal. This is sometimes referred to as a strategy of *denial*.

Deterrence works somewhat differently. Your jewels may not be heavily protected, but you let it be known that you have Eastwood and Associates on retainer and if anyone messes with your personal property they will hunt down the perpetrators and generally make life miserable for them. However, as Patrick Morgan points out, although deterrence and defense are analytically distinct, they are thoroughly related in practice. A good defense/denial capability may have the side effect of enhancing a state's deterrence.[33]

Deterrence is based on a psychological relationship between two people or countries. A tries to impress B with the idea that if B performs certain actions in the future, he will punish B. That is, he threatens B with *retaliation*. If this idea is to be successfully impressed on B, he must be made to believe two things: (1) that A has the *capability* to retaliate effectively, and (2) that A has the *will* or intention to retaliate as he has threatened. If both capability and will are present, we say that A's threat has *credibility*; it is believable. (It goes without saying that it is also necessary that the threatened punishment is something that B actually fears.)

If A's threat is credible, then B should be prevented (deterred) from taking action. If B actually believes that Eastwood and Associates will brutalize him in retaliation for his acts against A, it would not be in his best interest to steal A's property. The expected losses would exceed any expected gains. In deterrence, unlike defense, the goal is not to kill the enemy when he invades; the goal is to convince him that he *will* be killed if he *does* invade.

Deterrence theory, put very simplistically, argues that peace is kept through maintaining credible threats against one's opponents. Ultimately, the opponent must believe that under certain fairly clear circumstances you will fight him—that certain acts are not acceptable and you are willing to go to war if he steps over the boundaries of permissible action. War is prevented by the threat of war. Conversely, war occurs because the threat fails to be received credibly. That is, B either doesn't believe A has the capacity to retaliate effectively, or B doesn't believe A has the will to actually do what he has threatened, or both.

Perhaps the most compelling argument for deterrence theory and a foreign policy based on it has been constructed by James Payne in his book *The American Threat.*[34] It might be beneficial to review Payne's arguments in some detail. Payne argues that a state's most important instrument for inhibiting aggression is the threat of war, but threats must be communicated in ways that make them credible to the opponent. Threats are typically conveyed through words, but "words are cheap." Formal treaty agreements are somewhat better, but the best way to communicate one's deterrent threat is through past actions—especially through the execution of threats. Carrying out threats conveys a willingness to make sacrifices and take risks in order to meet commitments.

Countries should pay great attention to how to make their threats more credible. In this respect, Payne attacks Hans Morgenthau's dictum that nations should never put themselves in a position from which they cannot retreat without losing face.[35] Payne argues just the opposite, that it is necessary precisely to put yourself in a position from which you cannot retreat gracefully. It is only then that the opponent will be absolutely sure of your threat. If you can retreat gracefully, then you might not keep your word, and if you *might* not, then the opponent will believe you *will* not.[36] Threats become credible, Payne contends, to the extent that you can deprive yourself of freedom of action and choice. If this can be achieved, your opponents will believe you are automatically bound to carry out your commitment.

If this sounds familiar, it should. This was exactly the advise offered as a winning tactic in the game of chicken: convince your opponent that you are incapable of choosing to swerve, that you are committed to driving straight ahead even if it means destruction. This leaves the choice in your opponent's hands, and the rational thing for him to do is to back down. Thus, deterrence strategy is similar to the chicken strategy in important ways. Both require a clear enunciation of a threat, and both require that the threat be conveyed to the opponent in a highly credible manner. Of course, the problem with treating deterrence as a game of chicken is that both sides may make irrevocable commitments and freeze themselves into incompatible stances, producing the disaster each wanted to avoid.

In an interesting insight into the relationship of individual-level factors and dyadic-interaction factors, Charles Lockhart has made the observation that "hard-line" or hawkish statesmen are predisposed (perhaps by their operational codes) to see conflicts with rival states as chicken contests that require strong actions to signal one's commitment and credibility. On the other hand, "soft-line" or dovish leaders are more predisposed to view these encounters as prisoners' dilemma games that call for the development of cooperative and conciliatory strategies.[37]

One of the central paradigms of deterrence theory (and of Payne's work) is the Munich Crisis of 1938 and the outbreak of World War II a year later. A brief historical review might be in order here. In 1936 Hitler began a remilitarization of the Rhineland in violation of the Versailles Treaty. Britain and France objected, but took no action beyond this. In March 1938 Hitler bullied the Austrian leadership into accepting German military occupation and incorporation into the Third Reich. Once again France and Britain took no action. In the fall of 1938 Hitler pressured the government of Czechoslovakia for the cession of the Sudetenland to Germany. Although the Czechs had defense pacts with both France and Russia, they were unwilling to fight Germany over Czechoslovakia, and at the Munich Conference in October Britain agreed that the Czechs must cede the Sudetenland. In March 1939 German troops marched unopposed into the remainder of Czechoslovakia. The British and French refused to take immediate action, but threatened Hitler that if he attacked Poland, they would come to her defense. As everyone knows, Hitler was not dissuaded by the allied threat and Poland was attacked in the fall of 1939. Britain and France declared war and the second great conflagration of the twentieth century began.

What does Payne make of this scenario? What are the "lessons of Munich?" The major lesson is that nations that permit their opponents to commit aggression are likely to experience even more aggression.[38] The policy of *appeasement* lessens the coerciveness of a state's threat. Tolerance of aggression causes several unfortunate effects to occur simultaneously. The opponent feels a sense of "exhilaration"—his first acts of defiance and aggression have been successful and he is tempted to believe that further moves will meet with similar inaction. The warning signals of other nations begin to be discounted by the aggressor. Additionally, the fact that aggression has initially been successful will strengthen the hawkish faction internally against the doves who have cautioned restraint in the past. For all these reasons there is a high probability that aggression by the opponent will increase rather than abate.

The toleration of aggression has effects within the appeasing country as well. Appeasement cannot be sustained indefinitely. The cries of shame and cowardice by internal critics of the regime will eventually force a change in either government policy or personnel or both. Hawks will be brought to power as part of the reaction to the failed policies of the past. Eventually, a new policy of peace through strength will be implemented and new threats will be issued. Consequently, war becomes much more likely. On the one hand, the aggressor is predisposed (on the basis of past performances) to discount the appeaser's threats as empty rhetoric. But internal politics in the appeaser have now forced it to take a hard-line approach. The aggressor will make one more move and this time it will be met by force.

Payne concludes, therefore, that war occurs because a nation's threat has not been credible enough to deter its opponents. The logical solution is that it may be necessary to confront aggression forcefully in its early stages, even if this means war. It is better to fight a small war now than a larger war later. Additionally, it is probably safer to confront aggression in its early stages because at this point the aggressor is probably uncertain of the opponent's reaction and is more likely to disengage if confronted. It is frequently speculated, for instance, that Britain and France would have been successful in halting German aggression if they had taken forceful action from the start.

Payne also discusses a more contemporary situation in which the lack of a credible threat induced aggressive action—the Cuban Missile Crisis of 1962.[39] The question for Payne is "Why did the Soviets decide to pursue such a risky gambit as placing nuclear weapons in Cuba?" His answer is that the United States failed to keep its threat in good working condition. First, the new American president, John F. Kennedy, let himself be bullied by Khrushchev at the Vienna Summit in 1961. Second, the United States suffered a humiliating defeat in the Bay of Pigs Crisis when it failed to take risks and make sacrifices to assist anti-Castro guerrillas in a plot it had set in motion. Third, Kennedy chose to negotiate a compromise with the Communists in Laos rather than use military force to defend the government, even though a SEATO defense commitment was on the line. Fourth, the United States did not attempt to reverse the building of the Berlin Wall in 1961. Fifth, the United States declined to send ground troops to South Vietnam, refusing at this point to make a major commitment to an ally. Sixth, we had permitted the Soviets to contribute to a weapons buildup in Cuba itself. Through a series of weak responses to challenges to our interests, we therefore permitted the Soviets to think that we would not respond to further provocations. The result was that the two superpowers came very close to war.

Payne rather vehemently criticizes the stimulus-response theory (which he calls the "excitation" theory).[40] Remember that the stimulus-response theory portrays war as an inadvertent result of miscalculation and misunderstanding. The true intentions of the two sides are peaceful, but through a conflict spiral that escalates out of control, war breaks out even though neither side wanted it or planned it. The implication is that war is caused by a failure of one side to break the upward spiral of violence, a break that could best be brought about by cooperative and conciliatory acts in response to a pattern of provocation by the other.

Payne dismisses the stimulus response theory as empirically unfounded and as a dangerous guide for policy. Cooperation and conciliation are simply fancy words for appeasement to Payne. And appeasement doesn't lead to peace, but to an even higher probability of war. In his first edition, published in 1970, Payne ridicules the excitation/stimulus-response theory:

> The excitation theory advises us to turn the other cheek rather than respond firmly. . . . Communist China, for example, appears to be warlike and dangerous. The excitation theory suggests that the Chinese are belligerent because they are suspicious of us. They feel encircled and threatened. . . . To reduce Chinese hostility, therefore, we should abrogate collective defense treaties, withdraw from Vietnam, bring China into the United Nations, and the 7th Fleet home.[41]

After Payne's first edition went to press, this is exactly what the United States did! The Nixon administration extricated U.S. soldiers from Vietnam and signed the Paris Peace Treaty, made it possible for the People's Republic of China to enter the United Nations and take a seat on the Security Council, and arranged a triumphal summit with Chinese leaders in Peking. The Carter administration solidified this new relationship by abrogating its Mutual Defense Pact with the Republic of China (Taiwan) and by granting official recognition of the PRC. The result has been a much closer and more cooperative relationship between the United States and China—including efforts at joint military and intelligence cooperation aimed at the U.S.S.R.! Meanwhile, this interesting and awkwardly prescient passage is nowhere to be found in Payne's new and enlarged second edition written in 1981.

A second problem with the stimulus-response theory, as Payne sees it, is that it implies that no one is to blame for war and that no country consciously desires war or plans for it. However, traditional deterrence theorists such as Payne see states as "gain maximizers" who constantly seek "windows of opportunity" through which they may take advantage of others. It is only credible threats of retaliazation by defenders of the status quo that are able to keep these windows shut.[42] In Payne's theory (now outdated by the demise of the Soviet bloc and of the Cold War itself), it was assumed that there were good guys and bad guys and that it was clear who was who. The United States and the "Free World" were the good guys—defensive, status quo nations that sought a peaceful world. The Soviet Union and the "Communist Bloc" countries were the bad guys—aggressive, expansionist states that were desirous of upsetting the status quo.

Paynes also assumes the existence of a clearly defined international status quo, which represents a mutually perceived distribution of rights and territories between states.[43]

The status quo is primarily spatial and geographic, but it is also based on ideology. Essentially, it refers to a distribution of territories that are "ours" and "theirs." For the last several decades, "our" side has consisted of the territory of the United States itself, our allies, and nations within our "sphere of influence." "Their" side has consisted of the territory of the U.S.S.R. and its allies and nations within its "sphere of influence." It was fairly clear what belonged to whom, according to Payne. (This formulation of the status quo also has a clear Cold War basis, though the concept of the status quo still has general utility in the post–Cold War era.)

The status quo is an important concept in Payne's general theory of deterrence. A violation of the status quo provokes war; stopping short preserves peace. The threshold is crystal clear. Hostile states know exactly where and when to stop if they don't want war. But if a nation is determined to have a war, it can have it—by challenging the status quo. There can be no miscalculation. Wars are not accidental; they are conscious decisions made by the leaders of aggressive states.

Since Payne is developing not only an empirical theory concerning the cause of war, but also a normative theory concerning how best to conduct American foreign policy, he addresses several policy-related questions. One of the most important questions is "When and where must we respond with force to challenges to American interests?" One widely held answer is that the United States must respond with force in order to defend nations that are strategically valuable.[44] *Strategic value* might be based on the presence of any attribute that would contribute significantly to the military capability of a superpower opponent if it were to fall into his hands, thus changing the balance of military power. The implication is, of course, that states that do not possess any of these strategic resources may be safely sacrificed; they do not necessarily have to be defended.

Payne suggests an alternative policy. He contends that the United States should oppose any moves by the other superpower or its friends to alter the status quo, not because it would result in an alteration of the military balance of power, but because failure to act would decrease the credibility of our threat. From this perspective the American involvement in Vietnam was laudable. Although South Vietnam possessed no real strategic value, it was necessary for the United States to defend it in order to defend the credibility of our threat to resist aggression against ourselves and our allies.

The resulting irony, if Payne is correct, is that war is needed to prevent further war. War itself becomes an instrument of peace. Deterrence requires credibility, and credibility ultimately requires a nation to demonstrate its ability and willingness to engage in armed conflict.

Deterrence: Empirical Research

Although a tremendous amount has been written about the theory of deterrence—especially about the deterrence of nuclear war—relatively little empirical research on conventional deterrence has been undertaken until recently.

In their classic work *Deterrence in American Foreign Policy*, Alexander George and Richard Smoke analyzed the deterrent efforts of the United States in the Cold War period from 1948 to 1962.[45] Using a comparative case studies method, they rigorously examined and compared eleven cases of U.S. deterrent threats in an effort to explain how deterrence fails and how it succeeds. What leads a "potential initiator" to mount a challenge to deterrence? The most important factor seems to be the potential initiator's view of the risks involved in challenging the defender. In almost all the cases the authors find evidence that before taking action, the initiator concluded that the risks of the option he had chosen would be calculable and controllable in a way that would ensure that the risk would be acceptable. Such a feeling on the part of the initiator seems to George and Smoke to be a necessary—but not a sufficient—condition for a decision to challenge deterrence. On the other hand, the belief that the range of options available is not calculable or controllable is usually a sufficient condition for deterrent success.[46] The decision-makers in the challenging states seemed to be risk-averse loss minimizers rather than risk-acceptant gain maximizers.

A second major factor is the initiator's view of the defending state's commitment. Contrary to what one might expect, George and Smoke found that an American commitment per se was clearly insufficient to deter a potential initiator. If the opponent possessed an option for challenging the status quo that seemed likely to achieve his objectives at an acceptable cost/benefit ratio, deterrence could fail even in the presence of a credible U.S. commitment. The authors concluded that the initiator's perception of the presence of a defender's commitment may be a necessary condition for deterrent success, but not a sufficient condition.[47]

George and Smoke identify three distinct patterns of deterrent failure. Pattern 1 is termed a *fait accompli* since it involves actions designed to overturn the status quo quickly before the defender has a chance to decide he is committed to reversing the change. Fait accompli patterns occur when the initiator believes that no commitment by the defender actually exists. Of course, if the initiator is correct in his view that no commitment exists, one cannot properly say that there has been a failure of deterrence, since the defender was never committed in the first place.[48] The Soviet intervention in Hungary in 1956 surely fits this pattern. Soviet intervention was certainly intended to present a fait accompli to the West, but just as certainly the United States was never committed to retaliating against the U.S.S.R. for any aggression there. Sometimes, of course, a commitment does exist through the opponent believes otherwise. This was probably the situation in the North Korean attack on South Korea in 1950 as well as in the Iraqi attack on Kuwait in 1990.

The second pattern of deterrence failure discovered by George and Smoke is called the *limited probe*. Such actions occur when the initiator believes a defender's commitment is uncertain or ambiguous. He then initiates a controlled crisis to clarify the defender's commitment, presumably following Lenin's famous dictum that "if you strike steel, withdraw; if you strike mush push on." Examples of this pattern would include the initial phase of the Berlin Blockade in 1948 and the Quemoy Crisis in 1959.[49] The limited probe is frequently followed by a second phase, which George and Smoke identify as *controlled pressure*. If the initiator regards the defender's commitment as solid, he may still attempt to find a way around it if he can at the same time keep his options both calculable and controllable. Controlled pressure responses involve low-risk strategies involving minimum force. The late phases of the Berlin Blockade and the Quemoy Crisis illustrate the technique.[50]

George and Smoke conclude that deterrent threats by the United States against opponents that employ low-risk strategies have often been ineffective. Initiators frequently calculate that defenders may not be willing to adequately defend against low-level violations of the status quo. The fact that an initiator possesses multiple options for violating the status quo seems to be a crucial factor in determining whether initiators will risk challenging deterrence.[51]

In patterns 2 and 3, challenges to the status quo are mounted incrementally in a series of small steps, each of which is reversible if need be. This prompts one commentator to write:

> . . . it is not surprising that the effectiveness of deterrence is rather skimpy at the margins, hard to sustain when the challenges come at low levels in places of limited importance over matters not intrinsically of vital national interest. And it is hardly surprising that this is exactly the form in which most challenges appear.[52]

Another scholar who has been interested in deterrence theory is Bruce Russett. One of the earliest data-based studies on deterrence was reported in his article "The Calculus of Deterrence."[53] Like George and Smoke, Russett focused on *immediate extended deterrence*—that is, attempts by one state (the defender) to deter the impending use of military force by another state (the potential attacker) against a friendly third state (the protégé). Russett was particularly interested in discovering what determined whether a deterrent threat failed or succeeded. To investigate this question he examined data from seventeen cases of deterrence between 1935 and 1961 in which a Great

Power tried to prevent an attack on a smaller protégé. The seventeen cases were all situations in which an aggressor was deemed likely to take action against the client state.

Russett's analysis led him to some interesting conclusions. First, it did not seem that potential attacks against the more important protégés were more successfully deterred than those against less important clients. In fact, all cases of successful deterrence involved relatively unimportant protégés (in terms of gross national product and population). In other words, successful deterrence did not seem to be linked to the client's possession of *strategic value*. Second, an explicit commitment by the Great Power defender was found to be no guarantee of deterrent success. Third, neither local nor general military superiority in the hands of the Great Power defender seemed to guarantee successful deterrence. This last finding echoed a similar discovery in another early research effort. Raoull Naroll's study of deterrence over the last twenty centuries also concluded that superior strength alone was not sufficient to deter war. The fact that defensive states prepare militarily superior forces did not enhance the probability of peace; Naroll found that, if anything, armament tended to make war more likely.[54]

These are interesting results because deterrence theory suggests that clear military capability to retaliate coupled with explicit commitments should result in a credible threat, which should result in a successful deterrent effort. If these factors do not lead to successful deterrence, what does?

Russett discovered that the best predictor of successful deterrence seemed to be the existence of close military, economic, and political ties between the defender and the client. In all cases of successful deterrence strong military cooperation was present, with the defender supplying the protégé with both arms and advisers. In four of the six cases of successful deterrence there were close political ties, and in five of the six cases there was substantial economic interdependence between the client and defender as indicated by bilateral trade statistics.[55] The general breadth and intensity of relations between the defender and the pawn would seem to signal the credibility of the defender's commitment to the client state, thus enhancing the probability of successful deterrence.

Russett's early work on deterrence has now been significantly expanded. Russett and Paul Huth have identified fifty-four cases of immediate extended deterrence between 1900 and 1980.[56] Using an expected-utility model of deterrence, they assume that deterrence will be achieved if the cost-benefit calculation of the attacker concludes that the expected utility of an attack would be less than the expected utility of forgoing the attack. The potential attacker's calculations would logically include estimates of the defender's capability to defend the protégé and its commitment and willingness to do so. Huth and Russett devise indicators that indirectly tap such considerations: the relative military balance between the attacker and the defender and protégé, the economic and military ties that bind the defender to the protégé, the intrinsic (or strategic) value of the protégé, and the defender's previous behavior in deterrent situations (his reputation).

They find that deterrence was successful in thirty-one of the fifty-four cases. Deterrence attempts were most successful when there were strong economic (trade) and political (arms transfers) links between the defender and the protégé and when the local military balance favored the defender and the protégé. Formal alliance ties did not appear to enhance the chances for deterrent success, nor did the defender's past behavior in crisis, or even the defender's possession of nuclear weapons.[57]

Huth and Russett subsequently revised and expanded their data set to include the years 1885–1984, resulting in fifty-eight cases of immediate, extended deterrence. Their analysis of the period confirms that the immediate, short-term balance of military forces has an important impact on deterrence success, though neither the long-term military balance nor the possession of nuclear weapons plays a major role. Apparently, decision-makers do not initiate conflict with the intention of creating long-term wars of attrition, but with the desire to win quickly and establish a fait accompli that cannot be overturned by the defender. What matters most therefore is the ability of the defender to prevent such a quick victory. Deterrence through the denial of immediate gains seems more important than a credible threat of punishment in the long term.[58]

The British predicament in 1939 may be instructive of the difference. Alan Alexandroff and Richard Rosecrance argue that although Britain tried a strategy of long-run deterrence against Hitler—threatening to win a war of attrition—the only strategy that would have prevented Hitler's attack on Poland was a credible threat to deny Germany the immediate ability to take Poland, and this could not have been accomplished without British and French cooperation with the Soviet Union.[59]

Huth and Russett also examined the credibility of the defender's threat by looking at his pattern of diplomatic negotiation in previous deterrent situations and at his strategy of military escalation (his bargaining behavior) in the crisis. Their findings are illuminating. They discover that a reciprocol (TIT-FOR-TAT) strategy of military escalation is more likely to achieve a successful deterrent effect than either a policy of responding more forcefully to the opponent's actions (a "policy of strength") or a policy of responding at lower levels of military action (a "policy of caution"). Likewise, a reciprocal ("firm but flexible") strategy of diplomacy was more effective for the defender than either bullying or conciliatory strategies.[60] A past record of either bullying or conciliation (backing down) reduced the chances for successful deterrence. Bullying sometimes worked against a much weaker potential attacker, but it was a risky deterrent strategy against a state with similar military capabilities.[61]

As one would expect, if a defender was previously forced to concede by the same attacker, the defender's threat would lack credibility in the next crisis, creating a deterrent failure. However, bullying behavior by the defender in the previous encounter with the same attacker also decreased the chances that deterrence would succeed in the future! Once bullied, the potential attacker is less likely to retreat and suffer further damage to its reputation and prestige.[62] Paradoxically, previous deterrent success against the same potential attacker can reduce the chances for success in the future by increasing the loser's grievances.[63] In the long run, a stalemated previous crisis appeared safer than one in which the defender backed down or bullied his way to success. In fact, in Huth and Russett's study, a stalemate was the only past behavior not associated with the failure of deterrence.[64]

Deterrence theorists are becoming increasingly aware that for deterrence to work, the challenger must not only believe the defender's threats are credible, but the deterrent acts themselves must not increase the potential attacker's fear of preemptive military action, thus provoking escalation to war.[65] Deterrence can fail because conflict spirals are induced by states attempting to make credible threats.[66] Decision-makers in deterrent situations must walk a fine line. If they demonstrate too much toughness, they risk provoking an overly hostile reaction from a potential challenger who was not previously committed to risking war. If they don't demonstrate enough firmness, however, they may encourage wishful thinkers in the potential attacker to believe the defender will not make good on its commitment.[67] Leaders need to guard against both appeasement and provocation.

The studies of Huth and Russett seem to indicate that sometimes deterrence succeeds and sometimes it falls, but that the nature of deterrent successes and failures fails pretty well within the expectations of deterrence theory. Potential aggressors can be deterred by credible threats of retaliation by a defender, especially if the defender enjoys immediate local military advantages and if the defender's commitment to the protégé can be clearly discerned from its economic and political-military ties to the protégé. Formal alliance ties seem unimportant as evidence of the defender's commitment, but this can be explained by the potential attacker's attention to deeds rather than words and treaties. The defender's reputation for carrying out commitments seems to be important, but only with regard to the same potential challenger. Deterrent failures can be laid at the doorstep of less-than-credible military capabilities and less-than-clearcut commitments to the client state—all predicted by deterrence theory.

Criticism of Deterrence Research and Deterrence Theory

As you might imagine, these studies have not gone unchallenged. One of the major bones of contention among political scientists who study deterrence is how to select actual cases of deterrence. One criticism, originally raised concerning Russett's initial study but generally applicable to most studies of extended deterrence, is that if one looks only at cases in which the client is threatened, one may in fact miss the most successful cases of deterrence— those where the defender is able to project so great a deterrent threat that no opponents even seriously considered action against the pawn![68]

Another criticism is equally important. The existence of a case of immediate extended deterrence requires the presence of a potential attacker who is seriously interested in the immediate use of military force and the presence of a defender who actually engages in a serious effort to deter such a use of force. Critics have charged that Russett and Huth (as well as others) have been guilty of using cases in which (a) the potential attacker was not seriously contemplating the use of military force against a client state, thus leading to the erroneous impression of a deterrent success, or (b) the "defender" did not really engage in a serious effort to deter the attacker, thus giving the erroneous impression of a deterrent failure.[69]

For instance, Richard Ned Lebow and Janice Gross Stein, using far stricter definitions for the occurrence of immediate extended deterrence, conclude that of the fifty-four cases in Huth and Russett's original data set, only nine really fit the definition; they find only ten real instances of extended deterrence in the later fifty-eight-case set.[70] Of the nine cases of deterrence that they identify in the twentieth century, only three cases were deemed successful and only in the short run—Munich, Egypt's deterrence of an Israeli attack on Syria in May 1967, and American deterrence of a Turkish attack on Cyprus in 1964. They find immediate deterrence successes to be "uncommon, partial and tenuous."[71] Such a wide discrepancy concerning the relevant cases to be examined is astonishing. It points not only to the theoretical difficulty of identifying cases of deterrence, but also to the wariness with which we should treat the results of any statistical analysis based on a particular set of cases.

Not only is determining the existence of deterrence attempts problematic, so is determining whether such attempts have been successes or failures. It has already been suggested that some cases that appear to illustrate successful deterrence may, in fact, be (1) cases in which the adversary never really harbored any intention to act and thus did not need to be deterred, or (2) cases in which the adversary, while indeed wishing to challenge the status quo, was dissuaded from military action not by the expected costs that a defender might impose on him in retaliation, but by other considerations— ideological, political, moral, or legal.[72]

Just because an attack does not take place does not mean peace can be attributed to successful deterrence. As Morgan points out, identifying cases of successful deterrence involves proving why something that did not happen did not happen—a task that is a logical nightmare.[73] The old joke about the Ohio farmer may be instructive. It seems that one afternoon an eccentric old farmer rather ostentatiously erected an extremely large pole in the middle of his backyard. His neighbor, spying the novel ornament, asked him why he had placed this oversized bean pole in his backyard. The farmer replied that it helped to keep the elephants away. When the neighbor protested that there were no elephants in the area, the farmer exclaimed triumphantly, "See, it works!" Deterrence may be much the same type of phenomenon.

We have already seen than several scholars have argued that the number of deterrence successes found by Huth and Russett is rather inflated and that the number of deterrence failures is much more considerable. In fact, some theorists argue that the number of deterrence failures is so large and the manner in which deterrence fails is so much at odds with rational deterrence theory that the theory itself requires major renovations.

Remember that deterrence theory does not say that attempts at deterrence will always be successful; deterrence will fail if the defender's retaliatory threat is "absent, incredible, or less valuable than the prize." If deterrent attempts are badly designed or implemented, this does not add up to a falsification of deterrence theory.[74] What *would* falsify the theory is the prevalence of situations in which the defender meets the requirements of the theory, but the attacker strikes anyway. In other words, when the defender (a) specifically defines its commitment, (b) communicates this commitment to the potential attacker, (c) possesses sufficient military capabilities to carry out the commitment, and (d) demonstrates its willingness to carry them out, and the attacker *still* initiates military action, something is wrong. The challenger is not acting as the theory predicts.

Some critics contend that far too many such instances can be identified. Rational deterrence theory has been most often criticized by scholars who have examined deterrence through the use of comparative case studies. For instance, Lebow identifies eight brinkmanship crises in which the defender met all four of the standard conditions and failed to deter the potential attacker: Fashoda (1898), Korea (1903–1904), Agadir (1911), July (1914), Korea (1950), Cuban Missile Crisis (1962), Sino-Indian (1962), and Arab-Israeli (1967).[75] He argues that in each of these cases the defender's commitment and capabilities were solid, but they were not necessarily *perceived* as such by decision-makers in the challenging state. What was important was that the challenger perceived weaknesses in the defender's capabilities and commitment, not that such weaknesses actually existed. Cognitive factors at the individual level of analysis were crucial. The inability to correctly assess the capabilities and commitment of the protecting state led to deterrence failure under conditions where deterrence success would have been confidently predicted.[76]

Janice Gross Stein analyzed six cases in which the United States attempted to apply immediate extended deterrence in the Middle East in the 1960s and 1970s.[77] Four of these attempts failed; in the other two the challenger backed down, but it was difficult to determine conclusively whether this was due to the deterrent threat of the United States. In each of the cases the links between the United States and its protégés (Israel, Jordan, and Saudi Arabia) were clear and substantial; thus deterrence failed even though the challengers knew the links between the defender and the target were strong. Reputation was also less important than might have been predicted by deterrence theory; even though the United States "stood firm" in five of the six cases, deterrence failed in three of these five.[78]

Stein maintains that in each case the challenger's primary motivation was a perception that the costs of inaction were too high. The leaders in the challenging states were vulnerable to domestic and international pressures, increasing their motivation to challenge the status quo. She concludes that for challengers who are motivated primarily by their own internal weakness, a strategy of conciliation is perhaps better able to deter unwanted behaviors than a strategy of credible threats.

This approach is illustrated in the two cases in which the challenger was dissuaded from the threatened military action. Both cases involve American attempts to deter impending direct Soviet intervention in ongoing wars in the Middle East (in 1967 and 1973). In these instances success was achieved because deterrent actions by the United States were combined with American recognition of the legitimacy of Soviet interests and an attempt to reassure them that their demands would be met. In both cases the United States placed pressure on Israel (an act of compellence) to desist from its military actions against the threatened Soviet clients, Syria and Egypt, respectively. Stein concludes that the simultaneous practice of deterrence and *reassurance* is much more effective than the use of deterrence alone.

In summary, critics of deterrence theory argue that the traditional theory of deterrence is deficient in two fundamental ways. First, it assumes a rationality that may be lacking in real-world situations. In many cases the defender fulfills all the essential conditions posited by the theory and deterrence still fails. This is primarily due to individual level factors such as *misperception* and the distortion of crucial information about the cost/benefit ratio, the defender's commitment, or the likely outcome of a confrontation. A valid theory of deterrence must therefore take irrationality into account.[79]

Second, even when the potential attacker perceives the defender's military capability and commitment accurately, perceives the defender will intervene, and perceives his own attack will probably be unsuccessful, the potential attacker may nevertheless initiate action anyway because of factors that deterrence theory does not identify. Chief among these are domestic constraints and vulnerabilities that make the costs of inaction politically unacceptable. Challengers frequently initiate military action because they fear the domestic consequences of not acting. This makes deterrence based on threats both inadequate and unlikely to succeed.[80]

The decision of Anwar Sadat to initiate war against Israel in 1973 and the decision of the Japanese government to attack Pearl Harbor in 1941 are often cited as examples of this kind of situation. Another example can be found in the reasoning of the Argentine junta's decision to precipitate the Falklands War in 1982. If a consideration of the military balance was the main consideration, as traditional deterrence theory hypothesizes, then the Argentine generals should have waited another year before launching their challenge. By then the H.M.S. *Invincible* would have been transferred to the Australian navy, the *Hermes* gone, and the *Intrepid* and the *Fearless* would have been in the scrap heap. Paradoxically, the generals and admirals in control of Argentina were less concerned with military requirements (which suggested patience) than they were with their domestic political vulnerabilities (which dictated immediate action).[81]

Deterrence: Conclusion

What can we conclude about deterrence as a way of preventing war? First, it is hardly foolproof; it often fails. Second, even though local military superiority by the defender appears to be a substantial aid to successful deterrence, it does not guarantee success. In fact, as we might suspect from our understanding of the stimulus-response theory, it may even make the situation worse. Third, credibility is important if deterrence is to succeed. Explicit verbal commitment and paper guarantees aren't enough; the defender must demonstrate his commitment in more overt ways, especially through visible political, military, and economic ties to the pawn. Certainly, the commitment to back up one's threat must not appear ambiguous or uncertain to others. But even if credibility is apparent, deterrence may still fail. Finally, the potential aggressor must be faced with high risks in the event he initiates aggression; faced with only low-level risks, he may initiate probing actions that could blossom into full-scale armed conflict.

Significantly, most of the actions designed to enhance deterrence present the risk of provocation and escalation to unintended war. Our examination of stimulus-response theory has revealed that the security dilemma and the problem of conflict spirals apply to deterrence situations. Leaders in the deterring state must balance the need for enhanced credibility against the need to avoid inciting fear and provoking an overly hostile reaction from the opponent. Our examination of game theory warns us that although tough, noncooperative strategies designed to enhance credibility may be successful, they are also fraught with danger. Iterative chicken games between equal opponents may turn into conflict spirals as each player tries to demonstrate credibility to the other.

We have been discussing deterrence as a phenomenon that exists primarily at the interaction level of analysis, but critics of deterrence have reminded us that deterrence is linked to factors at individual, small-group, and state levels.

Remember that deterrence is in part a psychological concept: its success depends substantially on the target's perception of the threats that have been made against it. This lands us squarely in the individual level of analysis. Morgan wisely points out that threats may have different effects on different individuals, depending on their personalities. In fact, threats may provoke extreme, nonrational responses in some individuals. If this is so, threats may not be compatible with prompting governments to remain sensible and rational.[82] (Consider the inability of threats to persuade Saddam Hussein to order his army out of Kuwait.) We also know that crisis situations tend to reduce human rationality. And, of course, we have frequently referred to the pervasive inability of individuals to correctly perceive the attitudes and actions of others. Unfortunately, the combined effect of these phenomena must surely be that deterrent threats may not be received as intended and may not induce the completely logical responses desired. Robert Jervis makes this summation of attempted deterrence: "in almost no interactions do two adversaries understand each other's goals, fears, means-ends beliefs and perceptions."[83] Under such circumstances, the probabilities for the success of deterrence are relatively small.

Since deterrent threats are intended to affect government decision-makers, small-group decision processes come into play as well as factors at the individual level of analysis. What might be the effect of a deterrent threat on national leaders under the sway of the "groupthink" syndrome? Morgan suggests that the operation of groupthink does not bode well for the success of deterrence. The receiving group would be operating under the illusions of invulnerability and moral superiority, they would be overly optimistic in their assessment of their ability to manage the conflict through brinkmanship, and they might have a tendency to take risks they would ordinarily shun as individuals.[84] One ought to be aware also of the effects of bureaucratic politics on the receptivity of the government to threats. Threats normally strengthen the influence of those who take a hard line against the threateners. And, as we have seen, domestic political considerations play an important role in a potential attacker's calculations.

Deterrence is of course also affected by factors at higher levels of analysis such as the nature of the international system. Clinton Fink's analysis of Russett's study of deterrence points out that most of the cases of successful deterrence in Russett's study are to be found after World War II. The fact that seven of the eleven cases of attack occurred before 1940 suggests that the nature of the international system may be an important factor.[85] World War II marks a watershed. At the war's end the international system had made the transition from multipolarity to one characterized by tight bipolarity—split primarily between the United States and the Soviet Union and their respective allies. As a result, deterrence became bipolar as well: the two superpowers became committed to backing up their deterrent threats against the other. The status quo—to use Payne's terminology—had become more clearly delineated compared to the intricacies of the old multipolar past, presumably making deterrence easier.

With this last observation, it is appropriate that we turn our attention to the nature of global politics as a whole. In the next two chapters we devote our attention to the fifth and final level of analysis, the international system.

8

The International System: Anarchy and Power

> The trouble with the balance of power is not that it has no meaning, but that it has too many meanings.
>
> —Inis L. Claude, Jr.

We have arrived at the last level of analysis, the international system. Here we shift our focus to the "big picture"—to the way in which the world is structured and to the way in which nations interact as part of a global system. Attempts to build systemic level theories assume that there is in fact some order to the world—that events that appear to be random and unconnected are in reality part of a large-scale system of "organized complexity."[1] The behaviors of nations are seen as containing meaningful similarities and standardized sets of interaction patterns. In other words, they comprise an *international system*.

Definitions of systems are notoriously vague, but for starters let's just say that a system is any set of variables in interaction with each other. This interaction is patterned, recurring, and interdependent. Changes in one part of the system affect other parts of the system. In addition to possessing certain units that have a patterned relationship, all systems also have certain rules or norms, definable boundaries, an identifiable organization and structure, and a set of inputs and outputs.

The *units* that make up the international systems are assumed to be primarily sovereign states and organizations of states (such as alliances, trading blocs, and political organizations like the United Nations). But there are nonstate actors as well—multinational corporations, transnational interest groups, even individuals. The interactions between the major actors in the system have developed a regularity over time that conforms to established international legal *norms*, as well as to certain less formal norms that have developed through custom. Every system has *boundaries*, which distinguish the system from its external environment. International relations theorists have historically described the international system as the European Great Power system with non-European states making up the external environment of the system. The international system has gradually become a true global

224

system, however—leaving theorists in the uncomfortable position of being unable to find a true external environment to which the system responds.

The international system has a variety of *structures*. One essential aspect of the system's structure is its lack of an authoritative political organization with ability to issue and implement commands. In other words, the international system is characterized by *anarchy*; it is a political system that lacks a government. Paradoxically, we must try to envision a system that has order but has no "orderer."[2] Even though the international system may be anarchic, it may also possess a certain degree of stratification and hierarchy—such as the international distribution of political and social status. Arguably the most important aspect of the system's structure is the distribution of military and economic capability among its constituent units. In fact, the variation in the distribution of capabilities is, for many scholars, the defining characteristic of different types of international systems—unipolar, bipolar, multipolar.

Each system is also characterized by a set of *inputs* and *outputs*. Various inputs (or stimuli) from the system's own internal environment or from its external environment may disrupt the stability or equilibrium of the system. The system then responds with action (outputs) aimed at restoring a stable balance. Outputs of the system may reenter the system as inputs through the process called *feedback*, creating a continuous process. One may view the international system as being in the midst of a continuous balancing act; every system presumably responds to disturbances in ways that establish and preserve its essential structure. War may be seen as a way of maintaining the system's present structure or as the means through which the present structure is destroyed or transformed so drastically that an entirely new system is created.[3]

Most systems contain within them smaller (sub) systems. Systems may be thought of as fitting inside each other like a set of Chinese boxes, a concept that Robert North refers to as "nesting."[4] The global system is comprised of numerous issue-oriented or regional subsystems and each subsystem is made up of several states and other actors; each state contains within it a large number of organizational and decision-making subsystems; each decision-making group contains several individuals; each individual is a collection of interacting subsystems—physical, emotional, and so on.

At the systemic level of analysis the central assumption is that the structure of the international system plays the most important role in determining the behavior of nations.[5] The nature of the state or its leaders is relatively unimportant. The behavior of states is determined primarily by their positions in the international system (or regional subsystem).[6] Different states within the same international system will behave similarly despite differing national attributes.[7] The nature of the international system itself and the state's position within the system place certain limits on the behavior of states and compel or dispose states toward certain activities. Evan Luard suggests that the international system molds the character and behavior of its constituent units so that they become similar in their motives, means, roles, norms, institutions, and even in their internal structures. Perhaps most important, international "society itself teaches conflict to its members: tells them when to conflict, with whom and over what issues."[8]

War is typically explained as being linked to a particular kind of international system, brought about by a specific distribution of certain values within the system (military power, economic power, political prestige) or by a state's position within this overall structure. As you might imagine, there is considerable contention over which kind of international system is the most prone to war. Let's start our examination of the international system level by exploring the issue of anarchy.

International Anarchy

The French philosopher Jean-Jacques Rousseau used the now-famous *stag hunt analogy* to explore the social and political implications of anarchy. The analogy is as follows. Five men all suffer from hunger. Their hunger can be easily satisfied by the fifth of a stag, so they agree to cooperate to trap the unfortunate creature. The fly in the ointment is that the hunger of any single individual can be satisfied by a hare, so as a hare approaches one of the men chases it down and kills it. He thus satisfies his own hunger, but permits the stag to go free and his erstwhile friends to go hungry.[9]

Since this is an analogy, we should think of the men as representing states in the international system. But what does the analogy illustrate? First, this is a situation in which the immediate interest of the single individual prevails over the common interests of the group. What the hare snatcher did was good for himself and made a kind of rational sense. Although reason tells him that in the long run developing cooperative working relations with his neighbors is necessary, nevertheless, in the short run if someone else were to get the hare, he would have gone hungry instead.[10] States pursue their own national interests and they often do this at the expense of other states and at the expense of the interest of the international community. As you may have guessed from this discussion, the stag hunt analogy is essentially an extended prisoners' dilemma—involving many states rather than just two.

Second, the international system is, by definition, an *anarchic political system*. It is made up of sovereign, independent states each pursuing their own interests; no world government exists to constrain their actions and to compel them to cooperate in the pursuit of common goals. Because any state may refuse to cooperate, states must be constantly ready to engage in measures of self-help. And, to extend the analogy, because any state may use force, all states must be ready to use force in return. As Kenneth Waltz reminds us, in the state of nature one man (and, by analogy, one state) cannot begin to behave decently unless he has some assurance that others will not be able to ruin him.[11]

The absence of a world government that might regulate conflict is a primary structural element of the international system. The lack of world government means that international society is like a *Hobbesian world* in which there is a war of "every an against every man" or, in this case, every state against every state. International anarchy leads to constant suspicion, insecurity, conflict, and violence. Rousseau's argument is essentially that wars occur because there is nothing to prevent them.[12] The violence within the system doesn't depend on the nature of states themselves, but on the nature of the international system. Rousseau's famous analysis is appropriate here:

> It is quite true that it would be much better for all men to remain always at peace. But so long as there is no security for this, everyone, having no guarantee that he can avoid war, is anxious to begin it at the moment which suits his own interest and so forestall a neighbor . . . so that many wars, even offensive wars, are rather in the nature of unjust precautions for the protection of the assailant's own possessions than a device for seizing those of others.[13]

International Anarchy: Implications and Solutions

Robert Jervis has wisely noticed that two separate arguments about the nature of mankind are both consistent with the concept of international anarchy, but they lead the theoretician along totally different paths.[14] On the one hand, mankind (and therefore states) may be thought of as evil or power-seeking. In this case anarchy breeds aggressors and permits them leeway to act. Wars result from a failure of international government to deter or restrain the aggressive actions of states. This first path denotes the familiar deterrence model. On the other hand, mankind (and therefore states) may be assumed to be peaceful and cooperative by nature. In this case the lack of world government to enfore cooperation among states leads to aggression out of unwarranted fear that one's rivals won't be restrained. International anarchy leads to a tragedy in which war occurs despite the purely defensive intentions of all those involved. This second path is an expanded security dilemma or conflict spiral model. But whichever path one starts down, an anarchic international system still leads to war.

In either case the solution would appear to be the creation of some kind of supernational world government with real power to restrain the actions of its constituent members and to compel cooperation. If the problem is the absence of government, then the logical solution is the creation of government on a global scale.[15]

Anarchy and War: A Critique

The foregoing discussion has treated international anarchy as a constant condition in international relations. It may indeed play a role in permitting violence to exist between states, but constants are unlikely to be able to tell us why some historical periods were more war prone than others. If we wish to find why war itself is not constant, we need to find *variables* in the structure of the international system that vary with the changing rates of war. As a way out of this dilemma, theorists have suggested that either the international system is not truly anarchic or the degree of anarchy varies considerably over time. It is, of course, also possible that other systemic level variables have more to do with the causes of war than anarchy.

Several aspects of the structure of the intentional system have received especially close attention. International relations scholars have expended enormous energy examining the effects of status—in particular *status discrepancy*—on behavior. But political scientists have literally leveled entire forests in order to turn out academic papers concerning the *distribution of power* within the system. Similarly, much has been written about *changes* in the power distribution within the system. This is not to say that the decades of research have led to a consensus about the connection between these systemic variables and war. On the contrary, the theoretical debate at this level of analysis is characterized by high levels of disagreement and not a little bit of confusion.

Status Discrepancy

Status discrepancy theory (also known as rank disequilibrium theory) is based on the sociologist concept of stratification, which can be defined as the arrangement of units that make up a social system into "a hierarchy of positions that are unequal with regard to power, property, social evaluation and/or psychic gratification."[16] The units that make up the social system—individuals, groups, or states—carry out different roles in the social division of labor, and they can be ranked (stratified) on a number of different criteria or dimensions.[17] The chief assumption is that one's position within this stratified structure plays a role in determining one's behavior.

Since every social system, no matter what size, may be stratified, even the global system can be seen as a stratified social system. States might be ranked according to a wide variety of different criteria: military power, economic stability, literacy, technological sophistication, diplomatic reputation, productive capacity, possession of nuclear weapons, and so on. Maurice East prefers to collapse these criteria into three dimensions corresponding to sociologist Max Weber's classic categories: class (economic might), power (military force), and status (prestige).[18]

Image for simplicity's sake that states might rank in one of two positions—high or low—on these three criteria: economic power, military power, and status. If we refer to high ranking as *topdog* (T) and low ranking as *underdog* (U), then there are a limited number of possible configurations. Total topdogs to be ranked TTT on all three dimensions, while total underdogs will be ranked UUU on all three dimensions. Both these types of states are said to be in *rank equilibrium;* their ranks on all criteria are the same. On the other hand, states with rankings such as TTU, UTT, TUT, TUU, UTU, or UUT would be in *rank disequilibrium;* their rankings would not be totally consistent. Just as the profile of individual states will vary, international systems will also have widely differing profiles. Some international systems might be made up of states that are totally equilibrated, having no states with rank discrepancies; other system might include a large proportion of states with rank discrepant profiles.

Given these situations, two related sets of hypotheses have been put forward, one at the nation-state level and the other at the systemic level. Johann Galtung has suggested that states that are rank discrepant are more likely to participate in war than states that are in rank equilibrium. And East has hypothesized that the more rank discrepancy that is present in the international system, the more war it should experience.[19]

Why should status discrepancy lead to war? What is the theoretical explanation? A state's behavior is believed to be causally linked to its position in the international hierarchy. Total topdogs should be relatively peaceful because they have already attained most of the rewards available in the system and are thus satisfied members of the community. On the other hand, total underdogs may be deprived and thus dissatisfied, but they lack the necessary resources to successfully force a change. However, the situation for the rank discrepant states is different. They have suffered differential treatment—esteemed because of their achievements, say, in the military realm, but not esteemed because of their relative lack of economic development. This differential treatment produces a destabilizing pressure for upward mobility. Rank discrepant states treat total topdogs as their "reference group" and aspire to emulate them. If no peaceful channels are available, the upward mobility may be carried out through violence. Leaders of states, like ordinary individuals, may perceive aggression to be a necessary response to frustration.[20]

Rank discrepant states are relatively deprived (and thus dissatisfied) states, but unlike their cousins, the total underdogs, they possess capabilities that make an attempt to propel themselves upward a realistic possibility. They have motivation *and* resources. Galtung notes, however, that one should not expect rank discrepant states to initate wars to change their position in the system unless (a) other means of attaining total topdog status have been tried unsuccessfully and (b) the culture has some practice in violent aggression.[21]

Rank discrepancy would seem to be most dangerous if status lags behind the military and/or economic dimensions. This is the classic situation in which a state has *achieved* certain heights, but has been denied *ascribed* status by its peers. These "overachievers" are much more likely to feel they deserve a fairer deal than rank discrepant states that are "underachievers," with high ascribed status but low achievement on military or economic dimensions. Overachievers typically blame the system for constraining them. On the other hand, "underachievers" are usually placed in the position of having to defend their status against upwardly mobile "overachievers"—a potentially violent situation.[22]

With regard to the structure of the international system itself, East posits that systems with a fairly high degree of rank consistency will be more peaceful than those without such consistency. His reasoning is that rank congruence "makes for less ambiguous behavior, more clearly defined roles and role-expectations, and less incentive for social change."[23] Total topdogs will have little desire to change the system and total underdogs will have neither the material resources nor the inspiration to change. "It is only in the system with status discrepancy where the resources necessary for initiating social change are in the hands of those with the motivation and skill to better themselves."[24]

Rank disequilibrium—for states or for the international system as a whole—is not seen as a necessary condition for war; wars may occur in which neither participant is rank discrepant. Neither is rank discrepancy a sufficient condition: rank discrepant systems and rank discrepant states don't always become involved in war. The theory only suggests that given high levels of rank discrepancy for the system or for individual states, aggression becomes more probable.[25]

Well, you might ask, just what level of analysis are we dealing with here? Status discrepancy theorists make reference to individual psychological variables such as the desire of national leaders for achievement and their perceptions of the frustrations associated with the disequilibrated rankings of their state. And certainly there is a focus on the nature of certain states—whether they are status discrepant or not. However, a central assumption of the theory is that national leaders will react to the situation of rank disequilibrium in similar ways, so that individual personalities may be regarded as unimportant.[26] Likewise, regardless of their other differences, states that share similar ranks within the system will behave similarly. Finally, whether a state is rank discrepant or not can only be determined relative to other states in the context of the international system. Ultimately, therefore, the theory exists at the systemic level.

Status Discrepancy: Implications

Let us assume for a moment that this theory has some merit. What clues does it present for the possibility of peace? Generally, the theory implies that world leaders should devote their attention to creating and maintaining greater social justice in the system. Peaceful paths toward social mobility ought to be identified and pursued. At a minimum, states with substantial economic or military capabilities ought to be rewarded with political influence and access to positions that reflect their material attainments. For instance, peace was preserved in the Congress of Vienna era by permitting France to return as a full-fledged member of the Great Power system after the Napoleonic Wars. To have done otherwise would have been to create a permanently dissatisfied state. On the other hand, instability in Asia may have been due, at least in part, to the fact that while the Peoples' Republic of China emerged as a major power after the Communist victory in 1949, it had to wait over twenty years to obtain a seat in the United Nations and its rightful place in the international order.

Status Discrepancy: Empirical Evidence

Is there any evidence to support a status discrepancy explanation of war? Unfortunately, really strong confirmation is nowhere to be found, though there is some modest support. East investigated the association between status discrepancy (between economic and military ranking, on the one hand, and diplomatic prestige, on the other) and the presence of war in the international system between 1948 and 1964, using data for 120 nations. He was able to validate the systemic level hypothesis, but found only modest statistical correlations. Lagging the conflict variable two years behind status discrepancy increased the strength of the relationship somewhat.[27] Michael Wallace investigated a slightly longer period, from 1920 to 1964, and once again found a moderately clear association between the level of status discrepancy in the international system and battle fatalities (as well as increases in arms levels). Like East, he found that the relationships were stronger when the war data were lagged, this time approximately fifteen years.[28]

Investigations by James Lee Ray and by Charles Gochman have produced even more modest findings and great ambiguity of interpretation.[29] This may be due in part to the use of different indicators, but it may also be due to the fact that their studies are confined to the European system. Gochman limits his investigation to the major power subsystem from 1820 to 1970. This is a very nice temporal domain, but it is a severely limited political and spatial domain—containing only nine states whose variations in capabilities and status, at least compared to the variation in the rest of the world, are fairly restricted. For example, the United States is not considered to be part of the major power subsystem until 1899. This is standard historical opinion, based on the American victory over a minor European power, Spain. But if the United States had been included just one year earlier, Gochman would have had another example of a status discrepant power engaging in a war that results in the improvement of its position in the international system!

The point is that status discrepancy theory seems more appropriate for just these sorts of situations—where a state outside the major power subsystem achieves economic and military strength without attaining the political and diplomatic status that usually accompanies it, and then engages in aggression, the result of which is to bring her just that status which she seeks! Status discrepancy theory would seem to be most applicable, in other words, to those nations on the political periphery of the system who desire entrance to the club. Indeed, Gochman finds that his "inequity model" is most applicable to rising powers on the periphery (such as United States, China, and Japan), but does a rather poor job of explaining the war behavior of the traditional European topdogs (such as France, Germany, Austria-Hungary, Italy and, Russia/U.S.S.R.).

Ultimately, status discrepancy is probably only a subsidiary factor in the cause of war. Not all wars are related to status discrepancy and not all situations of status discrepancy lead to war. Even in those wars in which the participants are status discrepant, one may be hard-pressed to conclude that status disequilibrium itself was the primary cause of war. However, as we shall see later, status discrepancy is frequently linked to other, more important variables at the international systems level.

Polarity and Polarization: Definitions

Perhaps the most widely discussed aspect of the international system is the distribution of power among system's members. The notion that the *balance of power* within the system has an important effect on the behavior of states is an idea that can be traced back at least as far as Thucydides' history of the Pelopponesian Wars. It is a concept dear to the hearts of the realist school of thought. Since the 1960s social scientists have attempted to subject traditional realist hypotheses about the relationship between the balance of power and war to empirical tests.[30] These attempts have resulted in a steady stream of studies that have fed into a huge swamp of contention over definition of concepts, proper operationalization of variables, and conflicting results and interpretations. If there is any one area of war research that can rightly be called a quagmire, this is it! Now that you have been properly warned, we can plunge ahead.

The distribution of military power within the international system has been loosely associated with the concepts of *polarization* and *polarity*. Unfortunately, these terms have often been used to mean significantly different things by different people. David Garnham has distinguished four distinct meanings of polarity.[31]

1. Polarity is used to refer to the *size of the international system*. Some scholars use it to distinguish the number of Great Powers and others use it to distinguish the number of poles, a term vaguely described as "autonomous centers of power," which may be individual states or may instead be the number of alliances/blocs/clusters. International systems are then classified as either unipolar, bipolar, or multipolar on the basis of the number of Great Powers or the number of clusters. (Hardly anyone uses the term tripolar for some reason.)[32]

2. *Power polarity* (also known as power distribution) refers to the concentration or diffusion of national power within the system. Although national power is usually thought of as being primarily military power, it is also recognized that national power is a broader concept that also includes economic, technological, and demographic elements as well. Strictly speaking, power polarity refers to the degree to which capabilities are concentrated in the hands of a small number of states versus the degree to which it is diffused widely among a large number of states. Once again, international systems may be classified as unipolar, bipolar, or multipolar. Unipolar systems are characterized by power *preponderance*: power in the system is concentrated in the hands of a single state. Bipolar and multipolar systems are characterized (presumably) by *parity* of capabilities. Power is dispersed more or less equally between two superpowers (bipolarity) or among three or more major powers (multipolarity).

In some analyses, definitions A (size) and B (power polarity) seem to be indistinguishable. Although some scholars assume that an increase in the number of poles also increases the dispersion of power throughout the system, others have demonstrated that the number of poles is relatively independent of the distribution of power in the system.[33]

3. The term *polarization* (also known as *cluster polarity*) describes a specific pattern of alliance bonds. It refers to the degree to which coalitions of states form mutually exclusive blocs of actors with internally friendly and externally hostile relations. Polarization is a function of *tightness* (the degree of similarity of alliance ties *within* a cluster) and *discreteness* (the degree of dissimilarity of alliance ties *between* clusters.) Polarization occurs when there are many alliance bonds *within clusters*, but no bonds *across clusters*. A completely (or tightly) polarized system occurs when all the states in the system are members of one of two alliances and when no member of alliance A is also a member of alliance B. This is sometimes called cluster bipolarity.

A system that lacks polarization might have no blocs at all or it might be made up of several blocs with overlapping membership; in this case, the blocs are not mutually exclusive.[34] Nonpolarized systems may also be referred to as being cluster multipolar. (To muddy the waters even further, some scholars think that power distribution ought to be part of the definition of polarization; in other words, the two concepts ought to be combined.)[35]

4. Finally, researchers have also sometimes seen power distribution in terms of the *magnitude of alliance commitments*, that is, the number of alliance commitments in the system or the percent of nations in the system with alliance commitments.

Because the second and third concepts—power polarity and cluster polarity—are the most theoretically pregnant, we shall concentrate on them. We should start by noting that systems that are cluster bipolar are not necessarily power bipolar, nor vice versa. Similarly, systems that are cluster multipolar are not necessarily power multipolar, nor vice versa.[36]

Before confusion sets in, it might be helpful to look at the fourfold classification scheme in Table 8.1. We can identify international systems that occupy all four possible types. The nineteenth-century classical balance of power era in post-Napoleonic Europe was both cluster and power multipolar, with many great powers of similar strength arranged into shifting complex alliance arrangements. The World War II era and the years immediately preceding World War I are characterized by numerous relatively equal great powers (power multipolarity) arranged into two tightly polarized alliances. The early Cold War period that immediately followed the end of World War II is power bipolar, with two superpowers militarily dominant, and cluster bipolar, with two very tight alliance systems formed around each

Table 8–1

Types of International Systems Based on Combinations of Cluster Polarity and Power Polarity[37]

Distribution of military power	Polarization of blocs or alliances	
	Cluster multipolarity	Cluster bipolarity
Power multipolarity	Post-Napoleonic Europe (1812–1900) Interwar Europe (1919–1939)	Pre–World War I (1900–1914) World War II (1941–1945)
Power bipolarity	Post–Sino-Soviet split (1962–1989)	Early Cold War (1947–1962)

Source: Adapted from F. Wayman, "Bipolarity, Multipolarity and the Threat of War," in A. N. Sabrosky (ed.) *Polarity and War* (Boulder, CO: Westview, 1984), p. 120.

of the two superpowers. By 1962 the system was still power bipolar, but no longer cluster bipolar. The Soviet bloc had begun to break down: Yugoslavia had been evicted in 1948, Albania had gradually joined the Chinese camp, Rumania had become independent (at least in foreign affairs), and Peking had officially split with Moscow. The Western block had suffered deterioration as well, with the defection of the French from the united NATO command structure. The two superpowers were still militarily predominant, but their blocs had been weakened, and strong, nonaligned states such as India had begun to emerge. Empirical research has demonstrated that polarization declined consistently throughout the Cold War, with a rather abrupt decline between 1962 and 1963 and another between 1970 and 1972.[38]

Bipolarity and Multipolarity: The Theoretical Debate

The major theoretical debate among political scientists concerning the power in the international system has centered around the relative merits of bipolar versus multipolar systems.[39] This debate had its beginnings in the 1960s when the conceptual differences between cluster and power polarity had not been distinguished. Consequently, when theorists originally discussed bipolarity and multipolarity, there was a certain amount of confusion about the meaning of those terms. The debate involves issues of polarity and polarization, as well as system size.

It is probably wisest to look at the bipolar-multipolar debate as if bipolarity meant both cluster *and* power bipolarity and to think of multipolarity as meaning both cluster *and* power multipolarity—in other words, in terms of the early Cold War system versus the classic nineteenth-century balance of power system. With this in mind we may now proceed.

Two interrelated questions are involved in the debate. Which system is most stable? And which system is most peaceful? These questions are not totally distinct. *Stability* refers to the ability of the system to endure over time. The alternative is for the system to undergo transformation into a different type of international system—for instance, from bipolar to multipolar or unipolar. Such transformations, however, are generally thought to involve a cataclysmic general war that eliminates some of the major actors, creates larger states out of small states through territorial annexation or absorption, and/or splits large states and empires into several smaller, less powerful units. Thus, major wars lead to system transformation. Therefore, what theorists really mean by stability is whether the system can maintain itself over time without experiencing *major wars*.[40] Thus, the major theoretical questions become: Which system is most able to avoid wars? And which system is best able to avoid major wars? And, of course, what theoretical reasoning might be logically advanced to explain the difference between bipolar and multipolar systems?

Arguments for Multipolarity

Several explanations have been put forward for the reputed stability of multipolar systems.[41]

1. As the number of actors in the system increases (especially the number of major powers), the number of possible opportunities for cooperative interactions also increases. The increase in the number of interactions also produces *cross-pressures*, or cross-cutting loyalties among actors. This decreases the likelihood that any single relationship will become one of implacable opposition; instead, it is more likely that a state's opponent on one issue may be a friend on another issue. This creates a pluralistic system of complex relationships that prevents rigid cleavages and polarization, reducing the probability that conflicts will lead to war.

2. The larger the number of major actors, the larger the number of potential allies that might be arrayed against an aggressor and the greater the flexibility in alignment. The underlying assumption, based on realist thought, is that in a multipolar system, nations pursue a balance-of-power policy in which they agree to counter any attempt by a state or group of states to become too strong. Thus, the greater the number of major powers, the greater the deterrent capability of the system. (Sometimes, of course, deterrence fails and it is necessary to fight limited wars to prevent a state or a coalition of states from achieving dominance.)

3. The greater the number of actors, the larger the number of possible mediators who might be capable of resolving disputes.

4. Multipolar systems help to slow the rate of increase in the arms race, thus reducing tension and hostility. If there are only two major powers in the system and state A increases its armed forces from twenty divisions to twenty-three, state B will be forced to raise its forces by the same number. However, if there are several major powers and state A increases its divisions by three, then state B, C, and F will only have to raise their armies by one division each to offset the increase of state A.

5. In multipolar systems states are unable to become entirely preoccupied by a dispute with any one opponent; consequently, it becomes difficult to allocate sufficient levels of attention to any one state in order to decide for war with that state. It is assumed that a state needs to devote a certain minimum level of attention to another state in order to make a decision for war Deutsch and Singer estimate that limit to be 10% of the state's total foreign policy attention.[42] As the number of actors in the system increases

(especially the number of major actors), it becomes increasingly difficult to allocate a level of attention to any single actor sufficient to make war possible.

6. In a multipolar system the significance of Great Power conflict is reduced. Antagonism is spread out across the entire system, whereas in a bipolar system antogonism is reinforced and echoed throughout the system because of its presumed polarization.

7. Perhaps most important, multipolar systems are inherently full of ambiguity, uncertainty, and unpredictability owing to the large number of major actors and the complex linkages between them. Given the cross-cutting alliance systems, it would be difficult to predict with any precision who would line up on whose side if war were to break out, and therefore it would be difficult to predict the outcome of that war. Given the lack of certainty or predictability in the system, states are forced to act cautiously.

8. Finally, proponents of multipolarity argue that the historical record indicates that such systems have been characterized by a low intensity of conflict. Minor wars may break out in multipolar systems, but major wars are quite rare—witness the long century of relative peace from the Congress of Vienna in 1815 until World War I.

The theoretical underpinnings of the multipolarity argument derive in part from traditional balance of power notions put forward by the *realist* school of thought, which dominated the study of international relations in the United States from the 1940s to the 1960s—popularized by such luminaries as Hans Morgenthau, George Kennan, and Henry Kissinger. Realist theory has elements of both normative (policy oriented) and empirical theory and is based primarily on the lessons of diplomacy within the nineteenth-century multipolar environment of the European system.

Realists argue that the national interest of states would lead them to react to any attempt by rival states to change the balance of power. This could be done through a combination of the traditional means of the day, but it was achieved primarily through the construction of counterbalancing alliances and ultimately through war itself. The balance-of-power process is not unlike Adam Smith's economic market in that through each state's pursuit of its own interests—the preservation of its existence and the maximization of its power—stability is created and maintained for all. The predominance of any single actor or bloc is prevented, the preservation of all essential actors is achieved, and security is ensured.

For *neorealists*, like Waltz, the balance of power is rooted inescapably in the international system itself.[43] Given the structure of international anarchy and the relative power of the units, states are virtually compelled to act in certain ways. The nature of the international system pushes states toward certain kinds of policies and behaviors because some actions are simply more rational than others given the context of the global situation. The balance of power is simply a logical result of a global system based on the principle of anarchy.[44]

Realists and neorealists agree that one of the chief regularities of the system is the struggle for power among states, though realists tend to blame the nature of states (power seeking) for this and neorealists tend to blame the nature of the system (anarchic) for it. Whether the chicken came first or the egg, the result is that the chief regulator of the system is the balance-of-power mechanism. Aggression is checked in advance through the marshalling of countervailing power. The balance of power is essentially a deterrent system through which major wars are prevented.

It is assumed that the balance is essentially an *equal* balance—that preponderance in the hands of a single nation or a single bloc is dangerous. As Inis Claude has said, "There is danger when power confronts power, but there is a greater danger when power confronts weakness."[45] Strong powers are expected to be aggressors, since realists assume that all states attempt to increase their absolute power when possible, and the only thing that prevents this is the possibility of defeat. The construction of countervailing alliances means that would-be aggressors cannot expect to achieve gains at low cost.[46] Equality of power between the major powers is presumed to be effective in deterring war *at least between the major powers*, though it may not produce peace between major powers and lesser states.[47]

Arguments Against Multipolarity

Critics of the multipolarity/balance-of-power theory dispute the above reasoning. Some plausible counterarguments are listed below.[48]

1. An increased number of actors increases the number of potential opportunities for conflict as well as the potential opportunities for cooperation. The law of averages argues in favor of greater conflict as a result of greater interaction opportunities.

2. The greater the number of major powers, the more likely the system is to be characterized by diversity of interests and demands rather than by cooperation.

3. The level of attention argument assumes a fixed pie of attention to which states have access and a rather limited ability to reallocate attention among other states in the system. Both these assumptions are too restrictive.

4. The increased uncertainty that characterizes multipolar systems leads to a greater probability of misperception and miscalculation and therefore to a greater probability of war. Furthermore, ambiguity tempts aggressors to gamble rather than inducing them to be cautious.

5. If we accept the idea that equality of the distribution of resources among major powers is more conducive to peaceful relations than inequality,

mathematical probabilities indicate that the more states in the system, the more likely that resources are to be distributed unequally. This transition from equality to inequality is especially critical as the system moves from two states to three. And an increase in the number of great powers coupled with a decline in valued resources (such as the number of unaligned small states) would lead to a dramatic increase in inequality and instability.[49]

6. Finally, the balance-of-power argument, critics assert, requires states to be both risk averse and risk acceptant at the same time. It assumes that potential aggressors won't take the risk of launching war when faced with the possibility of a rival coalition. On the other hand, the balance-of-power theory assumes that some states are expansionistic and are willing to risk overthrowing the status quo.

Arguments and Bipolarity

The explanation put forward for the reputed stability of bipolar systems are as compelling as those in favor of multipolarity. The following should give you an idea of the debate.[50]

1. Because the two superpowers have interests everywhere, a solid balance is created, making expansion unlikely and preventing conflict.

2. Since the system is polarized and superpowers have interests all around the globe, a war anywhere could become a general war. This fear of major war and the realization that the stakes are very high in any contest induces caution all around.

3. Certainty and calculation are increased because of the simplicity of alignment in a bipolar system. This lessens the chance of war through misperception or miscalculation.

4. The superpowers are able to pressure their extremist allies or other small states to moderate their behavior.

5. Owing to rigid alliance structures and the salience of superpower issues, bipolar systems have essentially only one dyad across which war might break out—greatly reducing the probability of war—as opposed to multipolar systems, where war might break out across numerous dyads.

6. The balance of power is easier to achieve in a bipolar system. Adjustments and balance are automatic. In fact, balancing mechanisms become regularized, and superpowers develop routines for dealing with crises. A succession of crises even allows the superpowers to "fine-tune" conflict management techniques.

7. Shifts in alignment among the smaller states will not significantly threaten the balance of power due to the overwhelming military preponderance of the two superpowers. Since the balance of power is secure, changes in alignment do not need to lead to war.

8. Historically, tight bipolar systems—such as the post–World War II international system—have been extremely stable.

Arguments Against Bipolarity

Critics of this view offer several counterarguments.

1. The level of hostility in such a highly polarized system is extremely intense; antagonisms are automatically reciprocated. In effect, a bipolar system is a large zero-sum game in which whatever gains are made by one side must be achieved at the expense of the other. Regardless of whether an alignment shift actually changes the balance of power, the losing side will certainly perceive its loss as vital, precipitating a *causus belli*.

2. A completely polarized system lacks mediators that might be able to moderate or alleviate conflict between the two blocs.

3. Since Great Power interests are at stake everywhere, any conflict anywhere can become a general conflagration. The world is continually at the brink of war in such situations, and the crisis management capabilities of the superpowers are bound to fail at some point.

4. The superpower military stalemate may, paradoxically, lead to situations where Third World conflicts are tolerated by the bloc leaders because they fear that intervention could lead to direct confrontation.

5. Clarity and certainty of calculation may not be beneficial. It might be that nations go to war when they are more certain of the international environment than when they are uncertain. The lack of ambiguity may lead to more war rather than less.

Polarity: Implications

Before it escapes our attention, let us quickly address the question we have been continually asking about the theories we have discussed: How might insights from these theories enhance the prospects for peace? The proponents of bipolarity and multipolarity are essentially making the same argument: peace is maintained through the balance of power. They just happen to disagree on which type of international system is most conducive to maintaining a stable balance. They both argue for a policy that maintains an equal balance; some just happen to think this is easier in a system that has only two superpowers and lots of smaller states; others think it is easier when there are many states with equally strong capabilities. What theorists *do not* advocate is a conscious effort to change one system into the other. Bipolar theorists do not suggest, for example, that during periods of multipolarity we should attempt to reduce the number of great powers to two! Everyone understands that transitions from multipolarity to bipolarity (or vice versa) are frequently accompanied by major wars. Balance-of-power politics are therefore seen as methods of preserving the system as long as possible, whether it is bipolar or multipolar.

Polarization: Empirical Research

Have political scientists in their studies of polarity and polarization discovered any evidence that the structure of the international system is related to war? Let us first take up the research on polarization or *cluster polarity*.

Frank Wayman's study of major power wars finds that for the nineteenth century cluster multipolarity (that is, a lack of polarization) leads to war. Alliance clusters seem to have been disintegrating prior to the outbreak of war. The twentieth century shows just the opposite pattern: cluster multipolarity leads to peace, and alliance patterns become (bi)polarized prior to the outbreak of war. And since the wars of the twentieth century were more severe and were of greater magnitude and duration, high-cluster bipolarity (polarization) is therefore associated with severe general wars.[51]

Bruce Bueno de Mesquita finds somewhat similar patterns for the entire international system. Like Wayman he finds basic differences between the two centuries. Although he finds no relationship between polarization and war, he does find that *changes* in tightness (polarization) precede both Great Power wars and interstate wars in general, though only in the twentieth century. He discovers that 84% of the wars in the twentieth century began in years following a five-year rise in systemic tightness. This is doubtless to be interpreted as the result of alliance making, a process which has a drastic effect on the number of interaction opportunities, and which upsets previous patterns of relations. War almost never occurs in periods of declining tightness, according to Bueno de Mesquita, and no multilateral, complex wars occur during times of declining tightness.[52]

Using a different indicator of polarization, Michael Wallace finds a curvilinear relationship between polarization and the magnitude and severity of war.[53] Wallace's independent variable (polarity) is based on alliance membership, intergovernmental organization (IGO) membership, and diplomatic links. This is combined into a weighted index that takes into account each nation's military capabilities. Thus, his weighted index combines cluster polarity and power polarity. He finds that systems that have either very low or very high levels of polarization have the greatest probability of experiencing severe wars. Moderate levels of polarization minimize the probability of war. This pattern appears to be fairly strong for the twentieth century, but weak for the nineteenth century. Wallace concludes that when there are no alliances, weak and unprotected nations fall victim to the strong; when there is high polarization, rivalries are extremely intense—leading to large, multi-lateral wars. Tight polarization pulls all members into war.[54]

Jack Levy's historical analysis of major power wars from 1495 to 1975 gives aid and comfort to the opposition. He demonstrates that, contrary to the balance-of-power hypothesis, nearly all (five of the six) periods of the most highly flexible (and therefore unpolarized) alliance systems have been followed by relatively high levels of war.[55] The exception is the historically renowned Bismarckian system of 1871–1890. Unlike many of the other unpolarized systems, this one was characterized by a static system of complex, cross-cutting bonds rather than by rapidly changing coalitions. Levy concludes that although one can find instances of highly polarized alliance systems that precede war, one can also find examples of those that have resulted in highly stable periods of peace (for instance, the alliances that centered on the League of Augsburg against France's Louis XIV, compared to the later NATO/WTO polarization). One can find similarly disparate examples for loosely polarized systems.

Perhaps the only thing we can conclude with any certainty from these studies is that the relationship between polarization and wars is neither linear nor constant over time.[56] However, there does seem to be some evidence that increased polarization and alliance aggregation leads to war, at least in the twentieth century.

Empirical Research: Alliances

The research on polarization, especially the findings of Bueno de Mesquita and Wayman, find some support in the research on the magnitude of *alliance commitments*. Alliance aggregation and polarization are not, of course, one and the same. Although it seems logical that alliances, by reducing interaction opportunities and freedom of choice, would increase polarization, alliances can be constructed without greatly increasing the degree of polarization in the system. Alliances may instead be erected in such a way as to increase the complexity and the cross-pressures in the system rather than to reduce these things. Polarization will only be enhanced if the alliances created are exclusive and mutually inconsistent. Keeping this in mind, let us now press on to the research on alliance aggregation.

Singer and Small hypothesize that alliances will most probably reduce cross-pressures, interaction opportunities, and the number of uncommitted actors; it is therefore reasonable to expect that the greater the number of alliances, the greater the chance of war. Their investigation shows that at least in the twentieth century, the increase in the number of alliances is related to the magnitude and severity of war, although not to the onset of war. In other words, alliance aggregation is related to *large* wars in the twentieth century. However, this does not apply to the nineteenth century; in that period alliances were related to peace. Over the entire period Singer and Small find a low association between alliance formation and the amount of war.[57] Some observers note that had Singer and Small extended their study further (they stop at 1945) they would probably have discovered a reversion to the earlier trend of a strong negative relationship between alliance aggregation and war.[58]

An analysis of the 1816–1945 period by Charles Ostrom and Francis Hoole shows that within three years of alliance formation, as the number of alliance dyads increase, so do the number of war dyads. After three years this relationship vanishes, suggesting that the danger of war exists only in the immediate aftermath of alliance formation and then recedes.[59] Alan Ned Sabrosky, drawing on the single case study of World War I, suggests, however, that if there is a prolonged period of alliance aggregation around the same power center, the international system is more prone to war.[60] Timing aside, these studies are generally consistent with Bueno de Mesquita's finding that a change in tightness in the system is associated with war.

Jack Levy's analysis of Great Power wars from the sixteenth to the twentieth centuries also uncovers some interesting patterns. Levy discovers that except for the nineteenth century, the majority of alliances have been followed within five years by war involving at least one of the allies. In fact, all Great Power alliances in the sixteenth, seventeenth, and twentieth centuries have been followed by war within five years and many of these wars were Great Power wars. In the nineteenth century, however, only a very small percent of the alliances were followed by Great Power wars. Of the fourteen Great Power alliances, none was followed within five years by a war involving two of the allies, and only one was followed by a war involving one of the alliance members.[61]

What might explain the difference between the centuries? Several possibilities exist. Levy suggests that the purpose of alliances changed after 1815. He asserts that prior to 1815, most peacetime alliances were offensive in nature, with the treaty specifically calling for the initiation of war. After 1815 alliances were mostly defensive, with any military activity dependent on an attack on one of the alliance partners. The early alliances were generally ad hoc and formed as a deliberate prelude to war. However, nineteenth-century alliances were permanent rather than ad hoc and were intended for the purpose of maintaining the status quo and enhancing deterrence.[62] The nature of alliances changed again at the end of the nineteenth century, but in ways that are not totally understood.

Michael Wallace seems to agree that the purpose of the alliance may be an important factor in explaining the differences in the patterns found in various centuries. He asserts that in the nineteenth century alliances were equilibrating mechanisms; they could be formed and broken off without creating a serious threat to the security of any nation. On the other hand, alliances in the twentieth century have generally had as their purpose the building of winning coalitions in case of war. This created an arms race reaction in both camps, vastly increasing hostility and the probability of war.[63] It may indeed be true that the nature of the nineteenth-century alliance was different from those of both preceding and following centuries, but Levy's characterization of them as permanent and Wallace's description of them as flexible leads one to paraphrase President Kennedy and ask whether these two fellows visited the same century.

So far we have been interested primarily in studies that have investigated whether alliances are followed by war. We also need to determine the degree to which wars have been preceded by alliances. Levy does just that. He finds that wars were preceded by alliances less than a fifth of the time in the sixteenth century, less than a third of the time in the seventeenth, and less than one-half the time in the eighteenth. Only two of the twenty wars (and none of the Great Power wars) in the nineteenth century were preceded by Great Power alliances and about one-half of the twentieth century wars were preceded by alliances. Clearly, the large majority of wars have not been preceded by alliances. Levy therefore concludes that alliances are not a necesary cause of war.[64] Overall, the relationship between alliance formation and war (combined into ten-year periods) is negative and relatively low, contradicting the hypothesis that the greater the number of alliances in a given period, the greater the amount of war that is likely. On the other hand, it seems fairly clear as well that alliances neither prevent war nor foster peace.

John Vasquez argues that the association between alliances and war may be traced to the fact that the construction of alliances leads to the creation of counteralliances, which leads to greater insecurity and greater uncertainty owing to the probability that some alliance partners might welsh on their commitments.[65] He concludes:

> Since there is often an interval between the alliance and the outbreak of war, it is a legitimate inference that alliances do not directly cause war, but help to aggravate a situation that makes war more likely. They may do this in two ways: by promoting an atmosphere that polarizes the system and by encouraging arms races.[66]

Levy warns that even those positive correlations that do exist between the creation of alliances and the onset of war may be spurious. That is, although they occur nearly simultaneously, there may be no direct causal relationship. Instead, the correlation may simply reflect the fact that alliances and wars are both being generated by the same underlying factors.[67] Indeed, even when alliance *polarization* precedes war, direct causation may not be present. The construction of alliances and the resulting polarization may merely be *symptoms* that reflect a more basic cause of war. Alliances don't cause war; states merely form alliances because they believe war is near.

*   *   *

One of the few patterns that researchers seem to be able to agree on is that once wars begin, the presence of alliances serves to expand war activity throughout the system to more states.[68] Alliances act as contagion mechanisms for war, but alliance is not the only contagion mechanism. (Geographic contiguity is another.)[69]

The studies on polarization and on alliance formation indicate that alliance making that leads to polarization sometimes (but not always) produces wars of high magnitude, severity, and duration. Polarization increases the perception of threat; it leads to military expansion; it focuses attention on issues that divide states rather than those that bind them together; it reduces the effectiveness of cross-pressures; it reduces the number of effective mediators; and it may stimulate arms races. This is not the only pattern, but it is certainly one path by which war may be reached.

Polarity: Empirical Research

Studies of the *distribution of power* throughout the international system have produced widely varied and conflicting results. Some analysts claim to have found a pattern of war proneness in a particular kind of distribution; some have found relationships that differ according to the century investigated; and some have found no relationship at all between the distribution of power and war.

The often cited study by Singer, Bremer, and Stuckey of the 1820–1965 period focuses on the magnitude of war in the system (as indicated by the number of nation-months at war), rather than on the number of wars or the onset of war. The independent variable in this study is a statistic labeled CON, which indicates the degree to which military, industrial, and demographic capabilities are concentrated in the hands of a few states in the system or are rather widely dispersed throughout the states in the system.[70] The authors find that in the nineteenth century diffusion of power was associated with low war magnitude, whereas a high concentration of power was associated with a high magnitude of war. The pattern for the twentieth century was just the opposite. In the later period, systems with highly concentrated distributions of power (preponderance) were associated with a low magnitude of war, whereas a diffusion (or balance) of power was associated with a high magnitude of war.

Bruce Bueno de Mesquita reanalyzed the Singer-Bremer-Stuckey study using the presence or absence of war as the dependent variable instead of the level of war. He concludes that the distribution of power is not related to the occurrence of war in either century.[71] Neither the concentration of power in the system nor the change in concentration of power seemed to make a difference. A further replication by Wayman uses CON as well as a more controversial statistic he calls TWO CON, the percent of great power capabilities held by the two most powerful states in the system. Wayman finds that years that were power multipolar (that is, in which power was diffused rather than concentrated) were slightly less war prone, but the wars that broke out in these systems were massive. Three-quarters of the wars in such systems were of high magnitude. On the other hand, three-quarters of the wars in power bipolar systems (that is, in systems where power was highly concentrated) were of low magnitude. The bipolar giants seem to have been able to manage conflict in these systems and prevent them from becoming system engulfing.[72]

Midlarsky's historical analysis focuses on the transition from bipolar systems to those with a larger number of great powers.[73] His theoretical argument is that an increase in the *number* of great powers, coupled with a decline in the amount of valued resources in the system, would lead to a dramatic increase in inequality and therefore instability. Midlarsky notices that the Thirty Years' War (1618–1648) began as a transition from bipolarity (Catholic states and Lutheran states in Europe) to tripolarity (Catholic, Lutheran, and Calvinist states) was underway in Europe. World Wars I and II began as the number of resources (small, independent states and colonial areas) decreased while at the same time there was a mild increase in the number of Great Powers (for instance, the United States and Japan).

Jack Levy investigates the Great Power system for a larger period of history, 1495–1975, using a subjective classification of particular periods as multipolar, bipolar, or unipolar.[74] His interest is in wars between Great Powers and wars that involve at least one Great Power. Like Wayman, he concludes that although war occurs frequently in all systems, multipolar systems are slightly less prone to war than the other systems, though wars in multipolar systems tend to be more serious. Conversely, he discovers that large, "general wars" have not occurred in bipolar systems (for instance, 1495–1556 and 1945–1975). Wars between great powers were more frequent in bipolar systems, though bipolar systems had wars of less severity and magnitude. Bipolar and multipolar systems seem to be equally stable in terms of the relative number of years at peace. Unipolar systems were by far the most war prone, and general wars occurred most frequently in unipolar periods.

The results of the studies by both Levy and Wayman turn on its head the traditional realist wisdom that multipolar systems result in more frequent but less serious wars while bipolar systems result in less frequent but more serious wars. Their research suggests that just the opposite may be true.

What should we conclude from these efforts? First, the relationship between power distribution and war may vary over time. Second, research efforts produce different results when different indicators of polarity, stability, and war are used. Third, it seems that the distribution of power is only weakly related (if at all) to the onset of war, but is associated with certain types of war. If a war occurs, the distribution of power may have a major influence on the kind of war fought.[75] Fourth, war occurs frequently in all types of systems; none can be credited with making a significant contribution to peace. Given the differing methodologies used and the divergent results achieved by these research efforts, it is necessary to conclude that the relationship between power distribution and war is far from completely understood.

Combined Effects: Polarity and Polarization

Since neither the concepts of power polarity nor cluster polarity on their own seem to be overwhelmingly helpful, perhaps a combination of the two concepts would make more sense. Attempts to focus on one factor may be confounded or influenced by the effects of the other. Wayman prefers to combine the concepts of polarity and polarization so that international systems can be classified on the basis of the fourfold schema presented in Table 8.1. His research indicates that the systems that have been most prone to serious wars have been those that have been both cluster bipolar and power multipolar—that is, systems composed of a relatively large number of states with equal power that are aligned into two mutually exclusive blocs. The systems that have been most peaceful (at least in the twentieth century) have been both cluster multipolar and power bipolar.[76] Wayman contends that supporters of bipolarity are correct about the stability of bipolarity, as long as their argument is made in terms of *power* (bi)polarity. Likewise, proponents of multipolarity are correct about the stability of multipolarity, as long as they mean *cluster* (multi)polarity.

It should be kept in mind that other variables may interact with polarity and polarization in a way that reduces or increases the probability of war. Stoll and Champion suggest that differing results in research on bipolarity and multipolarity may be due to the relative strength of satisfied powers in the system.[77] Different distributions of satisfied/unsatisfied states should produce different behaviors. They hypothesize that when satisfied states hold a relatively low percent of systemic capabilities, there will be a strong positive relationship between concentration of capabilities (i.e., preponderance) and war. A test of this hypothesis gets mild support (though they use nation-months of war as the dependent variable rather than onset of war, and the determination of whether a state is satisfied or not is admittedly "soft"). They argue that if a dissatisfied major power wants to change the status quo, then an equal military distribution can keep the peace. Of course, if the level of satisfaction within the system is high, polarity is less relevant.

The difference between status quo states and revisionist states would seem to be important. Indeed, it is a distinction of great relevance not only to status discrepancy theory, but to the theory we will investigate next, power transition theory.

Power Transition Theory

We have been looking thus far at systemic variables in a fairly static way—focusing on the structure of the system at a given time, whether it is characterized by cluster bipolarity, or power multipolarity, or status disequilibrium. But we have also noticed the importance some scholars have attributed to *changes* in some of these variables. A. F. K. Organski has put forward a theory of war based primarily on changes in the distribution of power in the international system.[78]

Organski challenges the traditional balance-of-power thesis that equality of balance keeps the peace. This idea was based on the argument that equal power was sufficient to dissuade adventurism, while superiority tempted the possessor to gain power at the expense of others. As long as there was an equilibrium in the system that balanced power against power, war should be deterred. But as Inis Claude so clearly stated, "If an equilibrium means either side may lose, it also means that either side may win"—thus tempting both sides to initiate war.[79] This is Organski's starting point.

Organski argues that in each historical era a single dominant state usually leads the international order as head of a coalition of satisfied powers. (The international system is seen not as anarchic, but as more or less hierarchically organized.) As long as the leader of this status quo coalition enjoys a preponderance of power, peace is maintained. It is the inequality in the distribution of power between the hegemon and its primary challenger—combined with the support for the status quo by the hegemon's allies—that keeps the peace. Under these circumstances it would be foolish for the challenger to initiate war, and the dominant state has little to gain or to fear. However, as potential rivals undergo industrialization and modernization, the old leader is challenged, creating a situation that frequently leads to war. The source of war is the differences in size and rates of growth of the members of the system.

Conflicts are most likely when power transitions are underway. At the core of such shifts are simultaneous increases in productivity linked to industrialization, increased manpower due to demographic growth, and an increase in the capacity of political elites to mobilize national resources. Sudden changes in national capabilities upset the previous distribution of power. Specifically, major wars are asserted to be most likely when the challenger catches up to the dominant state, impelling a kind of "rear-end collision." Organski and Kugler assume the weaker challenger initiates the war against the stronger, dominant state. Powerful, satisfied states do not start wars; they are the primary beneficiaries of the present system and have no interest in changing it. On the other hand, the challenger is usually a newcomer to the ranks of the powerful and is therefore usually without the benefits that befit its capability. It is dissatisfied with the status quo in general and with its position in the international system in particular; it therefore desires to redraft the rules more to its liking. This should sound familiar. At least some of the explanatory logic for the power transition theory draws on the theory of status discrepancy.[80]

Organski and Kugler hypothesize that major wars are most likely when the power distribution between the dominant state and the challenger is approximately equal. Specifically, the challenger is believed most likely to initiate war *before* equality is actually attained, though there is some dispute about this point.[81]

Regardless of the exact timing involved, the theory argues that as the gap closes, each nation is likely to see the situation as threatening. The two rivals become increasingly anxious about the situation and sensitive to changes in the distribution of power. The dominant state fears that the challenger will surpass it in power, will be unwilling to accept a subordinant position in the international order, will challenge it for leadership, and will attempt to change the rules of the system. For these reasons the dominant state might institute a preemptive strike against the challenger, hoping to prevent the inevitable. However, war is most likely to occur because of an attempt by the challenger to hasten the passage, perhaps due to the overconfidence brought on by rapid growth and the temptation to make use of the opportunity to achieve a complete, outright victory. The lack of clarity in the balance of power creates a situation in which national leaders are likely to see either opportunities or threats in the external environment.

Premature aggression turns out to be strategic error on the challenger's part. The dominant nation's alliance is usually stronger. The challenger frequently neglects to entice away the hegemon's support and is therefore confronted with a superior coalition, leading to the defeat of the challenger and its bloc. Nevertheless, in the long run, the challenger recovers its power in fifteen to eighteen years and even surpasses some members of the winning coalition—a phenomenon Organski calls the "Phoenix Factor." Wars do not prevent the rise of challengers in the long run, and attempts to arrest the gains of fast-growing states may be doomed to failure.

Organski argues that the faster the rate of transition, the greater the probability of war. If the rate of growth is relatively slow, the warning time is greater for the hegemon, and both states will have a chance to prepare themselves for the future in a more reasoned and realistic manner. Mutually beneficial arrangements for the transition can be worked out between the challenger and the hegemon. Accommodations and compensations can be negotiated, and peaceful resolutions are more likely. On the other hand, if the rate of growth in the challenger is swift, neither nation is likely to be adequately prepared for the transition, and miscalculations and precipitous actions are much more likely.[82]

Power Transition Theory: Empirical Research

Organski and Kugler attempt to test the power transition theory against wars involving major powers in the nineteenth and twentieth centuries—the Franco-Prussian War, the Russo-Japanese War, and World Wars I and II. They find that wars occurred both when the hegemon-challenger dyad were equal and unequal in power. (They use gross national product as their indicator of power.) However, in each case where there was war between pairs of equal power, a power transition was under way. There were no cases of war between equal nations where one was not overtaking the other. They conclude, therefore, that wars among major power contenders occur only if a power transition is underway. Thus, power transition is a necessary, but not a sufficient, condition for war. They also find that the speed of transition is important, as hypothesized.[83]

Two Dutch scholars, Henk Houweling and Jan Sicamma, note that while Organski and Kugler test to see whether great power wars were preceded by power transitions, they do not investigate whether power transitions are always followed by wars. Using a broader measurement of national power that incorporated elements of both size and development, an expanded time frame, and a larger list of wars, they find that power transitions are an important predictor of the outbreak of war. Since they discover a strong relationship between power equality and the outbreak of war, their finding constitutes a major challenge to the traditional balance-of-power hypothesis that equality leads to peace.[84]

Richard J. Stoll and Michael Champion, using the COW composite indicators of relative capability, agree that all of Germany's wars with other great powers occurred when predicted by the power transition theory. The Autro-Prussian War, the Franco-Prussian War, and the two World Wars all broke out within five years of the intersection of capability scores between Germany and its major power rival at the time, thus lending support to the "parity leads to war" hypothesis. But they note also several transitions that did not result in war. War did not eventuate as the power capabilities of the United States surpassed those of the European powers; neither did the German overtaking of Russia in the 1870s lead to war.[85] The lack of war associated with these transitions might be due to the relative satisfaction of the rising challenger. One might certainly explain the former case (as Organski does) in this way.

Charles Gochman looks at the conflict involvement of major powers and non–major power rivals from 1816 to 1980.[86] His analysis generally supports the power transition hypotheses. He finds war is more likely among both major powers and non–major power rivals that are relatively equal in total (demographic-industrial-military) power. But parity alone is not sufficient to provoke war; a power transition must be underway. Gochman finds that both major power dyads and non–major power dyads are more likely to become involved in war when they are rapidly converging toward parity (or diverging away from it, though this finding isn't as strong). He discovers that great powers are generally more likely to engage in war when their own total capabilities are increasing rapidly, but not when they are decreasing. These findings are consistent with Organski's "rear-end collision" thesis. Gochman concludes:

> . . . rapid alterations in the relative strength of actors produce uncertainties with respect to intentions, or dissatisfaction with the distribution of benefits, for which the actors have insufficient time to adjust. More gradual change provides greater possibilities for accommodation or adjustment to new realities.[87]

Before we get overexcited that one of the theories in this chapter seems to have received universal validation, we ought to mention that a recent study by Woosang Kim provides weighty evidence to the contrary.[88] Kim investigates Organski's theory using an expanded list of wars and the same composite capability indicator as Stoll and Champion, but uses a different set of statistical tests. He finds most of Organski's hypotheses to be too weakly supported to grant confirmation. The dyadic equality of power simply does not explain the outbreak of war very well. The distribution of power between two states seems to have little to do with the incidence of war. In fact, neither the "equality of power leads to war" hypothesis nor the "preponderance leads to war" hypothesis is supported. In addition, Kim discovers a negative relationship between power transitions and war; war, in fact, seems *less likely* when one state is overtaking another. Furthermore, the speed of national growth seems to be unimportant, challenging the uneven national growth aspect of Organski's theory. The jury is still out on this one.

Perhaps now is the time to mention two things that may already have become apparent to the reader. First, the power transition theory is not a general theory of war; it only purports to explain certain exceptional cases—major encounters between the most powerful states in the system.[89] On the other hand, as Gochman demonstrates, it is certainly capable of being generalized to all states within a system, whether a central system or a regional subsystem. There seems to be no compelling theoretical reason why it should apply only to hegemonic contenders. Indeed, Organski and Kugler themselves apply it to the Russo-Japanese War.

Second, strictly speaking, the power transition theory is not an international system level theory of war; instead, it operates at the *dyadic interaction* level. It is concerned with the interrelationship between two states—a dominant power and a challenger. It is a version of the systemic distribution of power writ smaller. We have included it in this section because it essentialy deals with balance-of-power issues and because it is embedded in a theory about the structure of the international system—as typically led by a dominant power—in which peace in the international system is maintained by the preponderance of the system leader.

With this in mind we should note a few research efforts that focus not on power transitions between pairs of states, but on the *dyadic balance of power* and the occurrence of war. These studies tend to support the equality-leads-to-war argument of Organski, though toal agreement is lacking. Studies by Erich Weede on Asian dyads from 1950 to 1969 and by David Garnham on thirty dyads from 1816 to 1965 indicate that preponderance is more likely to lead to peace, while parity is more highly associated with war.[90] The peaceful impact of preponderance is also saluted by historian Geoffrey Blainey, who argues that decisive victories in major power wars have led to longer periods of peace precisely because they illustrated plainly the absolute preponderance of the victor, while wars that lacked decisive conclusion led to further wars because they left the system in a situation of relative parity where misperceptions concerning the true balance of power could lead all states to assume the balance was in their favor.[91]

However, just as significant disagreement exists concerning the relationship between power distribution and war at the systemic level, the same is true at the dyadic level. Impressive support for the "equality leads to peace" hypothesis comes from a study by Wayne Ferris. His analysis of the forty-two wars in the 1850–1965 period found that thirty-four (81%) exhibited a power disparity of 1.45 to 1.0 or greater between the contesting dyads. He concludes by stating, "Few wars are seen to occur when two sides to the conflict approach equality in power capabilities below the ratio level of 1.45. Once that threshold is exceeded, however, the number of war events increases markedly."[92] Preponderance seems to lead to war. Seyom Brown also maintains that while challenges to the prevailing balance (or imbalance) may trigger war, preponderance in a dyadic relationship may lead to war as well. He argues that if there is an intensely antagonistic relationship between two states and a large military imbalance, this tempts a dissatisfied superior state to escalate the conflict to war: for instance, Japan's attack on China, Hitler's aggression in Europe, North Korea's attack on South Korea, and India's attack on Pakistan in 1971.[93] Perhaps the key here is that the militarily superior power is deemed to be dissatisfied, while Organski and Kugler generally assume the opposite.

Power Transitions and Equality: Conclusions

While the validity of the power transition theory has by no means been determined, nevertheless it appears as one of the stronger attempts to explain great power war. It is clear that dyadic equality (or near equality) of power doesn't always lead to war between rivals; it is also clear that power transitions don't always eventuate in war. However, the coincidence of power transitions and dyadic parity does seem important. It appears that rapid changes in power capabilities, especially those that lead toward dyadic parity, make war between major powers and between non–major power rivals more likely. It is also likely that power transitions toward equality are associated with other factors—such as systemic power deconcentration, arms races, and perceptions of threat—which further contribute to the likelihood of war.

The power transition theory makes intuitive sense, it is consistent with our sense of the probable, it has internal logic, it is fairly parsimonious, it is supported by a small raft of evidence, and it is linked to important factors at other levels of analysis that also contribute to the initiation of war. Major shifts in the relative balance between states seem to be an important part of the war puzzle. And despite the studies by Kim and Ferris, a significant amount of evidence suggests that we should also have serious doubts about the traditional balance-of-power hypothesis that equality of power leads to peace.[94]

Let us continue our examination of the relationship between power preponderance and peace (and between power equality and war) by turning our attention to theories of the international system that focus on the cyclical rise and fall of global hegemonic leaders and the connection of these cycles to war.

9

The International System: Cyclical Theories and Historical-Structural Theories of War

> The old order changeth, yielding place to new.
> —Alfred, Lord Tennyson

Several theorists have turned their attention to the historical evolution of the international system and in particular to fluctuations in the concentration of power as reflected in the rise and decline of the system's leader and the wars that attend these phenomena. Proponents of these "historical-structural" theories believe that to understand the current structure of the international system, one needs to know how this system has evolved historically. In many ways the international system of the late twentieth tcentury constitutes merely a modification of the structures and processes of the international system that existed, say, in the sixteenth century. Many of the patterns and cyclical processes (including cycles of war) that are present now can be understood by examining their origins and development in previous international systems. Let us turn our attention now to several of these theories of war that deal with cycles of war between dominant states and challengers. The main contenders are Robert Gilpin's theory of hegemonic war, George Modelski's "long cycle" theory, Emmanuel Wallerstein's theory of the capitalist world system, and Charles Doran's cycle of relative power.

Gilpin's Theory of Hegemonic War

Robert Gilpin's theory is outlined in his *War and Change in World Politics*.[1] Like Organski's power transition theory, Gilpin's theory is not a general theory of war, but a medium-range theory that addresses wars fought between major powers for leadership in the international system— *hegemonic wars*. Also like Organski, his attention is focused on the dominant state in the system, which Gilpin calls a *hegemon*. These states' leadership of

254

the system has, historically, been set in motion by military victory. The hegemon's leadership is based on its simultaneous military and economic dominance and on its ability to provide certain public goods to system members: military security, investment capital, an international currency, a secure environment for trade and investment, a set of rules for economic transactions and the protection of property rights, and the general maintenance of the status quo. In return for the provision of these collective goods, the hegemon receives revenues and other benefits.[2] As you can imagine, the rules or the system and the distribution of values in the system reflect the interests of the hegemonic state.

Gilpin is interested primarily in wars fought for dominance in the international system. Hegemonic wars are direct contests between the dominant power(s) and a rising challenger over the governance and leadership of the international system. In his view, war arises because of an increasing disequilibrium between the political organization of the system, on the one hand, and the actual distribution of power, on the other. As the reigning hegemonic state gradually loses the dominant economic and military position it once held, the distribution of prestige and the distribution of power are no longer in conjunction. This state of affairs is largely due to the *law of uneven growth*, which virtually assures that the distribution of power in the system will be unstable. Uneven rates in the growth of national power result in a cycle of growth and decline for all states and the rise and fall of hegemonic powers.

Gilpin's conception of the law of uneven growth is somewhat similar to Lenin's use of the law of uneven development, which he asserted would lead to war between capitalist states. Gilpin, however, is a *neorealist*; he believes that the clash between major powers is not primarily economic, but is a more fundamental clash of strategic and national interests: it is a power struggle, not an economic struggle.[3] What is important here is the uneven growth of *power*, not the uneven development of national economies. Gilpin recognizes, however, that this uneven growth of power is created by changes in transportation, communication, industrial technology, population, prices, and the accumulation of capital, as well as by changes in military technology and strategy.

Gilpin places equal emphasis on the decline of the dominant power and the rise of the challenger. The decline in the relative position of the hegemon is virtually inevitable and is due to several factors: (a) the costs of maintaining dominance in the system—which include military expenditures, aid to allies, and provision of collective economic goods necessary to maintain the global economy; (b) the loss of economic and technological leadership to other states owing to uneven rates of growth, decreasing innovation and risk taking in the hegemon, and the tendency for the hegemonic state to emphasize consumption at the expense of investment; (c) the "advantage of backwardness" and the diffusion of military and economic technology away from the center; (d) the erosion of the hegemon's resource base; and (e) the tendency for power to shift from the center to the periphery as fighting among states in the central system weakens them all.

Incorporating a *rational choice model* in his theory, Gilpin argues that states will attempt to change the international system in response to developments that improve the cost/benefit ratio of attempting to change the status quo. The propensity to initiate change in the international system continues until an equilibrium is reached between costs and benefits.[4] The international system is stable as long as no state perceives that it is profitable to change it. Essentially, this means stability is ensured as long as the strongest states in the system are satisfied with the prevailing distribution of rights and benefits. The change in relative power alters the cost of changing the international system, granting some states a powerful incentive to seek change. As their relative power increases, rising nations attempt to change the rules of the system, the division of spheres of influence, and the distribution of benefits and territories, but only when the expected benefits of changing the system are perceived to exceed the expected costs.

War, of course, has historically been the primary method of resolving the disequilibrium between the structure of the international system and changing distribution of power. Who initiates this war? In Gilpin's theory, the rising challenger is expected to be the most likely culprit, as it attempts to expand its influence to the limits of its new capabilities. Gilpin, however, recognizes the possibility that the hegemon itself may attempt to weaken or destroy the challenger by initiating a preventive war to forestall its loss of position. Gilpin argues that there aren't too many examples historically of hegemonic powers willing to concede their dominance over the system to a rising challenger in order to avoid war. (Neither are there many examples of rising nations that prefer not to press their advantage.)[5]

Neither bipolarity nor multipolarity guarantees peace, according to Gilpin. The most important factor is not the distribution of power, but the dynamics of power relations over time. In both bipolar and multipolar systems, changes in the relative power among the principal actors lead to war and change.[6] (Without have said it in so many words, Gilpin has explained hegemonic wars in terms of power transitions.)[7] Implicit in Gilpin's theory of war and change is that there is an inverse relationship between the power of the hegemon and the likelihood of war. *Unipolar systems* (systems of "hegemonic governance") are seen as the most stable, while instability accompanies the decline of the hegemon's military preponderance—though the exact threshold at which this is presumed to take place is not clear. According to Gilpin, peace and stability have flourished during those times in which the prestige hierarchy has been clearly understood and unchallenged. A weakening of the hierarchy of prestige and increased ambiguity places the system on the road to war.[8]

The strong implication of Gilpin's theory is that the half-century of peace since 1945 has been due to the continued hegemony of the United States, but that a decline of American preponderance could usher in a new era of global warfare.[9] On the other hand, Gilpin argues that it is possible that systemic change be accomplished without hegemonic warfare. That this has not happened historially does not mean we are doomed to the pattern. Substitutes for war can be found.

Hegemonic War: Empirical Research

Gilpin's work only illustrates his theory with historical examples; it does not subject it to an empirical test. He is able neither to demonstrate that all hegemonic wars have resulted from the type of systemic disequilibrium he discusses, nor that all such systemic disequilibria have led to hegemonic wars. A recent test was made of Gilpin's hypothesized relationship between hegemonic decline and war by Edward Spiezio.[10] Since the creation of the modern international system in 1648 with the Peace of Westphalia, hegemonic governance has been accomplished only twice according to Gilpin, by the British (1815–1939) and the United States (1939 to the present).[11] Because the American cycle is incomplete, the period of British hegemonic rule is taken as a test case. Spiezio attempts to discern whether war was in fact inversely related to Britain's relative miltary and economic position, that is, whether war was more frequent during the period of hegemonic decline than the period of Britain's ascendancy. He concludes that Gilpin's theory is generally supported, but the relationship is not particularly strong, and there are some serious anamolies.

As hypothesized, the frequency of international conflict is inversely related to Britain's relative power during her entire cycle of leadership. However, although wars occurred more frequently during Britain's decline than during her ascendancy, the difference was not overwhelming (54% to 45%). Wars occurred frequently in both phases. Interestingly, ten of the twelve wars (involving a Great Power on one or both sides) that occurred during Britain's rising phase were actually clustered around the years 1845–1860, the highpoint of Britain's relative power in the system! On the other hand, the majority (79%) of wars involving Great Powers on both sides—the type of wars most relevant to the theory—did begin during Britain's declining phase. However, Spiezio concludes that ultimately, the degree of hegemonic power cannot be seen as a primary determinant of the occurrence of war.

Modelski's Long-Cycle Theory

A "long cycle" theory of international politics and war has been put forward by George Modelski and William Thompson.[12] According to this view, there are three principal structures in the world system: the global political system, the world economy, and the world cultural subsystem. The global political system is not entirely anarchic, but possesses a decentralized polity that lacks an overriding authority.[13] Management of the system is sometimes absent altogether or is often shared among several states, but from time to time the management of this interdependent global system is in the hands of a single unit. This state, which Modelski calls a *world power*, dominates the keeping of order in the system through its monopoly of military resources. The position of the world power prior to 1945, according to Modelski and Thompson, was based primarily on naval capabilities—the factor that contributes most to a state's command of "global reach."[14] The military preponderance of the world power makes it possible for this state to provide public goods such as military security, world organization, and a set of rules for international economic relations.

Since 1500 there has been a succession of world powers that have shaped the global system. The rise and fall of these world leaders has been cyclical in nature. Each cycle begins with a *global war*, which determines how the system is to be constituted and which world power will be able to organize the system. The war leaves military capabilities (particularly seapower) highly concentrated, at least temporarily, in the hands of a single actor. This actor also possesses, again temporarily, the world system's leading economy. Eventually, the power and the political legitimacy of this state decline and it attracts competitors. Order gives way to disorder, concentration of power to deconcentration. Thus, there are four stages of the *long cycle*: global war, world power, delegitimization, and deconcentration.

It is the world power state that is associated with peace and stability. Like Gilpin and Organski, the long cyclists believe that concentration of power in the hands of a world leader is associated with systemic stability, though this does not last. The long cycle of world leadership endures approximately one hundred years—three generations. The world power manages the system alone for the inital part of this cycle, but the system does not remain unipolar; as the legitimacy and power of the global leader erode, the system drifts from unipolarity to bipolarity and multipolarity. Long-cycle theorists claim the international system has completed four full cycles and part of a fifth, as illustrated by Table 9.1.

To what does Modelski attribute the cyclical nature of World leadership? First, each cycle is born in warfare—a situation that is not the most conducive to the creation of a stable world order. Second, monopolization of global power is a double-edged sword: monopolies create benefits, and benefits attract competition. Monopolization is also expensive. The burden of managing the system requires the expenditure of tremendous resources. Debt levels and the inability to secure uninterrupted access to credit are particularly important in the decline of world powers, especially the early global leaders.[15] Third, there is a tendency for the world power to respond to

Table 9–1
Long Cycles of World Leadership

Long cycle		World power	Global war
I	1494–1579	Portugal	Italian and Indian Ocean Wars (1494–1516)
II	1580–1689	Netherlands	Spanish-Dutch Wars (1580–1609)
III	1689–1792	Britain	Wars of Louis XIV (1688–1713) (Wars of the Grand Alliance)
IV	1792–1914	Britain	Wars of the French Revolution and Napoleon (1792–1815)
V	1914–	United States	World Wars I and II (1914–1945)

Source: G. Modelski and P. Morgan, "Understanding Global War," *Journal of Conflict Resolution* 29 (3), (September 1985), p. 396.

challenges by defending fixed positions and distant frontiers. Fourth, the long cycle is related to shifts in the distribution of economic resources among the states in the system, though this has more relevance for the post-1815 world system than for the pre–19th century. Finally, the coalition constructed in order to win the previous global war has a tendency toward fracturing. Thompson notes that in each of the long cycles one member of the winning coalition changed sides after the war and became the primary challenger in the next succession struggle.[16]

The long-cycle theory is concerned primarily with *global wars*—wars that result in the selection of a new world power (or the confirmation of the previous world power). Each global war has been relatively long-lasting and has taken place at intervals of approximately one hundred years. And each, according to Modelski, has had a distinctive oceanic-maritime component.[17] Although the primary focus of the theory is on global wars, the gradual deconcentration of power in the system is also related to smaller wars that serve as a prelude to the more cataclysmic global wars.[18] Long cyclists maintain that the cause of wars is to be found primarily in the processes and dynamics of the system, specifically the changing distribution of power that derives from uneven rates of development among members of the international system. Research by long-cycle theorists generally supports the contention by Organski that immediately prior to "global war" the challenger's capabilities are on the rise while those of the world power's are declining, though Modelski and Thompson argue that this does not necessarily mean the dissatisfied challenger will attack the leading power.

The conflict is usually initiated not by a direct confrontation between challenger and hegemon, but by the challenger's attempt at expansion on the European continent in what is initially a localized conflict, an attempt that frequently occurs before the challenger has actually surpassed the hegemon in power capabilities. With one exception (prior to the wars of the French Revolution), the global situation as been triangular: the rising continental power is confronted by two maritime powers, one of which is the world power. When the dust settles at the end of the global war, the challenger is defeated, and the other maritime power emerges as the successor to its ally as the new world power.[19] Thompson explains:

> Invariably, the challenger appears to act on the hope, belief, or mistaken assumption that one or more of the globally oriented powers will not oppose its continental expansion. These misperceptions may be mixed with impatience and overconfidence stemming from the challenger's rapid capability improvements and encouraged by a system characterized by declining order and increasing strife. But in any event, global wars tend to begin as relatively localized affairs, becoming global in scope only after the globally oriented power(s) decides to participate.[20]

The fact that global wars tend to start as local affairs seems to indicate that challengers may not have actually intended an all-out challenge to the status quo, raising the question of whether global wars for systemic leadership are (or need be) deliberate acts.[21]

Whether global wars are deliberate or nor, their results are similar. In fact, long cyclists uncover a pattern that virtually all cyclical theorists discover: the challenger invariably loses the military contest with the hegemon. The transfer of global leadership is often accomplished in a fairly cooperative manner, with the new leader frequently arising from the coalition of allies surrounding the old hegemon.[22] The events of the first half of the present century are instructive. German challenges were mounted—prior to World War I and World War II—before she overtook either Britain or the United States in economic terms, but especially important was her lack of naval power relative to either the declining hegemon (Britain) or the eventual new world power (the United States), thus limiting her "global reach" capabilities and leaving her vulnerable to naval blockades.[23] After World War II hegemony was smoothly transferred from the reigning world leader, Britain, to her coalition partner, the United States.

Long Cycles: Empirical Research

Remember that Modelski's long-cycle theory hypothesizes that unipolar systems will be the most stable and peaceful, followed by bipolarity, while multipolar systems are the most unstable. Thus, the level of stability (and order) in the system is directly related to the power structure of the international system. Thompson tests this set of propositions using a special indicator of polarity based on the distribution of seapower.

Thompson discovers that, with two exceptions, a unipolar or near-unipolar distribution of power does in fact emerge from periods of global warfare.[24] These periods are characterized by less warfare than would be expected by chance, and destabilizing warfare is least common in unipolar systems. As the distribution of power in the system becomes increasingly less concentrated, the amount of war increases, with multipolarity being the least stable system.[25] The 1816–1945 period deviates somewhat from this pattern in that bipolarity in this period resulted in a high proportion of weighted warfare. The British-German bipolar pair was especially war prone, while the bipolar system of British-Dutch rivalry in the seventeenth century, British-French rivalry in the eighteenth century, and British-German rivalry in the early twentieth century were not especially dangerous. Thus, the relative stability of bipolarity seems to be somewhat dependent on nonsystemic factors.[26] The important point remains, however, that unipolarity—at least as defined by long cyclists—is the most peaceful.

Thompson also investigates the possible connection between Organski's power transition and the hegemonic war cycle, examining the five long-cycle wars for evidence of power transitions. Using his own data on national power (based on naval capabilities), he finds each global war was preceded by a decline in the capability of the dominant state relative to the primary contender at the dyadic level, in part validating Organski's theory for the five global wars. He concludes that there may be some linkage between systemic and dyadic processes; if a world system cycle and a power transition occur simultaneously, even small local crises could trigger a global war.[27]

We know from the theories of Organski, Gilpin, and Modelski that the declining power of states, especially of hegemons, is a dangerous situation; however, declining power doesn't always lead to war. It would be helpful to know when it does and when it doesn't. Theorists have put forward various conditions.[28] It has been suggested that declining power leads to war when: (1) the transition is rapid and moves toward rough equality, (2) the magnitude of the shift is high, (3) there is a lack of tradition of friendship between the rivals, (4) the challenger is dissatisfied with the status quo, (5) offensive forces have a relative advantage over defensive forces and there is an expected probablity of the adversary initiating war first, (6) there is a probability of victory within tolerable costs, and (7) leaders in the inititing state are risk-acceptant. Whether all these need to be present, or just some, and in which combinations is not clear.

Long Cycles: Implications

As for the present situation, the "long peace" since 1945 can be explained by reference to the structural condition of the international system: for most of the last forty-five years (1946–1968 according to Thompson) it has been in the world power phase with clear American hegemony. Since 1969 it has entered a bipolar delegitimation phase, but the United States is still able to provide political, military, and economic order to the system. Indeed, Thompson demonstrates that the United States is in a stronger relative position than other world powers at a comparable point in the long cycle, along both naval concentration indicators and leading economic sector indicators.[29] The American position is buttressed by the anomalous situation in which the leading military contender and the leading economic contender have been different states, the U.S.S.R. and Japan, respectively! And in the past several years the military challenge from the Soviet Union has collapsed as that multinational state has fragmented. Thus, the structural conditions of the international system continue to discourage global war. However, the probability of global war might increase substantially in the next forty years.[30]

Long-cycle theorists argue that there is nothing inherent in the logic of long cycles that requires them to begin with global wars. Disequilibria in the international system could be resolved through peaceful change. Alternative mechanisms for the transfer of global leadership may be found. The cause of war in the contemporary world has simply been the lack of a substitute mechanism of the making of global decisions about political leadership.[31]

Long Cycles: Critique

Critics, of course, have challenged some of the analyses of long-cycle theorists. For instance, Jack Levy argues that the classification of global wars is a problem. Long-cycle theorists omit several major power wars with important consequences for the European system. The second phase of Charles V's Italian Wars with France (1672–1678) began early in the first long cycle's world-power phase; the Thirty Years' War (1618–1648) broke out during the world-power phase of the second cycle; the War of Jenkin's Ear/Austrian Succession (1739–1748) began barely a year after the end of the world-power phase of the third long cycle. That such important major power wars occurred during the very periods deemed to be most peaceful by the long-cycle theory undermines our confidence in the theory.[32]

A second concern is the emphasis on naval power at the expense of land-based military power and the deemphasis of the importance of dominant military position of the European continent. Levy summarizes:

> The primary cause of the great wars of the past . . . has been the perception by most of the great powers that one state was threatening to gain a dominant position in Europe. The great powers have always perceived the most serious threats . . . as coming from the great land powers of Europe—which could threaten their territorial integrity—rather than from the more wealthy naval and commercial powers. This is why the great European military coalitions have always been formed against the most threatening continental power rather than against the leading naval power.[33]

Wallerstein's World-Economy Approach

Immanuel Wallerstein is the leader of a rather diverse school of thought variously called the world-systems or world-economy approach.[34] The world-systems perspective is essentially a political economy approach to international relations that focuses on international inequality and dependence. Even though its primary focus is not on war, its influence on the study of war is widespread. You will notice also that it shares much with the approaches of Gilpin and Modelski.

As with the other historical-structural approaches, the world-systems perspective comes complete with its own terminology. Wallerstein classifies world systems into two types: *world empires*, in which a single political unit controls the world system's economy (i.e., the Roman Empire), and *world economies*, which are essentially multicentric, with no single state in control. Wallerstein argues that although limited world empires existed in the past, the modern age (beginning about 1450) has been characterized by the emergence of a European-based capitalist world economy that has gradually become a truly global economy. Although attempts have been made by certain states to construct a world empire, in the modern age none has succeeded.

Like the realists, Wallerstein emphasizes the anarchic nature of the international system. Essentially, the competitive nature of the system prevents monopolization, while the balance of power in the interstate system prevents any one state from controlling the world economy.[35] Political anarchy leads to a particular form of global economic system—a capitalist world economy with an international division of labor.

This world economy is divided by world-systems analysts into three segments: the core, the periphery, and the semiperiphery. *Core* states are the "haves"; they have the most efficient and productive economies and are the most technologically advanced. Production in core states is capital-intensive and uses skilled, high-wage labor. Core states also have the strongest military establishments. Needless to say, they also receive a disproportionate share of the world-economy's rewards.

The *periphery* is made up of economically weak states whose production is primarily in low-wage, labor-intensive goods. Their economies are highly dependent on those of the core state to which they are most closely associated. The *semiperiphery* constitutes an intermediate category of states, with some production that is similar to that of core areas and some similar to that found in the periphery. Thus, the semiperiphery acts in some respects as an exploiter (of periphery states) and as an exploited area (by the core states). There is constant conflict over membership in these groups; all states hope to be upwardly mobile. Mobility within the core area is also conflictual.

The core itself is divided between hegemonic powers and regular core states. A *hegemonic power* is a core state that develops a position of dominance throughout the entire world economy. Wallerstein sees this dominance primarily in terms of comparative advantage: the concentration of certain kinds of enterprises (called lead industries) within the core state. The hegemonic state holds a decisive superiority in agricultural-industrial productivity, in finance and investment, and it dominates world trade, ammassing the largest single share of the world market, and therefore the largest economic rewards. As a result, the hegemonic state is able to impose a set of rules on the system.

True hegemonic status has been achieved by only three states, and for only brief periods, according to Wallerstein: the United Provinces, 1620–1672; Great Britain, 1815–1873; and the United States, 1945–1967. *World wars* have played a key role in consolidating the hegemonic status of each.[36] The United Provinces' position was developed by the Thirty Years' War; British hegemony resulted from its victory over France in the Napoleonic Wars; and American hegemony resulted from World Wars I and II. Each attempt to impose world empire—by Louis XIV, by Napoleon, and by the Germans in the twentieth century—came during periods of relative hegemonic (that is, Dutch or British) weakness. Like Modelski, Wallerstein argues that the hegemonic states have been primarily maritime powers, though they become land powers as well to counter land-based challengers.

World-systems theorists place war in the framework of the development and expansion of the capitalist world economy. At bottom, "the capitalist system is a system that has pitted all accumulators of capital against one another."[37] Wallerstein argues that war can be seen as "struggles to shape the institutional structures of the capitalist world-economy so as to construct the kind of world market whose operation would automatically favour particular economic actors."[38]

Although world wars accommodate expanded levels of economic development, a point is reached when the political framework under the domination of the old hegemon is inadequate to facilitate world commodity production and distribution on a larger scale. Thus, says Christopher Chase-Dunn, "world wars and the rise and fall of hegemonic core powers . . . can be understood as the violent reorganization of production relations on a world scale," so as to increase the internationalization of capitalist production.[39] World wars are essentially attempts to restructure the interstate political structure to reflect changing economic realities and to convert the political-military strength of rising challengers into a greater share of the world surplus.[40]

World wars result in the crowning of a new hegemonic power; however, the victor's hegemony does not last. According to world-systems theorists, its demise has much more to do with economic factors than military ones. Maintaining hegemony is expensive in terms of military and bureaucratic overhead, and tax burdens rise within the hegemon. Uneven capitalist development leads to a change in the distribution of productive capabilities among the core states, and the hegemonic power loses its competitive edge in the production of leading industries; agricultural and industrial production declines. Wages in the hegemonic state tend to rise, reducing competitiveness, and profit rate differentials change, leading to the export of capital from the hegemon. The free market results in the flow of capital and technology to other states; innovations that have given the hegemonic power a competitive edge can always be copied by others. Hegemonic core states simply can't control this process.

It is important to understand that for Wallerstein these changing distributions of power are rooted in the underlying *economic* order and in uneven rates of *capitalist* development. Shifts in the balance of political-military power may be important, but they are brought about by economic processes.

Almost as soon as power is concentrated in the hands of the hegemon, it begins to wane, creating a cycle of concentration and diffusion of power among hegemonic powers and other core states. World-systems theorists describe a four phase cycle: (1) ascending hegemony, in which there is acute conflict among rival states to succeed the older hegemon; (2) hegemonic victory, in which the contender passes the declining, older hegemon; (3) hegemonic maturity, or true hegemony; and (4) declining hegemony, in which there is acute competition between the old hegemon and potential successors. (For some reason, the phases of ascending hegemony and declining hegemony do not overlap.)[41]

Hegemonic decline initiates a period of increasing military and economic competition. The hegemonic power's attempt to impose direct and exclusive control over the periphery leads to conflict between core states as well as resistance with the periphery. These conflicts are compounded by the increasingly stagnant world economy and by protectionist trade policies in the core. Over time, the hegemon's alliance system begins to disintegrate, and two states usually emerge as contenders—the winner usually being the one that remains allied with the declining hegemon. The United Provinces, Great Britain, and the United States all achieved their hegemonic positions after other competing core powers weakened themselves in intracore warfare, according to Chase-Dunn, but their success depended more on their economic competitive advantage then on their military superiority, though both were important.[42] The creation of a new hegemonic core state ushers in a long period of economic growth in which the hegemomic core state provies economic and military order and support. This is also a period of relative peace.[43] Thus, unicentricity is associated with relative peace and multicentricity with relatively higher levels of war.

World wars are not initiated by hegemonic core states, but by a rising challenger within the core. World-systems theorists agree with other theorists of war cycles that the challengers in these world wars have always failed. The reason seems to be twofold. The first reason is strategic. The challenger attempts to put areas under its control that are simply too large to be conquered and subjugated, and this error is combined with a failure to develop a strategy comptetitive production. The second reason derrives from the logic of the capitalist world economy itself. The challenger has a hard time lining up allies, a fact that is most likely due to a fear that their interests will not be well served by the construction of a world empire, but will probably be better secured by the continuance of the multicentric capitalist world economy.[44] In other words, the challenger finds it difficult to find other dissatisfied states; most core states are status quo powers. Thus, for world-systems theorists, the balance of power plays an important role in determining the outcome of world wars, but the objective basis of the balance of power is the nature of the capitalist world system itself.[45]

If the cycle of war is inherent in the basic logic of uneven development, exploitation, competition, and conflict found in the capitalist world economy, how is the war cycle to be broken? Presumably, the chances of peace will be enhanced with the dissolution of the present system and its replacement by a socialist world system. In one version (that of Chase-Dunn), a socialist world system would essentially mean that capitalism would be replaced with a collectivist economic rationality, and systemic leadership would be provided by a democratic and federal system of world government.[46]

Finally, we should take note of a problem that bedevils all the historical-structural theorists to some degree. It is universally agreed that prior to World War I (and World War II, for that matter) Britain was the hegemonic power and Germany was the primary challenger. What, then, are we to do with the fact that by 1914 the United States had already passed both Britain and Germany in terms of industrial production, leading sector position, and gross national product? The statistics for the pre–World War II period are even more lopsided in favor for the United States.[47] If the two world wars were truly wars of hegemonic succession, one would expect that the United States would be involved in the initial fighting either as the rising (and, indeed, overtaking) challenger or as the new defending hegemon. In neither case was the German challenge directed at the United States. Modelski is able to save the argument by pointing to British naval superiority even in the 1930s (though this still begs the question of the importance of seapower), but for those who emphasize economic and industrial criteria as the essence of hegemony, belated American participation in the two world wars presents a problem. If the United States is neither the initator nor the chief defender, how can these wars be about global leadership? The fact that the wars do indeed result in a change of global leadership is not enough. Results and causes should not be confused.

K-Waves

Both long cyclists and world-systems theorists have incorporated certain economic cycles called *Kondratieff waves* into their theories of the cycle of world leadership. The Russian economist Nikolai Kondratieff claimed in the 1920s to have discovered fifty-year waves (or cycles) in prices, production, and consumption in the economies of the major capitalist nations. He argued that these cycles were indicative of rhythms within the international economic system as a whole. His research also suggested that upswings in economic long waves were related to the occurrence of major war. He tentatively speculated that wars were due to the increased economic struggle for markets and raw materials that accompanied the accelerated pace of economic activity, rising prices, and growth in production that took place in upswing phases.[48] While many economists today do not believe that Kondratieff waves (*K-waves*) even exist, long cyclists not only claim to have found them, but insist that they operate parallel to world leadership cycles: one-hundred-year world leadership cycles are linked to pairs of K-waves. And since K-waves are linked to leadership cycles, they are also associated with cycles of global war.[49]

Thompson and Zuk demonstrate that most of the wars from 1780 to 1914, and most of the severe wars, were initiated in the upswing phase of a K-wave, as predicted by Kondratieff. The price upswings tended to precede major wars, and K-wave upper turning points also coincided with the termination of major wars.[50]

Thompson and Zuk also argue that major wars have been largely responsible for the shape of K-waves, particularly in reinforcing the upswing curve. They conclude that while it is difficult to say either that K-waves cause major wars or that major wars cause K-waves, a relationship does exist. It seems that global wars and K-waves reflect a common underlying process. Given the close linkages between the global political system and the world economy, instabilities in one structure will be transmitted to the other.[51]

Joshua Goldstein has compiled a marvelous set of economic indicators extending back to 1495.[52] Using several sets of economic data, he is able to map the trough and peak dates for fifty-year-long K-waves. In fact, he finds long waves in production, investment, innovation, prices, and wages. (These waves do not occur simultaneously, but sequentially, beginning with production.) Goldstein is unable to find any relationship between K-waves and the *frequency* of wars; the number of wars is roughly equal in upswing and downswing periods. However, Goldstein uncovers a clear association between K-waves and the cycle of war *severity* (average battle deaths per year). Like Thompson and Zuk, he finds that severe wars are more likely in the upswing phase of K-waves. For the nine waves that have occurred from 1495 to 1918, he finds that each peak in warfare occurs near the end of an upswing phase. He maintains that nine of the ten war severity peaks since 1500 have occurred near the end of the upward phase of the K-wave. The exception was World War II.[53] Typically, peaks in war severity are sandwiched between production and price upswings—with production upswings preceding war by ten years or so and war preceding price upswings by one to five years.

Goldstein's explanation for the link between K-waves and war is that increasing production produces a greater demand for resources, which in turn leads to international competition for these resources. This competition occurs during a period when production increases have made increased supplies of war materiel available to the military sector, drastically increasing the probability of war. (This is essentially a *lateral pressure* argument without the emphasis on population growth.) Since war is a costly endeavor, states prefer to engage in it when the resources are relatively plentiful. War is most likely to occur, then, near the end of the long-wave upswing.[54] Note, however, that Goldstein falls back on nation-state-level argument (the presence of economic wherewithal) to help explain a theory based on systemic-level factors (K-waves).

What does this have to do with Modelski's long-cycle theory? Goldstein argues that the hegemonic cycle and the economic long-wave cycle, though they are not in phase with each other, operate in conjunction with each other. Thus, hegemonic decline does not by itself lead to war; it is only dangerous when it coincides with an expansionary phase of the economic cycle. Economic expansion by itself is not dangerous either; it must be accompanied by hegemonic stagnation. For example, the economic expansion of the 1960s was not associated with major wars because of the strong hegemonic position of the United States. Goldstein predicts new economic upswings to coincide with the continuation of American hegemonic decline between 2000 and 2030.[55]

Jack Levy reexamines the issue, matching Goldstein's data on economic production cycles against the ten general wars of the last five centuries.[56] He is interested not in peaks of war severity, but in war initiation. When the production cycle alone is considered (after all, Goldstein's theory is based on the rise and fall of production, rather than on prices or other variables), Levy discovers a picture at odds with Goldstein's theory. Four of the ten wars were begun during the middle or end of a production downswing phase, and two occurred at the beginning of an upswing—rather than near the end of the upswing, as Goldstein's theory suggests. Many of the wars broke out near the transition from downswing to upswing, so that the casualties associated with them belonged in the upswing phase even though the wars might have begun in the downswing—explaining why Goldstein found an association between K-waves and *severity* of war, but not between K-waves and war *initiation*.

Not only do long cyclists see K-waves as important aspects of the structure of the world-economy, so do world-systems theorists.[57] The rise and decline of hegemonic powers is believed to be synchronized with pairs of

K-waves, though there appears to be no exact number of K-waves that make up a hegemonic cycle.[58] While Goldstein's research indicated that war severity peaks during the upswing phase of K-waves, specifically between the production cycle peak and the price cycle peak, Chase-Dunn turns this argument on its head. If war severity is at its apex *after* the production peak, this means war severity peaks after the beginning of the *downswings* in both the investment and production cycles. He is thereby able to make a more directly Marxist explanation. Downswings are periods in which states have a lot of resources available for war (as Goldstein suggests); simultaneously, overproduction during this phase leads to increased competition for foreign markets and investment opportunities. Pressure to use state power to protect or expand market shares and investment opportunities during an economic downturn becomes an important factor in the slide toward war.[59]

Doran's Relative Power Cycle Theory

Charles F. Doran's relative power cycle theory places a theory of decision-making about war in the context of the rise and decline of the relative power of major states.[60] Doran argues that the power capabilities of states, relative to other members of the Great Power central system, follow a cyclical path of growth, maturation, and decline. Though the highs and lows for each state will be different, as well as the length of time required to attains these peaks and troughs, nevertheless each Great Power will go through this cycle. The general pattern is that of an "accelerating rise in relative power that ultimately slows down until relative power peaks, and the decline in relative power that likewise ultimately proceeds at a slower pace."[61] The cycle is largely due to uneven rates of internal economic development. Since major powers tend to get involved in large wars, these power dynamics would seem to be helpful in explaining the timing of the larger wars in history, or what Doran calls *extensive wars*.[62]

Although this theory may seem to operate at the nation-state level, dealing with cycles of national power, it is really a systemic theory. Doran's power cycle is a cycle of *relative* power. A state's ride through the cycle depends as much on the power of others as on its own internal growth or decline. As with most theories that are systemic in nature, relative power cycle theory maintains that the policies and behaviors of states depend largely on their position in the system—in this case on their position in the cycle of relative power. War is most likely to occur as a state reaches four *critical points* along the cycle. At each of these points an abrupt inversion occurs in the path of relative capabilities. A complete cycle contains two *inflection points* and two *turning points*, as indicated in Figure 9.1.

The *lower turning point* (where most states enter the great power system) is the point at which the state's relative position changes from a

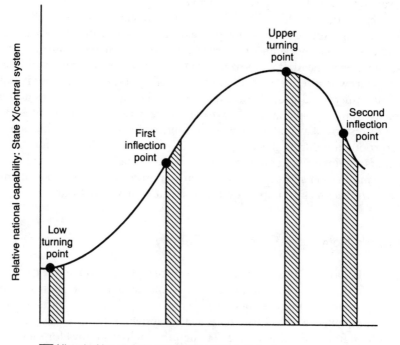

 Historical intervals in which probability is highest
for State X initiation of major war

Figure 9–1. The Cycle of Relative Power.

Source: C. F. Doran, "War and Power Dynamics: Economic Underpinnings," *International Studies Quarterly* 27 (1983), p. 420.

declining power to a rising power, as its capabilities, relative to others, begin to increase. The *first inflection point* represents the point at which the state's relative capabilities, while still rising, begin to rise at a much slower rate, signifying that the initial rapid relative power accumulation cannot go on indefinitely. The *upper turning point* is the point at which a state's capabilities, relative to those of other system members, begins to decline. The state changes from a rising power to a declining power. The *second inflection point* is the point at which the state's relative decline, which has been rapid at first, begins to drop more slowly, indicating that the future may be brighter.

The crucial theoretical question is why these specific circumstances should be particularly dangerous. The answer is complicated, but plausible. It incorporates theories about government planning and decision-making and national role conceptions as well as a theory of uneven development. Doran argues that national leaders make their long-range predictions by simply making a linear extrapolation (i.e., a straight-line projection) from past experience. If the past decade or so has seen a rapid rise in the state's power relative to others in the system, planning will be based on a continuation of this trend. However, each of the four critical points in the cycle represents a change in the previous trend. Each is essentially unpredictable, and each suddenly indicates that the previous thinking was radically mistaken, just at the point where being mistaken is the most threatening to the state's position.[63]

National behavior is based in part on the leader's conceptions of the state's role within the system; furthermore, this national role conception is based primarily on the state's position within the system in terms of its relative power capabilities. A change in relative capabilities will mean a change in roles (from leader to follower, for example). These transitions in role, triggered by passing through the critical points in the power cycle, are difficult for states to make. While critical points call for major role transformations, their sudden appearance eludes advanced detection; uncertainty is therefore high and national leaders are most vulnerable to overreaction and misperceptions that might lead them to choose war.[64]

The specific reasons for war differ, however, depending on which critical point the state has arrived at. Each point has its own logic and dynamic. For instance, as the state's relative power decreases, its role and interests should decrease accordingly, but states are usually reluctant to accept this reduction in status and influence. On the other hand, when a state's relative power increases, its interests and roles increase as well, but the other members of the system are frequently unwilling to permit the expansion of the rising state's activities. Thus, in both cases, disparities exist between a state's capabilities and its role, but in different ways.[65]

It is not just the reaction of the state that is undergoing the critical change which is important, but the reaction of other members of the system to the change as well.[66] Misperceptions and anxieties also afflict other system members. Under normal circumstances, all states in the system are able to plan for transitions in relative power, but these planning exercises break down for all nations when a major state undergoes a critical change. System-level phenomena (power shifts) trigger individual-level phenomena (perceptions of threat or opportunity) among the political elite in all major states.

Power cycle theory has implications for the behavior of nation-states, but it also has systemwide implications. When several states in the system simultaneously go through critical points in the relative power cycle, this has the unfortunate effect of generating pressures for role transformations while at the same time initiating changes in expectations about the relative balance of power. This leads to massive structural uncertainty in the system and detracts from the ability of system members to manage change. This disequilibrium makes the system extremely vulnerable to extensive wars, which may lead ultimately to a transformation of the international system itself.[67] This seems to have been what happened in the pre–World War I period. According to Doran, between 1885 and 1914 every member of the central great power system passed through at least one critical point in its power cycle.[68]

Systemic stability prevails when movement of system members though the power cycle is routine and anticipated. At these times the gap between interests and capabilities is small for major actors, and the system is in equilibrium. According to Doran, bipolar and multipolar systems are equally stable (or unstable). The decisive factor is not the difference in structure between the two systems, but the *transition* between multipolar and bipolar systems that occurs when a number of the major actors in the system pass through critical points in the cycle of relative power.[69]

The Cycle of Relative Power: Implications

Writing in the fall of 1989, just prior to the fragmentation of the Soviet Union into separate states, Doran saw the U.S.S.R. well past its first inflection point, dealing with slowing growth rates. The United States was past its peak in relative power, though not yet in "decline." Japan had reached its maximum growth rate at the first inflection point. He predicts a critical systems transformation will occur in the future when the following conditions are met: (1) the Soviet Union reaches its upper turning point, (2) U.S. relative power reaches the point of relative decline, (3) China reaches its maximum growth rate, (4) Japanese growth enters diminishing marginal returns, and (5) the European community enters the system as a major contender.[70] Although it is difficult to assess these points without the benefit of some historical perspective, the events of late 1989 through early 1992 indicate that points 1 and 2 have probably already been reached and points 4 and 5 are well on their way.

The Cycle of Relative Power: Empirical Research

Before we get too wrapped up in predictions, how does the theory fare in the face of empirical testing? Pretty well according to its proponents. Doran and Parsons investigated the cycles of the nine states that made up the major power system from 1816 to 1965. They hypothesized that the propensity to initiate extensive war was greatest during the four critical points and should diminish as the distance in time from such points increased. There were twenty-three critical periods during the years investigated and twenty-six wars were initiated during these critical periods. The more numerous non-critical periods contained fifty-one initations of war. However, the average magnitude, severity, and duration of wars were much higher for the critical periods, allowing Doran and Parsons to conclude that major powers are more likely to initiate wars that become extensive during one of the critical periods. The frequency of war is not related to relative power cycles. Only 34% of the wars fell during the critical periods, but wars that were initated by the great powers during a critical period escalated far beyond wars initiated at other times.[71] That is, relative power cycles are not associated with all wars, just *major wars* among great powers.

The inflection points seemed to be more prone to war initation than the turning points. Great powers seem most likely to start wars when their rate of growth in relative capabilities reaches a maximum (first inflection) or a minimum (second inflection). This runs somewhat contrary to popular thought, which presumes war to be most likely when states are at either the apex or nadir of their relative power curves.

Generally speaking, the nineteenth century after 1815 was free of major war because there was little movement of actors into or out of the system, and the leading powers of the system were traversing through the portions of their power trajectories that were smooth and predictable. Marginal adjustments based on early detection were routinely handled. Conversely, major power war engulfed the first half of the twentieth century because a large number of states entered critical points in their cycles and because new states entered the system (Germany in the late nineteenth century, followed by the United States and Japan) while some old members (Austria-Hungary) dropped out, radically transforming relative power positions and roles in the system. Together, these abrupt changes indicated a critical transformation in the system.[72]

Another test by Doran pitted Organski's power transition theory against his own power cycle theory. The test investigated the five wars from 1816 to 1975 that involved major power contenders (the top three or four states in the system) on both sides—Crimean War, Franco-Prussian War, World Wars I and II, and the Korean War. The results indicate that critical changes in relative power are much better predictors of extensive war among contenders than either equality of power or the presence of Organskian power transitions. Though many of the warring dyads were characterized by power symmetry (relative equality) and many were also characterized by a power transition, nevertheless, both symmetrical dyads and transitions led to war less than half the time. On the other hand, 90% of the critical points (100% if one counts the U.S.S.R. as a participant in the Korean War) led to major war. And while only 36.5% of the states experienced critical points in their power cycles during the period, all of the sixteen states at war either were undergoing a critical change or were fighting against a state that was. All the war participation of the noncritical point states was against a critical-point state. Perhaps most interesting of all, Doran found that in every case in which an Organskian power transition led to war, a critical point was also present. While it was not necessary for power transitions to take place in order for critical points to lead to war, power transitions led to war only when a critical point was also present.[73]

At present no empirical research has directly challenged Doran's realtive power cycle theory.

Power Transitions and Historical-Structural Theories: A Comparison

Despite significant differences, the power transition theory and the four historical-structural theories discussed here share several similarities. (1) Except for the power transition theory, they all apply to a modern state system that began around 1500. (2) They address major wars rather than all interstate wars. (3) Except for Doran's cycle of relative power theory, they focus on the struggle between the dominant state in the system and a rising challenger. (4) They all emphasize long-term causes of war. (5) In all the theories, uneven rates of growth among the system's members play an important role in creating a kind of systemic disequilibrium that may lead to war. (6) Most would accept the insights of status discrepancy theory and agree that a state's relative satisfaction or disatisfaction with its position in the international system is an important factor in its war behavior, though this is more important to some than to others. (7) With the exception of Doran, they all tend to see a unipolar concentration of power in the hands of a system leader as representing a relatively stable and peaceful situation, though they also agree that this situation cannot last indefinitely.

A theoretically interesting point that frequently emerges from research at the systemic level is that many of the factors proposed as having a causal effect on war may operate in conjunction with certain other systemic variables. For example: (1) Long cyclists and Wallersteinians both agree that power cycles somehow interact with K-waves to produce major wars, though they don't agree exactly why. (2) Waymon suggests that power multipolarity is most likely to lead to war when combined with cluster bipolarity. (3) Stoll and Champion suggest that a concentration of power within the system may be dangerous or peaceful, depending on the distribution of satisfaction in the system. (4) Doran has argued that Organskian power transitions only lead to war when combined with a nation's passing through one of its critical points in the power cycle. (5) Recent research by Daniel Geller also indicates that dyadic-level factors and systemic-level factors are interrealted. Focusing on the links between hegemonic stability theory and power transition theory, he concludes that power shifts among contender states had to be accompanied by conditions of systemic deconcentration in order for war to result.[74] (6) Thompson also found that the conjuction of deconcentration in the world system cycle with a dyadic power transition was especially dangerous. (7) Finally, Robert North has recently called for the "syngeristic convergence" of his lateral pressure theory with structural realist, power transition, and hegemonic stability approaches.[75]

Systemic Theories: Implications

To the extent that changing distributions of power and status in general and the decline of systemic leadership in particular precipitate war, how are we to preserve peace? We know that maintaining the status quo is impossible; if we have learned anything from systemic (and dyadic) level studies it is that differential rates of growth will make a stable balance of power impossible in the long run. Whatever stability exists, hegemonic or otherwise, must be merely temporary owing to the more general disequilibrium of uneven development.

As President Bush's repeated use of the term "New World Order" reminds us, the systemic changes that have taken place over the last few years have been truly earth-shattering. The decline of Soviet capabilities has been accompanied by the dissolution of the Soviet internal and external empires and the dismantling of the Soviet military bloc. NATO now appears an alliance without a mission. The creation of a unified Germany has brought a powerful new actor into the heart of Europe. Meanwhile, the relative capabilities of the United States (especially its economic capabilities) continue to decline relative to its chief competitors. The late 1980s and early 1990s have witnessed both a power transition of the first magnitude and the passing of several states through critical points in the power cycle. As polarization decreases and the distribution of power changes, we are witnessing a fundamental transformation of the international system. More systemic level changes are likely as we approach the millennium. All of which raises the question of whether, to paraphrase former President Reagan, we will be better off in the new world order than we were four years ago, or ten years ago.

A number of things can be said about the present transformation. First, the changes have been truly revolutionary. One analyst even refers to the transformation as the "functional equivalent of a hegemonic war" with out the violence.[76] Virtually all the systemic changes that structural-historical theorists talk about when they mention hegemonic transitions are currently taking place. A new distribution of power has developed; territorial adjustments have been undertaken in Europe and in the former U.S.S.R.; a new political alignment has taken place; a new hierarchy of prestige is evident; a new set of norms seems to be taking effect; and new procedures and institutions for the management of the system have been created.

Second, and perhaps most remarkable, these changes have been largely peaceful. Hegemonic or global wars have not been part of the package. Based on our previous discussion of systemic-level theories, this is an outcome one would not necessarily have expected. Explaining our good fortune will take some doing. The following analysis should be considered both rudimentary and preliminary.

First, a power transition has taken place, but it is not the war-inducing power transition that theorists usually talk about. This transition was one in which the declining state was the challenger (the former U.S.S.R.) rather than the hegemonic power (the United States). Neither was it a transition toward parity; rather, it was a shift away from the relative equality that the two superpowers had achieved over the years. Although there is some reason to believe that power transitions away from parity are dangerous, transitions in which potential challengers more toward parity with the dominant state have been more likely to lead to war.[77] Additionally, the decline in Soviet power has been partly offset by the fact that the United States and Russia are now engaged in a rapid mutual disarmament race. Soviet military power has declined precipitously, but the American military is being cut back as well.

Second, systemic polarization—what we have called cluster polarity— has decreased drastically. The Cold War bipolar alliance system no longer exists. The Warsaw Pact is defunct and many of its former members (including Boris Yeltsin's Russia!) have asked for membership in NATO, the one remaining alliance. It is difficult to know how to characterize this arrangement. One is tempted to call it unipolar, but military alliances have little meaning unless they are organized against another state or group of states. NATO no longer has this clarity of purpose and is likely to fade into the sunset in the near future. President Yeltsin's summit with President Bush early in 1992 produced a statement that the two countries are friends rather than enemies. It would seem more appropriate to simply classify this system as nonpolarized.

On balance, this lack of alliance polarization would seem to be a good thing. It has clearly been associated with reduced international tension. It has provided the background against which the Soviet-American arms race has been reversed. And to the extent that Russia will now be more likely to cooperate with the other major powers to reduce international conflict through the United Nations (as it did in the Persian Gulf crisis) or through regional organizations (such as the Conference on Security and Cooperation in Europe), the loss of polarization should prove to be beneficial to world peace.

However, while conflict between core members of the system may become less likely, the former superpowers may be less willing or able to constrain the actions of their former clients, leading to increased conflict in the periphery or semiperiphery. The current war between the newly independent states of Armenia and Azerbaijan over Nagorno-Karabakh may become the classic example.

So much for power transitions and polarization; what about power distribution (polarity)? The fashionable argument is that the demise of the Soviet Union has created a unipolar international system in which the United States is the only true superpower—the only state with superior capabilities on all relevant domains of power: military, economic, and technological.

President Bush, in his State of the Union message in January 1992, stated, "A world once divided into two armed camps now recognizes one sole and preeminent power: the United States of America."[78]

While it is undoubtedly true that the United States is the only state with the combined military-economic-technological capacity to be called a true superpower, nevertheless there is an element of multipolarity in the system. Russia remains a nuclear state on a par with the United States. China continues to grow both economically and militarily. Germany and Japan have surpassed the United States on some indicators of economic strength. The European community has become stronger politically as well as economically. It is doubtful that the United States could be classified as a hegemonic power. A few examples should suffice.

1. While the United States was clearly the only military power with the ability to transport and deploy sufficient force to counter Iraq's conquest of Kuwait, the insolvency of the American government meant that the United States had to go begging for contributions from its friends to defray the cost of the expedition.

2. The reunification of Germany, arguably the most important political and territorial adjustment in the post–Cold War world, was arranged primarily through a joint Soviet–West Germany treaty (on West Germany terms) with the United States playing the role of the uninvited guest.

3. The United States was unable to bring sufficient pressure on its friends in the European community to make concessions on agricultural subsidies during the last round of the General Agreement on Tariffs and Trade negotiations, thus bringing about a virtual collapse of those talks and the serious below for the American position of further arranging the world trading system around the principle of free trade.

4. The June 1992 "Earth Summit" in Rio saw the United States virtually isolated in its role opposing strong global environmental treaties.

Thus, we have to conclude (I apologize for the vagueness, but there is no way around it) that the system has elements of both power unipolarity and multipolarity. Is this good for peace? It probably doesn't matter much. What matters is that the transition itself was achieved peacefully. The critical point is not whether the system is unipolar, bipolar, or multipolar, but what happens in the transition from one distribution to another. We seem to have weathered the latest transition in good shape.

Systemic-level theories tell us that war is the result of broad socio-political-economic forces beyond the day-to-day control of individuals or governments. Individual decisions to start wars merely represent the culmination of these large-scale impersonal forces. Consequently, attempts to prevent the outbreak of wars and to manage international structural change will be precarious at best. National leaders have had, and will continue to have, little control over the long-term cycle of national growth and decline and the changes in political relations that flow from them.

Systemic theorists offer somewhat different analyses of the paths to peace. Polarity theorists rely on the ability of major actors to construct balances of power in either bipolar or multipolar environments. A few theorists (such as those in the world-economy school) pin their hopes on a peaceful transition to a new international system based on different principles. However, the message of most of the theories discussed at this level of analysis—status discrepancy, Gilpin's theory of hegemonic war, Organski's theory of power transitions, Modelski's theory of world leadership, and Doran's cycle of relative power—is that the major powers will need to peacefully and cooperatively manage the inevitable transitions in power, role, and status that occur in the international system. While in the past these changes have been accompanied by war, the destructiveness of war in the present era necessitates the development of peaceful mechanisms of change. Alternative institutions and processes must be created to deal with the changes that will inevitably occur in world politics.

Some of the theorists in this group, notably Gilpin and Modelski, believe this is possible. While systemic forces are crucial causal factors, they are not entirely deterministic; political responses to these phenomena are to some extent subject to freedom of choice. As this manuscript was being written, the world was witnessing what may be the first major systemic transformation to have taken place without large-scale interstate warfare. During this potentially explosive period, international leaders have taken great care to manage these momentous systemwide changes by building new international institutions or enhancing old institutions and by consciously seeking ways to reduce the grievances of the major loser (the former Soviet Union) in the transformation. Perhaps there is reason for optimism.

10
Conclusion

We have met the enemy and he is us.
—Pogo

I hope that in the preceding pages the reader has become acquainted with some of the complexities involved in discovering the origins of war. It is easy to be overwhelmed by the sheer multitude of hypotheses concerning the causes of war. By now you are probably hoping that the author will sum up by sorting among the various theories presented in the preceding pages and give the REAL ANSWER to the question of what causes war. However, such simple and easy answers don't exist. We have been unable to identify a single theory that alone can account for war as a general phenomenon. Instead, we have discovered several islands of theory that have achieved partial validation: they seem to apply to a good many wars, but not all wars; or they are useful in explaining wars between Great Powers, but not between states of lesser power; or they pertain to certain periods of time, but not all; or they apply under certain conditions, but not under all.

Although no single theory seems to have anywhere near universal validity, social scientific research has not been completely fruitless. Some theories have been identified as lacking a factual basis and have been relegated to the status of mythology. But several theories, having been validated often enough by real-world events, have emerged as more useful and warrant our sincerest attention. Certain patterns and tendencies have been identified as likely precursors to war; other reputed patterns have failed to be observed. Thus, a winnowing-out process is occurring in the scholarship of war studies. Even though the investigations undertaken by social scientists during the last four decades have not culminated in the creation of a single, unified theory of war, they have certainly added greatly to our understanding of the causes of war. And by so doing they have added as well to our understanding of how peace may be maintained.

One of the messages of this book is that instead of a single cause of war there are multiple causes. Most wars not only require several kinds of theoretical explanations, but require that these explanations be made at several levels of analysis. Not only is there a winnowing-out process going

on, but there is also a process of cross-level integration going on as researchers find important connections between levels of analysis. However, the
construction of a single, integrated, cross-level theory is still in its rudimentary stages.

Summing Up: Some Persistent Patterns

Perhaps the best that can be done at the moment—at least in the brief space
that can be allotted a concluding chapter—is to point out some tendencies
and recurrent patterns and to illustrate how factors at the various levels of
analysis might operate together in an interactive or reciprocal way to increase
the probability of war. One might, in fact, build a "model" of the typical
scenario for war—a hypothetical case that represents the coming together of
several factors which in combination might make war virtually inevitable.[1]

Let us place our initial focus on the occurrence of an international
security crisis between two (or more) states. The leaders of the states involved
perceive that the situation represents a serious threat to their nations' vital
interests and that the use of force (by them or their opponent) is within the
realm of possibility in the immediate future.

It seems that the major instigation to war is derived from the negative
and conflictual interaction of these states with each other—what has been
called here the "security dilemma." Realpolitik tactics—such as the use of
bullying, threats, ultimata, defiance, "brinkmanship," coercive actions, and
demonstrations of force—which are meant to demonstrate toughness and to
deter opponents are likely to lead to hostile reciprocal actions rather than to
the desired result of backing down. For reasons having to do with the
individual psychological makeup of leaders, with their operational codes,
and with the domestic political environment, realpolitik tactics are not likely
to be effective—especially between equals. Threats are met with counterthreats, defiance with intransigence, and demonstrations of resolve with
counterdemonstrations. The degree of hostility escalates and the nations
enter a conflict spiral. Security crises may begin as prisoners' dilemma games,
but they have a tendency to become transformed into games of chicken in
which leaders on both sides come to believe two things: that backing down is
(for themselves) unacceptable, but that their opponent(s) will relent when
confronted with clear evidence of commitment.

States may resort to arms buildups, which are then reciprocated and
become arms races. Military alliances may be concluded to enhance one's
security, and these alliances may be countered by similar compacts by the
opponent. The combined effect of these arms races and the building of
military alliances may be bloc polarization. All these factors lead to the
creation of higher and higher international tension. The early phases of the
arms accumulation process and the alliance construction process are proba-

bly the most critical, as they lead to greater fear and suspicion and therefore to arms races and counteralliance making. Unless the conflict spiral is broken through creative diplomacy, war becomes a high probability.

Within this context, attempts at deterrence have a limited possibility of success. In fact, even superior military capabilities and formal commitments may not suffice to deter violent conflict. Threats and coercive actions intended to prevent the violent actions of others in fact serve to confirm the "worst case" suspicions of one's opponents. The perceived threat to their own interests often impels them to initiate or continue belligerent activities of their own. Whether or not an original threat in fact existed, the result is the same: deterrence fails.

These dyadic interaction processes are perhaps triggered—and are certainly abetted—by factors at the individual, small-group, nation-state, and international-system levels. At each level of analysis, several factors may contribute to the likelihood of war or may retard the march toward violence.

Perceptions by national leaders at the individual level are inextricably tied to factors at higher levels of analysis. Actions that take place at every level of analysis are filtered through individual leaders' perceptual screens and are shaped and interpreted by their images and world views. The individual's response to these actions is given direction through his or her operational code.

Perceptions of economic upswings and downturns, internal unrest, power transitions, the lack of justice in the systemic distribution of status, the hostility of interactions with others, alliance formations, and the balance of power within the international system are important to the extent that they are *perceived* as important by political elites with the authority to make decisions about war and peace. Perhaps the best way to conceptualize the role of phenomena at the systemic, dyadic, and nation-state levels of analysis is as stimuli that trigger individual perceptions (and misperceptions), which then guide policy decisions about war and peace.

Misperceptions about the opponent's actions, his intentions and capabilities—and hence about the degree of threat to one's own security— may create the conditions necessary for the onset of a crisis. Once the crisis begins, these misperceptions may accelerate and exacerbate the level of tension. Particularly important are the combination of an overperception of the rival's hostility and treachery and an underperception of both the capabilities of the rival and the amount of risk involved. Unwarranted confidence in the ability to compel one's opponent(s) to back down short of war, or of one's ability to defeat the adversary with little cost if war does begin, seem to be an important part of the picture. A significant aspect of this is the perception that other states are not committed to assisting one's opponent or are unwilling or unable to carry out their commitments.

While images and perceptions play a decisive role in determining the extent to which leaders believe the interests of their states are being threatened, operational codes play a crucial role in determining how these leaders will respond to the pereived threats. Leaders with realpolitik operational codes, which are based on the belief that bullying and threats will work and which emphasize the use of aggressive tactics, are probably most likely to find themselves trapped in conflict spirals from which they cannot extricate themselves short of war.

Individual personality factors may also play a role here, affecting the ability of national leaders to realistically appraise and react to the international situation. Since many national leaders probably possess psychological characteristics such as power orientation and high dominance, and employ various ego defense mechanisms to protect against feelings of low-self esteem, the likelihood that they will be psychologically predisposed to back down in the face of threats from external opponents is probably fairly low. If you add to the aforementioned traits that of risk acceptance, the personal fuel mixture becomes highly volatile. Finally, psychological stress brought on by the crisis may have a deleterious effect on the ability of decision-makers to make rational calculations.

Ultimately, decisions for war are likely to be predicated on the assumption that war is inevitable, or that it can be waged successfully, or, at the very least, that it can be waged at an acceptable level of cost. These individual perceptions (or misperceptions) can be reinforced by factors at the small-group level.

At the small-group level, decision-makers may ignore warnings of impending policy failures and military disasters through the process of group think. Small-group dynamics may be coupled with individual cognitive processes that prevent the decision-makers from reexamining incorrect assumptions and from seriously considering points of view at variance with their own.

On the other hand, the dynamic of bureaucratic politics may be predominant. Crisis escalation is more likely if the decision process is dominated by political elites whose political-bureaucratic-economic interests will be maintained or enhanced by a decision to go to war.

One should be especially mindful of the effects of domestic political pressures on national leaders and of the tendency of "hawkish" factions to increase their power in times of crisis and confrontation. The fact that hawks dominate the decision-making machinery of the government means, almost by definition, that realpolitik-type tactics are more likely to be employed in the crisis.[2] Concomitantly, the need to mobilize the public against the external opponent and in favor of greater military expenditures requires that the enemy be painted as immoral, irrational, and implacably hostile. This has internal implications, granting greater influence to the hard-liners and making later face-saving gestures and compromises more difficult. Efforts to defuse conflict spirals are difficult because of one's own previous acts and pronouncements and because of the domestic implications of compromising or reversing previous hard-line policies. Elite fears that domestic opponents will be able to brand compromise and conciliation as appeasement stifle creative conflict resolution. That these dynamics occur in one country is bad enough, but the internal politics of both rivals are likely to be similarly affected, thus creating reciprocal, reinforcing effects.

The likelihood of crises escalating to war is probably enhanced in cases in which the rivalries and patterns of conflictual interaction are longstanding—especially if the present crisis has been preceded by other crises with the same opponent. If a regime in one (or both) of the states has recently been perceived as having "lost" a previous crisis encounter with its rival, the need to prevent a second (or third) loss of face makes necessary a demonstration of resolve and makes a policy of compromise and conciliation difficult to achieve. Internal political considerations may outweigh international consideration. The domestic insecurity or vulnerability of elites—especially if combined with economic problems—is probably a factor that promotes militant postures and the taking of risks and leads to the creation of crises and their escalation to war. Scapegoat wars, while not overly plentiful, are possible.

At the nation-state level, the propensity for the more powerful states to become disproportionately involved in war is a worrisome factor. The connection between large states and war is related to factors at the individual and the small-group levels. At the individual level, leaders of major powers are most likely to have national role conceptions that define their nations' roles as protectors, defenders, interveners, and activists in the global system who carry the burden of providing world order. At the subnational level, the more powerful states also have well-developed national security institutions (military-industrial complexes) whose leaders or supporters are likely to be well represented in the governing coalition.

Conflicts may also develop in part because of the internal demographic and economic growth that takes place within certain states and because of the greater claims on resources necessitated by such growth. Whether such growth leads to international conflict, however, depends on a multitude of factors at various levels of analysis. It will depend on decisions made by national leaders concerning how the state will go about attaining greater resources; it will depend on national role conceptions of national leaders; it will depend on the state's relative position within the international system and on the national elite's degree of satisfaction with this position.

The probability that crises will escalate to war depends not so much on the nature of a particular state's political or economic system as on the degree of political-economic difference between a pair of states. At least in modern times, democratic systems have refrained from mutual war, while wars between states with different systems have been commonplace. While sharing similar political systems tends to prevent war, sharing borders with states governed by different principles tends to add to the perception that vital national interests are at stake, and therefore to the severity of the crisis and its propensity to escalate to war.

Security crises may originate in part because of the nature of the international system, and the nature of the international system will certainly have an effect on the development of the crisis as it proceeds toward either peaceful resolution or war. The particular configuration of power within the system—unipolar, bipolar, tripolar, or multipolar—may not matter. Those conflict spirals (and the arms races and alliance construction that are related to them) which lead to bloc polarization seem to be particularly dangerous—by reducing the importance of cross-cutting issues, by increasing the perception of threat, by enlarging the possible theater of war, by compelling states to prepare for worst-case scenarios, and by reducing the possibility of successful mediation.[3]

The most serious great power crises are most likely to occur during periods of transition in the international system (or in regional subsystems) where there are significant shifts in the balance of power, especially between the dominant power in the system and its major rival(s)—but also between any set of rivals. These systemic and dyadic changes are triggered by national level changes; power transitions are rooted in the process of economic development within states—a process whose speed is by its very nature different for each state. Power transition issues ultimately involve issues of prestige and status. Thus, power transitions can set off conflict over the proper distribution of prestige and status within the system as well as conflict over the proper distribution of political, military, and economic power.

Any change in the structure of the international (or regional) system can be dangerous. Whether the structural transition is brought about by industrial-technological-demographic growth, by the conscious accumulation of military capabilities by a challenging state, or by the rearrangement of military alliances, the fortunes of some states are being diminished while the fortunes of others are being enhanced. The results are many: role transformations, status disequilibria, changes in the perceived degree of security, and increased systemic uncertainty. It is at these times that the degree of insecurity and threat in the international system is highest. Responses to these structural threats are likely to take on the characteristics of conflict spirals.

It would seem especially dangerous if several system-level phenomena were occurring simultaneously—as is likely. For instance, the concurrence of power transitions, critical points in the cycle of relative power, hegemonic decline, systemic deconcentration (toward greater power multipolarity), and alliance polarization—or just a few of these—would be much more dangerous than the existence of any single factor. Any of these structural changes at the international-systems level may trigger perceptions of threat by national leaders at the individual level. System- and dyadic-level factors are closely linked to individual and perceptual factors. This is an insight at least as old as Thucydides' summarization of the cause of the Pelopponesian War: "What made the war inevitable was the growth of Athenian power and the fear this caused in Sparta."

Is War Becoming Obsolete?

We would be remiss if we did not conclude with a brief discussion of the thesis that interstate war is now becoming obsolete—or at least that major wars among countries of the developed world are becoming obsolete. The two most important factors in this development seem to be the spread of democracy and the spread of peaceful norms.[4]

One of the most widely reported global trends of the 1980s has been the the replacement of autocratic governments with democratic governments. If we believe, as most theorists do, that the likelihood that democratic states will fight each other is virtually nil, and if we couple that law with the recognition that the number of democratic states in the world is continually increasing (while the number of autocratic states is decreasing), then we come to the conclusion that war is slowly and surely becoming obsolete.[5] And since democracy has found a home first in the developed countries of the world, it is in this area that peace is currently most prevalent.

John Mueller, a leading theorist on this issue, believes, however, that the connection between the spread of democracy and peace is spurious. He contends the primary causal factor is simply the geographic spread of the idea that interstate war is unacceptable. That idea has diffused throughout the globe in a manner similar to the diffusion of democracy: both started in the developed world. Thus, the countries in which "moral progress" has occurred with regard to war have also experienced democratic political progress. The two are associated geographically, but not causally.[6]

The notion that the likelihood of war is being decreased by the spread of peaceful norms has been put forward by several theorists, most notably by Mueller in his *Retreat from Doomsday: The Obsolescence of Major War.*[7] The argument is essentially that war is becoming obsolete among the states of the developed world because in those states attitudes about war are changing. War is no longer seen as normal part of international relations; it is no longer viewed as required by human nature; it is no longer believed to be necessary for human progress; and it is no longer seen as serving a necessary social-political-economic function. Instead, it is now widely viewed as irrational and immoral, and as unacceptable as part of the relations between civilized states. A new norm seems to have been established among states of the developed world: offensive war is not acceptable. The proposition that war ought to be abolished, says Mueller, is an idea whose time has come. (This is a change propelled in part by the enormous destruction of World

Wars I and II and the realization that future wars would be so costly as to be irrational.)

Mueller's primary argument is that war, like any other cultural institution, is subject to change over time. Changes in moral and aesthetic values lead eventually to changes in social institutions. While a good many societies at one time supported institutions such as slavery, dueling, and even human sacrifice, these institutions have been gradually discredited and then completely abandoned (not just replaced by other social institutions). The same is beginning to happen to attitudes about war in the developed world. One can point to the fact that several European states have forgone war for centuries now—the Swiss, the Scandinavians, and the inhabitants of The Netherlands for instance. And Europe itself, an area that was once the most war prone in the world, has not experienced interstate war since 1945.

Nevertheless, it should be emphasized that the trend Mueller discusses is not yet global in scope. (Indeed, the trend may not encompass all of Europe, as the recent conflict between Slovenia, Croatia, and Bosnia-Herzegovina against the remnants of the Yugoslav state led by Serbia illustrates.) The majority of the world's states are not members of the developed area (and neither are they democratic). War is not yet obsolete, it is only in the process of becoming obsolete—a process whose end is uncertain and whose time frame is unknown.

Mueller suggests that social scientist, by ignoring the autonomous power of ideas, have left out an important independent variable in their search for the origins of war. He suggests that war is ultimately an idea that has been adopted by large portions of international society, perhaps temporarily, as a method for dealing with conflict. Since it is required neither by human nature nor by the nature of the international system, it may be abolished like any other cultural creation. According to Mueller, war can disappear

> . . . without requiring that there be notable change or improvement on any of the level of analysis categories. Specifically, war can die out without changing human nature, without modifying the nature of the state or the nation-state, without changing the international system, without creating an effective world government or system of international law, and without improving the competence or moral capacity of political leaders. It can also go away without . . . enveloping the earth in democracy or prosperity; without devising ingenious agreements to restrict arms or the arms industry; . . . and without doing anything whatsoever about nuclear weapons.[8]

Mueller's argument draws our attention to a crucial variable in the war puzzle—and one that is generally underexplored—the operational code. Operational codes contain the attitudes of individual leaders toward war: Can war be just? Is it acceptable? Is it necessary? Is war an effective tool of foreign policy? Under what circumstances should war be used? What are the proper goals and purposes of war? How should war be pursued for best results? The answers to these questions are contained within the operational code.

We know from the historical studies of Evan Luard and K. J. Holsti that attitudes toward war have not remained constant over the ages.[9] The proper goals of war, the issues over which states choose to fight, and the moral evaluation of war have changed throughout history. Mueller's argument can be interpreted to say that in the twentieth century the operational codes of the leaders of the developed states have undergone a change with regard to war. Its morality has been seriously challenged; its efficacy as a tool of policy has been questioned; and its political-social acceptability has been denied.

Operational codes play a crucial role in the chain of events leading to war. Most paths to war pass through individual images and operational codes. They are situated at the crucial junction connecting variables at all other levels of analysis. The images and operational codes of individual leaders act as filters through which they view and interpret the actions of others. Acts of rivals (such as arms buildups, technological progress, alliance formation, verbal statements) as well as power transitions and shifts in the systemic or dyadic balance are all filtered through our images. Perceptions (and misperceptions) are formed and operational codes are engaged to help interpret and analyze events and choose responses.

Hard-line operational codes—which see war as a normal and effective tool of policy, which support aggressive tactics such as threats, ultimata, brinkmanshp, and bullying, which advocate a "peace through strength" approach to international relations, which prefer war to concessions and the loss of face, and which view cooperation, conciliation, and unilateral concessions with disdain—help to condition a response that overreacts to the behavior of others and leads to a conflict spiral.

Mueller is right in suggesting that peace may be brought about by changing norms about war. As the words of the UNESCO constitution remind us, "Since wars begin in the minds of men, it is in the minds of men that the defense of peace must be constructed." Peace will come when operational codes change, when realpolitik (and other hard-line) approaches to foreign policy are discredited, when our images of others change, when leaders learn to break out of conflict spirals, and when war is finally seen as unethical, improper, immoral, and illogical.

In the meantime, while we are waiting for the acceptance of peaceful norms to be universally accepted, perhaps a few modest suggestions are in order.

Some Modest Proposals

All of this should give the real-world practitioner of international affairs plenty to think about. The forgoing has probably painted an unrealistically gloomy picture of the possibility of war. We must remain optimistic that most wars, though perhaps not all, can be avoided. Just as recent research has given us some clues about the causes of war, it has also suggested some guidelines for the prevention of war. Here are some extremely modest suggestions for practitioners to think about.

1. Perceptions are important. Leaders should consciously engage in reality testing to guard against misperceptions. One should keep an open mind and be open to the suggestions of others that one's own interpretation of reality is unfounded. In this regard, some type of multiple-advocacy approach to policy making is desirable.

2. One must be wary against the automatic assumptions that threats work and that opponents will back down when confronted with superior force and clear-cut commitments. This is rare—especially between equals, but even states on the wrong side of the military balance frequently find it difficult to back down.

3. One must be wary of conflictual interactions spiraling out of control. Potential conflict spirals must be identified as quickly as possible, and attempts should be made early in such situations to defuse the spiral and reverse its course. Though they may not always work, reciprocating strategies such as TIT-FOR-TAT and GRIT are worth trying, especially if they are begun early enough.

4. One must be aware of the security dilemma and recognize that one's own actions may be perceived by adversaries as threatening even if that was not the intention. Security must be mutual; it cannot be achieved at the expense of others. Empathy is an important attribute for decision-makers.

5. Periods of power transitions and systematic changes are periods of danger. Statesmen would be well advised to manage these transitions cautiously, with equal regard for those whose power is declining and for those whose power is increasing. The former must be made to feel their legitimate interests will be protected even though they themselves are less able to do it, and the latter must be granted the status and responsibilities that correspond to their new capabilities.

6. National leaders need to recognize that their external adversaries may be responding as much to their own internal, domestic situation as to the international environment. Calculations that omit this factor are likely to lead to disappointments.

7. National leaders may have to be prepared to take their domestic lumps. Placing too much importance on the domestic political implications of crisis decisions creates problems. Do the right thing.

Notes

Chapter 1

1. St. Louis *Post Dispatch*, April 12, 1985, p. 2; quoted in Ronald J. Glossop, *Confronting War: An Examination of Humanity's Most Pressing Problem*, 2nd ed. (Jefferson, NC: McFarlane, 1987), p. 3.
2. Two excellent chapters on theory in international relations are Michael P. Sullivan, *International Relations: Theories and Evidence* (Englewood Cliffs, NJ: Prentice-Hall, 1976), Chapter 1, and Kenneth N. Waltz, *Theory of International Politics (Reading, MA: Addison-Wesley, 1979), Chapter 1.*
3. J. David Singer and Melvin Small, *The Wages of War, 1816–1965: A Statistical Handbook* (New York: Wiley, 1972).
4. Sullivan, p. 9.
5. J. David Singer, "Introduction," pp. 11–20 in J. D. Singer and Associates, *Explaining War: Selected Papers from the Correlates of War Project* (Beverly Hills, CA: Sage, 1979). See also David Dessler, "Beyond Correlations: Toward a Causal Theory of War," *International Studies Quarterly*, 35 (3) (September 1991), pp. 337–55.
6. Glenn H. Snyder and Paul Diesing, *Conflict Among Nations: Bargaining, Decision-making, and System Structure in International Crises* (Princeton, NJ: Princeton University Press, 1977), pp. 21–22.

Chapter 2

1. My thanks to Professor James Rosenau for this observation.
2. The terms "man" and "mankind" will occasionally be used here to refer collectively to human beings; they are not intended to denote only male members of the species.
3. William James, "The Moral Equivalent of War," in Bramson and Goethals (eds.) *War: Studies from Psychology, Sociology, Anthropology*, rev. ed. (New York: Basic Books, 1968).
4. Sigmund Freud, "Why War?" in M. Small and J. D. Singer (eds.), *International War: An Anthology* (Homewood, IL: Dorsey Press, 1985), pp. 158–63. Although Freud himself did not use the term "thanatos," others have used it as an appellation for the death instinct.
5. Konrad Lorenz, *On Aggression* (New York: Bantam Books, 1966).

6. Robert Ardrey, *African Genesis* (New York: Atheneum, 1961); *The Territorial Imperative* (New York: Atheneum, 1966); and *The Social Contract* (New York: Atheneum, 1970).
7. Lionel Tiger and R. Fox, *The Imperial Animal* (New York: Holt, Rinehart & Winston, 1971.
8. See, for instance, Raymond Dart, "The Predatory Transition from Ape to Man," *International Anthropological and Linguistic Review* 1 (1953), pp. 207–8.
9. Richard Leaky, *The Making of Mankind* (New York: Dutton, 1981),pp. 221–25.
10. Edward O. Wilson, *Sociobiology: The Abridged Edition* (Cambridge, MA: The Belknap Press of Harvard University Press, 1980), pp. 120–21.
11. Lorenz, *On Aggression*, p. 42.
12. See Samuel S. Kim, "The Lorenzian Theory of Aggression and Peace Research: A Critique," in Richard Falk and S. S. Kim (eds.), *The War System* (Boulder, CO: Westview, 1980), p. 84.
13. Lorenz, *On Aggression*, pp. 52–53, and *Studies in Animal and Human Behavior*, p. 320, quoted in Kim, "The Lorenzian Theory," p. 85.
14. Anthony Storr, "Aggression Is an Instinct," in D. Bender and B. Leone (eds.), *Are Humans Aggressive by Nature?* (St. Paul, MN: Greenhaven Press, 1983), pp. 16–21.
15. J. P. Scott, "That Old-Time Aggression," in Ashley Montagu (ed.), *Man and Aggression* (New York: Oxford University Press, 1968).
16. Ardrey, *The Territorial Imperative*, pp. 168–73, 179–83, and 333–338. This emphasis on innate needs is somewhat similar to psychologist Abraham Maslow's concept of "instincoid needs." See Maslow's *Motivation and Personality* (New York: Harper & Row, 1954).
17. Ardrey, *The Territorial Imperative*, pp. 180–82.
18. Leonard Berkowitz, *Aggression: A Social-Psychological Analysis* (New York: McGraw-Hill, 1962), pp. 9–11.
19. Quoted in Blaine Hardin, "Boring, Boring, Boring, Boring, Boring," *Washington Post*, January 31, 1982, pp. D1, D4.
20. Quoted in Kenneth Boulding, *Conflict and Defense: A General Theory* (New York: Harper & Row, 1962), p. 306.
21. See, for instance, Diane Fossey, *Gorillas in the Mist* (Boston: Houghton Mifflin, 1983), and Jane Goodall, *Through a Window: My Thirty Years with the Chimpanzees of Gombe* (Boston: Houghton Mifflin, 1990).
22. Goodall, see especially pp. 75–84, 98–111, and 206–16.
23. Kim, "The Lorenzian Theory," p. 88.
24. Ashley Montagu, "The New Litany of 'Innate Depravity' or Original Sin Revisited," in Ashley Montagu (ed.), *Man and Aggression*, pp. 9–11.
25. Kim, "The Lorenzian Theory," p. 97.
26. James A. Schellenberg, *The Science of Conflict* (New York: Oxford University Press, 1982), p. 30, and Scott, "That Old-Time Aggression," p. 53.
27. See, for instance, David Pilbeam, "The Fashionable View of Man as a Naked Ape Is: 1. An Insult to Apes, 2. Simplistic, 3. Male-Oriented, 4. Rubbish," *New York Times Magazine*, September 3, 1972, p. 10, cited in Ronald Glossop, *Confronting War* (Jefferson, NC: McFarland, 1987), p. 45. Most of these arguments were put forward prior to Goodall's observations about chimp behavior. On the territoriality of primates see Jane Goodall, "Life and Death at Gombe," *National Geographic* 155 (5) (May 1979), p. 599. See also Goodall's *Through a Window*, cited above.
28. Scott, "That Old-Time Aggression," p. 56.
29. Kim, "The Lorenzian Theory," pp. 101–2.

30. Ibid., p. 95.
31. Goodall, *Though a Window*, p. 210.
32. Edward O. Wilson, *Sociobiology: The New Synthesis* (Cambridge, MA: Harvard University Press, 1975). See also Wilson's *On Human Nature* (Cambridge: Harvard University Press, 1978).
33. Wilson, *On Human Nature*, pp. 20–22.
34. Ibid., pp. 99–100 and throughout Chapter 5, pp. 99–120.
35. Wilson, *Sociobiology*, 1980 edition, p. 122.
36. Ibid.
37. Wilson, *On Human Nature*, pp. 106–7 and p. 114, as well as pp. 101–2.
38. Ibid., pp. 116–17.
39. Ibid., p. 106.
40. Ibid., p. 119.
41. Ashley Montagu, "Introduction," in A. Montagu (ed.), *Sociobiology Examined* (New York: Oxford University Press, 1980), pp. 6–7.
42. Wilson, *Sociobiology*, 1975 edition, p. 345.
43. Montagu, *Sociobiology Examined*, pp. 7–8.
44. Ibid.
45. Ibid., pp. 8–10. See also Marshall Sahlins, *The Use and Abuse of Biology: An Anthropological Critique of Sociobiology* (Ann Arbor: University of Michigan Press, 1976).
46. On these points, see Evan Luard, *War in International Society* (New Haven, CT: Yale, 1986).
47. See, for instance, John A. Vasquez, "Foreign Policy, Learning, and War," in C. F. Hermann, C. W. Kegley, Jr., and J. N. Rosenau (eds.), *New Directions in the Study of Foreign Policy* (Boston: Allen and Unwin, 1987), p. 372.
48. Montagu, "The New Litany," pp. 6 and 16.
49. Leaky, *The Making of Mankind*, p. 229.
50. Ibid., pp. 229–30 and 237.
51. Andrew Bard Schmookler, *The Parable of the Tribes: The Problem of Power in Social Evolution* (Boston: Houghton Mifflin, 1984).
52. David Fabbro, "Peaceful Societies," in Falk and Kim (eds.), *The War System*, pp. 180—203.
53. Ibid., p. 181.
54. Ibid., p. 199.
55. Ibid., p. 181.
56. Elizabeth Thomas, *The Harmless People* (New York: Knopf, 1959), quoted in Seyom Brown, *The Causes and Prevention of War* (New York: St. Martin's, 1987), p. 14.
57. Gwynne Dyer, *War* (New York: Dorsey, 1985), p. 6.
58. Ibid., p. 9.
59. Ibid.
60. Ibid., p. 10.
61. Quincy Wright, *A Study of War* (Chicago: University of Chicago Press, 1965), p. 63.
62. Werner Levi, "The Causes of War and the Conditions of Peace," in Richard Falk and S.H. Mendlovitz (eds.), *Toward a Theory of War Prevention* (New York: World Law Fund, 1966).
63. Scott, "That Old-Time Aggression," p. 54.
64. See Margaret Mead, "Warfare Is Only an Invention—Not Biological Necessity," in Charles Beitz and Theodore Herman (eds.), *Peace and War* (San Francisco: WH Freeman, 1973), pp. 112–18.

65. See Albert Bandura, "The Social Learning Theory of Aggression," in Falk and Kim, *The War System*, pp. 141–56.
66. Edwin I. Megargee and Jack E. Hokanson, *The Dynamics of Aggression* (New York: Harper & Row, 1970), p. 43, cited in Lloyd Jensen, *Explaining Foreign Policy* (Englewood Cliffs, NJ: Prentice-Hall, 1982), p. 20.

Chapter 3

1. John Stoessinger, *Why Nations Go to War*, 3rd ed. (New York: St. Martin's, 1982), p. 135. Emphasis added.
2. The following draws from Ole Holsti, "Foreign Policy Decision-Makers Viewed Psychologically: 'Cognitive Process' Approaches," in James Rosenau (ed.), *In Search of Global Patterns* (New York: Free Press, 1972), p. 127, and from Margaret Hermann, "Effects of Personal Characteristics of Political Leaders on Foreign Policy," in M. East, S. Salmore, and C. F. Hermann (eds.), *Why Nations Act: Theoretical Perspectives for Comparative Foreign Policy Studies* (Beverley Hills, CA: Sage, 1978), pp. 51–52.
3. James Davies, "Violence and Aggression: Innate or Not?" *The Western Political Quarterly* 23 (1970), pp. 617–18, cited in Ralph Pettman, *Human Behavior and World Politics* (New York: St. Martin's, 1975), p. 219.
4. Abraham Maslow, "A Theory of Human Motivation," *Psychological Review* 50 (1943), p. 394.
5. Although empirical evidence exists for the presence of physical and security needs, and indeed for their hierarchical nature, empirical vaidation for the existence of Maslow's three higher needs is lacking. See Ross Fitzgerald, "Abraham Maslow's Hierarchy of Needs—An Exposition and Evaluation," in R. Fitzgerald (ed.), *Human Needs and Politics* (Rushcutters Bay, Australia: Pergamon Press, 1977), pp. 36–51.
6. Henry Kissinger, "Domestic Structure and Foreign Policy," in James Rosenau (ed.), *International Politics and Foreign Policy*, rev. ed. (New York: Free Press, 1969), p. 271.
7. Kenneth Terhune, "Studies in Motives, Cooperation, and Conflict Within Laboratory Microcosms," *Buffalo Studies* 4 (1968), pp. 29–58, cited in Lloyd Jensen, *Explaining Foreign Policy* (Englewood Cliffs, NJ: Prentice-Hall, 1982), pp. 22 and 23.
8. David G. Winter and Abagail J. Stewart, "Content Analysis as a Technique for Assessing Political Leaders," in M. G. Hermann (ed.), *A Psychological Examination of Political Leaders* (New York: Free Press, 1977), p. 60, cited in Jensen, *Explaining Foreign Policy*, p. 23.
9. Harold Lasswell, *Psychopathology and Politics* (Chicago: University of Chicago Press, 1930), and *Power and Personality* (New York: Norton, 1948).
10. K. W. Terhune and J. M. Firestone, "Psychological Studies in Social Interaction and Motives (SIAM), Phase 2: Group Motives in International Relations Games," CAL Report VX-2018-6-2, Cornell Aeronautical Laboratory, 1967, and D. G. Winter, *The Power Motive* (New York: Free Press, 1973), both cited in M. Hermann, "Effects of Personal Characterstics of Political Leaders on Foreign Policy," p. 66.
11. Winter and Stewart, "Content Analysis as a Technique for Assessing Political Leaders," p. 60, cited in Jensen, *Explaining Foreign Policy*, p. 23.
12. K. W. Terhune, "Motives, Situation, and Interpersonal Conflict Within Prison-

ers' Dilemma," *Journal of Personality and Social Psychology*, Monograph Supplement 8, No. 3, (1968) Part 2, pp. 1–23, cited in Hermann, "Effects of Personal Characteristics of Political Leaders on Foreign Policy," p. 66.

13. Milton Rokeach, *The Open and Closed Mind* (New York: Basic Books, 1960).

14. Milton Rokeach, "The Nature and Meaning of Dogmatism," *Psychological Review* 61 (May 1954), p. 200, cited in Jensen, *Explaining Foreign Policy*, p. 26.

15. T. W. Adorno, *The Authoritarian Personality* (New York: Harper & Row, 1950).

16. Jensen, *Explaining Foreign Policy*, p. 25.

17. Lloyd Etheredge, "Personality Effects on American Foreign Policy, 1898–1968," *American Political Science Review* 72 (June 1978), pp. 434–51, and Graham H. Shepard, "Personality Effects on American Foreign Policy, 1969–1984: A Second Test of Interpersonal Generalization Theory," *International Studies Quarterly* 32 (1) (March 1988), pp. 91–123.

18. Etheredge, p. 449. Shepard is unable to confirm any difference between the effects of introverted and extroverted personality on U.S. policy toward the Soviet Union in the 1969–1984 period.

19. R. Raskin, J. Novacek, and R. Hogan, "Narcissism Self-Esteem Management," *Journal of Personality and Social Psychology* 60, pp. 911–18; R. Raskin and H. Terry, "A Principle Components Analysis of the Narcissistic Personality Inventory and Further Evidence of its Construct Validity," *Journal of Personality and Social Psychology* 54, pp. 890–902; and L. Carroll, "A Comparative Study of Narcissism, Gender, and Sex Role Orientation Among Body Builders, Athletes and Psychology Students," *Psychological Reports* 64, pp. 99–1006.

20. U.S. House of Representatives, Committee on Foreign Affairs, "The Persian Gulf Crisis," Statement by Jerrold Post, December 11, 1990 (pp. 381–401), USGPO, Washington, DC, 1991, and the "McNeill-Lehrer News Hour," February 2, 1991, interview with Betty Glad and Jerrold Post.

21. See Bruce Bueno de Mesquita, "Risk, Power Distribution and the Likelihood of War," *International Studies Quarterly* 25 (IV) (December 1981), pp. 542–46, and Bueno de Mesquita, *The War Trap* (New Haven, CT: Yale University Press, 1981).

22. Robert Isaac, *Individuals and World Politics*, 2nd ed. (Monterey, CA: Wadsworth-Duxbury, 1981), p. 157.

23. Jerome Frank, *Sanity and Survival: Psychological Aspects of War and Peace* (New York: Random House–Vintage, 1967), p. 59.

24. Robert Tucker, *Stalin as Revolutionary: 1879–1929, a Study in History and Personality* (New York: Norton, 1973).

25. Alexander George and Juliet George, *Woodrow Wilson and Colonel House—A Personality Study* (New York: Dover Publications, 1964). See also the excellent review of the Georges' work in Fred Greenstein, *Personality and Politics* (New York: Norton, 1975), pp. 63–93. My summary draws heavily on Greenstein's analysis.

26. D. Jablow Hirshman and Julian Lieb, "Does the White House Need a Shrink?" *Washington Post*, February 12, 1989, p. C3.

27. James Barber, *The Presidential Character* (Englewood Cliffs, NJ: Prentice-Hall, 1972); Fawn Brodie, *Richard Nixon* (New York: Norton, 1981); Eli Chesen, *President Nixon's Psychiatric Profile* (New York: Peter Wyden, 1973); Lloyd Etheredge, "Hard Ball Politics: A Model," *Political Psychology* (Spring 1979); Bruce Mazlish, *In Search of Nixon* (Baltimore: Penguin, 1973). For an article that suggests that former President Reagan suffered from castration

anxiety, see Lloyd Demause, "The Making of a Fearful Leader: 'Where's the Rest of Me?'" *Journal of Psychohistory* 12 (Summer 1984).

28. Hirshman and Lieb, op. cit.
29. Herman C. Kelman, "Social-Psychological Approaches to the Study of International Relations," in H. Kelman (ed.), *International Behavior: A Social-Psychological Analysis* (New York: Holt, Rinehart & Winston, 1965).
30. Thomas Wiegele, "Decision-Making in an International Crisis: Some Biological Factors," *International Studies Quarterly* 17 (3) (September 1973), pp. 302–4.
31. Sally Squires, "Stress, Poor Communication Cited in Vincennes' Downing of Jet," *Washington Post*, October 17, 1988.
32. From Barry Schneider, *Danger and Opportunity: Decision Making, Bargaining, and Management in Three United States and Six Simulated Crises*, Ph.D. dissertation, Columbia University, New York, 1974, pp. 67–68, cited in Patrick Morgan, *Deterrence* (Beverly Hills, CA: Sage, 1977), pp. 186–87; Donald Kinder and Janet Weiss, "In Lieu of Rationality," *Journal of Conflict Resolution* 22 (4) December, 1978), p. 722; Ole Holsti; "Theories of Crisis Decision Making," in Paul Viotti and Mark Kauppi, *International Relations Theory* New York: Macmillan, 1987), pp. 244–81.
33. Ole Holsti, *Crisis, Escalation, War* (Montreal: McGill-Queens University Press, 1972), pp. 199–200, cited in Morgan, *Deterrence*, p. 187.
34. Hugh L'Etang, *The Pathology of Leadership* (New York: Hawthorne, 1970).
35. Ole Holsti, "Cognitive Dynamics and Images of the Enemy," in J. C. Farrell and A. P. Smith (eds.), *Image and Reality in World Politics* (New York: Columbia University Press, 1967), p. 18. See also, Kenneth Boulding, "The Learning and Reality Testing Process in the International System," in Farrell and Smith, *Image and Reality in World Politics*, and Boulding, *The Image* (Ann Arbor: University of Michigan Press, 1956).
36. Ole Holsti, "Foreign Policy Decision Makers Viewed Psychologically," p. 122.
37. Harvey Starr, *Henry Kissinger: Perceptions of International Politics* (Lexington: University Press of Kentucky, 1984), p. 47.
38. Harold Sprout and Margaret Sprout, *The Ecological Perspective on Human Affairs* (Princeton, NJ: Princeton University Press, 1965).
39. Alexander George, "The Operational Code: A Neglected Approach to the Study of Political Leaders and Decision-Making," in Erik Hoffman and Frederick Fleron (eds.), *The Conduct of Soviet Foreign Policy* (New York: Aldine, 1980), p. 170.
40. Nathan Leites, *A Study of Bolshevism* (Glencoe, IL: Free Press, 1953).
41. George, "The Operational Code," pp. 174–88.
42. Alexander George, "The Operational Code," pp. 172–73, and Ole Holsti, "Foreign Policy Decision Makers Vieweded Psychologically," p. 138.
43. See Starr, *Henry Kissinger*, p. 45 and p. 47.
44. Stephen G. Walker, "The Interface Between Beliefs and Behavior: Henry Kissinger's Operational Code and the Vietnam War," *Journal of Conflict Resolution* 21 (1) (March 1977), pp. 151–52.
45. Starr, *Henry Kissinger*, p. 159.
46. Robert Jervis, "Hypotheses on Misperception," in James Rosenau (ed.), *International Politics and Foreign Policy*, rev. ed. (New York: Free Press, 1969), p. 240.
47. The classic work is Leon Festinger, *A Theory of Cognitive Dissonance* (Evanston, IL: Row, Patterson, 1957).
48. Ole Holsti, "Cognitive Dynamics and Images of the Enemy," in John Farrell and Asa Smith (eds.), *Image and Reality in World Politics* (New York: Colum-

bia University Press, 1967), pp. 18–21. The tendency toward cognitive dissonance affects not only how new information is processed, but also how the images in our belief system are organized. For instance, some beliefs are created and maintained not on the basis of direct evidence, but because they are logically connected to other established beliefs. Consistency of belief requires they be present. On this point see John Steinbruner, *The Cybernetic Theory of Decision* (Princeton, NJ: Princeton University Press, 1974), pp. 97 and 114.

49. Ibid., 97. See also Dina Zinnes, "Some Evidence Relevant to the Man-Milieu Hypothesis," in J. Rosenau, V. Davis, and M. East (eds.), *The Analysis of International Politics* (New York: Free Press, 1972), p. 245.

50. Robert Jervis, *Perception and Misperception in International Politics* (Princeton, NJ: Princeton University Press, 1976), pp. 119–20.

51. Steinbruner, *The Cybernetic Theory of Decision*, p. 102.

52. See, for instance, Charles Krauthammer, "No, The Cold War Isn't Really Over," *Time*, September 5, 1988.

53. See Ole Holsti, "Cognitive Dynamics and Images of the Enemy," in Farrell and Smith, *Image and Reality in World Politics*, and "The Belief System and National Images: A Case Study," in James Rosenau (ed.), *International Politics and Foreign Policy*, rev. ed. (New York: Free Press, 1969), pp. 543–50.

54. Henry Kissinger, *The Necessity for Choice* (New York: Doubleday, 1962), p. 201.

55. Jervis, *Perception and Misperception in International Politics*, p. 308.

56. Karl Deutsch and Richard Merritt, "Effects of Events on National and International Images," in Herbert Kelman (ed.), *International Behavior*, pp. 132–87.

57. Jervis, *Perception and Misperception in International Politics*, p. 191.

58. Ibid., p. 145.

59. Ibid., p. 208.

60. Nancy Cooper and John Barry, "Seven Minutes to Death," *Newsweek*, July 18, 1988, pp. 18–24. A similar situation occurred in April 1989 when an Iraqi aircraft erroneously shot down a friendly Egyptian training jet armed with missiles that was flying to an international air show in Baghdad. The Iraqi air defense command had been at a heightened state of alert for several weeks after Israeli officials publically announced their concern over Iraq's civilian nuclear power program. Additionally, Iraqi air defenses had become accustomed to a shoot-first strategy furing the Iran-Iraq War. Patrick Tyler, "Iraqis May Have Thought Downed Jet Was Israeli," *Washington Post*, April 29, 1989, pp. A16 and A26.

61. Jervis, *Perception and Misperception in International Politics*, p. 217.

62. Steinbruner, *The Cybernetic Theory of Decision*, p. 116.

63. Two researchers, in fact, find no examples of historical analogies providing leaders with correct interpretations of a message within their sample of cases. Paul Diesing and Glen Snyder, *Systems, Bargains, Decisions* (Princeton, NJ: Princeton University Press, 1977).

64. Harry S. Truman, *Memoirs*, II (Garden City, NY: Doubleday, 1956), quoted in Ernest May, *"Lessons" of the Past: The Use and Misuse of History in American Foreign Policy* (New York: Oxford University Press, 1973), pp. 81–82.

65. The following draws on May, *"Lessons" of the Past*, pp. 91–101.

66. *Pentagon Papers*, II, Sen. Gravel ed. (Boston: Beacon Press, 1971), p. 650, quoted in May, *"Lessons" of the Past*, pp. 98–99.

67. Jervis, *Perceptions and Misperception in International Politics*, p. 267.

68. John Vasquez, "Foreign Policy, Learning, and War," in C. F. Hermann, C. W.

Kegley, Jr., and J. Rosenau (eds.), *New Directions in the Study of Foreign Policy*, p. 379.

69. Jervis, *Perceptions and Misperceptions in International Politics*, p. 244.
70. Ibid., p. 252.
71. Garry Wills, *Reagan's America* (New York: Penguin Books, 1985), pp. 286–307.
72. Jervis, *Perception and Misperception in International Politics*, p. 238.
73. K. J. Holsti, "National Role Conceptions in the Study of Foreign Policy," *International Studies Quarterly* 3 (September, 1970).
74. Michael Brecher, *Decisions in Israel's Foreign Policy* (New Haven, CT: Yale University Press, 1975), p. 334, cited in Richard Ned Lebow, *Between Peace and War: The Nature of International Crisis*, (Baltimore: Johns Hopkins University Press, 1981), p. 196.
75. Jack S. Levy, "Misperception and the Causes of War: Theoretical Linkages and Analytical Problems," *World Politics*, Vol. 36, No. 1 (October 1983), pp. 76–99.
76. Quoted in Jervis, *Perception and Misperception in International Politics*, p. 74.
77. Robert North, "Perception and Action in the 1914 Crisis," in Farrell and Smith, *Image and Reality in World Politics*, p. 122.
78. Stoessinger, *Why Nations Go to War*, p. 211.
79. Levy, "Misperception and the Causes of War," pp. 88–89.
80. Lebow, *Between Peace and War*, p. 200.
81. See articles in the *Washington Post* on August 3 and 4, 1990, and September 22, 1990.
82. Geoffrey Blainey, *The Causes of War* (New York: Free Press, 1973), p. 246.
83. Lebow, *Between Peace and War*, pp. 242–43.
84. William J. Barnds, *India, Pakistan and the Great Powers* (New York: Praeger, 1972), p. 200, cited in Stoessinger, *Why Nations Go to War*, pp. 125–26.
85. Lebow, *Between Peace and War*, pp. 245–46.
86. Levy, "Misperception and the Causes of War," p. 84.
87. Lebow, *Between Peace and War*, pp. 62 and 83.
88. Ibid., pp. 238–41.
89. Ibid., p. 97.
90. Ibid., pp. 164–66.
91. Jervis, *Perception and Misperception in International Politics*, p. 52.
92. Lebow, *Between Peace and War*, pp. 158–61.
93. Joseph de Rivera, *The Psychological Dimension of Foreign Policy*, pp. 247–57, cited in Lebow, *Between Peace and War*, p. 160.
94. Lebow, *Between Peace and War*, pp. 157–78.
95. Evan Luard, *War in International Society*, (New Haven, CT: Yale University Press, 1986), p. 329. Emphasis added.
96. Ibid., Chapter 8, pp. 329–78.
97. Levy, "Misperception and the Causes of War," p. 81.
98. For instance, Barbara Tuchman, *The Guns of August* (New York: Dell, 1962).
99. Lebow, *Between Peace and War*, p. 254. Fritz Fischer, *War of Illusions: German Policies from 1911 to 1914* (New York: Norton, 1975), pp. 45, 55, and 398–402.
100. Luard, *War in International Society*, pp. 360–61.
101. Lebow, *Between Peace and War*, pp. 264–65.
102. On these points see Blainey, *The Causes of War*, pp. 208–9, and Tuchman, *The Guns of August*, pp. 45–62 and 142.
103. Blainey, *The Causes of War*, pp. 57–67.

104. Ibid., and Levy pp. 91–93.
105. *Washington Post*, August 4, 1990, and October 21, 1990.
106. Blainey, *The Causes of War*, p. 53.
107. Lebow, *Between War and Peace*, p. 207.
108. Stoessinger, *Why Nations Go to War*, p. 72.
109. Ibid., p. 73.
110. Lebow, *Between Peace and War*, pp. 216–19.
111. Ibid., p. 102.
112. Irving Janis and Leon Mann, *Decision-Making: A Psychological Analysis of Conflict, Choice and Commitment* (New York: Free Press, 1977).
113. This discussion of Jervis and Mann is from Lebow, *Between Peace and War*, pp. 107–10.
114. Ibid., p. 111.
115. Ibid., pp. 275–76.
116. Ibid., p. 275.
117. Dina Zinnes, "Expression and Perception of Hostility in Prewar Crisis: 1914," in J. David Singer (ed.), *Quantitative International Politics* (New York: Free Press, 1968), pp. 85–123, and Robert North, Richard Brody, and Ole Holsti, "Some Empirical Data on the Conflict Spiral," *Peace Research Society (International)*, Vol. 1 (1964), pp. 1–15.
118. Dina Zinnes, Robert North, and Howard E. Koch, Jr., "Capability, Threat, and the Outbreak of War," in J. Rosenau (ed.), *International Politics and Foreign Policy* (New York: Free Press of Glencoe, 1961), pp. 469–83, and especially, Ole Holsti and Robert North, "History of Human Conflict," in Elton B. McNeil (ed.), *Nature of Human Conflict* (Englewood Cliffs, NJ: Prentice-Hall, 1965), pp. 155–72. The assertion that German leaders perceived a situation of relative weakness does not exactly square with Blainey's assertion that German leaders were optimistic about the impending war. Blainey explains that to some extent this is due to the fact that North and his colleagues were unaware of the documentary evidence of German optimism because Fritz Fischer's seminal *Germany's Aims in the First World War*, published in Germany in 1961, had not yet been translated into English at the time of North's original research. On this point see Blainey, *The Causes of War*, pp. 130–32.
119. O. Holsti, R. North, and R. Brody, "Perception and Action in the 1914 Crisis," in J. D. Singer (ed.), *Quantitative International Politics*, pp. 123–59.
120. O. Holsti, R. Brody, and R. North, "Measuring Affect and Action in International Reaction Models: Empirical Materials from the 1962 Cuban Crisis," *Peace Research Society (International)*, Vol. II (1965), pp. 170–90.

Chapter 4

1. For an explanation of the rational actor model see Graham T. Allison, *Essence of Decision: Explaining the Cuban Missile Crisis* (Boston: Little, Brown, 1971).
2. See Bruce Bueno de Mesquita, *The War Trap* (New Haven, CT: Yale University Press, 1981). Bueno de Mesquita sees governments as unitary decision-makers who approach the problems of war and peace as expected utility maximizers.
3. Charles W. Kegley, Jr., and Eugene R. Wittkopf, *American Foreign Policy: Pattern and Process*, 3rd ed. (New York: St. Martin's, 1987), p. 472.
4. McGeorge Bundy, *Danger and Survival: Choices About the Bomb in the First Fifty Years* (New York: Random House, 1988), p. 451.

5. Glenn H. Snyder and Paul Diesing, *Conflict Among Nations: Bargaining, Decision Making, and System Structure in International Crises* (Princeton, NJ: Princeton University Press, 1977), p. 369.

6. Paul A. Anderson, "What Do Decision Makers Do When They Make Foreign Policy? The Implications for the Comparative Study of Foreign Policy," in Charles F. Hermann, Charles W. Kegley, Jr., and James N. Rosenau, (eds.), *New Directions in the Study of Foreign Policy* (Boston: Allen & Unwin, 1987), pp. 285–308.

7. For instance, Herbert Simon, *Administrative Behavior* (New York: Macmillan, 1959), and *Models of Man* (New York: Wiley, 1957); James March and Herbert Simon, *Organizations* (New York: Wiley, 1958); Richard Cyert and James March, *A Behavioral Theory of the Firm* (Englewood Cliffs, NJ: Prentice-Hall, 1963).

8. If no acceptable alternative appears, decision-makers then lower the level of aspiration and review the options again. See Snyder and Diesing, p. 344.

9. See Snyder and Diesing, p. 342.

10. Anderson, pp. 296–97.

11. David Braybrooke and Charles Lindblom, "Types of Decision-Making," James Rosenau (ed.), *International Politics and Foreign Policy*, rev. ed. (New York: Free Press, 1969), pp. 207–216.

12. Braybrooke and Lindblom, p. 212.

13. Moreover, the goals of policy making continue to change as feedback from previous policy decisions sheds new light on what is possible and desirable.

14. Leslie Gelb and Richard Betts, *The Irony of Vietnam: The System Worked* (Washington, DC: Brookings Institution, 1979).

15. Gelb and Betts, p. 278.

16. Gelb and Betts, p. 295.

17. See Arthur Schlesinger, Jr., *The Bitter Heritage: Vietnam and American Democracy, 1941–1966*, (Boston: Houghton Mifflin, 1967).

18. See also Allison's "Conceptual Models and the Cuban Missile Crisis," *American Political Science Review* 63 (September 1969), pp. 689–718; Allison and Morton Halperin, "Bureaucratic Politics: A Paradigm and Some Policy Implications," in Raymond Tanter and Richard Ullman (eds.), *Theory and Policy in International Relations* (Princeton; NJ: Princeton University Press, 1972); and Halperin, *Bureaucratic Politics and Foreign Policy* (Washington, DC: Brookings Institution, 1974).

19. Allison and Halperin, op. cit. They also label the BPM a paradigm rather than a theory in this revised effort.

20. Allison, *Essence of Decision*, p. 67.

21. Snyder and Diesing, p. 373.

22. John Steinbruner, *The Cybernetic Theory of Decision* (Princeton, NJ: Princeton University Press, 1974). This cybernetic tinkering is, of course, a method by which large organizations can reduce the overwhelming complexity of the policy environment. The focus on a few variables helps to reduce complexity by eliminating variety. Keeping critical variables within a tolerable range reduces both complexity and uncertainty. Complexity is further reduced through the breaking down of problems into smaller "miniproblems"—each dealt with by separate organizational subunits.

23. Allison, *Essence of Decision*, p. 130.

24. Jack S. Levy, "Organizational Routines and the Causes of War," *International Studies Quarterly* 30 (2) (June 1986), pp. 193–222.

25. Levy, p. 211.

26. See Jerel Rosati, "Developing a Systematic Decision-Making Framework: Bureaucratic Politics in Perspective," *World Politics* 33 (January 1981), pp. 234–52, for a somewhat more restricted view of the central propositions of the BPM.
27. All of this is not to say that organizational players see only organizational interests at stake in policy decisions. They also have personal interests and goals that play a role. Some of these might be personal advancement, a run for the top rung of the political ladder, a place in history, the respect of one's colleagues, and the advancement of an ideological agenda.
28. Empirical evidence does indicate a causal relationship between attitudes and roles. See Kegley and Wittkopf, *American Foreign Policy*, p. 464, fn. 2. Conformity is especially evident in formal roles.
29. Kegley and Wittkopf, p. 466.
30. Roger Hilsman has developed a variant of the BPM that he calls the political process model. While Allison assumes that the organization is the single most important determinant of the policy that players espouse, and that larger, powerful bureaucracies are the most important determinants of policy outcomes, Hilsman regards government organizations as only one factor—and not necessarily the most important. He notes the importance of factionalism within government organizations so that, for instance, certain offices within the State Department align with certain offices within the Defense Department in opposition to rival factions in these same institutions. Most important, Hilsman's model gives a larger role to the effects of domestic politics on foreign policy and includes congressional politics as well as executive branch politics. It also gives more attention to interest groups and to the public. Roger Hilsman, *The Politics of Policy Making in Defense and Foreign Affairs* (Englewood Cliffs, NJ: Prentice-Hall, 1987), pp. 77–78.
31. In their study of international crises Snyder and Diesing found that all strategies put forward for consideration could be accounted for by bureaucratic politics (p. 407).
32. Charles F. Hermann, "The Impact of Single Group Decision Units on Foreign Policy." Paper presented at International Studies Association conference, St. Louis, March 1988. See also Margaret Hermann and Charles F. Hermann, "A Look Inside the 'Black Box': Building on a Decade of Research," Gerald Hopple (ed.), *Biopolitics, Political Psychology and International Politics* (New York: St. Martin's, 1982).
33. Lindblom has termed the process "partisan mutual adjustment." Charles Lindblom, *The Intelligence of Democracy* (New York: Free Press, 1965), p. 98 ff.
34. Allison, *Essence of Decision*, pp. 144–45.
35. C. F. Hermann, "The Impact of Single Decision Units."
36. Kenneth Arrow, *Social Choice and Individual Values* (New York: Wiley, 1951); see also Bruce Bueno de Mesquita, *The War Trap*, pp. 12–18, and C. F. Hermann, "The Impact of Single Decision Units."
37. See Miriam Steiner's critique of the BPM, "The Elusive Essence of Decision," *International Studies Quarterly* 21 (2) (June 1977), pp. 389–422.
38. Snyder and Diesing (p. 350) define a majority coalition as "a portion of the decision-making group that can carry out a strategy without the help of the remaining group members, and if necessary against their active opposition." Snyder and Diesing see the building of majority coalitions as the essence of the BPM, while Charles Hermann ("The Impact of Single Group Decision Units") seems to disagree, emphasizing compromise.

39. Snyder and Diesing, p. 353.
40. Snyder and Diesing, p. 519.
41. Ibid.
42. Bundy, *Danger and Survival*, p. 446.
43. Kegley and Wittkopf, p. 498. See also, Philip G. Roeder, "Soviet Policies and Kremlin Politics," *International Studies Quarterly* 28 (2) (June 1984), pp. 171–93, on the lack of consistency and coherence in Soviet foreign policy.
44. Philip Roeder has argued that "pluralistic" and "oligarcic" decision-making regimes in the Soviet Union are usually characterized by compromise, incrementalism, and aversion to risk. It appears that political competition leads to risk taking in the U.S.S.R. primarily in situations where a single leader who has consolidated his authority over foreign policy is being challenged by rivals. See Philip G. Roeder, "Soviet Policies and Kremlin Politics."
45. Roger Hilsman, *The Politics of Policy Making in Defense and Foreign Affairs*, p. 61.
46. Barbara Hill, "A General Model of International Conflict: Dynamics, Problems and Prospects." Paper presented to International Studies Association conference, St. Louis, March 1988, p. 25.
47. Robert Axelrod, "Bureaucratic Decisionmaking in the Military Assistance Program: Some Empirical Findings," in Morton Halperin and Arnold Kanter (eds.), *Readings in American Foreign Policy: A Bureaucratic Perspective* (Boston: Little, Brown, 1973), pp. 154–72.
48. Andrew K. Semmel, "Some Correlates of Attitudes to Multilateral Diplomacy in the United States Department of State," *International Studies Quarterly* 20 (2) (June 1976), pp. 301–24.
49. Stephen Krasner, "Are Bureaucracies Important? A Re-examination of Accounts of the Cuban Missile Crisis," *Foreign Policy* 7 (Summer 1972).
50. Anderson, p. 299.
51. Graham H. Shepard, "Personality Effects on American Foreign Policy, 1969–1984: A Second Test of Interpersonal Generalization Theory," *International Studies Quarterly* 32 (1) (March 1988), p. 121.
52. Hilsman, p. 87.
53. Krasner, op. cit.
54. Harriet Fast Scott, "Soviet Military Doctrine: From the Great Patriotic War to the Gorbachev Era." Address to the 2nd International Security Conference on Soviet Military Doctrine in an Era of Change, Norfolk, VA, May 26, 1989. Also, Michael Dobbs, "Soviet Cities Dissent on Afghan War," *Washington Post*, March 20, 1989.
55. Richard Betts, *Soldiers, Statesmen, and Cold War Crises* (Cambridge, MA: Harvard University Press, 1977), pp. 4, 210, and 216.
56. Snyder and Diesing, pp. 512 and 359.
57. Halperin and Kanter, pp. 9–10.
58. Krasner, "Are Bureaucracies Important?"; Jerel A. Rosati, "Developing a Systematic Decision-Making Framework: Bureaucratic Politics in Perspective," *World Politics* 33 (2) (January 1981), pp. 234–52; Amos Perlmutter, "The Presidential Political Center and Foreign Policy: A Critique of the Revisionist and Bureaucratic-Political Orientations," *World Politics* 27 (1) (October 1974); Robert Art, "Bureaucratic Politics and American Foreign Policy: A Critique," *Policy Sciences* (December 1974).
59. Perlmutter, p. 92.
60. Dan Caldwell, "Bureaucratic Foreign Policy Making," *American Behavioral Scientist* 21 (1) (October 1977), p. 97.

61. Rosati, op. Cit.
62. On this point see Fen Osler Hampson, "The Divided Decision-Maker: American Domestic Politics and the Cuban Crisis," *International Security* 9 (3) (1985).
63. Bundy, *Danger and Survival*, pp. 400–1.
64. See Rosati, p. 246, and Krasner, op. cit.
65. Wilfred Kohl, "The Nixon-Kissinger Foreign Policy System and U.S.-European Relations: Patterns of Policy Making," *World Politics* 28 (1) (October 1975), pp. 1–43. Kohl's alternative models included (a) Hilsman's democratic politics model, (b) the royal court model (sometimes called the strong man model), which emphasizes the personality and operating style of the top decision maker, (c) the shared images and perceptions model, (d) Alexander George's multiple advocacy model, and (e) Janis' groupthink model.
66. Snyder and Diesing, pp. 355–56.
67. On "intermestic politics" see Bayless Manning, "The Congress, the Executive and Intermestic Affairs: Three Proposals," *Foreign Affairs* 55 (2) (January 1977), pp. 306–24, and John Spanier and Eric Uslaner, *How American Foreign Policy Is Made*, 2nd ed. (New York: Holt, Rinehart & Winston/Praeger, 1978).
68. C. F. Hermann, "The Impact of Single Decision Units on Foreign Policy," and Bruce Bueno de Mesquita, *The War Trap*.
69. C. F. Hermann, "The Impact of Single Decision Units on Foreign Policy."
70. Snyder and Diesing, p. 512. Snyder and Diesing also see the BPM as more relevant to modern times, "when agencies other than the foreign offices have become involved in foreign policy making."
71. Kim Richard Nossal, "Bureaucratic Politics and the Westminster Model," in Robert O. Matthews, Arthur Rubinoff, and Janice Gross Stein (eds.), *International Conflict and Conflict Management* (Scarborough, Ontario: Prentice-Hall, 1984), pp. 120–27.
72. For example, H. Gordon Skilling and Franklin Griffiths focus on "interest groups" in the Soviet system in their *Interest Groups in Soviet Politics* (Princeton, NJ: Princeton University Press, 1971); Carl Linden uses a "conflict model" to examine the Khrushchev administration in *Khrushchev and the Soviet Leadership* (Baltimore: Johns Hopkins University Press, 1966); Dennis Ross emphasizes "coalition maintenance" in his "Coalition Maintenance in the Soviet Union," *World Politics* 32 (2) (January 1980), pp. 258–80. For a view that opposes oligarchic/pluralist perspectives and advocates a return to a totalitarian model of soviet policy making, see William Odom, "A Dissenting View on the Group Approach to Soviet Politics," *World Politics* 28 (4) (July 1976), pp. 542–67.
73. Jiri Valenta, *Soviet Intervention in Czechoslovakia, 1968: Anatomy of a Decision* (Baltimore: Johns Hopkins University Press, 1979), p. 4.
74. Ross, "Coalition Maintenance in the Soviet Union"; see also his "Risk Aversion in Soviet Decisionmaking," in Jiri Valenta and William Potter, (eds.), *Soviet Decisionmaking for National Security* (Boston: George Allen & Unwin, 1984), pp. 237–51.
75. Ross, "Risk Aversion in Soviet Decisionmaking," p. 240.
76. Ross, "Coalition Maintenance in the Soviet Union," p. 266.
77. For an edited reader of early BPM case studies see Morton Halperin and Arnold Kanter, *Readings in American Foreign Policy, A Bureaucratic Perspective* (Boston: Little, Brown, 1973); for a review of BPM case studies see Dan Caldwell, "Bureaucratic Foreign Policy-Making."
78. Baltimore: Johns Hopkins University Press, 1979.

79. Dina Rome Spechler, "The U.S.S.R. and Third World Conflicts: Domestic Debate and Soviet Policy in the Middle East, 1967–1973," *World Politics* 38 (3) (April 1986), pp. 435–61.

80. Max Jacobson, *The Diplomacy of the Winter War: An Account of the Russo-Finnish War, 1939–1940* (Cambridge, MA: Harvard University Press, 1961).

81. Valenta's study of Soviet decision to intervene in Afghanistan also suggests possible bureaucratic alignments and institutional concerns of the Soviet elites. Jiri Valenta, "Soviet Decisionmaking on Afghanistan, 1979," in Valenta and William Potter (eds.), *Soviet Decisionmaking for National Security*. Although it is beyond the scope of this study, it would be interesting to speculate about the development of a BPM explanation for the behavior of czarist Russia leading up to the Russo-Japanese War. With a weak czar, Nicholas II, the Russian government followed contradictory policies in the Far East owing to the shifting balance of power surrounding Finance Minister Witte and Foreign Minister Lamsdorff, on the one hand, and the "Bezobrazov group," War Minister Kuropatkin, and Interior Minister Plehve, on the other. For a classic review of the situation see William Langer, "The Origin of the Russo-Japanese War," in Carl E. Shorske and Elizabeth Shorske (eds.), *Explorations in Crisis* (Cambridge, MA: Belknap/Harvard University Press, 1969).

82. Robert Gallucci, *Neither Peace nor Honor* (Baltimore: Johns Hopkins University Press, 1975). David Halberstam's analysis of the American involvement in Vietnam, *The Best and the Brightest* (Greenwich, CT: Fawcett, 1972) is consistent with the BPM approach, although Halberstam never explicitly identifies his analytical framework as such.

83. James Thomson's proposition concerning this development, and one that is consistent with the BPM. is that the more sensitive the issue and the higher it rises in the bureaucracy, the more completely the experts are excluded while the senior generalists take over. James C. Thomson, "How Could Vietnam Happen? An Autopsy," in Halperin and Kanter (eds.), *Readings in American Foreign Policy*, pp. 98–110, especially pp. 101–2.

84. Thomson, p. 103.

85. Gallucci, p. 48.

86. On this point see Gelb and Betts, pp. 309–10.

87. Gallucci, p .49.

88. Hilsman, pp. 87–90.

89. In Tanter and Ulmann (eds.), *Theory and Policy in International Relations*.

90. Caldwell, p. 100.

91. On this point see David Dessler, "Beyond Correlation: Toward A Causal Theory of War," *International Studies Quarterly* 35 (3) (September 1991), pp. 337–55.

92. Irving Janis, *Groupthink*, 2nd ed. (Boston: Houghton Mifflin, 1982), p. 9.

93. Ibid., pp. 242–43.

94. Ibid., p. 13.

95. Ibid., p. 256.

96. Ibid., p. 258.

97. Ibid., pp. 12 and 127.

98. Richard Barnet, *Roots of War: The Men and Institutions Behind U.S. Foreign Policy* (New York: Penguin, 1981), p. 109, quoted in Kegley and Wittkopf, p. 503.

99. See, for instance, Dean Pruitt, "Choice Shifts in Group Discussion: An Introductory Review," *Journal of Personality and Social Psychology* 20 (1971), pp. 339–60.

100. See D. Cartwright, "Risk-taking by Individuals and Groups: An Assessment of Research Employing Choice Dilemmas," *Journal of Personality and Social Psychology* 20 (1971), pp. 261–78; and B. Wilpert, P. Burger, J. Doktor, and R. Doktor, "The Risky Shift in Policy Decision Making: A Comparative Analysis," *Policy Sciences* 7 (1976), pp. 365–70.

101. D. G. Myers and H. Lamm, "The Polarizing Effect of Group Discussion," in Irving Janis (ed.), *Current Trends in Psychology: Readings from the American Scientist* (Los Altos, CA: Kaufmann, 1977).

102. See Andrew K. Semmel, "Small Group Dynamics in Foreign Policymaking," in Gerald Hopple (ed.), *Biopolitics, Political Psychology, and International Politics* (New York: St. Martin's, 1982), pp. 94–113.

103. Ibid.

104. Semmel also finds that the psychological rigidity of group members is an important factor. Groups composed of more flexible members tended to be less risk-prone than those composed of members whose psychological profiles were more rigid (p. 108).

105. Gregory M. Herek, Irving L. Janis, and Paul Huth, "Decision Making During International Crisis: Is Quality of Process Related to Outcome?" *Journal of Conflict Resolution* 31 (2) (June 1987), pp. 203–26.

106. Janis, p. 196.

107. Ibid., p. 197.

108. C. F. Hermann, "The Impact of Single Group Decision Units."

109. Ibid.

110. Janis, pp. 262–71.

111. Alexander George, "The Case for Multiple Advocacy in Making Foreign Policy," *American Political Science Review* 66 (September 1972), pp. 751–85.

112. Richard K. Betts, "Analysis, War, and Decision: Why Intelligence Failures Are Inevitable," *World Politics* 31 (1) (October 1978), p. 76.

113. Richard Ned Lebow, *Between Peace and War: The Nature of International Crises* (Baltimore: Johns Hopkins University Press, 1981), pp. 296–305.

114. At least one study actually demonstrates that the presence of leaders who are high in power motivation encourages the development of groupthink. E. M. Fodor and T. Smith, "The Power Motive as an Influence on Group Decision Making," *Journal of Personality and Social Psychology* 42 (1982), pp. 178–85.

Chapter 5

1. See Michael P. Sullivan, *International Relations: Theories and Evidence* (Englewood Cliffs, NJ: Prentice-Hall, 1976), pp. 102–3.

2. Dina Zinnes, "Why War? Evidence on the Outbreak of International Conflict," in Ted Robert Gurr, *Handbook of Political Conflict* (New York: Free Press, 1980), p. 335.

3. J. David Singer and Melvin Small, *Wages of War, 1816–1965: A Statistical Handbook* (New York: Wiley, 1972), p. 287. The nations involved in the most wars in this period were Britain and France, nineteen; Turkey, seventeen; Russia, fifteen; Sardinia, twelve; and Spain, nine.

4. See Kenneth Waltz, *Man, the State and War* (New York: Columbia University Press, 1959), Chapter IV, from which this discussion draws heavily.

5. Edmund Burke, Letter to William Smith, January 9, 1795, quoted in John

Bartlett, *Famous Quotations*, 14th ed. Emily Morison Beck (ed.) (Boston: Little, Brown, 1968), p. 454.

6. A. J. P. Taylor, *Rumors of War* (London: Hamish Hamilton, 1952), p. 44, quoted in Waltz, *Man, the State and War*, p. 114. It should be mentioned that liberals suggest several other solutions. The Manchester liberals of the eighteenth and nineteenth centuries suggested that a policy of free trade would bind nations together economically in such a way as to make war unthinkable. War would make all states subject to international economic chaos since it would imperil the international trading system in which all nations were mutually dependent on each other for important goods and services. More modern liberals argue that a world government is the only long-term solution. Just as twentieth-century liberals argue that the central government should involve itself to a much greater degree in resolving economic conflicts within the state (abandoning laissez faire economics), they also argue that a world government is necessary to resolve political and economic conflicts between states.

7. Quincy Wright, *A Study of War*, Vol. II (Chicago: University of Chicago Press, 1942), pp. 833–42.

8. J. David Singer and Melvin Small, "The War Proneness of Democratic Regimes," *Jerusalem Journal of International Relations* 1 (1976), pp. 49–69.

9. Bruce Russett and R. J. Monsen, "Bureaucracy and Polyarchy as Predictors of Performance: A Cross-National Examination," *Comparative Political Studies* 8 (April 1975), pp. 5–31.

10. Michael Haas, "Societal Approaches to the Study of War," in Richard A. Falk and Samuel S. Kim (eds.), *The War System: An Interdisciplinary Approach* (Boulder, CO: Westview Press, 1980), pp. 354–55.

11. Dina Zinnes and Jonathan Wilkenfeld, "An Analysis of Foreign Conflict Behavior of Nations," in Wolfram F. Hanrieder (ed.), *Comparative Foreign Policy: Theoretical Essays* (New York: David McKay, 1971), pp. 167–213; Steven A. Salmore and Charles F. Hermann, "The Effects of Size, Development and Accountability on Foreign Policy," *Peace Research Society Papers* 14 (1970), pp. 15–30.

12. R. J. Rummel, "Libertarianism and International Violence," *Journal of Conflict Resolution* 27 (1) (March 1983), pp. 27–71. See also his "Libertarian Propositions on Violence Within and Between Nations: A Test Against Published Research Results," *Journal of Conflict Resolution* 29 (1) (September 1985), pp. 419–55.

13. Steve Chan, "Mirror, Mirror on the Wall . . . Are the Freer Countries More Pacific?" *Journal of Conflict Resolution* 28 (4) (December 1984), pp. 617–48.

14. Erich Weede, "Democracy and War Involvement," *Journal of Conflict Resolution* 28 (4) (December 1984), pp. 651–52.

15. T. Clifton Morgan and Sally H. Campbell, "Domestic Structures, Decisional Constraints, and War: So Why Kant Democracies Fight?" Paper delivered at International Studies Association conference, April 1990, Washington, DC. Morgan and Campbell also find that decisional constraints reduce the probability of war for major powers, but increase the probability of war for minor powers.

16. Found originally in R. J. Rummel, *Understanding Conflict and War, Vol. 4: War, Power and Peace* (Beverly Hills, CA: Sage, 1979), pp. 277–79.

17. Rummel, "Libertarianism and International Violence," p. 40.

18. Ibid., p. 42; and Singer and Small, "The War Proneness of Democratic Regimes," p. 67. On a dyadic basis, Singer and Small's data for the 1816–1965 period show that of the 325 war dyads, only 11—all marginal exceptions—

were pairs of democratic states. On this point see also Rummel, ibid., pp. 47 and 48.

19. Rummel, "Libertarianism and International Violence," p. 48.
20. Jack Levy, "Domestic Politics and War," in R. Rotberg and T. Rabb, *The Origin and Prevention of Major Wars* (Cambridge: Cambridge University Press, 1988), p. 88. A study by Dean V. Babst provides perhaps the original source of support for the joint freedom proposition: D. V. Babst, "A Force for Peace," *Industrial Research* (April 1972). See also Zeev Maoz and Nasrin Abdolali, "Regime Type and International Conflict, 1816–1976," *Journal of Conflict Resolution* 33 (1) (March 1989), pp. 3–35, which argues that while militarized disputes are less frequent among democracies than would be expected by chance, autocracies are also less likely to initiate disputes against other autocracies. Two recent studies show that the relationship between democracy and peace at the dyadic level is not spurious: Zeev Maoz and Bruce Russett, "Alliance, Contiguity, Wealth, and Political Stability: Is the Lack of Conflict Among Democracies a Statistical Artifact?" Paper presented at American Political Science Association Annual Meeting, San Francisco, 1990; and Stuart Bremer, "Dangerous Dyads: Conditions Affecting the Likelihood of Interstate War, 1816–1965," revised version of paper presented at Peace Science Society Meeting, Rutgers University, 1991.
21. John A. Hobson, *Imperialism: A Study* (Ann Arbor: University of Michigan Press, 1965), pp. 71–82.
22. Hobson, pp. 71–93.
23. Hobson, pp. 46–63.
24. V. I. Lenin, *Imperialism: the Highest Stage of Capitalism* (New York: International Publishers, 1939).
25. See Waltz, *Man, the State and War*, pp. 154–58.
26. Michael Haas, "Societal Approaches to the Study of War," p. 349 in Falk and Kim (eds.).
27. Kenneth N. Waltz, *Theory of International Politics* (Reading, MA: Addison-Wesley, 1979), p. 20. The discussion here draws on pp. 18–30.
28. D. K. Fieldhouse, "Imperialism: An Historiographical Revision," in Kenneth Boulding and Tapan Mukerjee (eds.), *Economic Imperialism* (Ann Arbor: University of Michigan Press, 1972), p. 110.
29. Herbert Feis, *Europe, the World's Banker, 1870–1914* (New York: August M. Kelley, 1930), p. 23. Cited in Waltz, *Theory of International Politics*, p. 24.
30. Robert Gilpin, *US Power and the Multinational Corporation* (New York: Basic Books, 1975), p. 74.
31. Waltz, *Theory of International Politics*, p. 24.
32. Ibid., p. 25.
33. William Appleman Williams, *Tragedy of American Diplomacy*, rev. ed. (New York: Dell, 1962). See especially pp. 18–50.
34. Waltz, *Theory of International Politics*, p. 25.
35. See Reuven Brenner, *Betting on Ideas: Wars, Invention, Inflation* (Chicago: University of Chicago Press, 1985), especially Chapter 1, cited in Bruce Russett, "Economic Decline, Electoral Pressure and the Initiation of Interstate Conflict," p. 124 in Charles Gochman and A. N. Sabrosky (eds.), *Prisoners of War? Nation-States in the Modern Era* (Lexington, MA: Lexington Books, 1990).
36. C. W. Ostrom and B. L. Job, "The President and the Political Use of Force," *American Political Science Review* 80 (1986), pp. 554–66.
37. Russett, "Economic Decline, Electoral Pressures, and the Initiation of Interstate Conflict," especially pp. 124–34.

38. Geoffrey Blainey, *The Causes of War* (New York: Free Press, 1973), pp. 89–90. See also Bruce Russett, "Prosperity and Peace," *International Studies Quarterly* 27 (1983), pp. 381–87.
39. Alec Laurence Macfie, "The Outbreak of War and the Trade Cycle," *Economic History* 3 (February 1938), pp. 89–97.
40. Joshua Goldstein, *Long Cycles: Prosperity and War in the Modern Age* (New Haven, CT: Yale University Press, 1988), pp. 239–48. Goldstein's work will be discussed more fully in Chapter 6, since he sees economic cycles not as national cycles, but as part of the structure of the international system.
41. Ibid., pp. 260–62. He adds a lateral pressure argument as well—that economic growth stimulates the need for greater resources, and this leads to lateral pressure, intersections, and war.
42. On this point see Russett, "Prosperity and Peace," p. 386.
43. Blainey, p. 93.
44. For Macfie it was not only the present mood of optimism that was important, but also a nervousness that the prosperity might not last. Blainey does not mention this and prefers to emphasize only the optimistic part.
45. Blainey, p. 94.
46. Dexter Perkins, *The American Approach to Foreign Policy*, rev. ed. (New York: Atheneum, 1968), pp. 136–55.
47. William R. Thompson, "Phases of the Business Cycle and the Outbreak of War," *International Studies Quarterly* 26 (June 1982), pp. 301–11. While Russett claims that American involvement in conflict since 1898 has been associated with weak economic conditions, his use of two- and three-year lags throws this conclusion into doubt. He also looks primarily at militarized disputes rather than war involvement. B. Russett, "Economic Decline, Electoral Pressures, and the Initiation of Interstate Conflict."
48. There are many different indicators of the "power" of states; among these would be geographic size, population, GNP or GNP per capita, iron and steel production, energy production or consumption, defense budget, and size of armed forces.
49. These same countries are in Diehl and Goertz's list of the ten countries most involved in territorial changes in the last century and a half (minus Austria-Hungary) and in Gochman and Maoz's list of the ten states most involved in militarized disputes (minus Spain). Paul Diehl and Gary Goertz, "Territorial Changes and Militarized Conflict," *Journal of Conflict Resolution*, 32 (1) (March 1988), pp. 103–22; Charles Gochman and Zeev Maoz, "Militarized Interstate Disputes, 1816–1976: Procedures, Patterns and Insights," *Journal of Conflict Resolution* 28 (1984), pp. 585–616. Of the sixteen wars (both interstate and extrasystemic) in which the most war-prone Great Powers were not involved, ten were in Latin America. See Singer and Small, *Wages of War*, Table 11.2, pp. 275–80 and Tables 4.2 and 4.4, pp. 60–69 and 72–75; see also the summary on pp. 286–87.
50. Melvin Small and J. David Singer, "Patterns in International Warfare, 1816–1965," *Annals of the American Academy of Political and Social Sciences* 391 (September 1970), pp. 151–52, quoted in Lloyd Jensen, *Explaining Foreign Policy* (Englewood Cliffs, NJ: Prentice-Hall, 1982), pp. 222–23.
51. Stuart Bremer, "National Capabilities and War Proneness," in J. David Singer (ed.), *The Correlates of War II: Testing Some Realpolitik Models* (New York: Free Press, 1980), pp. 57–82. Bremer also finds that while the top-ranked states in the system had the highest relative frequency of war involvement, the number 2 ranked state had the highest frequency of war initiation. Indeed, of the states

in ranks 1–5, the states ranked as number 1 had the lowest rate of initiation. This gives indirect support for those who emphasize the centrality of conflict between the systemic leader and its challenger(s). These theories will be addressed in Chapters 8 and 9.

52. Haas, "Societal Approaches to the Study of War," in Richard Falk and Samuel Kim (eds.), *The War System* (Boulder, CO: Westview, 1980), pp. 355–56 and p. 365. Other analysts also find a positive association between foreign conflict involvement and national power indicators. See Patrick McGowan and Howard Shapiro, *The Comparative Study of Foreign Policy* (Beverly Hills, CA: Sage, 1973).

53. See, for instance, Maurice A. East and Phillip Gregg, "Factors Influencing Cooperation and Conflict in the International System," *International Studies Quarterly* 11 (September 1967), p. 266; Lewis Richardson, *Statistics of Deadly Quarrels* (New York: Quadrangle/New York Times, 1960), p. xi; R. J. Rummel, "Some Attributes and Behavioral Patterns of Nations," *Journal of Peace Research* IV (2) (1967), p. 197; and R. J. Rummel, "The Relationship Between National Attributes and Foreign Conflict Behavior," in J. David Singer (ed.) *Quantitative International Politics*, (New York: Free Press, 1968), p. 204. See also R. Rosecrance, A. Alexandroff, B. Healy, and A. Stein, "Power, Balance of Power, and Status in Nineteenth Century International Relations," *Sage Professional Papers in International Studies*, Vol. 3 (Beverly Hills, CA: Sage, 1974). The authors find little association between capability indicators and conflict of the five great powers in Europe between 1870 and 1881.

54. See R. J. Rummel, "Testing Some Possible Predictors of Conflict Behavior Within and Between Nations," *Peace Research Society (International) Papers* 1 (1964), pp. 79–111; and R. J. Rummel, "The Relationship Between National Attributes and Foreign Conflict Behavior," in J. David Singer (ed.), *Quantitative International Politics: Insights and Evidence*, (New York: Free Press, 1968), pp. 187–214.

55. See especially Salmore and Hermann, "The Effects of Size, Development and Accountability on Foreign Policy," pp. 16–30; Maurice A. East, "Size and Foreign Conflict Behavior," *World Politics* 25 (July 1973), pp. 556–76; and Michael Sullivan's excellent discussion of the literature in *International Relations: Theories and Evidence*, pp. 109–14.

56. See James E. Dougherty and Robert L. Pfaltzgraff, Jr., *Contending Theories of International Relations*, 2nd ed. (New York: Harper & Row, 1981), pp. 66–68.

57. William L. Shirer, *The Rise and Fall of the Third Reich* (New York: Fawcett Crest, 1960), p. 77.

58. Dougherty and Pfaltzgraff, p. 67.

59. Adolf Hitler, *Mein Kampf*, American ed. (Boston, 1943), quoted in Shirer, *Rise and Fall*, p. 123.

60. Stuart Bremer, J. David Singer, and Urs Luterbacher, "The Population Density and War Proneness of European Nations, 1816–1964," *Comparative Political Studies* 6 (1973), pp. 329–48. See also J. David Singer, "The Correlates of War Project: An Interim Report and Rationale," *World Politics* 24 (January 1972), p. 267. Singer's findings refer to members of the European system.

61. Quincy Wright, *A Study of War*, Vol. II (Chicago: University of Chicago Press, 1942), p. 1132.

62. Nazli Choucri and Robert North, *Nations in Conflict: National Growth and International Violence* (San Francisco: W. H. Freeman, 1975), pp. 14–24.

63. Nazli Choucri and Robert North, "Lateral Pressure in International Relations: Concept and Theory," in Manus Midlarsky (ed.), *Handbook of War Studies*

(Boston: Unwin Hyman, 1989), p. 296. They conclude that the more immediate cause of war is "human and subjective."

64. Choucri and North, *Nations in Conflict*, pp. 234–54. See the discussion in the next chapter.

65. Richard Ashley, *The Political Economy of War and Peace* (New York: Nichols, 1980).

66. Choucri and North, "Lateral Pressure: Concept and Theory," p. 310.

67. Ibid., p. 311.

68. See Jensen's excellent discussion of the role of borders, from which this discussion draws. Lloyd Jensen, *Explaining Foreign Policy*, pp. 208–10.

69. On this point see Evan Luard, *War in International Society* (New Haven, CT: Yale University Press, 1986), Chapter 3. Luard's contention that territorial disputes are waning is supported by K. J. Holsti, *Peace and War: Armed Conflicts and International Order 1648–1989* (Cambridge: Cambridge University Press, 1991), pp. 307–11.

70. Erich Weede, "Nation-Environment Relations as Determinants of Hostilities Among Nations," *Peace Science Society (International) Papers* 20 (1973), pp. 67–90.

71. Robert Mandel, "Roots of Modern Interstate Border Disputes," *Journal of Conflict Resolution* 24 (1980), pp. 427–54.

72. Diehl and Goertz, "Territorial Changes and Militarized Conflict."

73. R. J. Rummel, *The Dimensions of Nations* (Beverly Hills, CA: Sage, 1972). The correlation between the number of borders and the number of wars is $r = +0.20$ (p. 459) and the number of borders loads on the foreign conflict factor with a 0.21 (p. 371).

74. Richardson, *Statistics of Deadly Quarrels*, p. 176. See also Manus Midlarsky, *On War* (New York: Free Press, 1975); also Harvey Starr and Benjamin Most, "A Return Journey: Richardson, 'Frontiers' and Wars in the 1946–1965 Era," *Journal of Conflict Resolution* 22 (September 1978). Starr and Most find the general relationship to be true, but demonstrate that it varies according to the time period, data set, states investigated, types of borders and statistics used. See also David Garnham, "Dyadic International War, 1816–1965: The Role of Power Parity and Geographic Proximity," *Western Political Quarterly* 29 (1976). Garnham uses distance between capitols rather than number of borders.

75. James Paul Wesley, "Frequency of Wars and Geographical Opportunity," *Journal of Conflict Resolution* 6 (December 1962), pp. 387–89.

76. See Harvey Starr and Benjamin Most, "The Substance and Study of Borders in International Relations Research," *International Studies Quarterly* 20 (December 1976), pp. 581–620. See also Most and Starr, "Diffusion, Reinforcement, Geopolitics and the Spread of War," *American Political Science Review* 74 (1980), pp. 932–46; and Stuart Bremer, "The Contagiousness of Coercion: The Spread of Serious International Disputes, 1900–1976," *International Interaction* 9 (1982), pp. 29–55; and Starr and Most, "Contagion and Border Effects on Contemporary African Conflict," *Comparative Political Studies* 16 (1983), pp. 92–117. Siverson and Starr affirm that both alliance membership and contiguity increase the probability that a state will become involved in an ongoing war, though the former is the most potent predictor of the two. Randolph M. Siverson and Harvey Starr, "Opportunity, Willingness and the Diffusion of War, 1816–1965," *American Political Science Review* (March 1990).

77. Paul F. Diehl, "Contiguity and Military Escalation in Major Power Rivalries, 1816–1980," *Journal of Politics* 47 (4) (1985), pp. 1203–11.
78. This is consistent with the later finding by Diehl and Goertz (op. cit.) that violent territorial transfers are more likely when the territory in question is contiguous to both disputants than when it is contiguous to one or neither disputant.
79. Diehl, "Contiguity and Military Escalation in Major Power Rivalries, 1816–1980," p. 1207.
80. Bruce Russett, *International Regions and the International System* (Chicago: Rand McNally, 1967), p. 200. Emphasis in the original.
81. Richardson, *Statistics of Deadly Quarrels*, p. 288.
82. Diehl, "Contiguity and Military Escalation in Major Power Rivalries, 1816–1980," p. 1207. See also Kenneth Boulding's discussion of the concept of the "loss of strength gradient" in his classic, *Conflict and Defense* (New York: Harper & Row, 1962).
83. For the relationship between proximity and cooperative interaction, see Roger W. Cobb and Charles Elder, *International Community* (New York: Holt, Rinehart & Winston, 1970).
84. Starr and Most, "A Return Journey," pp. 444–49.
85. Starr and Most, "A Return Journey," p. 445.
86. Manus Midlarsky, "Power, Uncertainty and the Onset of International Violence," *Journal of Conflict Resolution* 18 (1974), pp. 395–431. Midlarsky finds a strong relationship between the number of borders and the frequency of war for the major powers.
87. Harvey Starr, "'Opportunity' and 'Willingness' as Ordering Concepts in the Study of Wars," *International Interactions* 4 (1978), pp. 363–87. There is some debate about the relative war proneness of home borders and colonial borders. While Diehl and Goertz's study of territorial changes between 1816 and 1980 finds that territorial changes involving home territories were more likely to be violent than changes in colonial territory, Starr and Most's investigation of the 1946–1965 period discovers a much stronger correlation between colonial borders and war than between noncolonial borders and war. In part, the difference can be attributed to the nature of the post–World War II system, in which Great Powers have rarely engaged in direct conflict with each other across mutual borders. Instead, they have engaged in warfare primarily in colonial areas of the world through proxy wars. See Diehl and Goertz, "Territorial Changes and Militarized Conflict," and Starr and Most, "A Return Journey."
88. K. J. Holsti, *Peace and War*, pp. 307–11.
89. Starr and Most, "A Return Journey," p. 445.
90. Ostrom and Job, "The President and the Political Use of Force," and Bruce Russett, "Economic Decline, Electoral Pressures, and the Initiation of Interstate Conflict."
91. Richard Rosecrance, *Action and Reaction in World Politics* (Boston: Little, Brown, 1963). See especially p. 306.
92. Richard Ned Lebow, *Between Peace and War: The Nature of International Crises* (Baltimore: Johns Hopkins University Press, 1981), pp. 57–70.
93. Jack Levy, "The Diversionary Theory of War: A Critique," in Manus Midlarsky (ed.), *Handbook of War Studies* (Boston: Unwin Hyman, 1989), pp. 259–88.
94. In this case the Argentine government engaged in a diversionary action that they probably did not expect would lead to full-scale war with Britain. See M.

Hastings and S. Jenkins, *The Battle for the Falklands* (New York: Norton, 1983).

95. Blainey, p. 71.
96. Blainey, pp. 72–81.
97. Blainey, p. 82. Michael Haas seems to imply just the opposite. He cites the example that when internal disputes broke out in Switzerland in 1802 Napoleon dispatched 20,000 men to obtain an armistice that brought Switzerland under French domination. On the other hand, he mentions that large nations with vexing problems were seen by others as too difficult to control, thus deterring attempts at conquest. Michael Haas, "Societal Approaches to the Study of War," in Richard Falk and Samuel Kim (eds.), *The War System* (Boulder, CO: Westview, 1980), p. 352.
98. Blainey, p. 81.
99. See, for instance, Jack Levy, "The Diversionary Theory of War," pp. 272–74.
100. Zeev Maoz, "Joining the Club of Nations: Political Development and International Conflict, 1816–1976," *International Studies Quarterly* 32 (2) (June 1989), pp. 199–231.
101. The presence of revolutionary change within states has an international system-level effect as well. Maoz found that the level of stability in the international system is sensitive to the way in which new states join the system and to the way in which states transform themselves politically. The more revolutionary change in the system, the greater the number of militarized disputes in the system. K. J. Holsti's study of war and issues is indirectly supportive of Maoz's results. Holsti finds that the creation of nation-states has been a major source of war since the late eighteenth century and has been the most prevalent war-generating issue in the post-1945 era—a period in which over 50% of the wars were related to state creation. (See pp. 311–12 of Holsti's *Peace and War*.) Not all the wars involved with this issue, however, could be categorized as interstate wars. Many would be colonial wars or wars of national liberation.
102. Michael Haas, "Social Change and National Aggressiveness, 1900–1960," in J. David Singer (ed.), *Quantitative International Politics* (New York: Free Press, 1968), pp. 215–45.
103. R. J. Rummel, "Dimensions of Conflict Behavior Within and Between Nations," *General Systems: Yearbook of the Society for General Systems Research* 8 (1963), pp. 1–50. Also, Rummel, "The Reltionship Between National Attributes and Foreign Conflict Behavior," in J. David Singer (ed.) *Quantitative International Politics* (New York: Free Press, 1968), p. 202 and p. 208.
104. R. J. Rummel, "Testing Some Possible Predictors of Conflict Behavior Within and Between Nations," pp. 79–111.
105. The conclusion that intense levels of domestic conflict do not produce high levels of international conflict is also supported by the work of Leo Hazelwood, "Dimension Mechanism and Encapsulated Processes: The Domestic Conflict—Foreign Conflict Hypothesis Reconsidered," *Sage Foreign Policy Yearbook*, Vol. 3 (Beverly Hills, CA: Sage, 1975), pp. 213–43, and by Dina A. Zinnes and Jonathan Wilkenfeld, "An Analysis of Foreign Conflict Behavior of Nations," in Wolfram Hanreider (ed.), *Comparative Foreign Policy* (New York: David McKay, 1971), pp. 167–213.
106. Raymond Tanter, "Dimensions of Conflict Behavior Within and Between Nations, 1958–1960," *Journal of Conflict Resolution* 10 (March 1966), pp. 41–64; Phillip Gregg and Arthur Banks, "Dimensions of Political Systems: Factor Analysis of 'A Cross-Polity Survey'," *American Political Science Review*

59 (September 1965), pp. 602–14; and Zinnes and Wilkenfeld, "An Analysis of Foreign Conflict Behavior of Nations," pp. 167–213.

107. Jonathan Wilkenfeld, "Domestic and Foreign Conflict Behavior of Nations," *Journal of Peace Research* 5 (1) (1968), pp. 59–69.

108. See Levy, "The Diversionary Theory of War," pp. 272–274.

109. And, of course, all of this assumes that internal conflict precedes external conflict. The relationship may proceed from external conflict to internal conflict as well. In fact, there may be a reciprocal, interactive effect. See Levy, Ibid., pp. 259–88.

110. Arnold Toynbee, *A Study of History*, Vol. IX (London: Oxford University Press, 1954), pp. 322–23.

111. Blainey, p. 7.

112. Levy and Morgan suggest, however, that regime type may make a difference. It is possible that war may be positively addictive for some regime types and negatively addictive for others. Jack S. Levy and T. Clifton Morgan, "The War Weariness Hypothesis: An Empirical Test," *American Journal of Political Science* 30 (1986), p. 31.

113. Lewis Richardson, *Arms and Insecurity* (Chicago: Quadrangle, 1960), p. 232.

114. Richardson makes a feeble attempt to salvage what he can of the theory by suggesting that at least it provides a good explanation for the rapid demise of the French army and that government's subsequent surrender to the Nazis. He says, "The French had entered an inter-war breathing space in a mood of disillusionment and discouragement that had been registered in action eventually in France's collapse and capitulation in June 1940. . . ." Lewis F. Richardson, *Statistics of Deadly Quarrels*, p. 495.

115. Levy and Morgan, "The War Weariness Hypothesis: An Empirical Test," p. 28.

116. P. Karsten, *Soldiers and Society: The Effects of Military Service and War in American Life* (Westport, CT: Greenwood, 1978), cited in Francis A. Beer, *Peace and War* (San Francisco: W. H. Freeman, 1981), p. 293.

117. Robert J. Lifton, *Home from the War: Vietnam Veterans—Neither Victims nor Executioners* (New York: Simon & Schuster, 1973), and M. Janowitz, *The Professional Soldier* (Glencoe, IL: Free Press, 1960), cited in Beer, p. 298.

118. See, for instance, Richard J. Barnet, *The Roots of War: The Men and Institutions Behind U.S. Foreign Policy* (New York: Penguin, 1973)

119. See Blainey, p. 17 and pp. 108–124; and Levy and Morgan, pp. 28–29.

120. Singer and Small, *Wages of War*, pp. 283–84.

121. J. David Singer and Thomas Cusack, "Periodicity, Inexorability and Steermanship in International War," in Richard Merritt and Bruce Russett (eds.) *From National Development to Global Community*, (London: Allen and Unwin, 1981), pp. 413–15.

122. Ibid., pp. 415–17. This relationship is statistically significant for international wars, but not for interstate wars. Singer and Cusak find no relationship between the costliness of war and the length of the interwar interval.

123. David Garnham, "War-Proneness, War-Weariness, and Regime Type: 1816–1980," *Journal of Peace Research* 23 (3) (1986), pp. 279–89, and his "Explaining Major Power Bellicosity and Pacifism," paper presented at International Studies Association conference (April 1982).

124. Levy and Morgan, "War-Weariness and Other Hypotheses," pp. 35–39. Levy and Morgan conclude that while their findings on the distribution of war unambiguously contradict the war-weariness hypothesis, they are not strong enough to support the contrary hypothesis of positive contagion.

125. Levy and Morgan, "War-Weariness and Other Hypotheses," pp. 46–47.

126. Harold and Margaret Sprout, *The Ecological Perspective on Human Affairs with Special Reference to International Politics* (Princeton, NJ: Princeton University Press, 1965), p. 11.

Chapter 6

1. J. David Singer, "The Level of Analysis Problem in International Relations," in James Rosenau (ed.), *International Politics and Foreign Policy*, rev. ed. (New York: Free Press, 1969), p.23.
2. Anatol Rapoport, *Fights, Games and Debates* (Ann Arbor: University of Michigan Press, 1960), discussed in Russell Leng and Robert Goodsell, "Behavioral Indicators of War Proneness in Bilateral Conflicts," in Patrick J. McGowan (ed.), *Sage International Yearbook of Foreign Policy Studies*, Vol. II (Beverly Hills; CA: Sage, 1974), pp. 193–94.
3. Leng and Goodsell, p. 194.
4. Leng and Goodsell, pp. 207–17.
5. Joshua S. Goldstein and John R. Freeman, *Three-Way Street: Strategic Reciprocity and World Politics* (Chicago: University of Chicago Press, 1990).
6. Alternatively, we might choose to create a scale in which the cooperative acts are assigned positive values (say, from 1 to 4) and the noncooperative acts are given negative values (say, from -1 to -4). For a comparison of some frequently used event-interaction scales, see Joshua Goldstein, "Reciprocity in Superpower Relations: An Empirical Analysis," *International Studies Quarterly* 35 (June 1991), p. 200.
7. Russell Leng, "Reagan and the Russians: Crisis Bargaining Beliefs and the Historical Record," *American Political Science Review* 78 (June 1984), pp. 338–55.
8. William A. Gamson and Andre Modigliani, *Untangling the Cold War: A Strategy for Testing Rival Theories* (Boston: Little, Brown, 1971), reported in Michael P. Sullivan, *International Relations: Theories and Evidence* (Englewood Cliffs, NJ: Prentice-Hall, 1976), pp. 286–87.
9. Jan F. Triska and David D. Finley, "Soviet-American Relations: A Multiple Symmetry Model," in David V. Edwards (ed.), *International Political Analysis: Readings* (New York: Holt, Rinehart & Winston, 1969).
10. Ole Holsti, *Crisis, Escalation and War* (Montreal: McGill-Queens University Press, 1972).
11. Richard K. Ashley, *The Political Economy of War and Peace* (New York: Nichols, 1980; Michael Don Ward, "Cooperation and Conflict in Foreign Policy Behavior," *International Studies Quarterly* 26 (March 1982), pp. 87–126; William J. Dixon, "Measuring Interstate Affect," *American Journal of Political Science* 27 (November 1983), pp. 828–51.
12. See Frank Mogdis, "The Verbal Dimension in Sino-Soviet Relations: A Time Series Analysis," paper presented at American Political Science Association convention, September 1970, cited in Sullivan, *International Relations*, pp. 289–90.
13. Goldstein and Freeman, *Three-Way Street*, especially Chapter 3. See also Joshua Goldstein, "Reciprocity in Superpower Relations: An Empirical Analysis," which deals solely with U.S.-Soviet relations.
14. Ole Holsti, Robert North, and Richard Brody, "Perception and Action in the 1914 Crisis," in J. David Singer (ed.), *Quantitative International Politics* (New

York: Free Press, 1968); and North, Brody, and Holsti, "Some Empirical Data on the Conflict Spiral," *Peace Research Society (International) Papers* 1 (1964), pp. 1–14.

15. Leng and Goodsell, op. cit.
16. Jeffrey S. Milstein, "American and Soviet Influence, Balance of Power, and Arab-Israeli Violence," in Bruce Russett (ed.), *Peace, War and Numbers* (Beverley Hills, CA: Sage, 1972), pp. 139–62.
17. R. Burrowes and J. Garriga-Pico, "The Road to the Six Day War: Relational Analysis of Conflict and Cooperation," *Peace Science Society (International) Papers* 22 (1974), pp. 47–74.
18. J. M. McCormick, "Evaluating Models of Crisis Behavior: Some Evidence from the Middle East," *International Studies Quarterly* 19 (January 1975), pp. 17–45.
19. Jonathan Wilkenfeld, Virginia Lee Lussier, and Dale Tahtinen, "Conflict Interactions in the Middle East, 1949–1967," *Journal of Conflict Resolution* 16 (June 1972), pp. 135–54.
20. There are fifteen equations because the authors examined not only military actions, but two other types of foreign conflict behavior: "active hostility" and "verbal hostility."
21. Jonathan Wilkenfeld, "A Time Series Perspective on Conflict Behavior in the Middle East," in Patrick McGowan (ed.), *Sage International Yearbook of Foreign Policy Studies* III (1975), pp. 177–212.
22. Michael Don Ward, "Cooperation and Conflict in Foreign Policy Behavior: Reaction and Memory," *International Studies Quarterly* 26 (March 1982), pp. 87–126. Israel's response to U.A.R. behavior was also escalatory. She returned both conflict and cooperation received at a ratio of 1.7 to 1.0.
23. Russell J. Leng and Hugh B. Wheeler, "Influence Strategies, Success and War," *Journal of Conflict Resolution* 23 (December 1979), pp. 655–84.
24. Russell J. Leng, "Influence Strategies and Interstate Conflict," in J. David Singer (ed.), *Correlates of War II: Testing Some Realpolitik Models* (New York: Free Press, 1980), pp. 124–57. See especially p. 154.
25. Russell J. Leng and Charles S. Gochman, "Dangerous Disputes: A Study of Conflict Behavior and War," *American Journal of Political Science* 26 (November 1982), pp. 664–87.
26. Russell J. Leng, "When Will They Ever Learn? Coercive Bargaining in Recurrent Crises," *Journal of Conflict Resolution* 27 (September 1983), pp. 379–419. See also, Russell J. Leng, "Reagan and the Russians: Crisis Bargaining Beliefs and the Historical Record," *American Political Science Review* 78 (September 1984), pp. 338–55; and Russell J. Leng, "Crisis Learning Games," *American Political Science Review* 82 (March 1988), pp. 179–94.
27. Nazli Choucri and Robert North, *Nations in Conflict: National Growth and International Violence* (San Fransisco: Freeman, 1975). For their more recent work on lateral pressure, see Choucri and North, "Lateral Pressure in International Relations: Concept and Theory," in Manus Midlarsky (ed.), *Handbook of War Studies* (Boston: Unwin, Hyman, 1989), pp. 289–326; and Robert C. North, *War, Peace, Survival: Global Politics and Conceptual Synthesis* (Boulder, CO: Westview, 1990).
28. Choucri and North, *Nations in Conflict*, pp. 218–54; see especially pp. 248–49 and 254.
29. Raymond Tanter, "International System and Foreign Policy Approaches: Implications for Conflict Modelling and Management," *World Politics* 24 (Spring 1972), pp. 7–39; and G. T. Duncan and R. M. Siverson, "Markov Models for

Conflict Analysis: Results from Sino-Indian Relations," *International Studies Quarterly* 19 (September 1975), pp. 344–74.

30. Gordon Hilton, "A Closed and Open Model Analysis of Expressions of Hostility in Crisis," *Journal of Peace Research* 8 (3–4) (1971), pp. 249–62.

31. See J. Wilkenfeld, G. W. Hopple, P. J. Rossa, and S. J. Andriole, *Foreign Policy Behavior* (Beverly Hills, CA: Sage, 1980); and similar conclusions by William Dixon, "Reciprocity in United States–Soviet Relations: Multiple Symmetry or Issue Linkage?" *American Journal of Political Science* 30 (1986), pp. 421–45.

32. Samuel P. Huntington, "Arms Races: Prerequisities and Results," in C. J. Friedrich and S. E. Harris (eds.), *Public Policy*, Vol. 8 (Cambridge, MA: Graduate School of Public Administration, Harvard University, 1958), p. 41.

33. Lewis F. Richardson, *Arms and Insecurity* (Pittsburgh: Boxwood Press, 1960). For those interested, the precise equation is as follows: $dx/dt = ky - ax + g$. In which dx/dt = the rate at which one increases arms levels; x = one's own strength; y = the opponent's strength; k = one's readiness to accumulate arms; a = fatigue and cost; and g = the general level of grievance.

34. W. Ladd Hollist, "An Analysis of Arms Processes in the United States and Soviet Union," *International Studies Quarterly* 21 (September 1977), pp. 503–28; Benjamin S. Lambeth, "The Sources of Soviet Military Doctrine," in B. Horton et al. (eds.), *Comparative Defense Policy* (Baltimore: Johns Hopkins University Press, 1974); A. F. K. Organski and Jacek Kugler, *The War Ledger* (Chicago: University of Chicago Press, 1980); Stephen J. Majesky and David L. Jones, "Arms Race Modelling: Causality Analysis and Model Specification," *Journal of Conflict Resolution* 25 (1981), pp. 259–88; Charles Ostrom, Jr., "Evaluating Alternative Foreign Policy Decision Making Models," *Journal of Conflict Resolution* 21 (June 1977), pp. 235–66; and Ostrom and R. F. Marra, "U.S. Defense Spending and the Soviet Estimate," *American Political Science Review* 80(3) (September 1986), pp. 819–42.

35. Mike Horn, "Arms Races and the Likelihood of War," paper presented to International Studies Association convention, Atlanta, 1984.

36. Thomas R. Cusack and Michael Don Ward, "Military Spending in the United States, Soviet Union and the Peoples' Republic of China," *Journal of Conflict Resolution* 25 (September 1981), pp. 429–67. Studies of arms races in the Middle East have produced mixed results. For some periods and for some states there has been a Richardson-type reaction process, but this has not been found to hold true for all states and all time periods. For instance, see Hans Rattinger, "From War to War: Arms Races in the Middle East," *International Studies Quarterly* 20 (December 1976), pp. 501–31.

37. Hans Rattinger, "Armaments, Detente, and Bureaucracy: the Case of the Arms Race in Europe," *Journal of Conflict Resolution* 19 (December 1975), pp. 571–95. See also, W. Ladd Hollist, "Alternative Explanations of Competitive Arms Processes: Tests on Four Pairs of Nation," *American Journal of Political Science* 21 (May 1977), pp. 315–40.

38. Choucri and North, *Nations in Conflict.*

39. Arthur J. Marder, *From the Dreadnought to Scapa Flow* (New York: Oxford University Press, 1961), p. 121 quoted in Choucri and North, p. 206.

40. See Choucri and North, p. 207.

41. Choucri and North, pp. 208–9 and p. 218.

42. Choucri and North, p. 218.

43. Lloyd Jensen, *Explaining Foreign Policy* (Englewod Cliffs, NJ: Prentice-Hall, 1982), pp. 239–40.

44. Goldstein and Freeman, *Three-Way Street* (pp. 26–27). Note that, generally,

stimulus-response studies that use data aggregated on a yearly basis fail to find reciprocity, while those using data aggregated on a subannual basis generally do find reciprocity. They suggest this is because using annual aggregations lumps together reciprocal interactions and exchanges, thus masking them and washing out lagged correlations and making them appear simultaneous.

45. Michael Don Ward, "Differential Paths to Parity: A Study of the Contemporary Arms Race," *American Political Science Review* 78 (1984), pp. 297–317. Joshua Goldstein argues that event and spending data are both prone to biases that cause the significance of reciprocity to be understated in statistical analyses. The aggregation of such data over long periods of time tends to have the same effect. Studies based on annually aggregated military expenditure data rarely find evidence of reciprocol arms racing. J. S. Goldstein, "Reciprocity in Superpower Relations," p. 198.

46. Huntington, "Arms Races: Prerequisites and Results."

47. Huntington, p. 61.

48. Huntington, p. 65. Richardson's model points in a somewhat different direction. In his formulation, if armaments increase indefinitely, with little restraint, war will eventually break out. That is, a "runaway" arms race in which no equilibrium point is reached is the most dangerous.

49. Patrick Morgan, *Theories and Approaches to International Politics*, 3rd ed. (New Brunswick, NJ: Transaction, 1981), p. 268.

50. Huntington, pp. 75–76.

51. Huntington, p. 71–72.

52. Jonathan Adelman and Deborah Palmieri, *The Dynamics of Soviet Foreign Policy* (New York: Harper & Row, 1989), pp. 276–80.

53. *Washington Post*, December 22, 1988, pp. A1 and A27.

54. Michael D. Wallace, "Arms Races and Escalation: Some New Evidence," *Journal of Conflict Resolution* 23 (March 1979), p.7.

55. Wallace, "Arms Races and Escalation," p. 14.

56. On these points, see Erich Weede, "Arms Races and Escalation: Some Persisting Doubts," *Journal of Conflict Resolution* 24 (June 1980), pp. 285–87; and Randolph Siverson and Paul Diehl, "Arms Races, the Conflict Spiral, and the Onset of War," in Midlarsky (ed.), *Handbook of War Studies*, p. 203.

57. M. Altfeld, "Arms Races?—and Escalation?: A Comment on Wallace," *International Studies Quarterly* 27(2) (June 1983), pp. 225–231.

58. Paul F. Diehl, "Arms Races and Escalation: A Closer Look," *Journal of Peace Research* 20(3) (1983), pp. 206–7. This is a problem that Wallace himself addresses and partly resolves in a later study: Michael D. Wallace, "Armaments and Escalation: Two Competing Hypotheses," *International Studies Quarterly* 26 (March 1982), pp. 37–56. Using a stricter definition of arms races and a combination of dyads in which two or more allies entered simultaneously into war with a common enemy, his results are still quite supportive of the connection between war and arms races.

59. Erich Weede, "Arms Races and Escalation: Some Persisting Doubts." And see Wallace's reply, M. W. Wallace, "Some Persisting Findings: A Reply to Professor Weede," *Journal of Conflict Resolution* 24 (June 1980), pp. 289–92.

60. See Diehl, "Arms Races and Escalation: A Closer Look," pp. 207–11. Also, research by Lambelet, unconnected to the Wallace study, finds arms races and wars to be independent of each other. John Lambelet, "Do Arms Races Lead to War?" *Journal of Peace Research* 12(2) (1975).

61. James D. Morrow, "A Twist of Truth: A Reexamination of the Effects of Arms

Races on the Occurrence of War," *Journal of Conflict Resolution* 33 (September 1989), pp. 518–19.

62. Perhaps one reason that not all wars are preceded by arms races is that not all wars are between relative equals. Although arms races tend to escalate disputes between relative equals, they rarely play a role in disputes between nonequals. On this point see John Vasquez, "The Steps to War," *World Politics.* XL(1) (October 1987), p. 136, n. 85.
63. Morrow, "A Twist of Truth," p. 502.
64. Ibid.
65. See the review by Siverson and Diehl, op. cit. p. 214.
66. Morrow, "A Twist of Truth."
67. Another necessary condition seems to be that the dispute in question arises in an area contiguous to one of the rivals. Paul Diehl, "Arms Races to War: An Analysis of Some Underlying Effects," *Sociological Quarterly* 26 (1985), pp. 331–49.
68. Wallace finds no support either for the hypothesis that relative rates of military growth are related to the outbreak of war. Michael Wallace, "Armaments and Escalation," *International Studies Quarterly* 26 (1982), pp. 37–56. See also M. Wallace, "Armaments and Escalation: A Reply to Altfeld," *International Studies Quarterly* 27 (1983), pp. 233–35.
69. L. F. Richardson, *Arms and Insecurity.*
70. Theresa Clair Smith, "Arms Race Instability and War," *Journal of Conflict Resolution* 24 (June 1980), pp. 253–84; and T. C. Smith, "Curvature Change and War Risk in Arming Patterns," *International Interactions* 14 (1988), pp. 201–28. Smith includes only those races which last for four years or more.
71. Research by Diehl and Kingston suggests that large arms increases don't make states or a set of rivals more likely to be involved in disputes. That is, they find no evidence for a causal chain that starts with arms races and proceeds to disputes and then to war. Instead, it is more likely that disputes arise because of other reasons and then arms races develop due to the tensions involved in the preexisting disputes. Paul Diehl and J. Kingston, "Messenger or Message? Military Buildups and the Initiation of Conflict," *Journal of Politics* 49 (1987), pp. 789–99.
72. Robert Jervis, "Perception and Misperception: The Spiral of International Insecurity," in William Olson, David McLellan, and Fred Sondermann (eds.), *Theory and Practice of International Relations,* 6th ed. (Englewood Cliffs, NJ: Prentice-Hall, 1983), p. 201.
73. Jervis, p. 200.
74. Jervis, p. 201.
75. Jean-Jacques Rousseau, *A Lasting Peace Through the Federation of Europe,* translated by C. E. Vaughan (London: Constable, 1917), pp. 78–79, quoted in Jervis, p. 200.
76. Charles E. Osgood, "Graduated Unilateral Initiatives for Peace," in Clagett G. Smith (ed.), *Conflict Resolution: Contributions from the Behavioral Sciences* (Notre Dame, IN: University of Notre Dame, 1971), pp. 515–25. The following section draws on this work. See also Osgood, *An Alternative to War or Surrender* (Urbana: University of Illinois Press, 1962).
77. Osgood, "Graduated Unilateral Initiatives for Peace."
78. This applies as well to TIT-FOR-TAT, a strategy to be discussed later. On this point see Kenneth Oye, "Explaining Cooperation Under Anarchy: Hypotheses and Strateagies," *World Politics* 38 (October 1985), p. 16.
79. GRIT appears to be more effective than TIT-FOR-TAT in inducing early

cooperation. See Svenn Linskold and Michael Collins, "Inducing Cooperation by Groups and Individuals," *Journal of Conflict Resolution* 22 (December 1978), pp. 679–90; S. Lindskold, P. S. Walters, and H. Koutsourais, "Cooperators, Competitors, and Responses to GRIT," *Journal of Conflict Resolution* 27 (1983), pp. 521–32; and M. Pilisuk and P. Skolnick, "Inducing Trust: a Test of the Osgood Proposal," *Journal of Personality and Social Psychology* 8 (1968), pp. 122–33. For an excellent overall review of the experimental literature on GRIT, see Svenn Lindskold, "Trust Development, the GRIT Proposal, and the Effects of Conciliatory Acts on Conflict and Cooperation," *Psychological Bulletin* 85(4) (1978), pp. 772–93. See also Lindskold, "Conciliation with Simultaneous or Sequential Interaction," *Journal of Conflict Resolution* 23 (December 1979), pp. 704–14.

80. Goldstein and Freeman, *Three-Way Street*, Chapter 4.
81. Ibid., Chapter 5, especially pp. 134–36.
82. Ibid., p. 153.
83. Ibid., p. 152.

Chapter 7

1. Thomas Schelling, *The Strategy of Conflict* (New York: Oxford University Press–Galaxy Books, 1963), pp. 9–10.
2. Adapted from Martin Shubik, "Game Theory and the Study of Social Behavior: An Introductory Exposition," in Martin Shubik (ed.), *Game Theory and Related Approaches to Social Behavior* (New York: Wiley, 1964), pp. 15–17; See also the discussion in James Dougherty and Robert Pfaltzgraff, Jr., *Contending Theories of International Relations: A Comprehensive Survey*, 2nd ed. (New York: Harper & Row, 1981), pp. 515–16.
3. Dougherty and Pfaltzgraff, p. 516.
4. See Dougherty and Pfaltzgraff, pp. 514–17.
5. Glenn Snyder and Paul Diesing, *Conflict Among Nations: Bargaining, Decision Making, and System Structure in International Crises* (Princeton, NJ: Princeton University Press, 1977), pp. 118–22.
6. Kenneth Oye, "Explaining Cooperation Under Anarchy: Hypotheses and Strategies," *World Politics* 38 (October 1985), p. 14.
7. On the importance of repeated prisoners' dilemma interactions, see Robert Axelrod, *The Evolution of Cooperation* (New York: Basic Books, 1984), pp. 11–12.
8. Axelrod, p. 77.
9. Axelrod, p. 84.
10. Murnighan and Roth find that as the probability of continued play is increased, for particular games, cooperation is also increased. J. Keith Murnighan and Alvin E. Roth, "Expected Continued Play in Prisoner's Dilemma Games," *Journal of Conflict Resolution* 27 (June 1983), pp. 279–300.
11. Axelrod's matrix awards 1 point for each player for mutual defection and 3 points for each player for mutual cooperation; the defect/cooperate cells yield either 0 points or 5 points. Axelrod, *The Evolution of Cooperation*, p. 8.
12. See Axelrod, *The Evolution of Cooperation*; and Axelrod, "Effective Choice in the Prisoner's Dilemma," *Journal of Conflict Resolution* 24 (March 1980), pp. 3–25 and Axelrod, "More Effective Choice in the Prisoner's Dilemma," *Journal of Conflict Resolution* 24 (September 1980), pp. 379–403.

13. Axelrod, "More Effective Choice in the Prisoner's Dilemma," p. 394.
14. Axelrod, *The Evolution of Cooperation*, p. 54.
15. S. Oskamp, "Effects of Programmed Strategies on Cooperation in Prisoner's Dilemma and Other Mixed Motive Games," *Journal of Conflict Resolution* 15 (1971), pp. 225–59.
16. Russell J. Leng and Hugh B. Wheeler, "Influence Strategies, Success and War," *Journal of Conflict Resolution* 23 (December 1979), pp. 655–84; and Leng, "Reagan and the Russians: Crisis Bargaining Beliefs and the Historical Record," *American Political Science Review* 78 (June 1984), pp. 338–55; also Paul Huth and Bruce Russett, "Deterrence Failure and Crisis Escalation," *International Studies Quarterly* 32 (March 1988), pp. 29–45.
17. See, for instance, Raymond Dacey, and Norman Pendergraft, "The Optimality of TIT-FOR-TAT," *International Interactions* 15(1) (1988), p. 52.
18. Oye, p. 15. Martin Patchen believes TFT should be even more effective in chicken situations than in prisoners' dilemma because the rival suffers maximum damages when his noncooperative move is reciprocated. Martin Patchen, "Strategies for Eliciting Cooperation from an Adversary: Laboratory and Internation Findings," *Journal of Conflict Resolution* 31 (March 1987), p. 171.
19. Patchen, pp. 176–77. Leng also demonstrates the absolutely critical importance of initiating the interaction with a cooperative move. Without such initial strategies, it is almost inevitable that the two sides will become locked into an escalation that could lead to war. Leng attributes this escalation to "realpolitik" assumptions about bargaining strategies. Russell J. Leng, "Crisis Learning Games," *American Political Science Review* 82 (March 1988), pp. 179–94.
20. Theodore To, "More Realism in Prisoner's Dilemma," *Journal of Conflict Resolution* 32 (June 1988), pp. 402–8.
21. C. L. Gruder and R. J. Dulak, "Elicitation of Cooperation by Retaliatory and Nonretaliatory Strategies in a Mixed-Motive Game," *Journal of Conflict Resolution* 17 (1973), pp. 162–74.
22. Axelrod, *The Evolution of Cooperation*, p. 138.
23. Roy Behr, "Nice Guys Finish Last—Sometimes," *Journal of Conflict Resolution* 25 (June 1981), pp. 289–300. TIT-FOR-TAT was also the only strategy to lose to RANDOM. The scoring in Behr's tournament was: win = 2, tie = 1, and loss = 0. TIT-FOR-TAT did equally poorly when point differentials were used as the standard of success instead of won-loss records.
24. Dacey and Pendegrift, pp. 45–52; Oye, pp. 1–24. (The success of TIT-FOR-TAT is also affected by the number of players.)
25. Patchen, p. 176.
26. Steven Van Evera, "Why Cooperation Failed in 1914," *World Politics* 38 (October 1985), pp. 80–117.
27. Van Evera, p. 99.
28. Leng and Wheeler, "Influence Strategies, Success and War."
29. Svenn Lindskold and Michael Collins, "Inducing Cooperation by Groups and Individuals," *Journal of Conflict Resolution* 22 (December 1978), pp. 679–90.
30. Joshua S. Goldstein and John R. Freeman, *Three-Way Street: Strategic Reciprocity in World Politics* (Chicago: University of Chicago Press, 1990), Chapter 5.
31. For instance, Jack Levy's attempt to reconstruct the preference orderings of national leaders in Austria, Germany, France, Britain, Russia, and Serbia in the 1914 crisis helps to explain why it was virtually impossible to construct a cooperative solution in prewar Europe. Jack S. Levy, "Preferences, Constraint, and Choices in July 1914," *International Security* 15 (Winter 1990-1991), pp. 151–86.

32. George and Smoke define deterrence as "the persuasion of one's opponents that the costs and/or risks of a given action he might take outweigh the benefits." Alexander L. George and Richard Smoke, *Deterrence in American Foreign Policy: Theory and Practice* (New York: Columbia University Press, 1974), p. 11.

33. Patrick Morgan, *Deterrence: A Conceptual Analysis* (Beverly Hill, CA: Sage, 1977), p. 30.

34. James L. Payne, *The American Threat: The Fear of War as an Instrument of Foreign Policy* (Chicago: Markham, 1970), and the revised edition, Payne, *The American Threat: National Security and Foreign Policy* (College Station, TX: Lytton, 1981).

35. Payne (1970), p. 172.

36. Payne (1970), p. 139.

37. Charles Lockhart, "Problems in the Management and Resolution of International Conflicts," *World Politics* 29 (April 1977), pp. 378–403.

38. The following section is based on Payne (1970), pp. 1–22.

39. Payne (1970), pp. 43–61.

40. See especially Payne (1970), pp. 62–68.

41. Payne (1970), pp. 63–64.

42. Critics of deterrence theory call this the "theory of opportunity." See Richard Ned Lebow, "Windows of Opportunity: Do States Jump Through Them?" *International Security* 9 (Summer 1984), pp. 147–86; and Janice Gross Stein, "Extended Deterrence in the Middle East: American Strategy Reconsidered," *World Politics* 39 (April 1987), p. 329.

43. Payne (1970), p. 68; for a discussion of the status quo see pp. 68–104.

44. Payne (1970), p. 7 and pp. 113–26.

45. George and Smoke, *Deterrence in American Foreign Policy.*

46. George and Smoke, pp. 527 and 529.

47. George and Smoke, p. 526. Other factors that may play a secondary role in determining the success or failure of deterrence are: (1) the initiator's perception of the adequacy and appropriateness of the defender's military capability, (2) his perception of a defender's motivation, (3) his perception that only force can bring about the desired change, (4) his willingness to accept compensation elsewhere as an alternative to challenging the defender. (George and Smoke, pp. 530–31.)

48. On this point see Morgan, *Deterrence*, pp. 141–42.

49. George and Smoke, pp. 540–41.

50. George and Smoke, pp. 543–44.

51. George and Smoke, p. 508 and p. 532.

52. Morgan, *Deterrence*, p. 143.

53. Bruce Russett, "The Calculus of Deterrence," in James Rosenau (ed.), *International Politics and Foreign Policy*, rev. ed. (New York: Free Press, 1969), pp. 359–69.

54. Raoull Naroll, "Deterrence in History," in Dean G. Pruitt and Richard C. Snyder (eds.), *Theory and Research on the Causes of War* (Englewood Cliffs, NJ: Prentice-Hall, 1969), pp. 152 and 163. Wayne Ferris also finds that in five of nine wars initiated against Great Powers in the nineteenth and twentieth centuries, the nations that were attacked were appreciably stronger than the initiators. Superior strength is an insufficient deterrent. Wayne Ferris, *The Power Capability of Nations* (Lexington, MA: D. C. Heath, 1973).

55. Russett, "The Calculus of Deterrence," pp. 364–68.

56. Paul Huth and Bruce Russett, "What Makes Deterrence Work? Cases from 1900–1980," *World Politics* 36 (July 1984), pp. 496–526.

320 • *What Causes War?*

57. Ibid., pp. 516–18.
58. Paul Huth, "Extended Deterrence and the Outbreak of War," *American Political Science Review* 82 (June 1988), pp. 423–43; and Huth and Russett, "Deterrence Failure and Crisis Escalation." Their analysis of deterrence in this extended period was unable to support the earlier finding that strong economic and political ties between the defender and protégé increase the change of deterrent success. They attribute this to the inclusion of six new cases from the pre-1900 period. In this earlier era arms transfers were a less frequent and probably less relevant aspect of the political-military relationship between two states. On this point see Huth, "Extended Deterrence and the Outbreak of War," p. 436.
59. Alan Alexandroff and Richard Rosecrance, "Deterrence in 1939," *World Politics* 29 (April 1977), pp. 404–24.
60. Huth, "Extended Deterrence and the Outbreak of War," p. 436. While the behavior of the defender in most recent confrontations with the attacker had a significant impact on deterrent success, the past behavior of the defender in deterrent situations in general did not.
61. Huth and Russett, "Deterrence Failure and Crisis Escalation," p. 39.
62. Huth, "Extended Deterrence and the Outbreak of War," p. 438.
63. Robert Jervis, "Rational Deterrence: Theory and Evidence," *World Politics* 41 (January 1989), pp. 198–99.
64. Huth and Russett, "Deterrence Failure and Crisis Escalation," p. 39.
65. Huth, "Extended Deterrence and the Outbreak of War," p. 426.
66. Jervis, "Rational Deterrence: Theory and Evidence," p. 192.
67. John Orme, "Deterrence Failures: A Second Look," *International Security* 11 (Winter 1986–1987), p. 97. The idea that the attacker may be pushed into an attack on the client state is based, in part, on the idea that attackers have both defensive and offensive motivations for their actions and that this should be incorporated into deterrence theory. See Huth, "Extended Deterrence and the Outbreak of War," p. 424.
68. Clinton Fink, "More Calculations About Deterrence," *Journal of Conflict Resolution* 9 (1965), pp. 54–66.
69. A further problem is, according to George and Smoke, that Russett defines deterrence success as a situation that occurs when an attack on a pawn is (1) prevented or (2) repulsed without conflict between the attacking force and the regular combat units of the great power defender. The inclusion of point two leads Russett to include as examples of success some cases others would identify as failures—for example, the unsuccessful French and British attack on Egypt in 1956 and the Soviet blockade of Berlin in 1948. George and Smoke conclude that Russett seems to blur the distinction between successful deterrence and successful defense. George and Smoke, *Deterrence in American Foreign Policy*, pp. 516–17.
70. Richard Ned Lebow and Janice Gross Stein, "Deterrence: the Elusive Dependent Variable," *World Politics* 42 (April 1990), pp. 336–69. Critics of Lebow and Stein retort that by using too stringent criteria for the selection of deterrence cases they miss far too many real cases. See Paul Huth and Bruce Russett, "Testing Deterrence Theories: Rigor Makes a Difference," *World Politics* 42 (July 1990), pp. 466–501.
71. Lebow and Stein, "Deterrence: the Elusive Dependent Variable," p. 348.
72. Alexander George and Richard Smoke, *Deterrence in American Foreign Policy*, pp. 516–17. A third possibility also exists—one of mixed outcomes—cases in which some actions are deterred, but some other, lesser acts are not.
73. Morgan, *Deterrence*, p. 23.
74. Christopher H. Achen and Duncan Snidal, "Rational Deterrence Theory and

Comparative Case Studies," *World Politics* 41 (January 1989), p. 152. Additionally, a state can rationally choose to fight a war it thinks it will probably lose if the gains from winning and/or the costs of alternative policies are great enough. See Jervis, "Rational Deterrence: Theory and Evidence," p. 187.

75. Richard Ned Lebow, *Between Peace and War: The Nature of International Crisis* (Baltimore: Johns Hopkins University Press, 1981), pp. 82–87.

76. It should be mentioned that another scholar has reanalyzed these eight cases and has concluded that these deterrence failures are consistent with deterrence theory rather than refuting it. John Orme finds that in each case there are serious problems with the defender's position; either a weak commitment or a weak military capability "tempted an aggressive, perhaps risk-prone, but not necessarily irrational opponent." Orme, "Deterrence Failures: A Second Look," p. 121–22.

77. J. G. Stein, "Extended Deterrence in the Middle East." None of these deterrence attempts were undertaken to deter an impending military attack per se against an American protege; most were attempts to deter escalations of ongoing wars in the region.

78. Consistent with deterrence theory, Stein finds that in three of the four cases of failure, the deterrence strategy was weakly articulated, but she concludes that faulty articulation was, by itself, not a sufficient explanation of failure.

79. This is the message of Robert Jervis, R. N. Lebow and J. G. Stein's *Psychology and Deterrence* (Baltimore: Johns Hopkins University Press, 1985).

80. Leaders may be motivated by both opportunity and vulnerability under different circumstances or simultaneously; the two motivations are not mutually exclusive. See Achen and Snidal, "Rational Deterrence Theory and Comparative Case Studies," pp. 148–49, and Stein, "Extended Deterrence in the Middle East," pp. 329–34.

81. See R. N. Lebow, "Miscalculations in the South Atlantic: The Origins of the Falklands War," p. 122 in Jervis, Lebow, and Stein, *Psychology and Deterrence.*

82. Morgan, *Deterrence*, pp. 14 and 50.

83. Jervis, "Rational Deterrence: Theory and Evidence," p. 198.

84. Morgan, *Deterrence*, pp. 61–62.

85. Fink, "More Calculations About Deterrence."

Chapter 8

1. Michael Sullivan, *International Relations: Theories and Evidence* (Englewood Cliffs, NJ: Prentice-Hall, 1976), p. 144.

2. The presence of either anarchy or hierarchy comprises the basic principle by which international systems are ordered according to Kenneth Waltz, *Theory of International Politics* (Reading, MA: Addison-Wesley, 1979), p. 89.

3. James E. Daugherty and Robert L. Pfaltzgraff, Jr., *Contending Theories of International Relations*, 3rd ed. (New York: Harper & Row, 1990), p. 137.

4. Robert North, *War, Peace, Survival: Global Politics and Conceptual Synthesis* (Boulder, CO: Westview, 1990), p. 10.

5. For a contrary view—that the international system plays no determining role—see North, *War, Peace, Survival.*

6. International systems theory assumes that variables at other levels of analysis have a random effect on the behavior of states. Sullivan, *International Relations: Theories and Evidence*, p. 153.

7. Waltz, *Theory of International Politics*, p. 72.
8. Evan Luard, *War in International Society* (New Haven, CT: Yale University Press, 1986), p. 385. See also his *Types of International Society* (New York: Free Press, 1976).
9. Found in Rousseau's "A Discourse on the Origin of Inequality," in *The Social Contract and Discourses*, trans. G. D. H. Cole (New York: Dutton, 1950), p. 238.
10. Kenneth Waltz, *Man, the State and War* (New York: Columbia University Press, 1959), pp. 168–69.
11. Ibid., pp. 6 and 7.
12. Ibid., p. 188.
13. Jean-Jacques Rosseau, *A Lasting Peace Through the Federation of Europe*, trans. C. E. Vaughan (London: Constabale, 1917), pp. 78–79, quoted in Waltz, *Man, the State and War*, p. 180.
14. Robert Jervis, *Perceptions and Misperceptions in International Politics* (Princeton, NJ: Princeton University Press, 1976), pp. 58–113.
15. For the classic critique of world government, see Inis Claude, Jr., *Power and International Relations* (New York: Random House, 1962).
16. Melvin Tumin, *Social Stratification* (Englewood Cliffs: Prentice-Hall, 1967), p. 12.
17. Johann Galtung, "A Structural Theory of Aggression," *Journal of Peace Research* 1 (2) (1964), p. 96.
18. Maurice East, "Status Discrepancy and Violence in the International System: An Empirical Analysis," in James Rosenau, Vincent Davis and Maurice East (eds.), *The Analysis of International Politics* (New York: Free Press, 1972), p. 300.
19. Galtung, "A Structural Theory of Aggression;" East, "Status Discrepancy and Violence: An Empirical Analysis."
20. Galtung, pp. 99 and 96. It seems, however, on the basis of data from individual-level studies, that a considerable amount of discrepancy needs to be present before aggression takes place. See Galtung, p. 102, on this point.
21. Ibid., p. 99. Since aggression is not likely to be an immediate response to rank discrepancy, a time lag is probably involved. See Ibid., p. 105.
22. Ibid., p. 103.
23. East, p. 303.
24. Ibid.
25. An interesting aspect of the theory is that it postulates an exact parallel between several levels of analysis—individual, nation-state, and international system—with rank disequilibrium and aggression being related at each level. Thus, there exists the possibility of a causal link between levels. Disequilibrium at one level can lead to disequilibrium at another level. See Galtung, p. 106.
26. Sullivan, p. 177.
27. East, op. cit.
28. Michael D. Wallace, "Status, Formal Organization, and Arms Levels as Factors Leading to the Onset of War, 1820–1964," in Bruce Russett (ed.), *Peace, War and Numbers* (Beverly Hills, CA: Sage, 1972) and Wallace, "Power, Status, and International War," *Journal of Peace Research* 8 (1) (1971), pp. 23–36. See also Michael Wallace, *War and Rank Among Nations* (Lexington, MA: Heath, 1973).
29. James Lee Ray, "Status Inconsistency and War Involvement in Europe, 1816–1970," *Peace Science Society (International) Papers* 23 (1974), pp. 69–80, and Charles S. Gochman, "Status, Capabilities, and Major Power Conflict," in J.

David Singer (ed.), *The Correlates of War: II* (New York: Free Press, 1980), pp. 83–123.

30. For a review of empirical tests of realist assumptions see John Vasquez, *The Power of Power Politics: A Critique* (New Brunswick, NJ: Rutgers, 1983).

31. This classification is drawn from David Garnham, "The Causes of War; Systemic Findings," in Alan Ned Sabrosky (ed.), *Polarity and War: The Changing Structure of International Conflict* (Boulder, CO: Westview, 1985), pp. 7–23.

32. For an approach that calls for a twofold classification based on the number of military centers of power and the number of political centers of decision, see Patrick James and Michael Brecher, "Stability and Polarity: New Paths for Inquiry," *Journal of Peace Research* 25 (1) (1988), pp. 31–42.

33. Jack S. Levy, "The Polarity of the System and International Stability: An Empirical Analysis," in Sabrosky (ed.), *Polarity and War*, p. 47.

34. Levy defines nonpolarized systems as characterized by the presence of a number of alliances and the absence of two well-defined clusters and either (a) a series of cross-cutting alliance bonds or (b) rapidly shifting alliance partners. Jack S. Levy, "Alliance Formation and War Behavior: An Analysis of the Great Powers, 1495–1975," *Journal of Conflict Resolution* 25 (1981), p. 607.

35. Michael Wallace, "Polarization: Toward a Scientific Conception," in Sabrosky (ed.), *Polarity and War*, pp. 95–113.

36. Frank Wayman demonstrates that power polarity and cluster polarity are two uncorrelated and empirically separate dimensions. Frank Wayman, "Bipolarity, Multipolarity, and the Threat of War," in Sabrosky (ed.), *Polarity and War*, pp. 115–44. See also Jeffrey Hart, "Symmetry and Polarization in the European International System, 1870–1879: A Methodological Study," *Journal of Peace Research* 11 (1974), pp. 229–44, and Jeffrey Hart, "Power and Polarity in the International System," in Sabrosky (ed.), *Polarity and War*, pp. 25–40. See also Levy, "The Polarity of the System and International Stability," pp. 47–48.

37. For a somewhat similar classification, see Seyom Brown, *The Causes and Prevention of War* (New York: St. Martin's, 1987), p. 72.

38. David Rapkin, William R. Thompson, and Jon Christopherson, "Bipolarity and Bipolarization in the Cold War Era," *Journal of Conflict Resolution* 23 (2) (June 1979), pp. 261–95. They use a "bloc flow" approach to the measurement of (bi)polarization, which determines the extent to which conflict behavior (of a variety of types, not necessarily military) is concentrated between blocs and cooperative behavior is concentrated within blocs.

39. Several analysts suggest that alternative systems that contain elements of both bipolarity and multipolarity may provide the most stability. For instance, Richard Rosecrance examines the system of "bimultipolarity" and Manus Midlarsky discusses a system of "hierarchical equiilibrium." See Richard Rosecrance, "Bipolarity, Multipolarity, and the Future;" and Midlarsky, op. cit. Both Rosecrance's "bimultipolarity" and Midlarsky's "hierarchical equilibrium" model share some features with Morton's Kaplan's "loose bipolar" model (and his "very loose bipolar" model). See Morton Kaplan, "Variants on Six Models of the International System" in Rosenau (ed.), *International Politics and Foreign Policy*, pp. 291–303.

40. See Henry Kissinger, *A World Restored: The Politics of Conservatism in a Revolutionary Age* (New York: Grossett and Dunlap, 1964).

41. See Karl W. Deutsch, and J. David Singer, "Multipolar Power Systems and International Stability," *World Politics* 16 (3) (1964), pp. 390–406, and Lloyd Jensen, *Explaining Foreign Policy* (Englewood Cliffs: Prentice-Hall, 1982), p. 255.

42. Deutsch and Singer, op. cit.
43. "Neorealism" is an attempt to refine classical realist thought by injecting greater theoretical rigor, especially by defining concepts more clearly and by developing testable hypotheses. Power is still the key variable for neorealists, but the focus has been shifted from the nation-state level to the international-system level. Waltz is the primary proponent of this approach, but one might count Robert Gilpin as another.
44. Waltz, *Theory of International Politics.* This is not to say that the system's structure completely determines state behavior; it simply exerts a strong constraining influence. In return, the units of the system shape the structure of the system. "Neorealists" emphasize that states in different international structures will behave differently. Waltz identifies three aspects of international structure that are important in this respect: (1) the principle by which the system is organized—hierarchy or anarchy, (2) the specification of functions of the units (there is none in anarchy), and (3) the distribution of capabilities among the units. Waltz, *Theory of International Politics*, p. 82.
45. Claude, p. 62.
46. Jacek Kugler and A. F. K. Organski, "The Power Transition: A Retrospective and Prospective Evaluation," in Manus Midlarsky (ed.), *Handbook of War Studies* (Boston: Unwin Hyman, 1989), p. 176.
47. Randolph Siverson and Michael Sullivan, "The Distribution of Power and the Onset of War," *Journal of Conflict Resolution* 27 (3) (September 1983), p. 477. See also Richard J. Stoll and Michael Champion, "Capability Concentration, Alliance Bonding, and Conflict Among the Major Powers," in Sabrosky (ed.), *Polarity and War*, pp. 67–94. Stoll and Champion remind us that the realists associated an equal balance with stability, not with peace (pp. 73–75).
48. One of the classic critiques of the Deutsch and Singer argument for the stability of multipolarity is found in Richard Rosecrance, "Bipolarity, Multipolarity, and the Future," in James Roseanu (ed.), *International Politics and Foreign Policy*, rev. ed. (New York: Free Press, 1969), pp. 325–35.
49. Manus Midlarsky, "Hierarchical Equilibria and the Long-Run Instability of Multipolar Systems," in Midlarsky (ed.), *Handbook of War Studies*, pp. 64–74.
50. The classic formulation in support of bipolarity is found in Kenneth Waltz, "International Structure, National Force, and the Balance of World Power," in Rosenau (ed.), *International Politics and Foreign Policy*, pp. 304–14. See also his *Theory of International Politics.*
51. Wayman, op. cit. Wayman's measure of cluster polarity is the ratio of the actual poles (alliance blocs and nonaligned great powers) to the number of potential poles.
52. Bruce Bueno de Mesquita, "Systemic Polarization and the Occurrence and Duration of War," *Journal of Conflict Resolution* 22 (June 1978), pp. 241–67.
53. Wallace, *War and Rank Among Nations* and "Alliance Polarization, Cross-Cutting, and International War, 1815–1964," *Journal of Conflict Resolution* 17 (December 1973), pp. 576–604.
54. Similar results were found by two other scholars, Charles Kegley and Gregory Raymond, "Alliance Norms and War: A New Piece in an Old Puzzle," *International Studies Quarterly* 26 (December 1982). They find that extremely flexible and rigid alliances are associated with a high magnitude and severity of war.
55. Jack S. Levy, "Alliance Formation and War Behavior," p. 608.
56. This is a point made by Michael Wallace, "Polarization: Toward a Scientific Conception," p. 110.
57. J. David Singer and Melvin Small, "Alliance Aggregation and the Onset of War,

1815–1945," in Singer (ed.), *Quantitative International Politics* (New York: Free Press, 1967), pp. 247–86.

58. Daugherty and Pfaltzgraff, p. 352.
59. Charles W. Ostrom and Francis W. Hoole, "Alliances and War Revisited: A Research Note," *International Studies Quarterly* 22 (June 1978), pp. 215–36.
60. Alan Ned Sabrosky, "From Bosnia to Sarajevo," *Journal of Conflict Resolution* 19 (March 1975), pp. 3–24.
61. Levy, "Alliance Formation and War Behavior."
62. Ibid., pp. 590 and 605.
63. Wallace, "Polarization: Towards a Scientific Conception."
64. Levy, "Alliance Formation and War Behavior," p. 600.
65. Ibid., p. 123.
66. John Vasquez, "The Steps to War: Toward a Scientific Explanation of Correlates of War Findings," *World Politics* 40 (1) (October 1987), p. 121.
67. Ibid., p. 123.
68. See, for instance, Randolph Siverson and Joel King, "Alliances and the Expansion of War," in J. David Singer and Michael Wallace (eds.), *To Auger Well: Early Warning Indicators in World Politics* (Beverly Hills, CA: Sage, 1982), pp. 37–49. Also, Siverson and Harvey Starr, "Opportunity, Willingness, and the Diffusion of War, 1816–1965," *American Political Science Review* (March 1990).
69. Benjamin Most and Harvey Starr, "Diffusion, Reinforcement, Geopolitics, and the Spread of War," *American Political Science Review* 74 (December 1980), pp. 941–44. Both geographic proximity and alliance ties are correlated with war involvement, though alliance membership has the greater effect of the two. However, the combined effects of both factors have an effect greater than either variable by itself. See B. Most, P. Schrodt, R. Siverson, and H. Starr, "Border and Alliance Effects in the Diffusion of Major Power Conflict, 1816–1965," pp. 209–29 in C. Gochman and A. N. Sabrosky (eds.), *Prisoners of War? Nation-States in the Modern Era* (Lexington, MA: Lexington Books, 1990).
70. J. David Singer, Stuart Bremer, and John Stuckey, "Capability Distribution, Uncertainty, and Major Power War, 1820–1965," pp. 19–48 in Bruce Russett (ed.), *Peace, War and Numbers.* CON ranges from 0 to 1.0; it is 0 when the distribution of capabilities is perfectly equal across the system, and it is 1.0 when one state holds 100% of the capabilities in the system.
71. Bruce Bueno de Mesquita, "Measuring Systemic Polarity," *Journal of Conflict Resolution* 19 (June 1975), pp. 187–216.
72. Wayman, op. cit.
73. Midlarsky, p. 70.
74. Levy, "The Polarity of the System and International Stability," pp. 41–66.
75. On this point see John Vasquez, "The Steps to War," p. 128.
76. Wayman, pp. 138–39. However, Wayman's research is unable to confirm the relationship between cluster multipolarity and peace for the nineteenth century.
77. Stoll and Champion, op. cit.
78. A. F. K. Organski, *World Politics* (New York: Knopf, 1958, 1968); see also A. F. K. Organski and Jacek Kugler, *The War Ledger* (Chicago: University of Chicago Press, 1980).
79. Claude, p. 56.
80. Note also that Organski's theory suggests that war is rank related; states with higher power rankings are presumed to be more highly involved in war. On this point see Henk Houweling and Jan Siccama, "Power Transitions as a Cause of War," *Journal of Conflict Resolution* 32 (1) (March 1988), pp. 87–102.

81. See William R. Thompson, "Succession Crises in the Global Political System: A Test of the Transition Model," in A. L. Bergeson (ed.), *Crises in the World-System* (Beverly Hills, CA: Sage, 1983).
82. Organski admits that balance-of-power theory may have had some validity in the preindustrial era, but that in the twentieth century, where rapid industrialization fuels rapid shifts in power, balances are too unstable to keep the peace.
83. Organski and Kugler, op. cit.
84. Houweling and Siccama, op. cit.
85. Stoll and Champion, op, cit.
86. Charles Gochman, "Capability-Driven Disputes," pp. 141–59 in Gochman and A. N. Sabrosky (eds.), *Prisoners of War?*.
87. Gochman, "Capability Driven Disputes," p. 157.
88. Woosang Kim, "Power, Alliance, and Major Wars, 1816–1975," *Journal of Conflict Resolution* 32 (2) (June 1989), pp. 255–73.
89. It may actually describe an even more limited set of cases since its emphasis on industrialization limits it to the period after the midnineteenth century and since Organski and Kugler's list of appropriate wars seems confined almost entirely to the wars of attempted German expansion. On this point, see Siverson and Sullivan, op. cit.
90. In Weede's study of Asian dyads, preponderance is defined as an overwhelming 10 to 1 disparity, and lesser levels are interpreted as equality. Erich Weede, "Overwhelming Preponderance as a Pacifying Condition Among Contiguous Asian Dyads, 1950–1969," *Journal of Conflict Resolution* 20 (September 1976), pp. 395–411; David Garnham, "Dyadic International War, 1816–1965: The Role of Power Parity and Geographical Proximity," *Western Political Quarterly* 29 (June 1976), pp. 231–42. See also the review in Siverson and Sullivan, op. cit.
91. Geoffrey Blainey, *The Causes of War* (New York: Free Press, 1973), pp. 108–24.
92. Wayne Ferris, *The Power Capabilities of Nation-States* (Lexington, MA: Lexington Books, 1973), p. 76.
93. Brown, pp. 103–5.
94. One complication here is that the traditional balance-of-power theory argues that an important aspect of equality or inequality of power is found in alliance bonds. The dyadic balance is not the only consideration of states contemplating aggression; they will seek to assess how alliance commitments affect the balance. In other words, peace is kept not by the dyadic balance alone, but by the balance between alliances. Therefore, looking solely at the dyadic balance may be misleading. Two studies give some support to this thesis, though their results produce as many disagreements as agreements: Randolph Siverson and Michael Tennefoss, "Power, Alliance, and the Escalation of International Conflict, 1815–1965," *American Political Science Review* 78 (1984), pp. 1057–69; and Kim, op. cit.

Chapter 9

1. Robert Gilpin, *War and Change in World Politics* (Cambridge: Cambridge University Press, 1981).
2. Other theorists of hegemonic stability emphasize the construction and maintenance of a liberal, free-trading regime by the hegemon, which contributes to peace and stability in the system. See, for instance, Stephen Krasner, "State Power and the Structure of International Trade," *World Politics* 28 (April 1976),

pp. 317–47; Robert O. Keohane, "The Theory of Hegemonic Stability and Changes in International Economic Regimes, 1967–77," in Ole Holsti, Randolph Siverson, and Alexander George (eds.), *Change in the International System* (Boulder, CO: Westview, 1980), pp. 131–62; and Robert Keohane and Joseph Nye, *Power and Interdependence* (Boston: Little, Brown, 1977). Gilpin mentions this, but prefers not to emphasize it; he argues that when Britain was unable to contain the imperial ambitions of its continental rivals owing to its declining hegemonic position, it began to practice a kind of "preclusive" imperialism to minimize losses to its rivals. Thus, hegemonic powers do not always practice free trade.

3. Gilpin, p. 83.
4. Ibid., pp. ix–xii.
5. Ibid., pp. 208–9. Other options are, of course, open to the hegemon as well, such as an increase in the resources dedicated to hegemony or a reduction in commitments.
6. Ibid., pp. 92–93.
7. On this point see Robert North, *War, Peace, Survival*, (Boulder, CO: Westview, 1990), p. 222.
8. Gilpin, p. 31. Like Blainey, Gilpin argues that the more decisive the initial military victory by the hegemon, the more clear-cut the postwar hierarchy, and therefore, the less likely war is to occur.
9. For an assessment of historical-structural perspectives and their views of the future, see Jack Levy, "Long Cycles, Hegemonic Transitions and the Long Peace," pp. 147–76 in Charles W. Kegley (ed.), *The Long Postwar Peace: Contending Explanations and Projections* (New York: Harper Collins, 1991).
10. K. Edward Spiezio, "British Hegemony and Major Power War, 1815–1939: An Empirical Test of Gilpin's Model of Hegemonic Governance," *International Studies Quarterly* 34 (2) (June 1990), pp. 165–81.
11. Although some historical-structural theorists see Portugal and the United Provinces as hegemonic states (Modelski, for instance) or at least the United Provinces (Wallerstein), Gilpin prefers not to classify either as having achieved hegemonic status. The 1648–1815 period was characterized by the European balance of power rather than by cycles of hegemonic succession, according to Gilpin, and the premodern age was characterized by a succession of empires (p. 116).
12. George Modelski, "The Long Cycle of Global Politics and the Nation-State," *Comparative Studies in Society and History* 20 (2) (April 1978), pp. 214–35; and William R. Thompson, *On Global War: Historical-Structural Approaches to World Politics* (Columbia: University of South Carolina, 1988). The long-cycle perspective does not claim to be an extensive theory; it is still evolving as its proponents continue to refine it. Thompson prefers to call it a "perspective" or an "analytic framework." William R. Thompson, "Uneven Economic Growth, Systemic Challenges, and Global Wars," *International Studies Quarterly* 27 (1983), pp. 341–55.
13. Thompson, *On Global War*, p. 45, p. 118. Modelski, "The Long Cycle of Global Politics and the Nation-State," p. 215.
14. William R. Thompson, "Polarity, the Long Cycle, and Global Power Welfare," *Journal of Conflict Resolution* 30 (4) (December 1986), pp. 587–615.
15. Karen Rasler and William R. Thompson, "Global Wars, Public Debts, and the Long Cycle," *World Politics* 35 (4) (July 1983). See also Paul Kennedy, *The Rise and Fall of Great Powers: Economic Change and Military Conflict from 1500 to 2000* (New York: Random House, 1988).
16. Thompson, *On Global War*, pp. 49–50.

17. George Modelski and Patrick Morgan, "Understanding Global War," *Journal of Conflict Resolution* 29 (3) (September 1985), p. 399.
18. On this point see William R. Thompson, "Succession Crises in the Global Political System: A Test of the Transition Model," in Albert Bergesen (ed.), *Crises in the World-System* (Beverly Hills, CA: Sage, 1983), p. 109.
19. See George Modelski and William R. Thompson, "Long Cycles and Global War," in Midlarsky (ed.), *Handbook of War Studies* (Boston: Unwin Hyman, 1989), p. 39, and also Thompson, "Succession Crises in the Global Political System: A Test of the Transition Model."
20. Thompson, "Uneven Economic Growth, Systemic Challenges, and Global Wars," p. 349.
21. See Levy's comments on this point: Jack Levy, "Theories of General War," *World Politics* 37 (3), pp. 361–63.
22. Modelski and Morgan, pp. 400–1, and Rasler and Thompson, p. 500.
23. Thompson, "Uneven Economic Growth, Systemic Challenges, and Global Wars," pp. 349–51.
24. Thompson, *On Global War*. On this point see also William R. Thompson and Karen A. Rasler, "War and Systemic Capability Reconcentration," *Journal of Conflict Resolution* 32 (June 1988). Global wars also tend to facilitate an increase in the new world power's leading economic sectors.
25. This, of course, conflicts with Singer, Bremer, and Stuckey's finding that in the nineteenth century there is a positive correlation between capability concentration and ongoing war. Thompson argues that the Correlates of War findings are dependent on the classification of nations as Great Powers, the selection of the 1820 starting point, the use of a capability index giving equal weight to demographic, military, and industrial measures, and the use of nation-months as the measure of war. William R. Thompson (ed.), *Contending Approaches of World System Analysis* (Beverly Hills, CA: Sage, 1983).
26. Thompson, "Polarity, the Long Cycle, and Global Power Warfare," *Journal of Conflict Resolution* 30 (4) (December 1986), pp. 587–615; and Thompson, *On Global War*, Chapter 9.
27. Thompson, "Succession Crises in the Global Political System," p. 112.
28. These are summarized in Jack Levy, "Declining Power and the Preventive Motivation for War," *World Politics* 40 (1) (October 1987), pp. 85–88, and in Levy, "Long Cycles, Hegemonic Transitions and the Long Peace." Levy draws on Organski, *World Politics* (1968), p. 376; Stephen Van Evera, "The Cult of the Offensive and the Origins of World War I," *International Security* 9 (Summer 1984), pp. 58–107; and Jack L. Snyder, "Perceptions of the Security Dilemma in 1914," in Robert Jervis, Richard Ned Lebow, and Janice Gross Stein (eds.), *Psychology and Deterrence* (Baltimore: Johns Hopkins Press, 1985), pp. 153–79.
29. Thompson, *On Global War*, pp. 277–80.
30. Modelski and Thompson, "Long Cycles and Global War," p. 50.
31. Modelski and Morgan, p. 403; Modelski and Thompson, p. 42.
32. Levy, "Long Cycles, Hegemonic Transitions, and the Long Peace," p. 158. Long Cycle theorists also omit the Seven Years' War (1755–1763) and the Dutch War of Louis XIV (1672–1678) from their list of global wars.
33. Ibid., 0. 159.
34. Wallerstein's major works include *The Modern World-System* (New York: Academic Press, 1974); *The Capitalist World-Economy* (New York: Cambridge University Press, 1979); and *The Modern World-System II: Mercantilism and the Coordination and the Consolidation of the European World Economy, 1600–*

1750 (New York: Free Press, 1980). For a short summary of his ideas, see his *Historical Capitalism* (London: Verso, 1983).

35. Christopher Chase-Dunn, "Interstate System and Capitalist World-Economy: One Logic or Two?" *International Studies Quarterly* 25 (1) (March 1981), pp. 27 and 31.

36. World wars are defined as conflicts in which one state seeks to take over, and thus destroy, the (multicentric) interstate system or as struggles that determine leading power status. Christopher Chase-Dunn, *Global Formation: Structure of the World-Economy* (Cambridge, MA: Basil Blackwel, 1989), p. 159.

37. Wallerstein, *Historical Capitalism*, p. 62.

38. Ibid., p. 64.

39. Chase-Dunn, "Interstate System and Capitalist World-Economy: One Logic or Two?" p. 23.

40. Chase-Dunn and Sokolovsky, p. 364.

41. Research Group on Cyclical Rhythms and Secular Trends, "Cyclical Rhythms and Secular Trends of the Capitalist World-Economy," *Review* 2 (Spring 1979), pp. 483–500. Cited in Thompson, *Global War*, p. 72.

42. Chase-Dunn, *Global Formation*, pp. 183–84.

43. Christopher Chase-Dunn and Joan Sokolovsky, "Interstate System, World-Empires and the Capitalist World-Economy: A Response to Thompson," *International Studies Quarterly* 27 (September 1983), p. 361.

44. Chase-Dunn, "Interstate System and Capitalist World-Economy: One Logic or Two?" pp. 38–40.

45. Wallerstein, *Historical Capitalism*, p. 58.

46. Chase-Dunn, *Global Formation*, pp. 84–85 and 343–45.

47. North, *War, Peace, Survival*, pp. 222–23.

48. N. D. Kondratieff, *The Long Wave Cycle* (New York: Richardson and Snyder, 1984). (Original edition 1928).

49. Modelski, "The Long Cycle of Global Politics and the Nation-State," pp. 227–30; Modelski and Morgan, p. 402; and Rasler and Thompson.

50. William R. Thompson and Gary Zuk, "War, Inflation, and the Kondratieff Long Wave," *Journal of Conflict Resolution* 26 (4) (December 1982), pp. 621–44.

51. Thompson, *On Global War*, pp. 53–54.

52. Joshua S. Goldstein, *Long Cycles: Prosperity and War in the Modern Age* (New Haven, CT: Yale University Press, 1988).

53. Joshua S. Goldstein, "Kondratieff Waves as War Cycles," *International Studies Quarterly* 29 (4) (December 1985), pp. 411–44; Goldstein, "Long Waves in War, Production, Prices, and Wages," *Journal of Conflict Resolution* 31 (4) (December 1987), pp. 573–600; and Goldstein, *Long Cycles*.

54. Levy notes, however, that since K-waves are systemic phenomena, all great powers should benefit from the upswings and thus the balance of power should remain generally unchanged. Levy, "Long Cycles, Hegemonic Transitions, and the Long Peace," p. 165.

55. Goldstein, *Long Cycles*, Chapter 15, and pp. 350–57.

56. Levy, "Long Cycles, Hegemonic Transitions, and the Long Peace."

57. World-systems theorists see the structure of the modern world-system as characterized by three constants, three cycles, and four secular trends. The three constants are: (1) commodity production, (2) the core-periphery division of labor, and (3) the state system with relatively strong core states and relatively weak periphery states. The three cycles are: (1) long waves (K-waves) of increases and decreases in the rate of capital accumulation and overall economic activity in

the system, (2) a unicentric-multicentric cycle of competition among core states, and (3) swings from free trade to controlled trade in core-periphery economic relations. The four secular trends are: (1) the expansion of the system over time, (2) the intensification and deepening of commodity relations, (3) the increasing power and control of states, and (4) the increasing size of economic enterprises. Christopher Chase-Dunn, "Comparative Research on World-System Characteristics," *International Studies Quarterly* 23 (4) (December 1979), pp. 607–8.

58. Goldstein, *Long Cycles*, pp. 287–88.
59. Chase-Dunn, *Global Formation*, p. 164. Wallerstein's view is slightly different. He argues that core states step up their exploitation of peripheral areas during the contraction phase as a way of minimizing the effects of the stagnation of the world economy. This is done primarily through attempts to seek out lower-wage workforces and incorporate them into the world-economy rather than through a search for new markets. See Wallerstein, *Historical Capitalism*, p. 39.
60. Though Doran's writings on this subject are numerous, see especially Charles F. Doran, "War and Power Dynamics: Economic Underpinnings," *International Studies Quarterly* 27 (1983), pp. 419–44; "Systemic Disequilibrium, Foreign Policy Role, and the Power Cycle: Challenges for Research Design," *Journal of Conflict Resolution* 33 (3) (September 1989), pp. 371–401; "Power Cycle Theory of Systems Structure and Stability: Commonalities and Complementarities," in Manus Midlarsky (ed.), *Handbook of War Studies*, pp. 83–110; and Doran and Wes Parsons, "War and the Cycle of Relative Power," *American Political Science Review* 74 (1980), pp. 947–65.
61. Doran, "Power Cycle Theory of Systems Structure: Commonalties and Complementarities," p. 88.
62. Ibid., p. 952; Doran, "War and Power Dynamics: Economic Underpinnings," p. 420.
63. Doran, "War and Power Dynamics: Economic Underpinnings," pp. 421–22, and Doran, "Power Cycle Theory of Systems Structure and Stability: Commonalities and Complementarities," p. 104.
64. Doran and Parsons, pp. 949–50.
65. Doran, "War and Power Dynamics: Economic Underpinnings," pp. 422–26; and Doran, "Power Cycle Theory of Systems Structure and Stability: Commonalities and Complementarities," p. 89.
66. Doran, "Power Cycle Theories," p. 90.
67. Doran, "Power Cycle Theory of Systems Structure and Stability: Commonalities and Complementarities," p. 84. The passage of a major nation through a critical point can also increase the importance of other, more long-standing systemic structures and processes such as status discrepancy, hegemonic decline, or power concentrtion/deconcentration. Ibid., p. 90.
68. Ibid., p. 92.
69. Doran, "War and Power Dynamics: Economic Underpinnings," pp. 429–30.
70. Doran, "Systemic Disequilibrium, Foreign Policy Role, and the Power Cycle: Challenges for Research Design," pp. 397–98.
71. Doran and Parsons, pp. 460–62.
72. Doran, "War and Power Dynamics: Economic Underpinnings," p. 430.
73. Doran, "Systemic Disequilibrium, Foreign Policy Role, and the Power Cycle: Challenges for Research Design," pp. 384–87.
74. Daniel Geller, "Toward a Unified Theory of War," paper delivered at International Studies Association conference, Washington, DC, April 1990.
75. North, *War, Peace, Survival*, pp. 153–56.

76. John Mueller, "Is War Still Becoming Obsolete?" paper presented at annual meeting of the American Political Science Association, Washington, DC, August 1991, p. 48.
77. Charles Gochman, "Capability-Driven Disputes," pp. 141–59 in Gochman and A.N. Sabrosky (eds.), *Prisoners of War? Nation-States in the Modern Era* (Lexington, MA: Lexington Books, 1990).
78. *Washington Post*, January 29, 1992, p. A–14.

Chapter 10

1. For an extremely good review of research findings on the causes of war by political scientists see John Vasquez, "The Steps to War: Toward a Scientific Explanation of the Correlates of War Findings," *World Politics* XL (1) (October 1987), pp. 108–45. Insights from this synopsis are scattered throughout this final chapter.
2. It is probably true that certain cultures tend to be more accepting of martial values than others and this affects the content of its leaders' operational codes. In these cultures bullying tactics are more generally acceptable, and political elites who represent these values tend to gain and retain a substantial degree of legitimacy.
3. Vasquez, p. 128
4. Other factos have been put forward as well, such as (1) the rising costliness of war, accelerated tremendously by the creation and proliferation of nuclear weapons and (2) the increase in internatioal interdependece and global complexity. On the former, see Kenneth Waltz, "Nuclear Myths and Political Realities," *American Political Science Review* 84 (3) (September 1990), pp. 731–45; John Mearsheimer, "Back to the Future: Instability in Europe After the Cold War," *International Security* 15 S(1) (Summer 1990), pp. 5–56; Bruce Bueno de Mesquita and William Riker, "An Assessment of the Merits of Selective Nuclear Proliferation," *Journal of Conflict Resolution* 26 (1982), pp. 287–306; Carl Kaysen, "Is War Obsolete?" *International Security* 14 (4) (Spring 1990). On the latter, see Normal Angell, *The Great Illusion* (New York: Knickerbocker Press, 1913); see also James Rosenau, "A Wherewithal for Revulsion," paper presented to the American Political Science Association conference, Washington, DC (August 1991).
5. Drawing on the arguments of Bueno de Mesquita and Lalman, Ray notes that, at least in the short term, the increase in the number of democracies may increase the opportunities for war since it may increase the number of democratic/nondemocratic dyads. But once the proportion of democratic states arrives at 50%, the number of democratic/nondemocratic dyads will decrease, thereby decreasing the opportunities for war. James Lee Ray, "The Future of International War," paper presented to the American Political Science Association conference, Washington, DC (August 1991).
6. John Mueller, "Is War Still Obsolete?" paper presented at Annual Meeting of the American Political Science Association, Washington, DC (August 1991).
7. John Mueller, *Retreat from Doomsday: The Obsolescence of Major War* (New York: Basic Books, 1989). Also, Mueller, "Changing Attitudes Towards War: The Impact of the First World War," *British Journal of Political Science* 21 (1991), pp. 1–28; and Mueller, "Is War Still Obsolete?" See also James Lee Ray, "The Abolition of Slavery and the End of International War," *International Organization* 43 (1989), pp. 405–39; and Ray, "The Future of International War;" Kalevi J. Holsti, *Peace and War: Armed Conflicts and International Order 1648–1989* (Cambridge: Cambridge University Press, 1991), especially pp. 325–30. Also,

James Rosenau, "A Wherewithal for Revulsion: Notes on the Obsolescence of Interstate War;" and Michael Howard, *The Lessons of History* (New Haven, CT: Yale University Press, 1991).

8. Mueller, "Is War Still Becoming Obsolete?" pp. 54–55.
9. Evan Luard, *War in International Society* (New Haven, CT: Yale University Press, 1986) and Kalevi J. Holsti, *Peace and War.*

Bibliography

Achen, C. H. and D. Snidal (1989) "Rational Deterrence Theory and Comparative Case Studies." *World Politics* 41:143–69.

Adelman, J. and D. Palmieri (1989) *The Dynamics of Soviet Foreign Policy*. New York: Harper & Row.

Adorno, T. W. (1950) *The Authoritarian Personality*. New York: Harper & Row.

Alexandroff, A. and R. Rosecrance (1977) "Deterrence in 1939." *World Politics* 29:404–24.

Allison, G. (1969) "Conceptual Models and the Cuban Missile Crisis." *American Political Science Review* 63:689–718.

—— (1971) *Essence of Decision: Explaining the Cuban Missile Crisis*. Boston: Little, Brown.

Allison, G. and M. Halperin (1972) "Bureaucratic Politics: A Paradigm and Some Policy Implications," pp. 40–79 in R. Tanter and R. Ullman (eds.), *Theory and Policy in International Relations*. Princeton, NJ: Princeton University Press.

Altfeld, M. (1983) "Arms Races? -and Escalation?: A Comment on Wallace." *International Studies Quarterly* 27(2): 225–31.

Anderson, P. A. (1987) "What Do Decision Makers Do When They Make Foreign Policy? The Implications for the Comparative Study of Foreign Policy," pp. 285–308 in C. F. Hermann, C. W. Kegley, and J. N. Rosenau (eds.), *New Directions in the Study of Foreign Policy*. Boston: Allen and Unwin.

Angell, N. (1913) *The Great Illusion*. New York: Knickerbocker Press.

Ardrey, R. (1961) *African Genesis*. New York: Atheneum.

—— (1966) *The Territorial Imperative*. New York: Atheneum.

—— (1970) *The Social Contract*. New York: Atheneum.

Arrow, K. (1951) *Social Choice and Individual Values*. New York: Wiley.

Art. R. (1974) "Bureaucratic Politics and American Foreign Policy: A Critique." *Policy Sciences* (Summer).

Ashley, R. (1980) *The Political Economy of War and Peace*. New York: Nichols.

Axelrod, R. (1973) "Bureaucratic Decisionmaking in the Military Assistance Program: Some Empirical Findings," pp. 154–72 in M. Halperin and A. Kantor (eds.), *Readings in American Foreign Policy: A Bureaucratic Perspective*. Boston: Little, Brown.

—— (1980a) "Effective Choice in the Prisoners' Dilemma." *Journal of Conflict Resolution* 24:3–25.

—— (1980b) "More Effective Choice in the Prisoners' Dilemma." *Journal of Conflict Resolution* 24:379–403.

—— (1984) *The Evolution of Cooperation*. New York: Basic Books.

Babst, D. V. (1972) "A Force for Peace." *Industrial Research* 14:55–58.

Bandura, A. (1980) "The Social Learning Theory of Aggression," pp. 141–56 in R. Falk and S.S. Kim (eds.), *The War System*. Boulder, CO: Westview.

Barber, J. D. (1972) *The Presidential Character*. Englewood Cliffs, NJ: Prentice-Hall.

Barnds, W. J. (1972) *India, Pakistan and the Great Powers*. New York: Praeger.

Barnet, R. (1973) *Roots of War: The Men and Institutions Behind U.S. Foreign Policy*. New York: Penguin.

Beer, F. A. (1981) *Peace Against War*. San Fransisco: W.H. Freeman.

Behr, R. (1981) "Nice Guys Finish Last—Sometimes." *Journal of Conflict Resolution* 25:289–300.

Beitz, C. and T. Herman (1973) (eds.) *Peace and War*. San Fransisco: W. H. Freeman.

Bender, D. L. and B. Leone (1983) (eds.) *Are Humans Aggressive by Nature?* St. Paul, MN: Greenhaven Press.

Bergeson, A. (1983) (ed.) *Crises in the World-System*. Beverly Hills, CA: Sage.

Berkowitz, L. (1962) *Aggression: A Social-Psychological Analysis*. New York: McGraw-Hill.

Betts, R. K. (1977) *Soldiers, Statesmen and Cold War Crises*. Cambridge, MA: Harvard University Press.

——— (1978) "Analysis, War, and Decision: Why Intelligence Failures Are Inevitable." *World Politics* 31(1):61–89.

Blainey, G. (1973) *The Causes of War*. New York: Free Press.

Boulding, K. (1956) *The Image*. Ann Arbor: University of Michigan Press.

——— (1962) *Conflict and Defense: A General Theory*. New York: Harper & Row.

——— (1967) "The Learning and Reality Testing Process in the International System," pp. 1–15 in J. C. Farrell and A. P. Smith (eds.), *Image and Reality in World Politics*. New York: Columbia University Press.

Braybrooke, D. and C. Lindblom (1969) "Types of Decision-Making," pp. 207–16 in J. Rosenau (ed.), *International Politics and Foreign Policy*. New York: Free Press.

Brecher, M. (1975) *Decisions in Israel's Foreign Policy*. New Haven, CT: Yale University Press.

——— (1988) "Stability and Polarity: New Paths for Inquiry." *Journal of Peace Research* 25:31–42.

Bremer, S. (1980) "National Capabilities and War Proneness," pp. 57–82 in J. D. Singer (ed.), *The Correlates of War II: Testing Some Realpolitik Models*. New York: Free Press.

——— (1982) "The Contagiousness of Coercion: The Spread of Serious International Disputes, 1900–1976." *International Interaction* 9:29–55.

——— (1991) "Dangerous Dyads: Conditions Affecting the Likelihood of Interstate War, 1816–1965." Revised version of paper presented at Peace Science Society Meeting, Rutgers University.

Bremer, S., J. D. Singer, and U. Luterbacher (1973) "The Population Density and War Proneness of European Nations, 1816–1965." *Comparative Political Studies* 6:329–48.

Brodie, F. (1981) *Richard Nixon*. New York: Norton.

Brown, S. (1987) *The Causes and Prevention of War*. New York: St. Martin's.

Bueno de Mesquita, B. (1975) "Measuring Systemic Polarity." *Journal of Conflict Resolution* 19:187–216.

——— (1978) "Systemic Polarization and the Occurrence and Duration of War." *Journal of Conflict Resolution* 22:241–67.

——— (1981a) *The War Trap*. New Haven, CT: Yale University Press.

——— (1981b) "Risk, Power Distribution and the Likelihood of War." *International Studies Quarterly* 25(4):541–68.

Bueno de Mesquita, B. and W. Riker (1982) "An Assessment of the Merits of Selective Nuclear Proliferation." *Journal of Conflict Resolution* 26:287–306.

Bundy, McG. (1988) *Danger and Survival: Choices About the Bomb in the First Fifty Years*. New York: Random House.

Burrows, R. and J. Garriga-Pico (1974) "The Road to the Six Day War: Relational Analysis of Conflict and Cooperation." *Peace Science Society (International) Papers* 22:47–74.

Caldwell, D. (1977) "Bureaucratic Foreign Policy Making." *American Behavioral Scientist* 21 (2):87–110.

Cartwright, D. (1971) "Risk-taking by Individuals and Groups: An Assessment of Research Employing Choice Dilemmas." *Journal of Personality and Social Psychology* 20:261–78.

Chan, S. (1984) "Mirror, Mirror on the Wall . . . Are the Freer Countries More Pacific?" *Journal of Conflict Resolution* 28(4):617–48.

Chase-Dunn, C. (1979) "Comparative Research on World-System Characteristics." *International Studies Quarterly* 23(4);601–23.

——— (1981) "Interstate System and Capitalist World-Economy: One Logic or Two? *International Studies Quarterly* 25(1):119–42.

——— (1989) *Global Formation: Structure of the World-Economy*. Cambridge, MA: Basil Blackwell.

Chase-Dunn, C. and J. Sokolovsky (1983) "Interstate System, World-Empires and the Capitalist World-Economy: A Response to Thompson." *International Studies Quarterly* 27:357–67.

Chesen, E. (1973) *President Nixon's Psychiatric Profile*. New York: Peter Wyden.

Choucri, N. and R. North (1975) *Nations in Conflict: National Growth and International Violence*. San Fransisco: W. H. Freeman.

——— (1989) "Lateral Pressure in International Relations: Concept and Theory," pp. 289–326 in M. Midlarsky (ed.), *Handbook of War Studies*. Boston: Unwin Hyman.

Claude, I. (1962) *Power and International Relations*. New York: Random House.

Cobb, R. W. and C. Elder (1970) *International Community*. New York: Holt, Rinehart & Winston.

Cusack, T. R. and M. D. Ward (1981) "Military Spending in the United States, Soviet Union and the Peoples' Republic of China." *Journal of Conflict Resolution* 25:429–67.

Cyert, R. and J. March (1963) *A Behavioral Theory of the Firm*. Englewood Cliffs, NJ: Prentice-Hall.

Darcey, R. and N. Pendegraft (1988) "The Optimality of TIT-FOR-TAT." *International Interactions* 15(1):45–57.

Dart, R. (1953) "The Predatory Transition from Ape to Man." *International Anthropological and Linguistic Review* 1.

Davies, J. (1970) "Violence and Aggression: Innate or Not?" *Western Political Quarterly* 23.

de Rivera, J. (1968) *The Psychological Dimension of Foreign Policy*. Columbus, OH: Charles Merrill.

Demause, L. (1984) "The Making of a Fearful Leader: 'Where's the Rest of Me?'" *Journal of Psychohistory* 12:5–21.

Dessler, D. (1991) "Beyond Correlations: Toward a Causal Theory of War." *International Studies Quarterly* 35:337–55.

Deutsch, K. and R. Merritt (1965) "Effects of Events on National and International Images," pp. 132–87 in H. Kelman (ed.) *International Behavior*. New York: Holt, Rinehart & Winston.

Deutsch, K. and J. D. Singer (1964) "Multipolar Power Systems and International Stability." *World Politics* 16(3):390–406.

Diehl, P. F. (1983) "Arms Races and Escalation: A Closer Look." *Journal of Peace Research* 20(3):205–12.

—— (1985a) "Contiguity and Military Escalation in Major Power Rivalries, 1816–1980." *Journal of Politics* 47(4):1203–11.

—— (1985b) ""Arms Races to War: An Analysis of Some Underlying Effects." *Sociological Quarterly* 26:331–49.

Diehl, P. F. and G. Goertz (1988) "Territorial Changes and Militarized Conflict." *Journal of Conflict Resolution* 32(1):103–22.

Diehl, P. F. and J. Kingston (1987) "Messenger or Message? Military Buildups and the Initiation of Conflict." *Journal of Politics* 49:789–99.

Dixon, W. J. (1982) "Measuring Interstate Affect." *American Journal of Political Science* 27:828–51.

—— (1986) "Reciprocity in United States–Soviet Relations: Multiple Symmetry or Issue Linkage?" *American Journal of Political Science* 30:421–45.

Doran, C. F. (1983) "War and Power Dynamics: Economic Underpinnings." *International Studies Quarterly* 27:419–44.

—— (1989a) "Systemic Disequilibrium, Foreign Policy Role, and the Power Cycle: Challenges for Research Design." *Journal of Conflict Resolution* 33(3):371–401.

—— (1989b) "Power Cycle Theory of Systems Structure and Stability: Commonalities and Complementarities," pp. 83–110 in M. Midlarsky (ed.) *Handbook of War Studies.* New York: Unwin Hyman.

Doran, C. F. and W. Parsons (1980) "War and the Cycle of Relative Power." *American Political Science Review* 74:947–65.

Dougherty, J. E. and R. L. Pfaltzgraff, Jr. (1981) *Contending Theories of International Relations,* 2nd ed. New York: Harper & Row.

Duncan, G. T. and R. M. Siverson (1975) "Markov Models for Conflict Analysis: Results from Sino-Indian Relations." *International Studies Quarterly* 19:344–74.

Dyer, G. (1985) *War.* New York: Dorsey.

East, M. A. (1972) "Status Discrepancy and Violence in the International System: An Empirical Analysis," pp. 299–319 in J. N. Rosenau, V. Davis, and M. A. East (eds.), *The Analysis of International Politics.* New York: Free Press.

East, M. A. and P. Gregg (1967) "Factors Influencing Cooperation and Conflict in the International System." *International Studies Quarterly* 11:224–69.

East, M. A., S. Salmore, and C. F. Hermann (1978) (eds.) *Why Nations Act: Theoretical Perspectives for Comparative Foreign Policy.* Beverley Hills, CA: Sage.

Etheridge. L. (1978) "Personality Effects on American Foreign Policy, 1898–1968." *American Political Science Review* 72:434–51.

—— (1979) "Hard Ball Politics: A Model." *Political Psychology* Spring.

Fabbro, D. (1980) "Peaceful Societies," pp. 180–203 in R. Falk and S. S. Kim (eds.) *The War System.* Boulder, CO: Westview.

Falk, R. and S. S. Kim (1980) (eds.) *The War System.* Boulder, CO: Westview.

Fann, K. T. and D. C. Hodges (1977) (eds.) *Readings in U.S. Imperialism.* Boston: Porter Sargeant.

Ferris, W. (1973) *The Power Capability of Nations.* Lexington, MA: D. C. Heath.

Festinger, L. (1957) *A Theory of Cognitive Dissonance.* Evanston, IL: Row, Patterson.

Fieldhouse, D. K. (1972) "Imperialism: An Historiographical Revision," in K.

Boulding and T. Mukerjee (eds.), *Economic Imperialism.* Ann Arbor: University of Michigan Press.

Fink, C. (1965) "More Calculations About Deterrence." *Journal of Conflict Resolution* 9:54–66.

Fischer, F. (1975) *War of Illusions: German Policies from 1911 to 1914.* Trans. M. Jackson, New York: Norton.

Fodor, E. M. and T. Smith (1982) "The Power Motive as an Influence on Group Decision Making." *Journal of Personality and Social Psychology* 42:178–85.

Fossey, D. (1983) *Gorillas in the Mist.* Boston: Houghton Mifflin.

Frank, J. (1967) *Sanity and Survival: Psychological Aspects of War and Peace.* New York: Vintage.

Freud, S. (1985) "Why War?" pp. 158–63 in M. Small and J. D. Singer (eds.) *International War: An Anthology.* Homewood, IL: Dorsey Press.

Gallucci, R. (1975) *Neither Peace nor Honor.* Baltimore: Johns Hopkins University Press.

Galtung, J. (1964) "A Structural Theory of Aggression." *Journal of Peace Research* 1:95–119.

Gamson, W. A. and A. Modigliani (1971) *Untangling the Cold War: A Strategy for Testing Rival Theories.* Boston: Little, Brown.

Garnham, D. (1976) "Dyadic International War, 1816–1965: The Role of Power Parity and Geographic Proximity." *Western Political Quarterly* 29:231–42.

——— (1985) "The Causes of War: Systemic Findings," pp. 7–23 in A. N. Sabrosky (ed.), *Polarity and War.* Boulder, CO: Westview.

——— (1986) "War-Proneness, War-Weariness, and Regime Type: 1816–1980." *Journal of Peace Research* 23(3):279–89.

Gelb, L. and R. Betts (1979) *The Irony of Vietnam: the System Worked.* Washington, DC: Brookings Institution.

Geller, D. (1990) "Toward a Unified Theory of War." Paper presented to International Studies Association conference, Washington, DC.

George, A. L. (1972) "The Case for Multiple Advocacy in Making Foreign Policy." *American Political Science Review* 66:751–85.

——— (1980) "The Operational Code": A Neglected Approach to the Study of Political Leaders and Decision Making," pp. 165–90 in E. Hoffman and F. Fleron (eds.), *The Conduct of Soviet Foreign Policy.* New York: Aldine.

George, A. L. and J. George (1964) *Woodrow Wilson and Colonel House—A Personality Study.* New York: Dover Publications.

George, A. L. and R. Smoke (1974) *Deterrence in American Foreign Policy: Theory and Practice.* New York: Columbia University Press.

Gilpin, R. (1981) *War and Change in World Politics.* Cambridge: Cambridge University Press.

Glossop, R. J. (1987) *Confronting War: An Examination of Humanity's Most Pressing Problem.* Jefferson, NC: McFarlane.

Gochman, C. (1980) "Status, Capabilities, and Major Power Conflict," pp. 83–123 in J. D. Singer (ed.), *The Correlates of War II.* New York: Free Press.

——— (1990) "Capability-Driven Disputes," pp. 141–59 in C. Gochman and A. N. Sabrosky (eds.), *Prisoners of War? Nation-States in the Modern Era.* Lexington, MA: Lexington Books.

Gochman, C. and Z. Maoz (1984) "Militarized Interstate Disputes, 1816–1976: Procedures, Patterns and Insights." *Journal of Conlict Resolution* 28:585–616.

Gochman, C. and A. N. Sabrosky (1990) (eds.) *Prisoners of War? Nation-States in the Modern Era.* Lexington, MA: Lexington Books.

Goldstein, J. (1985) "Kondratieff Waves as War Cycles." *International Studies Quarterly* 29(4):411–44.

———— (1987) "Long Waves in War, Production, Prices,and Wages." *Journal of Conflict Resolution* 31(4):573–600.

———— (1988) *Long Cycles: Prosperity and War in the Modern Era*. New Haven, CT: Yale University Press.

———— (1991) "Reciprocity in Superpower Relations: An Empirical Analysis." *International Studies Quarterly* 35(2):195–209.

Goldstein, J. and J. R. Freeman (1990) *Three-Way Street: Strategic Reciprocity and World Politics*. Chicago: Chicago University Press.

Goodall, J. (1990) *Through a Window: My Thirty Years with the Chimpanzees of Gombe*. Boston: Houghton Mifflin.

Greenstein, F. (1975) *Personality and Politics*. New York: Norton.

Gregg, P. and A. Banks (1965) "Dimensions of Political Systems: Factor Analysis of 'A Cross-Polity Survey'." *American Political Science Review* 59:602–14.

Gruder, C. L. and R. J. Dulak (1973) "Elicitation of Cooperation by Retaliatory and Nonretaliatory Strategies in a Mixed-Motive Game." *Journal of Conflict Resolution* 17:162–74.

Gurr, T. R. (1980) (ed.) *Handbook of Political Conflict*. New York: Free Press.

Haas. M. (1968) "Social Change and National Aggressiveness, 1900–1960," pp. 215–45 in J. D. Singer (ed.) *Quantitative International Politics*. New York: Free Press.

———— (1980) "Societal Approaches to the Study of the War," pp. 347–68 in R. A. and S. S. Kim (eds.), *The War System: An Interdisciplinary Approach*. Boulder, CO: Westview.

Halberstam, D. (1972) *The Best and the Brightest*. Greenwich, CT: Fawcett.

Halperin, M. (1974) *Bureaucratic Politics and Foreign Policy*. Washington, DC: Brookings Institution.

Halperin, M. and A. Kantor (1973) (eds.) *Readings in American Foreign Policy: A Bureaucratic Perspective*. Boston: Little, Brown.

Hampson, F. O. (1985) "The Divided Decision-Maker: American Domestic Politics and the Cuban Crisis." *International Security* 9(3):130–65.

Hart, J. (1974) "Symmetry and Polarization in the European International System, 1870–1879: A Methodological Study." *Journal of Peace Research* 11:229–44.

———— (1985) "Power and Polarity in the International System," pp. 25–40 in A. N. Sabrosky (ed.), *Polarity and War*. Boulder, Westview.

Hastings, M. and S. Jenkins (1983) *The Battle for the Falklands*. New York: Norton.

Hazelwood, L. (1975) "Dimension Mechanism and Encapsulated Processes: The Domestic Conflict—Foreign Conflict Hypotheses Reconsidered." *Sage Foreign Policy Yearbook* 3:213–43.

Herek, M, I. L. Janis, and P. Huth (1987) "Decision Making During International Crises: Is Quality of Process Related to Outcome?" *Journal of Conflict Resolution* 31(2): 203–26.

Hermann, C. F. (1988) "The Impact of Single Group Decision Units on Foreign Policy." Paper presented at International Studies Association conference, St. Louis.

Hermann, C. F., C. W. Kegley, Jr., and J. N. Rosenau (1987) (eds.) *New Directions in the Study of Foreign Policy*. Boston: Allen and Unwin.

Hermann, M. (1978) "Effects of Personal Characteristics of Political Leaders on Foreign Policy," pp. 49–68 in M. East, S. Salmore, and C. F. Hermann (eds.), *Why Nations Act: Theoretical Perspectives for Comparative Foreign Policy*. Beverley Hills, CA: Sage.

Hermann, M. and C. F. Hermann (1982) "A Look Inside the 'Black Box:' Building on a Decade of Research," pp. 1–36 in Gerald Hopple (ed.), *Biopolitics, Political Psychology and International Politics*. New York: St. Martin's.

Hill, B. (1988) "A General Model of International Conflict: Dynamics, Problems and Prospects." Paper presented to International Studies Association conference, St. Louis.

Hilsman, R. (1987) *The Politics of Policy Making in Defense and Foreign Affairs*. Englewood Cliffs, NJ: Prentice-Hall.

Hilton, G. (1971) "A Closed and Open Model Analysis of Expressions of Hostility in Crisis." *Journal of Peace Research* 8:249–62.

Hobson, J. A. (1965) *Imperialism: A Study*. Ann Arbor: University of Michigan Press.

Hollist, W. L. (1977a) "An Analysis of Arms Processes in the United States and Soviet Union." *International Studies Quarterly* 21:503–28.

—— (1977b) "Alternative Explanations of Competitive Arms Processes: Tests on Four Pairs of Nations." *American Journal of Political Science* 21:315–40.

Holsti, K. J. (1970) "National Role Conceptions in the Study of Foreign Policy." *International Studies Quarterly* 14(3):233–309.

—— (1991) *Peace and War: Armed Conflicts and International Order 1648–1989*. Cambridge: Cambridge University Press.

Holsti, O. (1967) "Cognitive Dynamics and Images of the Enemy," pp. 16–39 in J. C. Farrell and A. P. Smith (eds.), *Image and Reality in World Politics*. New York: Columbia University Press.

—— (1969) "The Belief System and National Images: A Case Study," pp. 543–50 in J. Rosenau (ed.), *International Politics and Foreign Policy*, rev. ed. New York: Free Press.

—— (1972a) "Foreign Policy Decision-Makers Viewed Psychologically: 'Cognitive Process' Approaches," pp. 120–44 in J. Rosenau (ed.), *In Search of Global Patterns*. New York: Free Press.

—— (1972b) *Crisis, Escalation, War*. Montreal: McGill-Queens University Press.

—— (1987) "Theories of Crisis Decision Making," pp. 244–81 in P. Viotti and M. Kauppi (eds.), *International Relations Theory*. New York: Macmillan.

Holsti, O., R. Brody, and R. North (1965) "Measuring Affect and Action in International Reaction Models: Empirical Materials from the 1962 Cuban Crisis." *Peace Research Society (International)* 2:170–90.

Holsti, O. and R. North (1965) "History of Human Conflict," pp. 155–72 in E. B. McNeil (ed.), *Nature of Human Conflict*. Englewood Cliffs, NJ: Prentice-Hall.

Holsti, O., R. North, and R. Brody (1968) "Perception and Action in the 1914 Crisis," pp. 123–59 in J. D. Singer (ed.), *Quantitative International Politics*. New York: Free Press.

Holsti, O., R. Siverson, and A. George (1980) (eds.) *Change in the International System*. Boulder, CO: Westview.

Horn, M. (1984) "Arms Races and the Likelihood of War." Paper presented to International Studies Association conference, Atlanta.

Houweling, H. and J. Siccama (1988) "Power Transitions as a Cause of War." *Journal of Conflict Resolution* 32(1):87–102.

Howard, M. (1991) *The Lessons of History*. New Haven, CT: Yale University Press.

Huntington, S. P. (1958) "Arms Races: Prerequisites and Results," pp. 41–86 in C. J. Friedrich and S. E. Harris (eds.), *Public Policy*. Vol. 8. Cambridge, MA: Graduate School of Public Administration, Harvard University.

Huth, P. (1988) "Extended Deterrence and the Outbreak of War." *American Political Science Review* 82:423–43.

Huth, P. and B. Russett (1984) "What Makes Deterrence Work? Cases from 1900–1980." *World Politics* 36:496–526.

——— (1988) "Deterrence Failure and Crisis Escalation." *International Studies Quarterly* 32:29–45.

——— (1990) "Testing Deterrence Theories: Rigor Makes a Difference." *World Politics* 42:466–501.

Isaac, R. (1981) Individuals and World Politics, 2nd ed. Monterey, CA: Wadsworth-Duxbury.

Jacobson, M. (1961) *The Diplomacy of the Winter War: An Account of the Russo-Finnish War, 1938–1940.* Cambridge, MA: Harvard University Press.

James, W. (1968) "The Moral Equivalent of War," pp. 21–31 in L. Bramson and G. Goethals (eds.), *War: Studies from Psychology, Sociology, Anthropology,* rev. ed. New York: Basic Books.

Janis, I. L. (1982) *Groupthink,* 2nd ed. Boston: Houghton Mifflin.

Janis. I. L. and L. Mann (1977) *Decision-Making: A Psychological Analysis of Conflict, Choice and Commitment.* New York: Free Press.

Jensen, L. (1982) *Explaining Foreign Policy.* Englewood Cliffs, NJ: Prentice-Hall.

Jervis, R. (1969) "Hypotheses on Misperception," pp. 239–54 in J. Rosenau (ed.), *International Politics and Foreign Policy,* rev. ed. New York: Free Press.

——— (1976) *Perception and Misperception in International Politics.* Princeton, NJ: Princeton University Press.

——— (1983) "Perception and Misperception: The Spiral of International Insecurity," pp. 200–207 in W. Olson, D. McLellan, and F. Sondermann (eds.), *Theory and Practice of International Relations,* 6th ed. Englewood Cliffs, NJ: Prentice-Hall.

——— (1989) "Rational Deterrence: Theory and Evidence." *World Politics* 41(2): 183–207.

Jervis, R., R. N. Lebow, and J. G. Stein (1985) *Psychology and Deterrence.* Baltimore: Johns Hopkins University Press.

Kaplan, M. (1969) "Variants on Six Models of the International System," pp. 291–303 in J. Rosenau (ed.), *International Politics and Foreign Policy.* New York: Free Press.

Karsten, P. (1978) *Soldiers and Society: The Effects of Military Service and War in American Life.* Westport, CT: Greenwood.

Kaysen, C. (1990) "Is War Obsolete? *International Security* 14(4):42–64.

Kegley, C. W. (1991) *The Long Postwar Peace: Contending Explanations and Projections.* New York: Harper Collins.

Kegley, C. W. and G. Raymond (1982) "Alliance Norms and War: A New Piece in an Old Puzzle." *International Studies Quarterly* 26:572–95.

Kegley, C. W. and E. R. Wittkopf (1987) *American Foreign Policy: Pattern and Process,* 3rd ed. New York: St. Martin's.

Kelman, H. C. (1965) "Social-Psychological Approaches to the Study of International Relations," pp. 3–39 in H. Kelman (ed.), *International Behavior: A Social-Psychological Analysis.* New York: Holt, Rinehart & Winston.

Kennedy, P. (1988) *The Rise and Fall of Great Powers: Economic Change and Military Conflict from 1500 to 2000.* New York: Random House.

Keohane, R. O. (1980) "The Theory of Hegemonic Stability and Changes in International Economic Regimes, 1967–77," pp. 317–47 in O. Holsti, R. Siverson, and A. George (eds.) *Change in the International System.* Boulder, CO: Westview.

Keohane, R. O. and J. Nye (1977) *Power and Interdependence.* Boston: Little, Brown.

Kim, S. S. (1980) "The Lorenzian Theory of Aggression and Peace Research: A Critique," pp. 82–115 in R. Falk and S. S. Kim (eds.), *The War System*. Boulder, CO: Westview.

Kim, W. (1989) "Power, Alliance, and Major Wars, 1816–1975." *Journal of Conflict Resolution* 32(2): 255–73.

Kinder, D. and J. Weiss, (1978) "In Lieu of Rationality." *Journal of Conflict Resolution* 22(4):707–35.

Kissinger, H. (1964) *A World Restored: The Politics of Conservatism in a Revolutionary Age*. New York: Grosset & Dunlap.

——— (1969) "Domestic Structure and Foreign Policy," pp. 261–75 in J. Rosenau (ed.), *International Politics and Foreign Policy*. New York: Free Press.

Kohl, W. (1975) "The Nixon-Kissinger Foreign Policy System and U.S.-European Relations: Patterns of Policy Making." *World Politics* 28(1):1–43.

Kondratieff, N. D. (1984) *The Long Wave Cycle*. New York: Richardson and Snyder. (Original edition 1928.)

Krasner, S. (1972) "Are Bureaucracies Important? A Re-examination of Accounts of the Cuban Missile Crisis." *Foreign Policy* 7:159–79.

——— (1976) "State Power and the Structure of International Trade." *World Politics* 28:317–47.

Kugler, J. and A. F. K. Organski (1989) "The Power Transition: A Retrospective and Prospective Evaluation," pp. 171–94 in M. Midlarsky (ed.) *Handbook of War Studies*. Boston: Unwin Hyman.

Lambelet, J. (1975) "Do Arms Races Lead to War?" *Journal of Peace Research* 12(2).

Lambeth, B. S. (1974) "The Sources of Soviet Military Doctrine," in B. Horton et al. (eds.), *Comparative Defense Policy*. Baltimore: Johns Hopkins University Press.

Langer, W. (1969) "The Origin of the Russo-Japanese War," pp. 3–45 in C. E. Schorske and E. Schorske (eds.), *Explorations in Crisis*. Cambridge, MA: Harvard University Press.

Lasswell, H. (1930) *Psychopathology and Politics*. Chicago: University of Chicago Press.

——— (1948) *Power and Personality*. New York: Norton.

Leaky, R. (1981) *The Making of Mankind*. New York: Dutton.

Lebow, R. N. (1981) *Between Peace and War: The Nature of International Crises*. Baltimore: Johns Hopkins University Press.

——— (1984) "Windows of Opportunity: Do States Jump Through Them?" *International Security* 9:147–86.

——— (1985) "Miscalculations in the South Atlantic: The Origins of the Falklands War," pp. 89–124 in R. Jervis, R. N. Lebow, and J. G. Stein, *Psychology and Deterrence*. Baltimore: Johns Hopkins University Press.

Lebow, R. N. and J. G. Stein (1990) "Deterrence: the Elusive Dependent Variable." *World Politics* 42:336–69.

Leites, N. (1953) *A Study of Bolshevism*. Glencoe, IL: Free Press.

Leng, R. J. (1980) "Influence Strategies and Interstate Conflict," pp. 124–57 in J. D. Singer (ed.), *Correlates of War II: Testing Some Realpolitik Models*. New York: Free Press.

——— (1983) "When Will They Ever Learn? Coercive Bargaining in Recurrent Crises." *Journal of Conflict Resolution* 27:379–419.

——— (1984) "Reagan and the Russians: Crisis Bargaining Beliefs and the Historical Record." *American Political Science Review* 78: 338–55.

——— (1988) "Crisis Learning Games." *American Political Science Review* 82:179–94.

Leng, R. J. and C. S. Gochman (1982) "Dangerous Disputes: A Study of Conflict Behavior and War." *American Journal of Political Science* 26:664–87.

Leng, R. J. and R. Goodsell (1974) "Behavioral Indicators of War Proneness in Bilateral Conflicts," pp. 191–226 in P. J. McGowan (ed.), *Sage International Yearbook of Foreign Policy Studies.* Vol. II. Beverly Hills, CA: Sage.

Leng, R. J. and H. B. Wheeler (1979) "Influence Strategies, Success and War." *Journal of Conflict Resolution* 23:655–84.

Lenin, V. I. (1939) *Imperialism: the Highest Stage of Capitalism.* New York: International Publishers.

L'Etang, H. (1970) *The Pathology of Leadership.* New York: Hawthorne.

Levi, W. (1966) "The Causes of War and the Conditions of Peace," in R. Falk and S. Mendlovitz (eds.), *Toward a Theory of War Prevention.* New York: World Law Fund.

Levy, J. S. (1981) "Alliance Formation and War Behavior: An Analysis of the Great Powers, 1495–1975." *Journal of Conflict Resolution* 25:581–614.

———— (1983) "Misperception and the Causes of War: Theoretical Linkages and Analytical Problems." *World Politics* 36(1):76–99.

———— (1985a) "Theories of General War." *World Politics* 37(3):344–74.

———— (1985b) "The Polarity of the System and International Stability: An Empirical Analysis," pp. 41–66 in A. N. Sabrosky (ed.), *Polarity and War.* Boulder, CO: Westview.

———— (1986) "Organizational Routines and the Causes of War." *International Studies Quarterly* 30(2):193–222.

———— (1987) "Declining Power and the Protective Motivation for War." *World Politics* 40(1):82–107.

———— (1988) "Domestic Politics and War," pp. 79–99 in R. Rotberg and A. Rabb (eds.), *The Origin and Prevention of Major Wars.* Cambridge: Cambridge University Press.

———— (1989) "The Diversionary Theory of War: A Critique," pp. 259–88 in M. Midlarsky (ed.), *Handbook of War Studies.* Boston: Unwin Hyman.

———— (1990–1991) "Preferences, Constraint, and Choices in July 1914." *International Security* 15:151–86.

———— (1991) "Long Cycles, Hegemonic Transitions and the Long Peace," pp. 147–76 in C. W. Kegley (ed.), *The Long Postwar Peace.* New York: Harper Collins.

Levy, J. S. and T. C. Morgan (1986) "The War Weariness Hypothesis: An Empirical Test." *American Journal of Political Science* 30:26–50.

Lindblom, C. (1965) *The Intelligence of Democracy.* New York: Free Press.

Linden, C. (1966) *Khrushchev and the Soviet Leadership.* Baltimore: Johns Hopkins University Press.

Linskold, S. (1978) "Trust Development, the GRIT Proposal, and the Effects of Conciliatory Acts on Conflict and Cooperation." *Psychological Bulletin* 85(4):772–93.

———— (1979) "Conciliation with Simultaneous or Sequential Interaction." *Journal of Conflict Resolution* 23:704–14.

Linskold, S. and M. Collins (1978) "Inducing Cooperation by Groups and Individuals." *Journal of Conflict Resolution* 22:679–90.

Linskold, S., P. S. Walters, and H. Koutsourais (1983) "Cooperators, Competitors, and Responses to GRIT." *Journal of Conflict Resolution* 27:521–32.

Lockhart, C. (1977) "Problems in the Management and Resolution of International Conflicts." *World Politics* 29:378–403.

Lorenz, K. (1966) *On Aggression.* New York: Bantam.

Luard, E. (1976) *Types of International Society.* New York: Free Press.
——— (1986) *War in International Society.* New Haven, CT: Yale University Press.
Macfie, A. L. (1938) "The Outbreak of War and the Trade Cycle." *Economic History* 3:89–97.
Majeski, S. J. and D. L. Jones (1981) "Arms Race Modelling: Causality Analysis and Model Specifications." *Journal of Conflict Resolution* 25:259–88.
March, J. and H. Simon (1958) *Organizations.* New York: Wiley.
Mandel, R. (1980) "Roots of Modern Interstate Border Disputes." *Journal of Conflict Resolution* 24:427–54.
Manning, B. (1977) "The Congress, the Executive and Intermestic Affairs: Three Proposals." *Foreign Affairs* 55(2):306–24.
Maoz, Z. (1989) "Joining the Club of Nations: Political Development and International Conflict, 1816–1976." *International Studies Quarterly* 32(2):199–231.
Maoz, Z. and N. Abdolali (1989) "Regime Type and International Conflict, 1816–1976." *Journal of Conflict Resolution* 33(1):3–35.
Maoz, Z. and B. Russett (1990) "Alliance, Contiguity, Wealth, and Political Stability: Is Lack of Conflict Among Democracies a Statistical Artifact?" Paper presented at American Political Science Association conference, San Francisco.
Maslow, A. (1943) "A Theory of Human Motivation." *Psychological Review* 50.
——— (1954) *Motivation and Personality.* New York: Harper & Row.
Matthews, R. O., A. Rubinoff, and J. G. Stein (1984) (eds.) *International Conflict and Conflict Management.* Scarborough, Ontario: Prentice-Hall.
May, E. (1973) *"Lessons" of the Past: The Use and Misuse of History in American Foreign Policy.* New York: Oxford University Press.
Mazlish, B. (1973) *In Search of Nixon.* Baltimore: Penguin.
McCormick, J. M. (1975) "Evaluating Models of Crisis Behavior: Some Evidence from the Middle East." *International Studies Quarterly* 19:17–45.
McGowan, P. and H. Shapiro (1973) *The Comparative Study of Foreign Policy.* Beverly Hills, CA: Sage.
Mead. M. (1973) "Warfare Is Only an Invention—Not Biological Necessity," pp. 112–18 in C. Beitz and T. Herman (eds.), *Peace and War.* San Fransisco: W. H. Freeman.
Mearsheimer, J. (1990) "Back to the Future: Instability in Europe After the Cold War." *International Security* 15(1):5–56.
Megargee, E. I. and J. E. Hokanson (1970) *The Dynamics of Aggression.* New York: Harper & Row.
Midlarsky, M. (1974) "Power, Uncertainty and the Onset of International Violence." *Journal of Conflict Resolution* 18:395–431.
——— (1975) *On War.* New York: Free Press.
——— (1989a) (ed.) *Handbook of War Studies.* Boston: Unwin Hyman.
——— (1989b) "Hierarchical Equilibria and the Long-Run Instability of Multipolar Systems," pp. 64–74 in M. Midlarsky (ed.), *Handbook of War Studies.* Boston: Unwin Hyman.
Milstein, J. S. (1972) "American and Soviet Influence, Balance of Power, and Arab-Israeli Violence," pp. 139–62 in B. Russett, (ed.), *Peace, War and Numbers.* Beverly Hills, CA: Sage.
Modelski, G. (1978) "The Long Cycle of Global Politics and the Nation-State." *Comparative Studies in Society and History* 20(2):214–35.
Modelski, G. and P. Morgan (1985) "Understanding Global War." *Journal of Conflict Resolution* 29(3):391–417.
Modelski, G. and W. R. Thompson (1989) "Long Cycles and Global War," pp. 23–54 in M. Midlarsky (ed.), *Handbook of War Studies.* Boston: Unwin Hyman.

Montagu, A. (1968) *Man and Aggression*. New York: Oxford University Press.

—— (1980) (ed.) *Sociobiology Examined*. New York: Oxford University Press.

Morgan, T. C. and S. Campbell (1990) "Domestic Structures, Decisional Constraints, and War: So Why Kant Democracies Fight?" Paper presented at International Studies Association conference, Washington, DC.

Morgan, P. (1977) *Deterrence: A Conceptual Analysis*. Beverley Hills, CA: Sage.

—— (1981) *Theories and Approaches to International Politics*, 3rd ed. New Brunswick, NJ: Transaction Books.

Morrow, J. D. (1989) "A Twist of Truth: A Reexamination of the Effects of Arms Races on the Occurrence of War." *Journal of Conflict Resolution* 33(3):500–29.

Most, B., P. Schrodt, R. Siverson, and H. Starr (1990) "Border and Alliance Effects in the Diffusion of Major Power Conflict, 1816–1965," pp. 209–29 in C. Gochman and A. N. Sabrosky (eds.), *Prisoners of War? Nation-States in the Modern Era*. Lexington, MA: Lexington Books.

Most, B. and H. Starr (1980) "Diffusion, Reinforcement, Geopolitics and the Spread of War." *American Political Science Review* 74:932–46.

Mueller, J. (1989) *Retreat from Doomsday: The Obsolescence of Major War*. New York: Basic Books.

—— (1991a) "Changing Attitudes Towards War: The Impact of the First World War." *British Journal of Political Science* 21:1–28.

—— (1991b) "Is War Still Becoming Obsolete?" Paper presented to American Political Science Association conference, Washington, DC.

Murnighan, J. K. and A. E. Roth (1983) "Expected Continued Play in Prisoner's Dilemma Games." *Journal of Conflict Resolution* 27:279–300.

Myers, D. G. and H. Lamm (1977) "The Polarizing Effect of Group Discussion," in I. Janis (ed.), *Current Trends in Psychology: Readings from the American Scientist*. Los Altos, CA: Kaufmann.

Naroll, R. (1969) "Deterrence in History," pp. 150–64 in D. G. Pruitt and R. C. Snyder (eds.) *Theory and Research on the Causes of War*. Englewood Cliffs, NJ: Prentice-Hall.

North, R. C. (1967) "Perception and Action in the 1914 Crisis," pp. 103–22 in J. C. Farrell and A. P. Smith (eds.), *Image and Reality in World Politics*. New York: Columbia University Press.

—— (1990) *War, Peace, Survival: Global Politics and Conceptual Synthesis*. Boulder, CO: Westview.

North, R. C., R. Brody and O. Holsti (1964) "Some Empirical Data on the Conflict Spiral." *Peace Research Society (International)* 1:1–15.

Nossal, K. R. (1984) "Bureaucratic Politics and the Westminster Model," pp. 120 27 in R. O. Matthews, A. Rubinoff, and J. G. Stein (eds.) *International Conflict and Conflict Management*. Scarborough, Ontario: Prentice-Hall.

Odom, W. (1976) "A Dissenting View on the Group Approach to Soviet Politics." *World Politics* 28(4):542–67.

Organski, A. F. K. (1958) *World Politics*. New York: Knopf.

Organski, A. F. K. and J. Kugler (1980) *The War Ledger*. Chicago: University of Chicago Press.

Orme, J. (1986–1987) "Deterrence Failures: A Second Look." *International Security* 11:96–124.

Osgood, C. E. (1962) *An Alternative to War or Surrender*. Urbana: University of Illinois Press.

—— (1971) "Graduated Unilateral Initiatives for Peace," pp. 515–25 in C. G. Smith (ed.), *Conflict Resolution: Contributions from the Behavioral Sciences*. Notre Dame, IN: Notre Dame University Press.

Oskamp, S. (1971) "Effects of Programmed Strategies on Cooperation in Prisoner's Dilemma and Other Mixed Motive Games." *Journal of Conflict Resolution* 15:225–59.

Ostrom, C. W. (1977) "Evaluating Alternative Foreign Policy Decision Making Models." *Journal of Conflict Resolution* 21:235–66.

Ostrom, C. W. and F. W. Hoole (1978) "Alliances and War Revisited: A Research Note." *International Studies Quarterly* 22:215–36.

Ostrom, C. W. and B. L. Job (1986) "The President and the Political Use of Force." *American Political Science Review* 80:554–66.

Ostrom, C. W. and R. F. Marra (1986) "U.S. Defense Spending and the Soviet Estimate." *American Political Science Review* 80:819–42.

Oye, K. (1985) "Explaining Cooperation Under Anarchy: Hypotheses and Strategies." *World Politics* 38(1):1–24.

Patchen, M. (1987) "Strategies for Eliciting Cooperation from an Adversary: Laboratory and Internation Findings." *Journal of Conflict Resolution* 31:164–85.

Payne, J. L. (1970) *The American Threat: The Fear of War as an Instrument of Foreign Policy*. Chicago: Markham.

——— (1981) *The American Threat: National Security and Foreign Policy*. College Station, TX: Lytton.

Perkins, D. (1968) *The American Approach to Foreign Policy*, rev. ed. New York: Atheneum.

Perlmutter, A. (1974) "The Presidential Political Center and Foreign Policy: A Critique of the Revisionist and Bureaucratic-Political Orientations." *World Politics* 27(1):87–106.

Pilisuk, M. and P. Skolnick (1968) "Inducing Trust: a Test of the Osgood Proposal." *Journal of Personality and Social Psychology* 8:122–33.

Pruitt, D. (1971) "Choice Shifts in Group Discussion: an Introductory Review." *Journal of Personality and Social Psychology* 20:339–60.

Rapkin, D., W. R. Thompson, and J. Christopherson (1979) "Bipolarity and Bipolarization in the Cold War Era." *Journal of Conflict Resolution* 23:261–95.

Rapoport, A. (1960) *Fights, Games and Debates*. Ann Arbor: University of Michigan Press.

Rasler, K. and W. R. Thompson (1983) "Global Wars, Public Debts, and the Long Cycle." *World Politics* 35(4):489–516.

Rattinger, H. (1975) "Armaments, Detente, and Bureaucracy: The Case of the Arms Race in Europe." *Journal of Conflict Resolution* 19:571–95.

——— (1976) "From War to War: Arms Races in the Middle East." *International Studies Quarterly* 20:501–31.

Ray, J. L. (1974) "Status Inconsistency and War Involvement in Europe, 1816–1970." *Peace Science Society (International) Papers* 23:69–80.

——— (1989) "The Abolition of Slavery and the End of International War." *International Organization* 43:405–39.

——— (1991) "The Future of International War." Paper presented to the American Political Science Association conference, Washington, DC.

Richardson, L. F. (1960a) *Statistics of Deadly Quarrels*. New York: Quadrangle-/New York Times.

——— (1960b) *Arms and Insecurity*. Chicago: Quadrangle.

Roeder, P. G. (1984) "Soviet Politics and Kremlin Politics." *International Studies Quarterly* 28(2):171–93.

Rokeach, M. (1954) "The Nature and Meaning of Dogmatism." *Psychological Review* 61 (May).

——— (1960) *The Open and Closed Mind*. New York: Basic Books.

Rosati, J. (1981) "Developing a Systematic Decision-Making Framework: Bureaucratic Politics in Perspective." *World Politics* 33(2):234–52.

Rosecrance, R. (1963) *Action and Reaction in World Politics.* Boston: Little, Brown.

——— (1969) "Bipolarity, Multipolarity, and the Future," pp. 325–35 in J. Rosenau (ed.), *International Politics and Foreign Policy*, rev. ed. New York: Free Press.

Rosecrance, R., A. Alexandroff, B. Healy, and A. Stein (1974) "Power, Balance of Power, and Status in Nineteenth Century International Relations." *Sage Professional Papers in International Studies* 3:2–29.

Rosenau, J. N. (1969) (ed.) *International Politics and Foreign Policy.* New York: Free Press.

——— (1991) "A Wherewithal for Revulsion: Notes on the Obsolescence of Interstate War." Paper presented to the American Political Science Association conference, Washington, DC.

Ross, D. (1980) "Coalition Maintenance in the Soviet Union." *World Politics* 32(2):258–80.

——— (1984) Risk Aversion in Soviet Decisionmaking," pp. 237–51 in J. Valenta and W. Potter (eds.), *Soviet Decisionmaking for National Security.* Boston: Allen and Unwin.

Rotberg, R. and T. Rabb (1988) (eds.) *The Origin and Prevention of Major Wars.* Cambridge: Cambridge University Press.

Rousseau, J. (1917) *A Lasting Peace Through the Federation of Europe.* Trans. by C. E. Vaughan. London: Constable.

——— (1950) *The Social Contract and Discourses.* Trans. by G. D. H. Cole. New York: Dutton.

Rummel, R. J. (1963) "Dimensions of Conflict Behavior Within and Between Nations." *General Systems: Yearbook of the Society for General Systems Research* 8:1–50.

Rummel, R. J. (1964) "Testing Some Possible Predictors of Conflict Behavior Within and Between Nations." *Peace Research Society (International) Papers* 1:79–111.

——— (1967) "Some Attributes and Behavioral Patterns of Nations." *Journal of Peace Research* 4(2).

——— (1968) "The Relationship Between National Attributes and Foreign Conflict Behavior," pp. 187–214 in J. D. Singer (ed.), *Quantitative International Politics.* New York: Free Press.

——— (1972) *The Dimensions of Nations.* Beverly Hills, CA: Sage.

——— (1979) *Understanding Conflict and War, Volume 4: War, Power and Peace.* Beverly Hills, CA: Sage.

——— (1983) "Libertarianism and International Violence." *Journal of Conflict Resolution* 27(1):27–71.

———(1985) "Libertarian Propositions on Violence Within and Between Nations: A Test Against Published Research Results." *Journal of Conflict Resolution* 29(1):419–55.

Russett, B. (1967) *International Regions and the International System.* Chicago: Rand McNally.

——— (1969) "The Calculus of Deterrence," pp. 359–69 in J. Rosenau (ed.), *International Politics and Foreign Policy*, rev. ed. New York: Free Press.

——— (1972) (ed.) *Peace, War and Numbers.* Beverly Hills, CA: Sage.

——— (1983) "Prosperity and Peace." *International Studies Quarterly* 27:381–87.

——— (1990) "Economic Decline, Electoral Pressure and the Initiation of Interstate Conflict," pp. 123–40 in C. Gochman and A. N. Sabrosky (eds.) *Prisoners of War? Nation-States in the Modern Era.* Lexington MA: Lexington Books.

Russett, B. and R. J. Monsen (1975) "Bureaucracy and Polyarchy as Predictors of

Performance: A Cross-National Examination." *Comparative Political Studies* 8:5–31.

Sabrosky, A. N. (1975) "From Bosnia to Sarajevo." *Journal of Conflict Resolution* 19:3–24.

——— (1985) (ed.) *Polarity and War: The Changing Structure of International Conflict.* Boulder, CO: Westview.

Sahlins, M. (1976) *The Use and Abuse of Biology: An Anthropological Critique of Sociobiology.* Ann Arbor: University of Michigan Press.

Salmore, S. A. and C. F. Hermann (1970) "The Effects of Size, Development and Accountability on Foreign Policy." *Peace Research Society Papers* 14:15–30.

Schellenberg, J. A. (1982) *The Science of Conflict.* New York: Oxford University Press.

Schelling, T. (1963) *The Strategy of Conflict.* New York: Oxford University Press–Galaxy Books.

Schmookler, A. B. (1984) *The Parable of the Tribes: The Problem of Power in Social Evolution.* Boston: Houghton Mifflin.

Scott, J. P. (1968) "That Old-Time Aggression," pp. 136–43 in A. Montague (ed.) *Man and Aggression.* New York: Oxford University Press.

Semmel, A. K. (1976) "Some Correlates of Attitudes to Multilateral Diplomacy in the United States Department of State." *International Studies Quarterly* 20(2):301–24.

——— (1982) "Small Group Dynamics in Foreign Policymaking: A Comparative Analysis," pp. 94–113 in G. Hopple (ed.), *Biopolitics, Political Psychology, and International Politics.* New York: St. Martin's.

Shepard, G. H. (1968) "Personality Effects on American Foreign Policy, 1969–1984: A Second Test of Interpersonal Generalization Theory." *International Studies Quarterly* 32(1):91–123.

Shirer, W. L. (1960) *The Rise and Fall of the Third Reich.* New York: Fawcett Crest.

Shubik, M. (1964) (ed.) *Game Theory and Related Approaches to Social Behavior.* New York: Wiley.

Simon, H. (1959) *Administrative Behavior.* New York: Macmillan.

Singer, J. D. (1968) (ed.) *Quantitative International Politics.* New York: Free Press.

——— (1969) "The Level of Analysis Problem in International Relations," pp. 20–29 in J. Rosenau (ed.) *International Politics and Foreign Policy,* rev. ed. New York: Free Press.

——— (1972) "The Correlates of War Project: An Interim Report and Rationale." *World Politics* 24:243–70.

——— (1979) "Introduction," pp. 11–20 in J. D. Singer and associates (eds.), *Explaining War: Selected Papers from the Correlates of War Project.* Beverly Hills, CA: Sage.

——— (1980) (ed.) *The Correlates of War II: Testing Some Realpolitik Models.* New York: Free Press.

Singer, J. D., S. Bremer, and J. Stuckey (1972) "Capability Distribution, Uncertainty, and Major Power War, 1820–1965," pp. 19–48 in B. Russett (ed.), *Peace, War and Numbers.* Beverly Hills, CA: Sage.

Singer, J. D. and T. Cusak (1981) "Periodicity, Inexorability and Steersmanship in International War," pp. 404–22 in R. Merritt and B. Russett (eds.), *From National Development to Global Community.* London: Allen and Unwin.

Singer, J. D. and M. Small (1967) "Alliance Aggregation and the Onset of War, 1815–1945," pp. 246–86 in J. D. Singer (ed.), *Quantitative International Politics.* New York: Free Press.

——— (1972) *The Wages of War, 1816–1965: A Statistical Handbook*. New York: Wiley.

Singer, J. D. and M. Wallace (1982) (eds.) *To Augur Well: Early Warning Indicators in World Politics*. Beverly Hills, CA: Sage.

Siverson, R. M. and P. Diehl (1989) "Arms Races, the Conflict Spiral, and the Onset of War," pp. 195–218 in M. Midlarsky (ed.) *Handbook of War Studies*. Boston: Unwin Hyman.

Siverson, R. M. and J. King (1982) "Alliances and the Expansion of War," pp. 37–49 in J. D. Singer and M. Wallace (eds.), *to Augur Well: Early Warning Indicators in World Politics*. Beverly Hills, CA: Sage.

Siverson, R. M. and H. Starr (1990) "Opportunity, Willingness and the Diffusion of War, 1816–1965." *American Political Science Review* 84:47–67.

Siverson, R. M. and M. Sullivan (1983) "The Distribution of Power and the Onset of War." *Journal of Conflict Resolution* 27(3):473–94.

Siverson, R. M. and M. Tennefoss (1984) "Power, Alliance, and the Escalation of International Conflict, 1815–1965." *American Political Science Review* 78:1057–169.

Skilling, H.G. and F. Griffiths (1971) *Interest Groups in Soviet Politics*. Princeton, NJ: Princeton University Press.

Small, M. and J. D. Singer (1970) "Patterns in International Warfare, 1816–1965." *Annals of the American Academy of Political and Social Sciences* 391:145–55.

——— (1976) "The War Proneness of Democratic Regimes." *Jerusalem Journal of International Relations* 1:49–69.

——— (1985) (eds.) *International War: An Anthology*. Homewood, IL: Dorsey Press.

Smith, T. C. (1980) "Arms Race Instability and War." *Journal of Conflict Resolution* 24:253–84.

——— (1988) "Curvature Change and War Risk in Arming Patterns." *International Interactions* 14:201–28.

Snyder, G. H. and P. Diesing (1977) *Conflict Among Nations: Bargaining, Decision-making, and System Structure in International Crises*. Princeton, NJ: Princeton University Press.

Snyder, J. L. (1985) "Perceptions of the Security Dilemma in 1914," pp. 153–79 in R. Jervis, R. N. Lebow, and J. G. Stein (eds.), *Psychology and Deterrence*. Baltimore: Johns Hopkins University Press.

Spanier, J. and E. Uslaner (1978) *How American Foreign Policy is Made*, 2nd ed. New York: Holt, Rinehart & Winston.

Spechler, D. R. (1986) "The U.S.S.R. and Third World Conflicts: Domestic Debate and Soviet Policy in the Middle East, 1967–1973." *World Politics* 38(3):435–61.

Spiezio, K. E. (1990) "British Hegemony and Major Power War, 1815–1939: An Empirical Test of Gilpin's Model of Hegemonic Governance." *International Studies Quarterly* 34(2):165–81.

Sprout, H. and M. Sprout (1965) *The Ecological Perspective on Human Affairs*. Princeton, NJ: Princeton University Press.

Starr, H. (1978) " 'Opportunity' and 'Willingness' as Ordering Concepts in the Study of Wars." *International Interactions* 4:363–87.

——— (1984) *Henry Kissinger: Perceptions of International Politics*. Lexington: University Press of Kentucky.

Starr, H. and B. Most (1976) "The Substance and Study of Borders in International Relations Research." *International Studies Quarterly* 20:581–620.

——— (1978) "A Return Journey: Richardson: 'Frontiers' and Wars in the 1946–1965 Era." *Journal of Conflict Resolution* 22:441–67.

—— (1983) "Contagion and Border Effects on Contemporary African Conflict." *Comparative Political Studies* 16:92–117.

Stein, J. G. (1987) "Extended Deterrence in the Middle East: American Strategy Reconsidered." *World Politics* 39(3):326–52.

Seinbruner, J. (1974) *The Cybernetic Theory of Decision.* Princeton, NJ: Princeton University Press.

Steiner, M. (1977) "The Elusive Essence of Decision." *International Studies Quarterly* 21(2):389–422.

Stoessinger, J. (1982) *Why Nations Go to War,* 3rd ed. New York: St. Martin's.

Stoll, R. J. and M. Champion (1985) "Capability Concentration, Alliance Bonding, and Conflict Among the Major Powers," pp. 67–94 in A. N. Sabrosky (ed.), *Polarity and War.* Boulder, CO: Westview.

Storr, A. (1983) "Aggression is an Instinct," pp. 16–21 in D. Bender and B. Leone (eds.), *Are Humans Aggressive by Nature?* St. Paul, MN: Greenhaven Press.

Sullivan, M. P. (1976) *International Relations: Theories and Evidence.* Englewood Cliffs, NJ: Prentice-Hall.

Tanter, R. (1966) "Dimensions of Conflict Behavior Within and Between Nations, 1958–1960." *Journal of Conflict Resolution* 10:41–64.

—— (1972) "International System and Foreign Policy Approaches: Implications for Conflict Modelling and Management." *World Politics* 24:7–39.

Taylor, A. J. P. (1952) *Rumors of War.* London: Hamish Hamilton.

Terhune, K. W. (1968) "Motives, Situation, and Interpersonal Conflict Within Prisoners' Dilemma." *Journal of Personality and Social Psychology,* Monograph Supplement 8, No. 3, Part 2, pp. 1–23.

Thomas, E. (1959) *The Harmless People.* New York: Knopf.

Thompson, W. R. (1982) "Phases of the Business Cycle and the Outbreak of War." *International Studies Quarterly* 26:301–11.

—— (1983a)"Succession Crises in the Global Political System: A Test of the Transition Model," pp. 93–116 in A. L. Bergeson (ed.), *Crises in the World-System.* Beverly Hills, CA: Sage.

—— (1983b) "Uneven Economic Growth, Systemic Challenges, and Global Wars." *International Studies Quarterly* 27:341–55.

—— (1986) "Polarity, the Long Cycle, and Global Power Warfare." *Journal of Conflict Resolution* 30(4):587–615.

——(1988) *On Global War: Historical-Structural Approaches to World Politics.* Columbia: University of South Carolina Press.

Thompson, W. R. and K. A. Rasler (1988) "War and Systemic Capability Reconcentration." *Journal of Conflict Resolution* 32:335–66.

Thompson, W.R. and G. Zuk (1982) "War, Inflation, and the Kondratieff Long Wave." *Journal of Conflict Resolution* 26(4):621–44.

Thomson, J.C. (1973) "How Could Vietnam Happen? An Autopsy," pp. 98–110 in M. Halperin and A. Kantor (eds.), *Readings in American Foreign Policy: A Bureaucratic Perspective.* Boston: Little, Brown.

Tiger, L. and R. Fox (1971) *The Imperial Animal.* New York: Holt, Rinehart Winston.

To T. (1988) "More Realism in Prisoner's Dilemma." *Journal of Conflict Resolution* 32:402–8.

Toynbee, A. (1954) *A Study of History.* Vol. IX. London: Oxford University Press.

Triska, J. F. and D. D. Finley (1969) "Soviet-American Relations: A Multiple Symmetry Model," in D. Edwards (ed.), *International Political Analysis: Readings.* New York: Holt, Rinehart Winston.

Tuchman, B. (1962) *The Guns of August* New York: Dell.

Tucker, R. (1973) *Stalin as Revolutionary: 1879–1929, A Study in History and Personality*. New York: Norton.

Valenta, J. (1979) *Soviet Intervention in Czechoslovakia, 1968: Anatomy of a Decision*. Baltimore: John Hopkins University Press.

———(1984) "Soviet Decisionmaking on Afghanistan," pp. 218–36 in J. Valenta and W. Potter (eds.), *Soviet Decisionmaking for National Security*. Boston: Allen and Unwin.

van Evera, S. (1984) "The Cult of the Offensive and the Origins of World War I." *International Security* 9:58–107.

———(1985) "Why Cooperation Failed in 1914." *World Politics* 38:80–117.

Vasquez, J. A. (1983) *The Power of Power Politics: A Critique*. New Brunswick, NJ: Rutgers University Press.

———(1987a) "Foreign Policy, Learning, and War," pp. 366–83 in C.F. Hermann, C. W. Kegley, Jr., and J. N. Rosenau (eds.), *New Directions in the Study of Foreign Policy*. Boston: Allen and Unwin.

——— (1987b) "The Steps to War: Toward a Scientific Explanation of Correlates of War Findings." *World Politics* 50(1):108–45.

Viotti, P. and M. Kauppi (1987) *Interntional Relations Theory*. New York: Macmillan.

Walker, S.G. (1977) "The Interface Between Beliefs and Behavior: Henry Kissinger's Operational Code and the Vietnam War." *Journal of Conflict Resolution* 21(1):129–68.

Wallace, M.D. (9171) "Power, Status, and International War." *Journal of Peace Research* 8(1):23-36.

———(1972) "Status, Formal Organization, and Arms Levels as Factors Leading to the Onset of War, 1820–1964," pp. 49–69 in B. Russett (ed.), *Peace, War and Numbers*. Beverly Hills, CA: Sage.

——— (1973a) *War and Rank Among Nations*. Lexington, MA: D.C. Heath.

——— (1973b) "Alliance Polarization, Cross-Cutting, and International War, 1815–1964." *Journal of Conflict Resolution* 17:576–604.

——— (1979) "Arms Races and Escalation: Some New Evidence." *Journal of Conflict Resolution* 23:3–16

——— (1980) "Some Persisting Findings: A Reply to Professor Weed." *Journal of Conflict Resolution* 24:289–92.

——— (1982) "Armaments and Escalation: Two Competing Hypotheses." *International Studies Quarterly* 26:37–56.

——— (1983) "Armaments and Escalation: A Reply to Altfeld." *International Studies Quarterly* 27:233–35.

——— (1985) "Polarization: Toward a Scientific Conception," pp. 95–114 in A. N. Sabrosky (ed.), *Polarity and War*. Boulder, CO: Westview.

Wallerstein, E. (1974) *The Modern World-System*. New York: Academic Press.

——— (1979) *The Capitalist World-Economy*. New York: Cambridge University Press.

——— (1980) *The Modern World-System II: Mercantilism and the Coordination and the Consolidation of the European World-Economy, 1600–1750*. New York: Free Press.

——— (1983) *Historical Capitalism*. London: Verso.

Waltz, K. N. (1959) *Man, the State and War*. New York: Columbia University Press.

——— (1969) "International Structure, National Force, and the Balance of World Power," pp. 304–14 in J. Rosenau (ed.), *International Politics and Foreign Policy*, rev. ed. New York: Free Press.

——— (1979) *Theory of International Politics*. Reading, MA: Addison-Wesley.

—— (1990) "Nuclear Myths and Political Realities." *American Political Science Review* 84(3):731–45.

Ward, M.D. (1982) "Cooperation and Conflict in Foreign Policy Behavior." *International Studies Quarterly* 26:87–126.

Waymon, F. (1985) "Bipolarity, Multipolarity, and the Threat of War," pp. 115–44 in A. N. Sabrosky (ed.), *Polarity and War*. Boulder, CO: Westview.

Weede, E. (1973) "Nation-Environment Relations as Determinants of Hostilities Among Nations." *Peace Science Society (International) Papers* 20:67–90.

—— (1976) "Overwhelming Preponderance as a Pacifying Condition Among Contiguous Asian Dyads, 1950–69." *Journal of Conflict Resolution* 20:395–411.

—— (1980) "Arms Races and Escalation: Some Persisting Doubts." *Journal of Conflict Resolution* 24:285–87.

—— (1984) "Democracy and War Involvement." *Journal of Conflict Resolution* 28(4):649–64.

Weil, H. (1975) "Can Bureaucracies Be Rational Actors? Foreign Policy Decision-Making in North Vietnam." *International Studies Quarterly* 19(4):432–68.

Wesley, J. P. (1962) "Frequency of Wars and Geographical Opportunity." *Journal of Conflict Resolution* 6:387–89.

Wiegele, T. (1973) "Decision-Making in an International Crisis: Some Biological Factors." *International Studies Quarterly* 17:295–333.

Wilkenfeld, J. (1968) "Domestic and Foreign Conflict Behavior of Nations." *Journal of Peace Research* 5(1): 56–69.

—— (1975) "A Time Series Perspective on Conflict Behavior in the Middle East," pp. 177–212 in P. J. McGowan (ed.), *Sage International Yearbook of Foreign Policy Studies* III. Beverly Hills, CA: Sage.

Wilkenfeld, J., G. W. Hopple, P. J. Rossa, and S. J. Andriole (1980) *Foreign Policy Behavior*. Beverly Hills, CA: Sage.

Wilkenfeld, J., V. L. Lussier, and D. Tahtinen (1972) "Conflict Interactions in the Middle East, 1949–1967." *Journal of Conflict Resolution* 16:135–54.

Williams, W. A. (1962) *Tragedy of American Diplomacy*, rev. ed. New York: Dell.

Wills, G. (1985) *Reagan's America*. New York: Penguin.

Wilpert, B., P. Burger, J. Doktor, and R. Doctor (1976) "The Risky Shift in Policy Decision Making: A Comparative Analysis." *Policy Sciences* 7:365–70.

Wilson, E.O. (1975) *Sociobiology: The New Synthesis*. Cambridge, MA: Harvard University Press.

—— (1978) *On Human Nature*. Cambridge, MA: Harvard University Press.

Winter, D. G. (1973) *The Power Motive*. New York: Free Press.

Winter, D. G. and A. J. Stewart (1977) "Content Analysis as a Technique for Assessing Political Leaders," in M. G. Hermann (ed.), *A Psychological Examination of Political Leaders*. New York: Free Press.

Wright. Q. (1965) *A Study of War*, 2nd ed. Two volumes. Chicago: University of Chicago Press.

Zinnes, D. (1968) "Expression and Perception of Hostility in Prewar Crisis: 1914," pp. 85–119 in J. D. Singer (ed.), *Quantitative International Politics*. New York: Free Press.

—— (1972) "Some Evidence Relevant to the Man-Milieu Hypothesis," pp. 209–51 in J. Rosenau, V. Davis, and M. East (eds.), *The Analysis of International Politics*. New York: Free Press.

—— (1980) "Why War? Evidence on the Outbreak of International Conflict," pp. 331–60 in T.R. Gurr (ed.), *Handbook of Political Conflict*. New York: Free Press.

Zinnes, D., R. North, and H. E. Koch (1961) "Capability, Threat, and the Outbreak of War," pp. 469–83 in J. Rosenau (ed.), *International Politics and Foreign Policy*. New York: Free Press.

Zinnes, D. and J. Wilkenfeld (1971) "An Analysis of Foreign Conflict Behavior of Nations," pp. 167–213 in W. Hanreider (ed.), *Comparative Foreign Policy*. New York: David McKay.

Index